PERSONAL DATA PROTECTION IN THE UNITED STATES AND THE EUROPEAN UNION

PERSONAL DATA PROTECTION IN THE UNITED STATES AND THE EUROPEAN UNION

Sylvia Lissens

INTERSENTIA
LEFEBVRE GROUP

Intersentia
Lefebvre Belgium SA
Avenue Jean Monnet 4
1348 Louvain-la-Neuve
Belgium
Email: contact@larcier-intersentia.com

Distribution for the UK, Ireland and
Rest of the World (excl. France, Belgium and Luxembourg)
Ingram Publisher Services UK
1 Deltic Avenue, Rooksley
Milton Keynes MK13 8LD
United Kingdom
Tel: +44 1752 202 301 | Fax: +44 1752 202 331
Email: ipsuk.customercare@ingramcontent.com

Distribution for France and Rest of the World (excl. Ireland and the UK)
Interforum Editis
Avenue de France 92
75013 Paris
France

Distribution for Belgium and Luxembourg
Larcier-Intersentia
Avenue Jean Monnet 4
1348 Louvain-la-Neuve
Belgium

Cover design: Danny Juchtmans / www.dsigngraphics.be
Cover image: Generated by artificial intelligence (AI)

ISBN 978-1-83970-656-1
D/2026/06040/0375
NUR 828

British Library Cataloguing in Publication Data. A catalogue record for this book is available from the British Library.

ACKNOWLEDGEMENTS

This book is based on my four-year PhD research, and it brings together the experiences from all my university years and many exchanges. Many people and meaningful friendships have guided me along the way to where I am today. My mother telling me it will be okay when I had just started university and was scared in my first hesitant years at KU Leuven as a bachelor's student of law and criminology. The shy law student that arrived in Finland with two suitcases, wondering why I thought it was a good idea to even go there, but who grew through the people I met and entertained with the songs I played on my guitar. The strong woman I became in Venice, inspired by my female professor, a martial arts professional, where I enjoyed "my last months as a student"; was I wrong thinking that! The love for nature I re-discovered in Bielsko-Biała, where I spent time with my mother's family. The nuanced approach in life that I learned from my classmates at Duke University, and which brought me to the topic of my PhD research. My interests in law, criminology, international cooperation, and mutual understanding were brought together in my doctoral years at KU Leuven and UJ Cracow, and I sincerely appreciate the opportunity I was given to conduct my PhD research.

Many people accompanied me on this way, and when you read this, you know who you are. All of you behind the scenes (and in the spotlight) who supported me throughout my PhD, at KU Leuven, UMASS, UJ Cracow, University of Primorska, Catolica, NOVA, even all the way to Brazil and Chile; this book could not have been written without your everlasting support, at moments where even I struggled to still see my own end goal. All the great people I got to know on this academic road, and you are with a lot, I really thank you from the deepest of my heart for everything.

When you start your studies at KU Leuven, they always tell you: "and you may find your true love in this city". Well, as with everything in my life, that took quite a while though … a bachelor's degree, a master's degree, another master's degree, and finally a PhD degree! It took many years, but it was worth waiting for, and I am really blessed with you in my life. Each one of the years I was patiently waiting, allowed me to grow and to understand who I am and what I want, making me the strong person I am today. Thank you for your everlasting support, patience, and love.

In the end, I did not become a singer (although my Helsinki friends would disagree), I did not become a songwriter (even though I still express myself best in writing), but I did end up being … a writer. This is the result, and I am honestly very proud of it.

CONTENTS

ABBREVIATIONS

Article 29 WP	Article 29 Working Party
BCRs	Binding Corporate Rules
CCPA	California Consumer Privacy Act
CLPO	Civil Liberties Protection Officer
CRS	Congressional Research Service
CoE	Council of Europe
CJEU	Court of Justice of the European Union
DPF	Data Privacy Framework
DPA	Data Protection Authority
DPRC	Data Protection Review Court
1995 Directive	Directive 95/46/EC
ECHR	European Convention on Human Rights
ECtHR	European Court of Human Rights
EDPB	European Data Protection Board
EDPS	European Data Protection Supervisor
EU	European Union
EO	Executive Order
FBI	Federal Bureau of Investigation
FTC	Federal Trade Commission
FISA	Foreign Intelligence Surveillance Act
FISC	Foreign Intelligence Surveillance Court
GDPR	General Data Protection Regulation
GCHQ	Government Communications Headquarters
IoT	Internet of Things
MLA	Mutual Legal Assistance

OECD	Organization for Economic Cooperation and Development
NSA	National Security Agency
SCCs	Standard Contractual Clauses
TEU	Treaty on the European Union
TFEU	Treaty on the Functioning of the European Union
HEW	U.S. Department of Health, Education, and Welfare
SCOTUS	U.S. Supreme Court
VCDPA	Virginia Consumer Data Protection Act

INTRODUCTION

The transatlantic data transfer frameworks of Safe Harbour, Privacy Shield, and the Data Privacy Framework all share the same aim: protecting European personal data while enabling commercial transactions and data flows with the United States. The United States and the European Union are key players in the technology and digital area. Why is it so difficult for them to reach an agreement on the adequate protection of personal data that is used for transatlantic commercial transactions?

This book addresses the question of what the core differences between the U.S. and EU legal approaches towards personal data (protection) are and if there are signs of convergences. To this end, functional comparative law research was conducted on three levels to reflect the perspectives of the three main stakeholders: the private sector, civil society, and the public sector, consisting of government intelligence and law enforcement agencies. The United States and the European Union seem to understand and qualify personal data differently in words and deeds, but upon closer inspection they have more in common than may seem at first sight. Consequently, it was possible to develop a roadmap for how the U.S. and EU approaches can co-exist, based on the convergences between the U.S. and EU approaches towards data privacy on all three levels.

The first introductory chapter provides an overview of the digital evolution from regular to 'smart' devices, the benefits and risks of personal data collection, and an introduction to profiling practices and personalized services. Secondly, the transatlantic data transfer frameworks are introduced together with the CJEU's case law where two of these frameworks were invalidated. The second chapter explains the methodological approach and additionally clarifies certain terminological choices used throughout this book.

The third chapter argues that the private sector needs globally accepted general data privacy principles to adequately protect people's privacy interests while enabling businesses to engage in data commerce. Six data privacy categories, consisting of several data privacy principles, are developed in this book, which can serve as a basis for transnational economic data privacy regulation in an overarching legal framework for the EU and the United States to co-exist, securing data privacy and supporting commerce. The first finding states that the data protection rules currently in place have become too strict and procedural, resulting in a mechanical instrument to 'tick the boxes' rather than restoring people's individual control and decisional power. Clear minimum standards preventing the most flagrant abuses of personal data are needed, enabling people to decide based on clear and understandable information whether they want to share their personal data for commercial purposes.

The fourth chapter argues that the expectations of civil society are converging between the two sides of the Atlantic, but that they are often overshadowed by the results of market failure, dominant public opinion, and the weight of certain lobby-driven stakeholders on the development of data privacy policies. The United States and the European Union seem to qualify data privacy substantially differently, but this qualification essentially reflects an evolutionary digital interpretation of the right to privacy. Data protection consists of data security measures necessary to protect (data) privacy interests, but has recently tilted too much towards the protection of the data as such (the procedural aspect) as opposed to the protection of the people behind the data. The second finding states that a reconceptualization is needed to bring the focus back on people's privacy interests by embracing a privacy harmful activities framework which takes account of the material as well as the psychological harm that can be caused by the mismanagement of people's personal data.

The fifth chapter argues that the public sector, consisting of intelligence and law enforcement agencies, needs a separate legal framework for its specific operations. The 'omnibus' regulatory approach of the European Union seems in stark contrast with the United States' sectoral approach, but actually includes many public sector and national security exemptions, bringing it closer to the U.S. model in this regard. The courts' scrutiny on both sides of the Atlantic also revealed that many EU Member States engage in similar far-reaching surveillance practices to the United States, leading to the third finding that the U.S. national security exception is not that different from the national security exceptions employed by Member States of the European Union.

The sixth chapter brings the findings from chapters three to five together in a comparative analysis, which is followed by the conclusion. This book discusses each of the three levels, namely the private sector, civil society, and the public sector, consisting of government intelligence and law enforcement agencies, in detail in order to reveal the core differences and convergences between the United States and the European Union in the area of data privacy. Many assumptions and prejudices will be rebutted to show that, beneath the surface, both regions take in essence a very similar approach.

CHAPTER 1

DATA COLLECTION AND EU-U.S. AGREEMENTS: AN INTRODUCTION

This introductory chapter sets the stage and context for the following sections of this book by explaining how personal data has evolved over time and why the collection and processing of personal data can simultaneously be useful and problematic. A unique approach is taken where personal data protection and processing is tackled from all relevant angles, namely private sector interests (*Chapter 3*), the perspective of civil society (*Chapter 4*), and public sector interests (*Chapter 5*). These three perspectives are introduced in this chapter and need to be tackled in a combined way to understand the underlying problems and find potential solutions for EU-U.S. personal data transfers. Given the extensive personal data flows between the European Union and the United States, EU-U.S. agreements were negotiated to enable data transfers from one legal system to the other, while ensuring an adequate level of protection for this data. Two adequacy findings were, however, invalidated by the Court of Justice of the European Union, and the question still remains whether the latest remedied adequacy finding of 2023 will survive the Court's scrutiny. The following sections provide a broader framework to understand both regions' perspective and focus additionally on the (problematic) aspects identified by the Court.

§ 1. SMART DEVICES, THE INTERNET OF THINGS, AND USER PROFILING

The scale of personal data collection and processing has significantly increased since the entry of 'smart' devices, and the subsequent development of the Internet of Things. At the same time, not only have products started to collect a large amount of personal data on their users, but services have also begun to collect their customers' data for profiling purposes in order to provide more relevant and personalized services. The different purposes and aspects of personal data (collection) will be exemplified by specific situations and practices to show how these new technologies can be used, and, unfortunately also, misused. Many people still do not grasp the full scale of how their personal data is processed and with which (private or public) actors it may be shared. This section aims to clarify the potential uses and risks, and to show the relevance of this book's content for each one of us.

A. SMART ENVIRONMENTS

Smart devices – The best-known 'smart' device used in daily life is probably the smartphone. The smartphone is still related to its predecessor, the regular portable cell phone, which enabled phone calls and text messages. Smart devices are equipped with an internet connection, upgrading regular devices to 'smart' ones. Applied to the cell phone, the smart feature allows for a much larger offer of features, such as the ability to check one's emails, social media, receive traffic directions, or check the weather forecast, just to name a few. Many of these features are provided by different 'applications' or 'apps'. Apps are "software applications designed for a specific task which organize information in a way suitable for and targeted at the specific characteristics of a particular (set of) smart device(s)".[1] Apps installed on smartphones or tablets can provide quick and easy access to services, such as email, social media, or the weather forecast, but they can also serve as a command connection or 'interface' for other smart devices, such as a smart vacuum cleaner, refrigerator, or heating system. In the latter situation, two types of smart device interactions can be distinguished, namely active and passive interactions. During active interactions, users tap on buttons in the app or talk to their smartphone, which transfers the commands to the smart device concerned. During passive interactions, the apps wait for the users' action or listen for a trigger word that will activate them.[2]

Internet of Things (IoT) – The network of all connected smart devices is called the 'Internet of Things' or 'IoT', and can be found in smart homes, smart cars, and even entire smart cities. The devices in these networks collect and exchange data in order to assist their users in everyday life. When the alarm rings in the morning, the smart coffee machine will start to prepare an espresso, and the smart fridge will suggest possible breakfast recipes based on its content. Smart homes enable users to remotely monitor their houses as they can control features, such as lighting or heating,

1 Colin Rooney, 'Data on smart devices – are data subjects being protected?' (2013) 13 PDP 8, 8.

2 Article 29 WP, 'Opinion 8/2014 on the Recent Developments on the Internet of Things' (WP223, 16 Sep 2014) 4; Steven Alter, 'Making Sense of Smartness in the Context of Smart Devices and Smart Systems' (2020) 22 ISF 381, 383-385; Anupam Chander, 'The Internet of Things' (2019) 18 WTR s9, s10; Jeremy de Beer, Jules Belanger, and Mohit Sethi, 'Consumer Contracts, Copyright Licensing, and Control over Data on the Internet of Things' (2020) 18 CJLT 161, 177-183; FTC, *Mobile Privacy Disclosures: Building Trust Through Transparency* (Staff Report, 2013) i and 2; Nicolas Karsenti, 'Privacy and Connected Objects' (2019) 17 CJLT 34, 34; Michael McTear, Zoraida Callejas, and David Griol, *The Conversational Interface* (1st edn, Springer 2016) 11-22 and 283-292; Louise Taylor, 'Wearable technology' (2014) 20 CTLR 95, 95.

through their smartphones. Smart cars may provide real-time navigation support or recommend nearby restaurants based on the driver's preferences.[3] The five dominant big tech companies at the time of writing are Google, Apple, Samsung, Amazon, and Meta.[4] Meta is currently one of the major social media players, being the parent company of Facebook, Instagram, and WhatsApp.[5] Amazon, Apple, Google, and Meta have their headquarters in the United States, while Samsung has its headquarters in South Korea.[6] Each of these companies are developing 'their own' smart devices which can be linked to a respective personal assistant. Meet Alexa from Amazon, Siri from Apple, Bigsby from Samsung, Google Assistant from Google, and the newest acquisition Meta AI from Meta.[7] It is, however, almost impossible to connect a smart device of one brand to a personal assistant of another brand, complicating interoperability and competition. Users will likely prefer to control all their smart devices through one application or assistant, which will limit users' choices when setting up smart homes, or even smart cities.[8] The limited interoperability will be left out of the scope of discussion, which will focus on EU-U.S. personal data flows more broadly.

Data Collection – Regular devices are evolving into 'smart' internet-connected devices at unprecedented speed.[9] To provide personalized services and enhance user experience, smart devices consist of sensors and technology capable of collecting large amounts of data on not only their users, but also on the environment these devices are

---

3 Article 29 WP, 'Opinion 8/2014' (n2) 4; Chander (n2) s10; de Beer *et al.* (n2) 162-176; Maxine Finding and Mark Taylor, 'Smart homes' (2016) 22 CTLR 147, 147; Angela Guimaraes Pereira, Alice Benessia, and Paula Curvelo, *Agency in the Internet of Things* (Eur.Comm. JRC Scientific and Policy Reports, 2013) 7-16; Bradley Limpert, 'App. 13.15 – The Internet of Things' [2016] TechContracting 1, 1-13; McTear *et al.* (n2) 15 and 406-409; Monica Salgado, 'Internet of things revisited' (2014) 15 PDP 12, 12; Sofia Scasserra and Carolina Martínez Elebi, *Digital Colonialism: Analysis of Europe's Trade Agenda* (Transnational Institute Amsterdam: Trade & Investment Policy Briefing, 2021) 5; Harald Sundmaeker and others (eds), *Vision and Challenges for Realising the Internet of Things* (CERP-IoT 2010) 11 and 43-52; Bridget Treacy and Anita Bapat, 'The "internet of things" – already in a home near you?' (2013) 14 PDP 11, 11; Ovidiu Vermesan and Joël Bacquet (eds), *Next Generation Internet of Things* (River Publishers 2018) 23-30.

4 de Beer *et al.* (n2) 181-184 and 200; Scasserra and Martínez Elebi (n3) 4.

5 'Our Mission' (*Meta*, 2023); 'Meta' (*Computer Hope*, 11 Jun 2021).

6 'Amazon Headquarters' (*headquartersoffice.com*, 2023); 'Apple Inc. Headquarters' (*headquartersoffice.com*, 2023); 'Google Headquarters Information' (*headquartersinfo.com*, 2023); 'Meta Headquarters' (*Chamber of Commerce*, 2023); '20 Things You Didn't Know About Samsung Headquarters in Suwon' (*Samsung News*, 29 Sep 2014).

7 de Beer *et al.* (n2) 178; Meta, 'Meet Your New Assistant: Meta AI, Built With Llama 3' (*fb.com*, 18 Apr 2024).

8 Article 29 WP, 'Opinion 8/2014' (n2) 13; de Beer *et al.* (n2) 182-184; Thomas Hoppner and Anastasia Gubanova, 'Regulatory challenges of the internet of things' (2015) 21 CTLR 227, 231; Scasserra and Martínez Elebi (n3) 5.

9 Hoppner and Gubanova (n8) 227; Karsenti (n2) 34; Xin Su and others, 'User biometric information-based secure method for smart devices' (2018) 30 CCPE 1, 1; Sundmaeker *et al.* (n3) 13; Taylor (n2) 95.

used in.[10] Private companies make, as a consequence, not only profit from the devices they sell, but also, and even more, from the data that is collected by these devices, which is often sold for processing and profiling to third parties. These business plans do not anymore solely focus on the devices or services themselves, but even more on the movements, behavior, and thoughts of the devices' users, leading to the famous observation that 'data is the new gold or the new oil'.[11] The more people use the devices and services, the more data will be collected and processed to train the algorithm, leading to even more accurate and personalized results and suggestions. The increased level of accuracy and personalization will then again incentivize more people to use or acquire the device or service, resulting in a 'cycle of increasing returns',[12] as the algorithm will again have more data to be trained with to optimize its results, leading once more to an increase in users.[13] These data collection and processing practices, combined with the complex wording of terms and conditions,[14] can even result in tracking and profiling practices that users could not foresee or could not be aware of. A smartphone's camera or GPS data reveals, for example, people's location almost precisely, enabling surveillance as people carry their phones almost everywhere with them.[15] Location-based services may also pick up the phone's location and display personalized advertisements, restaurant suggestions, or the nearest public transportation information. Some of these features can be beneficial to users and have their preference. In other cases, services 'pushed' to users against their will can create privacy issues. Metadata seemed, in this context, initially, an 'innocent' alternative to the more protected content data, as it provides information about content data, such as the sender/receiver of a call or message, the location, or the duration of the communication.[16] At first sight, these may seem only small irrelevant parts of data,

---

10 Article 29 WP, 'Opinion 8/2014' (n2) 4; Alter (n2) 384; Chander (n2) s12; FTC, *Mobile Privacy Disclosures* (n2) i and 2; Karsenti (n2) 35; Treacy and Bapat (n3) 11; Vermesan *et al.* (n3) 30-31.

11 Chris Hoofnagle, Bart van der Sloot, and Frederik Zuiderveen Borgesius, 'The European Union general data protection regulation' (2019) 28 ICT Law 65, 65; Matt Shepherd, 'Is Data the New Gold?' (*CEO Today*, 4 Apr 2018).

12 McTear *et al.* (n2) 20.

13 Anuj Anand, 'Shall we make the machines smart?' (2017) 23 CTLR 116, 117-118; de Beer *et al.* (n2) 162 and 186-187 and 201; FTC, *Mobile Privacy Disclosures* (n2) i and 2; Hoppner and Gubanova (n8) 228-229; Karsenti (n2) 35; Yevhen Laniuk, 'Freedom in the Age of surveillance capitalism' (2021) 11 Ethics&Bioethics 67, 67-70; Limpert (n3) 1-18; McTear *et al.* (n2) 20 and 283-285; Jason Millar, 'Core privacy' in Ian Kerr, Valerie Steeves, and Carole Lucock (eds), *Lessons from the Identity Trail* (OUP 2009) 99-108; Nadezhda Purtova, 'From knowing by name to targeting' (2022) 12 IDPL 163, 164-173; Rooney (n1) 8-9; Teresa Scassa and Anca Sattler, 'Location-Based Services and Privacy' (2011) 9 CJLT 99, 99 and 112; Vermesan *et al.* (n3) 30-31.

14 See *Chapter 4, § 1, B., ii)*.

15 Steven Farmer, 'European privacy body opines on geolocation services on smart mobile devices' (2011) 17 CTLR 115, 115; Scassa and Sattler (n13) 112-115.

16 Article 29 WP, 'Opinion 04/2014 on surveillance of electronic communications for intelligence and national security purposes' (WP215, 10 Apr 2014) 4; Glenn Greenwald, *No Place to Hide* (Hamish Hamilton 2014) 132; Daniel Solove, 'Data Is What Data Does' (2024) 118 NwUnivLRev 1081, 1116.

but the longer this information is collected, the more detailed people's daily activities can be deducted, and the more sensitive this information becomes as most people are nowadays permanently online. Metadata can, moreover, be put together, or aggregated with other data, such as Google Search engine queries or social media content, revealing patterns and a comprehensive insight into someone's private life.[17]

Privacy and security – Hackers – Manufacturers often focus predominantly on their devices' and services' advantages, which may overshadow their technical and privacy security risks. Firstly, smart devices can be hacked or security flaws exploited. These situations and privacy breaches do not have to occur intentionally by manufacturers, but can be the result of a general lack of interest or experience in security.[18] In a 2015 Internet of Things Research Study conducted by Hewlett-Packard,[19] 80% of smart devices (including home security systems) were found not to require strong passwords, and 70% did not encrypt communications, facilitating potential hackers' access and exploitation of this data.[20] Home security cameras, smart lights, or smart garage doors as part of a home security system have already been targeted, with freely accessible websites livestreaming footage from poorly secured cameras or hacked baby monitors that were used to talk and curse to children.[21] More dangerously, hackers can obtain access to the main Wi-Fi router in someone's home through a weakly secured smart device connected to it that they can use as a gateway. Since the router is the main device that all smart devices have to connect to in order to get internet access, hacking this device, or obtaining access to it, endangers all the information and devices

17 Article 29 WP, 'Opinion 04/2014' (n16) 4-5; Alter (n2) 390; Anand (n13) 117-118; Lee Bygrave, *Data Protection Law* (Kluwer 2002) 105; de Beer *et al.* (n2) 201-202; Farmer (n15) 115-116; FTC, *Mobile Privacy Disclosures* (n2) i; Greenwald, *No Place to Hide* (n16) 133-134; Limpert (n3) 5-13; Millar (n13) 99-103; Scassa and Sattler (n13) 99-113 and 133; Monika Zalnieriute, 'A Struggle for Competence' (2022) 85 MLR 198, 200.

18 Anand (n13) 117; Chander (n2) s12-s13; Finding and Taylor (n3) 148; Hoppner and Gubanova (n8) 228-231; Taylor (n2) 96; Vermesan *et al.* (n3) 103-134.

19 Anand (n13) 117; Finding and Taylor (n3) 148; Hewlett-Packard Enterprise, *Internet of Things Research Study* (Report, 2015) 1-6; Hoppner and Gubanova (n8) 229.

20 Hewlett-Packard Enterprise (n19) 4.

21 Spencer Ackerman, 'CIA Chief: We'll Spy on You Through Your Dishwasher' (*Wired*, 15 Mar 2012); de Beer *et al.* (n2) 176; Mat Honan, 'Hackers Are Exploiting Baby Monitors, But We Know How to Stop Them' (*Wired*, 15 Oct 2013); Karsenti (n2) 36; Angelina King and Jason Lo, 'Private moments captured on home security cameras being live streamed again on website' (*CBC News*, 29 Jun 2021); Adam Levin, '9 Household Products That May Be Spying on You' (*ABC News*, 18 Aug 2013); Limpert (n3) 12-18; Sarah Min, 'Your smart TV might be spying on you, FBI warns' (*CBS News*, 3 Dec 2019); Tara Seals, 'Google Nest Security Cam Bugs Allow Device Takeover' (*Threat Post*, 19 Aug 2019); Guy Sheetrit, 'Smart Home and Data Protection: Between Convenience and Security' (*Readwrite*, 18 Nov 2020); Ms. Smith, 'Peeping into 73,000 unsecured security cameras thanks to default passwords' (*CSO News*, 6 Nov 2014); Alex Sundby, 'Hacker spoke to baby, hurled obscenities at couple using Nest Camera, dad says' (*CBS News*, 31 Jan 2019); Sundmaeker *et al.* (n3) 51-53; David Whelan, 'For the Record: Internet of Things' (2014) 35 For the Defence 1, 1.

connected to it.[22] In order to prevent hacking and discover security flaws, private companies and government authorities hire so-called 'white' or 'ethical' hackers. These hackers search for vulnerabilities in order to remedy them before hackers with bad intentions can exploit the security flaws for malicious purposes. In 2012, a white-hat hacker managed to obtain access to and control a smart insulin pump of a diabetic person, providing the hacker with the opportunity to deliver a fatal insulin dose to, and hence kill, the diabetic person. Similar security issues were found in other medical equipment, such as smart pacemakers or defibrillators.[23] Hacking and security-related issues will, for the remainder of this book, be left out of the discussion's scope.

Privacy and security – Private companies – Secondly, manufacturers may also deliberately hide privacy and/or security risks behind nicely formulated benefits to convince users to share their personal information and data without really understanding how their data is subsequently processed.[24] It was mentioned above that big tech companies like Google, Amazon, or Apple have equipped their devices with a voice-activated personal assistant function that will react when hearing a specific command. 'Hey Google', 'Alexa', or 'Hey Siri' will, respectively, activate the related devices to conduct the particular task commanded. In order to 'hear' these commands, users' devices must always be listening and can, consequently, listen in on all private conversations. When these conversations are also recorded, even if anonymously for algorithm training purposes, one can legitimately question where this data will eventually end up. Users have the possibility to request deletion of the collected data, but due to frequent and extended sharing with third parties, it may be difficult or impossible to adequately exercise and comply with this request.[25] Given the many (manufacturing, distributing, processing …) actors involved in the Internet of Things, users face difficulties to determine who they should contact or hold accountable in case of a (suspected) security breach.[26] Similarly, smart TV spying practices caused public outrage in the United States when some of these devices were not only found to collect their users' watching behavior information (such as selected movies or preferred advertisements), but also that they were equipped with webcams

---

22 Anand (n13) 117; Limpert (n3) 17; Min (n21); Whelan (n21) 2; 'Your Smart TV May Be Spying on You' (*Arizona Financial*, 6 Mar 2020).

23 Bill Hancock, 'Experts: Use caution with white-hat hackers' (1999) 18 ComputSecur 285, 285; Levin (n21); Limpert (n3) 17.

24 Chander (n2) s12; Alexa Fox and Mariea Grubbs Hoy, 'Smart Devices, Smart Decisions?' (2019) 38 JPPM 414, 427; Karsenti (n2) 36; Limpert (n3) 17; Sheetrit (n21); Whelan (n21) 1-2; 'Your Smart TV' (n22).

25 de Beer *et al.* (n2) 187 and 201; Editorial Staff, 'Voice-Activated Device Privacy, What You Need to Know' (*Tripwire*, 22 Jun 2021); Forbes Technology Council, 'Nine Things Voice-Activated Tech Users Should Know About Their Devices' (*Forbes*, 17 Apr 2019); Karsenti (n2) 37 and 55; Makena Kelly and Nick Statt, 'Amazon confirms it holds on to Alexa data even if you delete audio files' (*The Verge*, 3 Jul 2019); Limpert (n3) 17.

26 FTC, *Mobile Privacy Disclosures* (n2) i and 2-3; Guimaraes Pereira *et al.* (n3) 9; Karsenti (n2) 55.

and microphones to actually 'watch' the users. In 2013, LG was involved in a privacy scandal for sharing its users' personal data without permission. In 2015, Samsung TVs turned out to be equipped with permanently switched on microphones and webcams. In 2017, Vizio faced a privacy scandal for not disclosing how and when users' personal data was collected, and for transmitting this data unencrypted.[27] Some of these features can be adjusted by users in the permission settings, but these are not always clear and user-friendly. Users may also not have the time or adequate technical knowledge to go through all the different settings and find the ones they would like to disable.[28] Additionally, settings' names are not always straightforward. 'Automatic Content Recognition', 'Viewing Information Services' (on Samsung), 'Viewing Data' or 'Smart Interactivity' (on Vizio) or 'Live Plus' (on LG) all cover personal data collection features on smart TVs, making it even more difficult for consumers to understand what these features encompass.[29] Private companies sometimes also 'punish' users that do not want to acquire certain (smart) devices or use certain services. Non-smart or 'dumb' versions of certain devices may disappear or become rare. Lengthy and complex privacy policies make it difficult for users to adjust settings according to their preferences, and even if users succeed in adjusting the settings, disabling some of them may make the acquired devices unusable. Opting out of certain options may also hinder, otherwise automatically received, security updates, making the devices vulnerable as detected security flaws are not remedied automatically. Consequently, users are left with a minor choice, if it can be considered a choice at all.[30] This book will, in the following chapters, focus on this second type of data privacy breaches, where personal data is (mis)used by private companies and additionally by law enforcement alike.

B. USER PROFILING AND PERSONALIZED SERVICES

Economic value – The two most well-known practices where collected personal data is used to offer personalized services are user profiling and targeted advertising. Users' personal data is fed to algorithms which subsequently not only predict users' preferences at the moment, but also what users' future interests (likely) will be. 'Direct profiling' occurs when private companies assume that users' personal data, collected in the online world, provides an overview of their interests and characteristics, and build user profiles based on this

---

27 de Beer *et al.* (n2) 186-187; Limpert (n3) 11-17; Min (n21); David Naylor and Robert Blamires, 'Smarter thinking – connected TV, law and regulation' (2012) 23 EntLR 123, 123; Sayb Saad, 'How to Stop Your Smart TV Spying on You (2025 Guide)' (*WizCase*, 31 May 2025); Kyla Taylor and Mark Taylor, 'Television and its role in the internet of things' (2015) 21 CTLR 66, 67; Whelan (n21) 1; 'Your Smart TV' (n22).

28 de Beer *et al.* (n2) 161; Scassa and Sattler (n13) 117; Sheetrit (n21).

29 Saad (n27).

30 de Beer *et al.* (n2) 190-200; Saad (n27); Sheetrit (n21); Whelan (n21) 1; 'Your Smart TV' (n22).

information. People may also prefer to receive this type of personalized services and advertisement as it is tailored to their preferences and interests.[31] 'Indirect profiling' occurs when user groups sharing similar characteristics are created and people are categorized within these groups based on some characteristics that they have in common.[32] Lee Bygrave identifies two components in profiling processes, namely, profile generation consisting of "the inference of a set of characteristics (profile) about an individual person", and profile application consisting of "the subsequent treatment of that person or other persons in the light of these characteristics, (which) will typically relate to the behavior (actual or expected) of a person".[33,34] The "process of creating and applying ... a sort of portraits ... used to characterize an individual, (or) a demographic group ... does not merely describe an individual or a group, but also predicts their behavior based upon what is typical for the individual or group in question".[35] This prediction of future behavior is then applied to determine user preferences and offer targeted advertisements.[36] The increased availability and collection possibilities of personal data have even led to the emergence of data brokers specialized in consolidating and selling almost complete user profiles.[37]

Inaccuracies – User profiles constructed by private companies or data brokers are not always accurate and can lead to human rights infringements. Julie Cohen explains that "there is much about individual behavior that is predictable ... yet there also is much about individual behavior that is not".[38] The constructed profiles and derived assumptions can be inherently flawed as "they are the outcomes of probability equations ... (which may) ... contain some margin of error".[39,40] Human agency differs in motivation and is influenced by independent factors, which can change the outcome of predictions based on generally expected behavior.[41] The constructed profiles can also be flawed if they are based on inaccurate or incomplete information, especially in the case of user groups, resulting in predictions that will not always be applicable to or relevant for all

---

31 Nadezhda Purtova, *Property Rights in Personal Data* (Kluwer 2012) 50.

32 Bygrave, *Data Protection Law* (n17) 303; Serge Gutwirth and others (eds), *Reinventing Data Protection?* (Springer 2009) 242-251; Purtova, *Property Rights* (n31) 23 and 49-50.

33 Bygrave, *Data Protection Law* (n17) 301.

34 *Ibid.* 302.

35 Purtova, *Property Rights* (n31) 23.

36 Bygrave, *Data Protection Law* (n17) 304; Paul Quinn and Gianclaudio Malgieri, 'The Difficulty of Defining Sensitive Data' (2021) 22 GLJ 1583, 1608.

37 Lee Bygrave, *Data Privacy Law* (OUP 2014) 4-5; Eleni Kosta and Irene Kamara (eds), *Data Retention in Europe and Beyond* (OUP 2025) 472-480.

38 Julie Cohen, 'Examined Lives' (2000) 52 SLR 1373, 1405.

39 Bygrave, *Data Protection Law* (n17) 309.

40 *Ibid.* 302-309 and 363.

41 Cohen (n38) 1405-1406; Gutwirth *et al.* (n32) 112-113.

users.[42] Privacy issues may also arise when some members of the user group reveal information that other group members may have preferred not to share, but since both persons belong to the same user group, the algorithm will infer that this information is applicable to and relevant for all the group members. "People's decisions about their own privacy (can consequently also) affect society"[43] or at least people sharing similar characteristics, which is enhanced by machine learning[44] practices, but which is not necessarily a correct deduction.[45]

Political extension – Personalized services are not only offered in the economic sphere but have also increasingly been employed in the context of political opinions and (democratic) elections. During the Belgian 2019 elections, the far right political party *Vlaams Belang* became the second-biggest political party in the region of Flanders due to a surprisingly high number of votes from the younger population.[46] *Vlaams Belang* was also the only political party that had spent the majority of its campaign budget on social media advertisement at that time.[47] During the 2020 U.S. elections, Facebook adjusted its algorithm to reduce the display of like-minded information by 1/3 in the framework of a study.[48] This adjustment did not impact users' behavior, but the study explains that the large degree of already existing electoral polarization in the United States may play a dominant role in these findings.[49] People may, of course, also engage with certain online content because they are actually interested in it, and not just because the algorithm selected that content for them.[50] Given the distorted world view that political personalized services may cause, political personal information

42 Bygrave, *Data Protection Law* (n17) 363; Gutwirth *et al.* (n32) 112-113; Orla Lynskey, *The foundations of EU data protection law* (1st edn, OUP 2015) 196-210; Purtova, *Property Rights* (n31) 23-24.

43 Daniel Solove, 'Introduction: Privacy Self-Management and the Consent Dilemma' (2013) 126 HarvLRev 1880, 1881.

44 Machine learning is a method of programming computer software whereby an algorithm has to perform a task. The algorithm is trained using example data and gains experience to differentiate one type of data from another. Based on the feedback that the algorithm receives (namely, correctly or mistakenly differentiated), it learns itself how to improve its decisions. The main aim is for the algorithm to make a correct decision when confronted with new data or new circumstances.: Ethem Alpaydın, 'Machine learning' (2011) 3 WIREs CompStat 195, 195; Przemysław Pałka, 'Data Management Law for the 2020s' (2020) 68 BuffLRev 559, 594.

45 Pałka, 'Data Management' (n44) 563-565 and 592-596; Yves Poullet, 'Data protection legislation' (2009) 25 CLSR 211, 214.

46 Tobias Santens, 'Vlaams Belang grote winnaar van de verkiezingen, partij wordt tweede in Vlaanderen' (*VRT NWS*, 26 May 2019).

47 Tim Van Opstal, 'Opiniestuk: het effect van social media op de recente (Vlaamse) verkiezingen. Of hoe het pamflet vervangen is door Instagram en Facebook' (*LinkedIn*, 28 May 2019).

48 Nick Petrić Howe, 'Facebook 'Echo Chamber' Has Little Impact on Polarized Views, According to Study' (*Nature*, 27 Jul 2023).

49 *Ibid.*

50 Brent Kitchens, Steven Johnson, and Peter Gray, 'Understanding Echo Chambers and Filter Bubbles' (2020) 44 MIS Quarterly 1619, 1627.

should not be used for profiling purposes, especially not around the time of elections. Instead, social media providers should display a variety of political advertisements to preserve a democratic debate and enhance the exchange of political ideas. Empirical evidence about the impact of 'echo chambers'[51] on elections and voting behavior is inconclusive,[52] but it is a phenomenon that should be brought to people's attention.

Many aspects – The examples above show that collected personal data can be used for different, sometimes even conflicting, purposes. Firstly, personal data is a commercial asset for private companies to personalize services and make a profit by selling their users' personal data to third parties for profiling purposes. Secondly, government authorities can also use this collected personal data as a source of intelligence for national security purposes, as will be shown in the next section. Thirdly, personal data is always closely linked to the person concerned, and a large amount of detailed information can provide 'a comprehensive insight into someone's private life', endangering people's privacy. Limiting the ability of private companies to collect personal data is beneficial for users, but hampers trade models where this data is used as a commercial asset. Government authorities need personal data to collect intelligence information, but the use and collection of this information should be regulated adequately to prevent the development of authoritarian and dictatorial regimes. It is, as a consequence, difficult to find the right balance between the different aspects and purposes of personal data collection.[53]

§ 2. EU-U.S. PERSONAL DATA FLOWS

Transatlantic divide – The different purposes and aspects of personal data collection have also inspired different approaches towards personal data on both sides of the Atlantic. Where the United States focuses predominantly on the commerce and intelligence dimension of personal data, the EU focuses more on the protection of personal data and data privacy in its regulatory framework. There are arguments for and against regulatory intervention. Consumer organizations may favor "a strong regulatory framework that is properly enforced (which) is needed to ensure that consumers' rights and autonomy are respected",[54] while technology specialists warn

---

51 Echo Chambers are a phenomenon on social media where users are categorized within polarized groups 'echoing' the same ideas as they hold, filtering out dissenting opinions. See *Chapter 4, § 2, A., iii)*.

52 Daniel Geschke, Jan Lorenz, and Peter Holtz, 'The Triple-filter Bubble' (2019) 58 BJSP 129, 130; Kamile Grusauskaite and others, 'Debating (In) Echo Chambers' [2023] NewMediaSoc 1, 3 and 18; Kitchens *et al.* (n50) 1620-1621 and 1642; Petrić Howe (n48).

53 Chander (n2) s15; Karsenti (n2) 48; Taylor (n2) 96; Treacy and Bapat (n3) 12-13.

54 Guimaraes Pereira *et al.* (n3) 30.

that "the key challenge for the industry is that, as is often the case with emerging technologies, the law is playing catchup with issues raised by … technology and until it does so, it falls to the industry to grapple with these issues".[55] A gap emerges between these two approaches, but in a globalized world, countries and regions must cooperate to effectively protect citizens' personal data, while ensuring international data flows.[56] Many EU citizens use the services of U.S. big tech companies daily for work, communication, and leisure. In order to allow these services to operate, an extensive amount of personal data is transferred over the Atlantic, as detailed personal data from European citizens is collected and processed by U.S. companies.[57] EU-U.S. personal data flows are even one of the highest in the world,[58] and keeping transatlantic services operational is hence an economic and social necessity. To overcome the regulatory differences, frameworks for EU-U.S. personal data transfers were developed in the form of adequacy decisions.

A. SAFE HARBOUR AND *SCHREMS I*

2000 Safe Harbour – The 1995 EU Data Protection Directive[59] stated in article 25.1 that "the transfer to a third country of (European) personal data which are undergoing processing or are intended for processing after transfer may take place only if … the third country in question ensures an adequate level of protection",[60] restricting the possibilities for personal data transfers outside the EU.[61] While the prescribed procedure requires the European Commission to adopt an adequacy decision, where the adequacy of the foreign system to the level of protection in the EU is established, this procedure involves in practice negotiations and agreements with third countries where, if needed, (adequate) rules, practices, and safeguards are introduced by the third country in order to obtain an adequacy decision. In U.S. literature, adequacy decisions are, consequently, often referenced as 'agreements' with the EU. In accordance with this procedure, the European Commission

55 Taylor (n2) 97.

56 Michael Birnhack, 'The EU Data Protection Directive' (2008) 24 CLSR 508, 510-511; Federico Fabbrini, Edoardo Celeste, and John Quinn, *Data protection beyond borders* (Hart Publishing 2021) 10 and 25; Maria Tzanou, 'European Union Regulation of Transatlantic Data Transfers and Online Surveillance' (2017) 17 HRLR 545, 546-547.

57 Bygrave, *Data Privacy Law* (n37) 123; Chander (n2) s14; Anthony Gardner, *Stars with Stripes* (Springer 2020) 163-164.

58 Walter Berka, 'CETA, TTIP, TiSA, and Data Protection' in Stephan Griller, Erich Vranes, and Walter Obwexer (eds), *Mega-Regional Trade Agreements* (OUP 2017) 175.

59 Directive 95/46/EC of 24 Oct 1995 on the protection of individuals with regard to the processing of personal data and on the free movement of such data [1995] OJ L 281/31; See *Chapter 3, § 3, B., i), b).*

60 Article 25.1 Directive 95/46/EC.

61 Daniel Solove and Woodrow Hartzog, 'The FTC and the New Common Law of Privacy' (2014) 114 ColumLRev 583, 603-604.

adopted the 2000 *Safe Harbour adequacy decision*[62] for the United States to allow the transfer of Europeans' personal data for commercial purposes. As was agreed, the U.S. Department of Commerce issued a document with the 'Safe Harbor Privacy Principles' and the Frequently Asked Questions (FAQs) "under its statutory authority to foster, promote, and develop international commerce".[63] Recital 5 of Safe Harbour stated that "the adequate level of protection for the transfer of data from the (EU) to the United States recognised by this Decision, should be attained if organisations comply with (1) the safe harbour privacy principles for the protection of personal data transferred from a Member State to the United States … and (2) the frequently asked questions … providing guidance for the implementation of the (safe harbour privacy) Principles … (3) the organisations should publicly disclose their privacy policies and (4) be subject to the jurisdiction of the Federal Trade Commission (FTC) under Section 5 of the Federal Trade Commission Act which prohibits unfair or deceptive acts or practices in or affecting commerce, or that of another statutory body that will effectively ensure compliance with the Principles implemented in accordance with the FAQs".[64] U.S. companies could voluntarily self-certify to the U.S. Department of Commerce that they met those requirements.[65] The enforcement mechanism prescribed by Safe Harbour can be qualified as a "hybrid self-regulatory system (as) it involve(d) both industry self-regulation and some government enforcement",[66] in the form of the FTC.[67] Remarkably, the different EU and U.S. approach towards privacy was acknowledged in the first paragraph of Annex I to Safe Harbour, but in the 6th paragraph U.S. law was chosen to "apply to questions of interpretation and compliance with the Safe Harbor Principles (including the Frequently Asked Questions) and relevant privacy policies by safe harbor organizations …".[68,69] Additionally, the scope of application of the Safe Harbour adequacy decision was restricted, as "adherence to these Principles (could) be limited: (a) to the extent necessary to meet national security, public interest, or law enforcement requirements …".[70,71]

Criticism – The German (Hessian) Chief Data Protection Commissioner Spiros Simitis, also called 'the godfather of European data protection', stressed already in 1999 that "personal data are not bananas",[72] meaning that personal data cannot

62 Commission Decision 2000/520/EC of 26 Jul 2000 pursuant to Directive 95/46/EC on the adequacy of the protection provided by the safe harbour privacy principles and related frequently asked questions issued by the U.S. Department of Commerce [2000] OJ L 215/7.

63 Annex I Decision 2000/520/EC, 10.

64 Recital 5 Decision 2000/520/EC.

65 Recital 7 Decision 2000/520/EC; Bygrave, *Data Privacy Law* (n37) 195.

66 Dorothee Heisenberg, *Negotiating Privacy* (Lynne Rienner Publishers 2005) 74.

67 Solove and Hartzog (n61) 585 and 603-604.

68 Annex I Decision 2000/520/EC, 11.

69 Bygrave, *Data Privacy Law* (n37) 196.

70 Annex I Decision 2000/520/EC, 10.

71 Bygrave, *Data Privacy Law* (n37) 195; Solove and Hartzog (n61) 603-604.

72 Berka (n58) 175; Lee Bygrave, 'International agreements to protect personal data' in Graham Greenleaf and James Rule (eds), *Global Privacy Protection* (Edward Elgar 2010) 15.

be equaled to regular goods or trade barriers.[73] Privacy protection is, moreover, exempted from WTO jurisdiction, resulting in privacy conflicts not being solvable in this framework, to which the EU and United States had usually recourse for trade conflicts.[74] The European Parliament as well as the Article 29 Working Party (Article 29WP)[75] opposed the adequacy finding by the EU Commission, but had no power to halt its adoption.[76] Dorothee Heisenberg and Lee Bygrave observe that the primary aim of Safe Harbour was to preserve the transatlantic commercial interests and keep EU-U.S. personal data transfers possible, rather than to 'adequately' protect Europeans' privacy and personal data.[77]

Snowden revelations – Thirteen years after Safe Harbour was concluded, whistleblower Edward Snowden shared top-secret documents about large-scale data collection programs and surveillance practices by U.S. intelligence agencies with newspaper *The Guardian*.[78] The first case revealed a court order issued by the U.S. Foreign Intelligence Surveillance Court (FISC[79]) mandating Verizon, the largest U.S. telecom provider, to share "all call detail records or 'telephony metadata' created by Verizon for communications (i) between the United States and abroad; or (ii) wholly within the United States, including local telephone calls"[80] with the U.S. National Security Agency (NSA), excluding the content of the communications.[81] The second case involved the controversial 'PRISM' program which provided the NSA and the FBI direct access to servers of leading U.S. companies and internet providers, such as Microsoft, Google, Facebook, YouTube, or Skype, to obtain intelligence material, such as emails, messages, photos, documents, etc., including not only metadata, but also content information. The PRISM program had its legal basis in an overly extensive interpretation of Section 702 of the Foreign Intelligence Surveillance Act

73 Berka (n58) 175.
74 Julia Fromholz, 'The European Union Data Privacy Directive' (2000) 15 BTLJ 461, 474; Heisenberg (n66) 3.
75 See *Chapter 3, § 3, B., i), b)*.
76 Heisenberg (n66) 8-17 and 94-96.
77 Bygrave, *Data Privacy Law* (n37) 195; Heisenberg (n66) 11 and 160.
78 David Bender, 'Having mishandled Safe Harbor, will the CJEU do better with Privacy Shield?' (2016) 6 IDPL 117, 118; Iain Cameron, 'European Union Law Restraints on Intelligence Activities' (2020) 33 IJIC 452, 456; Barton Gellman and Laura Poitras, 'U.S., British intelligence mining data from nine U.S. Internet companies in broad secret program' (*The Washington Post*, 6 Jun 2013); Glenn Greenwald, 'NSA collecting phone records of millions of Verizon customers daily' (*The Guardian*, 6 Jun 2013); Glenn Greenwald and Ewen MacAskill, 'NSA Prism program taps in to user data of Apple, Google and others' (*The Guardian*, 6 Jun 2013); Ewen MacAskill and others, 'GCHQ taps fibre-optic cables for secret access to world's communications' (*The Guardian*, 21 Jun 2013); Tarzie, 'Edward Snowden: Frenemy of the State' (2017) 76 AJES 348, 348-380.
79 See *Chapter 5, § 2*.
80 U.S. FISA Court, Order requiring the production of tangible things from Verizon Business Network Services, 25 Apr 2013.
81 Greenwald, 'NSA collecting' (n78); Greenwald, *No Place to Hide* (n16) 27-29 and 58; Newton Lee, *Facebook Nation* (3rd edn, Springer 2021) 11.

(FISA[82]).[83] The third case concerned a unique mass tapping operation called 'Tempora' which tapped information directly from the "transatlantic fibre-optic cables where they land on British shores carrying data to Western Europe from telephone exchanges and internet servers in North America".[84] Tempora was set up by the American NSA, but carried out by the British Government Communications Headquarters (GCHQ)[85] intelligence agency, and provided the latter with access to all the information and internet flows between the two sides of the Atlantic.[86] The 'Upstream' program was the U.S. counterpart to Tempora, and provided the NSA with direct access to metadata and content information from communications flowing through the transatlantic fiber-optic cables.[87]

Reactions Post-Snowden – Snowden's revelations caused public outrage in the United States and EU alike and had a negative impact on the transatlantic relationship and trust.[88] In response, an ad hoc EU-U.S. Working Group on data protection[89] was set up in July 2013 to assess the large-scale U.S. data collection and surveillance practices. The Working Group identified the following issues:

1) U.S. law allows that personal data transferred to the United States or processed by U.S. companies is collected and processed on a large scale for foreign intelligence purposes;

---

82 See *Chapter 5, § 2.*

83 *Big Brother Watch and Others v United Kingdom* App nos 58170/13, 62322/14, and 24960/15 (ECtHR, 13 Sep 2018) paras 15-17; *Big Brother Watch and Others v United Kingdom* App nos 58170/13, 62322/14, and 24960/15 (ECtHR, 25 May 2021) para 22-24; Bygrave, *Data Privacy Law* (n37) 195-196; Gellman and Poitras (n78); Barton Gellman, Julie Tate, and Ashkan Soltani, 'In NSA-intercepted data, those not targeted far outnumber the foreigners who are' (*The Washington Post*, 5 Jul 2014); Greenwald and Macaskill (n78); Greenwald, *No Place to Hide* (n16) 18-21 and 73-74; Lee (n81) 11-16.

84 Macaskill *et al.* (n78).

85 GCHQ is the United Kingdom's intelligence, security, and cyber agency, similar to the NSA in the United States.: GCHQ, 'Welcome to GCHQ' (*gov.uk*, 2025).

86 *Big Brother Watch 2018* (n83) paras 9-11; *Big Brother Watch 2021* (n83) paras 14-16; Gellman and Poitras (n78); Greenwald, *No Place to Hide* (n16) 119; Macaskill *et al.* (n78).

87 *Big Brother Watch 2018* (n83) para 18; *Big Brother Watch 2021* (n83) para 25.

88 Article 29 WP, 'Opinion 04/2014' (n16) 2; Berka (n58) 175-184; Bygrave, *Data Privacy Law* (n37) 196-197; European Commission, 'Restoring Trust in EU-US data flows – Frequently Asked Questions' MEMO(2013) 1059 final; European Commission, 'Towards a more dynamic transatlantic area of growth and investment: Speech by Viviane Reding' SPEECH(2013) 867 final; Leonhard Menges, 'Did the NSA and GCHQ Diminish Our Privacy?' (2020) 7 MOPP 29, 29-48.

89 Consisting of "on the EU side, the Commission and the Presidency of the Council of the European Union, representatives of the Presidency, the Commission services (DG Justice and DG Home Affairs), the European External Action Service, the incoming Presidency, the EU Counter-Terrorism Coordinator, the Chair of the Article 29 Working Party, as well as ten experts from Member States, selected from the area of data protection and law enforcement/security" and "on the U.S. side, senior officials from the Department of Justice, the Office of the Director of National Intelligence, the State Department and the Department of Homeland Security".: EC, 'Restoring Trust – FAQ' (n88) 8-10.

2) Higher safeguards are applicable to U.S. citizens and the collection of their data (including targeting and minimization requirements and constitutional protections such as the First and Fourth Amendment), which do not apply to EU citizens;
3) The legal bases used in the United States to engage in large-scale data collection and surveillance practices remain unclear;
4) U.S. as well as EU citizens whose personal data is collected and processed based on secret FISC orders cannot exercise their rights to access, rectify, or erase their data, and have no administrative or judicial redress options;
5) While a certain degree of oversight is present in the current U.S. system, judicial approval is not required for the 'queries' or 'selectors' entered to collect the data.[90]

Subsequently, the EU and the United States worked to restore the transatlantic relationship. Companies operating in the transatlantic region were, after all, faced with conflicting obligations by, on the one hand, having to respect EU data protection law, while, on the other hand, having to grant U.S. intelligence authorities access to their customers' data when requested.[91] The EU communicated that the U.S. national security exception enshrined in Safe Harbour could only be used "to an extent that is strictly necessary and proportionate".[92] Additional instruments were also put forward to provide remediation, such as the Umbrella Agreement in the field of law enforcement and police and judicial cooperation, or the Mutual Legal Assistance Agreement (*both discussed below*). President Barack Obama granted the EU's request by promulgating Presidential Policy Directive 28 (PPD-28)[93] in 2014, which extended safeguards to non-U.S. citizens, and U.S. Congress enacted the 2015 USA Freedom Act[94] to limit foreign signals intelligence and bulk data collection programs.[95]

2015 *Schrems I* – Safe Harbour was challenged and invalidated in the *Schrems I*[96] case by the Court of Justice of the European Union (CJEU) in 2015. Austrian privacy activist Maximilian Schrems filed a complaint about the inadequate protection of his personal data provided by Facebook in the aftermath of the Snowden revelations. The EU Commission had, after all, noted that "personal data of EU citizens sent to the

90 EC, 'Restoring Trust – FAQ' (n88) 9-10.
91 Article 29 WP, 'Opinion 04/2014' (n16) 7.
92 European Commission, 'Communication from the Commission to the European Parliament and the Council: Rebuilding Trust in EU-US Data Flows' COM(2013) 846 final.
93 The White House, Presidential Policy Directive/PPD-28, 17 Jan 2014; See *Chapter 5, § 2*.
94 Uniting and Strengthening America by Fulfilling Rights and Ensuring Effective Discipline Over Monitoring Act, 114th Congress, 2 Jun 2015, 129 Stat. 268 (USA Freedom Act); See *Chapter 5, § 2*.
95 Bender (n78) 120-122; EC, 'Restoring Trust – FAQ' (n88); EC, 'Rebuilding Trust' (n92); Shara Monteleone and Laura Puccio, *From Safe Harbour to Privacy Shield* (EPRS, 2017) 10; Emily Sheketoff, 'USA Freedom Act of 2015 passes' (2015) 76 C&RL News 401, 401.
96 C-362/14 *Maximilian Schrems v Data Protection Commissioner* [2015] (*Schrems I*).

(United States) under the Safe Harbour may be accessed and further processed by U.S. authorities in a way incompatible with the grounds on which the data was originally collected in the EU and the purposes for which it was transferred to the (United States and) a majority of the U.S. internet companies that appear to be more directly concerned by these programmes are certified under the Safe Harbour scheme".[97,98] Schrems was a Facebook user and as "all of the data provided to Facebook in Ireland is transferred from Facebook's Irish subsidiary to servers located in the United States, where it is processed",[99] U.S. intelligence agencies, such as the NSA, could potentially gain access to his personal data. Whilst surveillance laws can serve "necessary and indispensable objectives in the public interest",[100] the mass scale and undifferentiability of the data collection concerned "demonstrated 'significant over-reach' on the part of the NSA and other federal agencies".[101] This type of extensive surveillance compromised "the essence of the fundamental right to respect for private life, as guaranteed by article 7 of the (EU) Charter".[102] Third countries were not required to have identical data protection regimes to the one of the European Union in order to obtain an adequacy decision, but fundamental rights and freedoms had to be protected in an essentially equivalent manner. The Court found that Safe Harbour stipulated that "national security, public interest, or law enforcement requirements' have primacy over the Safe Harbour principles, primacy pursuant to which self-certified United States organisations receiving personal data from the European Union are bound to disregard those principles without limitation where they conflict with those requirements and therefore prove incompatible with them".[103] U.S. public authorities were not subject to the rules set out in Safe Harbour. It was, therefore, irrelevant whether U.S. companies complied with the Safe Harbour requirements; U.S. public authorities could, in any case, access transferred Europeans' personal data. Additionally, the CJEU noticed that "the first subparagraph of article 3(1) of (Safe Harbour) must … be understood as denying the national supervisory authorities the powers …, where a person, in bringing a claim …, puts forward matters that may call into question whether a Commission decision that has found … that a third country ensures an adequate level of protection is compatible with the protection of the privacy and of the fundamental rights and freedoms of individuals",[104] leaving no inquiry and redress options for EU citizens against an adequacy finding. Finally, the U.S. oversight mechanism was found to be ineffective as some certified

97 EC, 'Rebuilding Trust' (n92) 4.

98 *Schrems I* (n96) paras 14 and 22; EC, 'Communication: Rebuilding Trust' (n78); European Commission, 'Communication from the Commission to the European Parliament and the Council on the Functioning of the Safe Harbour from the Perspective of EU Citizens and Companies Established in the EU' COM(2013) 847 final, 16.

99 Global Freedom of Expression, 'Schrems v. Data Protection Commissioner' (*columbia.edu*, 2015).

100 *Ibid.*

101 *Ibid.*

102 *Schrems I* (n96) para 94.

103 *Ibid.* para 86.

104 *Ibid.* para 102.

companies did not comply with the Safe Harbour Principles, resulting in an illegal competitive advantage for these non-compliant companies.[105] Consequently, the CJEU invalidated Safe Harbour as the decision did not provide "a supervisory authority of a Member State … (the opportunity to examine) the claim of a person concerning the protection of his rights and freedoms in regard to the processing of personal data relating to him which has been transferred from a Member State to that third country when that person contends that the law and practices in force in the third country do not ensure an adequate level of protection",[106] which was incompatible with article 25.6 of the 1995 Directive read in the light of articles 7, 8, and 47 of the EU Charter.[107]

B. PRIVACY SHIELD AND *SCHREMS II*

2016 Privacy Shield – Safe Harbour's invalidation caused uncertainty regarding the legal framework governing EU-U.S. personal data flows. The alternative Standard Contractual Clauses (SCCs) provided for in article 26.2 of the 1995 Directive were, after all, insufficient as contractual clauses cannot bind third parties; in this case, U.S. public authorities (*see below*). To ensure that transatlantic data transfers would not be hampered, the Article 29 WP installed a moratorium, consisting of *"a legally authorized period of delay in the performance of an obligation"*.[108,109] In February 2016, the EU Commission and the United States finally reached a deal in the form of the 2016 *Privacy Shield adequacy decision*.[110] The United States tried to remedy the issues identified by the CJEU with substantial improvements. A redress mechanism for EU citizens was introduced, requiring U.S. companies to respond within a specified timeframe to EU citizens' complaints regarding the use of their personal data. A new Ombudsperson was created to investigate complaints regarding potential data access by national intelligence authorities. The system of self-certification

105 *Ibid.* paras 15 and 21.

106 *Ibid.* para 107.

107 Article 29 WP, 'Statement of the Article 29 Working Party' (16 Oct 2015) 1; Bender (n78) 117-138; Berka (n58) 183; Athena Christofi and Valerie Verdoodt, *Exploring the essence of the right to data protection and smart cities* (CiTiP Working Paper, 2019) 22-23; Lothar Determann, 'Adequacy of data protection in the USA' (2016) 6 IDPL 244, 244-250; Gardner (n57) 149-189; Samuel Gibbs, 'What is 'safe harbour' and why did the EUCJ just declare it invalid?' (*The Guardian*, 6 Oct 2015); Global Freedom of Expression (n99); Simon McGarr, 'Do Facebook and the USA violate EU data protection law? The CJEU hearing in Schrems' (*EU Law Analysis*, 29 Mar 2015); Monteleone and Puccio (n95) 1-16; Derek Scally, 'EU cannot guarantee citizens' privacy when transferring data to US, court told' (*The Irish Times*, 25 Mar 2015).

108 'Moratorium' (*Merriam-Webster*, 25 Jul 2023).

109 Berka (n58) 183.

110 Commission Implementing Decision (EU) 2016/1250 of 12 Jul 2016 pursuant to Directive 95/46/EC on the adequacy of the protection provided by the EU-U.S. Privacy Shield [2016] OJ L 207/1.

for U.S. companies was maintained, but the privacy principles, renamed to the 'EU-U.S. Privacy Shield Framework Principles', were broadened from only three pages in Safe Harbour to twenty pages in Privacy Shield.[111] The introduction of the new safeguards made Privacy Shield almost triple the size[112] of its Safe Harbour predecessor. Interestingly, the U.S. distinction between 'consumer privacy' (private sector) and 'dignity, respect and privacy interests in the handling of personal information' (public sector) was enshrined in Privacy Shield.[113] In the EU, on the contrary, privacy and personal data protection are considered fundamental rights that have to be equally respected by the private as well as the public sector. The controversial U.S. national security exception, which led in part to the invalidation of Safe Harbour, was maintained in Privacy Shield,[114] but the United States assured the EU that U.S. public authorities' access to Europeans' personal data for national security purposes would "be subject to clear limitations, safeguards and oversight mechanisms",[115] and that no more mass surveillance would occur. Yearly monitoring of the data protection level in the United States by the European Commission had to provide compliance and adequacy oversight.[116] The retention of the U.S. national security exception was criticized by European privacy watchers, human rights advocates, the European Consumer Organization, and the Article 29 WP.[117] Regardless of the U.S. government's commitment to limit and safeguard intelligence agencies' access to Europeans' personal data, the principles set out in Privacy Shield were still subject to far-reaching limitations to meet national and public security interests.[118]

2020 *Schrems II* – The CJEU confirmed the criticisms in the 2020 *Schrems II*[119] case, and invalidated Privacy Shield. Maximilian Schrems re-submitted his claim to the Irish Data Commissioner arguing that "(U.S.) law requires Facebook Inc.

---

111 Recital 65 and Article 1 & 3-4 Decision 2016/1250/EU; European Commission, 'EU Commission and United States agree on new framework for transatlantic data flows: EU-US Privacy Shield' IP(2016) 216 final.

112 Consisting of 112 compared to 41 pages.

113 Annex IV Attachment A and Annex VI Decision 2016/1250/EU, 85 and 103-104.

114 Annex II: I.5. Privacy Shield: "Adherence to these Principles may be limited: (a) … to meet national security, public interest, or law enforcement requirements" and Annex II: III.16.c. Privacy Shield: "absence of notice in accordance with … the Notice Principle shall not prevent or impair an organization's ability to respond to any lawful request".

115 EC, 'EU-US Privacy Shield' (n111) 1.

116 *Ibid.*

117 Article 29 WP, 'Opinion 01/2016 on the EU–U.S. Privacy Shield draft adequacy decision' (WP238, 13 Apr 2016).

118 Berka (n58) 183-184; EC, 'EU-US Privacy Shield' (n111); Gardner (n57) 172-184; Chris Linebaugh and Edward Liu, *EU Data Transfer Requirements and U.S. Intelligence Laws: Understanding Schrems II and Its Impact on the EU-U.S. Privacy Shield* (CRS, 2021) 1 and 6; Monteleone and Puccio (n95) 16-36; Iain Thomson, 'Safe Harbor ripped and replaced with Privacy Shield in last-minute US-Europe deal' (*The Register*, 2 Feb 2016).

119 C311/18 *Data Protection Comr v Facebook Ireland Ltd, Maximillian Schrems* [2020] (*Schrems II*).

to make personal data transferred to it available to certain (U.S.) authorities, such as the … (NSA) and the … (FBI)".[120] The Data Commissioner conducted an investigation and found that "personal data of EU citizens transferred to the United States were (still) likely to be consulted and processed by the (U.S.) authorities in a manner incompatible with articles 7 and 8 of the (EU) Charter and that (U.S.) law did (still) not provide those citizens with legal remedies compatible with article 47 of the Charter",[121] and pointed out that "the standard data protection clauses in the annex to the SCC Decision are not capable of remedying that defect, since they confer only contractual rights on data subjects against the data exporter and importer, without, however, binding the United States authorities".[122] Consequently, the action was brought before the Irish High Court to refer the question again to the CJEU.[123] The U.S. government intervened in the second hearings before the Irish High Court, as opposed to the first hearings which had led to the *Schrems I* case, which granted the opportunity to explain and clarify U.S. privacy and national security law.[124] The CJEU concluded, however, that, even though the national security exception was partially remedied, U.S. national security laws still allowed "bulk collection … of a relatively large volume of signals intelligence information or data under circumstances where the Intelligence Community cannot use an identifier associated with a specific target … to focus the collection", and that moreover, "surveillance programmes based on E.O. 12333[125] (allow) access to data in transit to the United States without that access being subject to any judicial review, (which) does not, in any event, delimit in a sufficiently clear and precise manner the scope of such bulk collection of personal data".[126,127] The newly introduced Ombudsperson did not have "the power to adopt decisions that are binding on (U.S.) intelligence services",[128] leading the CJEU to conclude that legislation which does not provide "for any possibility for an individual to pursue legal remedies in order to have access to personal data relating to him or her, or to obtain the rectification or erasure of such data, does not respect the essence of the fundamental right to effective judicial protection".[129,130] Consequently, "the existence of such a lacuna in judicial protection in respect of interferences with intelligence programmes … makes it impossible to conclude … that (U.S.)

120 *Ibid.* para 55.
121 *Ibid.* para 56.
122 *Ibid.* para 56.
123 *Ibid.* para 57.
124 Gardner (n57) 183.
125 See *Chapter 5, § 2.*
126 *Schrems II* (n119) para 183.
127 Linebaugh and Liu (n118) 5.
128 *Schrems II* (n119) para 196.
129 *Ibid.* para 187.
130 Linebaugh and Liu (n118) 6.

law ensures a(n essentially equivalent) level of protection",[131] and resulted in the invalidation of Privacy Shield.[132]

C. DATA PRIVACY FRAMEWORK AND *SCHREMS III*?

Implications – Privacy Shield's invalidation caused severe trade disruptions but did not preclude EU data transfers to the United States altogether. The CJEU left "data exporters (with the possibility to) take supplementary measures where necessary to ensure compliance with the level of protection required under EU law"[133] in the form of article 46 GDPR Standard Contractual Clauses (SCCs) to transfer personal data to a third country "without requiring any specific authorization from a supervisory authority".[134] SCCs change the 'adequacy' requirement into an 'accountability' requirement, where the data importer and exporter commit themselves to comply with the rules[135] set out in the SCCs, and "to verify, on a case-by-case basis ... whether the law of the third country of destination ensures adequate protection, under EU law, of personal data transferred pursuant to (the SCCs) ...".[136,137] The CJEU strengthened the requirements for SCCs in the *Schrems II* case by bringing them closer to article 45 GDPR's adequacy. The CJEU stated that SCCs must "ensure that data subjects whose personal data are transferred to a third country ... are afforded a level of protection essentially equivalent to that guaranteed within the (EU by the GDPR), read in the light of the (EU) Charter".[138,139] Private company clauses can, however, not bind third country public authorities and cannot eliminate public authorities' power to access transferred personal data.[140] In the case of the United States, the CJEU has already found twice that the U.S. data privacy system does not fulfill the requirements set out by EU law. Article 46 GDPR 'accountability' and potential sanctioning of private companies impedes their

131 *Schrems II* (n119) para 191.

132 European Commission, 'EU-US data transfers: How personal data transferred between the EU and US is protected' (*europa.eu*, 2025); Linebaugh and Liu (n118) 1-13; U.S. Department of Commerce, 'FAQs – EU-U.S. Privacy Shield Program Update' (*privacyshield.gov*, 2022).

133 Linebaugh and Liu (n118) 1.

134 Article 46.2 GDPR.

135 These include "enforceable data subject rights and effective legal remedies for data subjects".: Article 46.1 GDPR.

136 *Schrems II* (n119) para 134.

137 Gutwirth *et al.* (n32) 269-272.

138 *Schrems II* (n119) para 105.

139 Article 46 GDPR; Chiara Bertoldi, 'The New European Commission Decision on Standard Contractual Clauses?' (2022) 6 EurPap 1363, 1363; Laura Bradford, Mateo Aboy, and Kathleen Liddell, 'Standard contractual clauses for cross-border transfers of health data after *Schrems II*' (2021) 8 JLawBiosci 1, 9-18; Linebaugh and Liu (n118) 1 and 6; Edward McLaughlin, 'Schrems's Slippery Slope' (2021) 90 FordhamLRev 217, 217-227.

140 Colin Bennett, *Regulating Privacy* (Cornell University Press 1992) 131; Fromholz (n74) 478.

engagement in personal data transfers to a third country with an inadequate data privacy system. If an EU-based "controller or processor ... is not able to take adequate additional measures to guarantee such protection, (the CJEU) ... require(s) to suspend or end the transfer of personal data to the third country concerned".[141] Suspending or ending data transfers to the United States is, however, unrealistic as most daily services used in Europe are provided by U.S. private companies. Anu Bradford explains that "the problem with SCCs (and Binding Corporate Rules and Certification mechanisms etc.) is that they are contractual mechanisms ... that do not bind other governments ... therefore, where third country law or practice is inconsistent with the GDPR (as found by the CJEU for the United States), SCCs (or other contractual mechanisms for that matter) cannot remedy that problem".[142,143] The alternative personal data transfer mechanisms to adequacy decisions provided by the EU GDPR share, as a consequence, a common flaw; they cannot bind third parties. The alternative to build data centers in the EU to keep Europeans' personal data within the EU also falls short, as U.S. national security laws (FISA and EO 12333)[144] allow U.S. intelligence agencies to access and collect foreign intelligence information anywhere in the world, regardless of the location of data centers and servers.

2023 Data Privacy Framework – The negotiations for a new third transatlantic data privacy framework were reinitiated by the Secretary of Commerce on the U.S. side and the Commissioner for Justice on the EU side, reflecting the categorization of data privacy as respectively part of commerce and part of justice.[145] Shortly after, EU Commission President Ursula von der Leyen and U.S. President Joe Biden announced a new transatlantic data transfer framework in March 2022.[146] U.S. President Joe Biden addressed the issues identified by the CJEU and implemented the Court's exact wording in Executive Order (EO) 14086,[147] which was promulgated in October 2022.[148] Firstly, the United States committed to undertake "signals intelligence collection ... only where necessary to advance legitimate national security objectives, (without) disproportionately impact(ing) the protection of individual privacy and civil liberties".[149] Secondly,

141 *Schrems II* (n119) para 135.
142 Bradford *et al.* (n139) 15.
143 *Ibid.* 11-16.
144 See *Chapter 5, § 2.*
145 European Commission, 'European Commission and United States Joint Statement on Trans-Atlantic Data Privacy Framework' IP(2022) 2087 final.
146 Mark Scott and Vincent Manancourt, 'US eyes breakthrough on data dispute with EU as Biden visits Brussels' (*Politico*, 24 Mar 2022).
147 Executive Order 14086 Enhancing Safeguards for United States Signals Intelligence Activities, 87Fed.Reg.198, 62283, 7 Oct 2022 (EO 14086).
148 EO 14086, 62283-62297; Steven De Schrijver, 'Privacy Shield 2.0 – een stap naar Schrems III?' (2023) 1 Computerr 1, 1 2; See *Chapter 5, § 2.*
149 The White House, 'Fact Sheet: United States and European Commission Announce Trans-Atlantic Data Privacy Framework' (*archives.gov*, 25 Mar 2025).

a "new multi-layer redress mechanism (including) an independent Data Protection Review Court (DPRC) (consisting) of individuals chosen from outside the U.S. Government (with) full authority to adjudicate claims and direct remedial measures as needed"[150] was introduced in the U.S. system to address EU citizens' data privacy related complaints.[151] In response, the EU Commission adopted a draft EU-U.S. Data Privacy Framework (DPF) adequacy decision for the United States in December 2022.[152] In February 2023, the European Data Protection Board (EDPB) stated in its non-binding Opinion 5/2023[153] that there are improvements in the DPF, but that clarification is still needed regarding the interpretation of the newly introduced European concepts and regarding the new redress mechanism in the form of the Data Protection Review Court to determine EU adequacy.[154] In its equally non-binding Resolution[155] of 11 May 2023, the European Parliament welcomed the introduction of the European data protection concepts of 'necessity and proportionality' in the U.S. system and the introduction of a new redress mechanism in the form of the DPRC, but expressed concern that EO 14086 "can be amended or revoked at any time by the U.S. President",[156] that there are still insufficient safeguards against bulk collection of metadata as well as content data, that U.S. law enforcement and intelligence authorities can still access the collected data, and that "the decisions of the DPRC would ... not (be) made public or available to the complainant, who would only be informed that the review either did not identify any covered violations or that the DPRC had issued a determination requiring appropriate action, thereby undermining complainants' right to access or rectify their data ... the proposed redress process does (moreover) not provide for an avenue for appeal in a federal court".[157,158] The EU Parliament concluded "that the EU-U.S. Data Privacy Framework fails to create essential equivalence

---

150 *Ibid.*

151 Laura Drechsler and others, *Third time is the charm? The draft Data Privacy Framework for international personal data transfers from the European Union to the United States* (CiTiP Working Paper, 2023) 17-19; EC, 'Joint Statement' (n145).

152 De Schrijver (n148) 1-2; Drechsler *et al.* (n151) 4-5; European Commission, 'Data protection: Commission starts process to adopt adequacy decision for safe data flows with the US' IP(2022) 7631 final; NOYB, 'Statement on EU Commission adequacy decision on US' (*noyb.eu*, 13 Dec 2022).

153 EDPB, 'Opinion 5/2023 on the European Commission Draft Implementing Decision on the adequate protection of personal data under the EU-US Data Privacy Framework' (*europa.eu*, 28 Feb 2023).

154 Drechsler *et al.* (n151) 18; EDPB, 'Opinion 5/2023' (n153) 6; NOYB, 'New US Executive Order unlikely to satisfy EU law' (*noyb.be*, 7 Oct 2022); NOYB, 'Statement' (n152).

155 European Parliament, Adequacy of the protection afforded by the EU-U.S. Data Privacy Framework European Parliament resolution of 11 May 2023 on the adequacy of the protection afforded by the EU-US Data Privacy Framework (2023/2501(RSP)) OJ C 15 Dec 2023.

156 *Ibid.* 5.

157 *Ibid.* 4.

158 Drechsler *et al.* (n151) 19; EP, DPF Resolution (n155) 3-5.

in the level of protection".[159] Despite the criticisms of the EDPB and the EU Parliament, the EU Commission carried on and adopted the *EU-U.S. Data Privacy Framework adequacy decision*[160] in July 2023.[161] The United States implemented the CJEU's wording and comments within the confines of the specificities of its legal system, but retained its (far-reaching) surveillance laws. The question remains whether this new transatlantic data transfer framework will pass the CJEU's test or whether we are facing a *Schrems III*.[162] The issues identified by the CJEU and the characteristics of the EU and the U.S. legal systems will be explored and contextualized in this book to determine whether both systems are really that different or whether they can find a way to co-exist and enable transatlantic data transfers that respect both national security and data privacy.

D. OTHER EU-U.S. LEGAL INSTRUMENTS

In addition to the specific data privacy adequacy decisions, four other legal instruments in the area of data privacy, trade, and law enforcement are, were, or could be relevant for transatlantic data transfers when the previous adequacy decisions were invalidated. These legal instruments will briefly be introduced in this section and include (non-exhaustively) the 2003 Mutual Legal Assistance Agreement, the 2013 Transatlantic Trade and Investment Partnership, the 2013 Trade in Services Agreement, and the 2016 Umbrella Agreement.

2003 Mutual Legal Assistance Agreement – The 2003 Agreement on mutual legal assistance between the European Union and the United States of America (MLA)[163] aims to facilitate "cooperation … for the purpose of gathering and exchanging (personal) information, and requesting and providing assistance to obtain evidence located in another country".[164] Legal assistance in criminal matters between the EU and the United States is facilitated through the exchange of personal information, bank information, and through "legal frameworks for the use of new techniques such as joint investigative teams, (while establishing) a comprehensive and uniform framework for limitations on the use of personal and

159 EP, DPF Resolution (n155) 6.
160 Commission Implementing Decision EU 2023/1795 of 10 Jul 2023 pursuant to Regulation (EU) 2016/679 on the adequate level of protection of personal data under the EU-US Data Privacy Framework [2023] OJ L 231/118.
161 European Commission, 'Data Protection: European Commission adopts new adequacy decision for safe and trusted EU-US data flows' IP(2023) 3721 final.
162 Kristin Archick and Rachel Fefer, *U.S.-EU Privacy Shield and Transatlantic Data Flows* (CRS Report, 2021); Scott and Manancourt (n146); The White House, 'Data Privacy Framework' (n149).
163 Agreement on mutual legal assistance between the European Union and the United States of America [2003] OJ L 181/34 (MLA).
164 EC, 'Restoring Trust – FAQ' (n88).

other data".[165] The MLA Agreement tends to prioritize, however, security over freedom as the (personal) data exchanged between law enforcement and judicial authorities is confidential. The 2016 Umbrella Agreement (*discussed below*) includes data protection safeguards which supplement the MLA Agreement where necessary. Personal information exchanges in criminal matters between the EU and the United States must, consequently, comply with the rules set out in both the MLA and the Umbrella Agreement.[166]

2013 Transatlantic Trade and Investment Partnership – The EU and the United States entered negotiations in 2013 to set up an EU-U.S. free trade area under the Transatlantic Trade and Investment Partnership (TTIP). The TTIP aimed at removing and reducing transatlantic trade barriers between the world's two largest economies in order to increase trade relations, and to possibly not only set transatlantic standards, but also global ones. The United States wanted to include data (privacy) protection principles in these negotiations, but the EU refused as the TTIP focused on trade and investment, while the EU perceived data protection as a fundamental right. EU Commission Vice-President Viviane Reding voiced clearly that "data protection is not red tape or a tariff ... it is a fundamental right and ... is not negotiable".[167] This statement also set the tone for the position of the EU in the transatlantic adequacy decisions. Data (privacy) protection was eventually excluded from the TTIP negotiations, even though U.S. business advocates argued to not restrict US-EU data flows. The TTIP negotiations ended in 2016 without a deal, and were formally closed in 2019, resulting in the end of the TTIP.[168]

---

165 Executive Summary of Mutual Legal Assistance between the United States of America and the European Union (EU), signed on Jun 25, 2003, at Washington, together with 25 bilateral instruments that subsequently were signed between the United States and each European Union Member State in order to implement the Agreement with the EU, and an explanatory note that is an integral part of the Agreement, 109th Congress, Treaty Document 109-13 (EU-US MLA), VI.

166 EU-US MLA (n165); Giacomo Di Federico, 'Cartel Criminalization and International Cooperation' in Catherine Flaesch-Mougin and Lucia Rossi (eds), *La dimension extérieure de l'espace de liberté, de sécurité et de justice après le Traité de Lisbonne* (Bruylant 2013) 626-629; EC, 'Restoring Trust – FAQ' (n88); Eur-Lex, 'Agreement with the United States on mutual legal assistance' (*europa.eu*, 16 Apr 2019); U.S. Department of Justice, 'U.S./EU Agreements on Mutual Legal Assistance and Extradition Enter into Force' (*justice.gov*, 2010); Theodore Georgopoulos, 'What kind of treaty making power for the EU?' (2005) 30 ELR 190, 190-202; Valsamis Mitsilegas, 'The New EU–USA Cooperation on Extradition, Mutual Legal Assistance and the Exchange of Police Data' (2003) 8 EFAR 515, 523-536.

167 EC, 'Towards a more dynamic' (n88) 5.

168 Berka (n58) 181-182; EC, 'Rebuilding Trust' (n92); EC, 'Towards a more dynamic' (n88); EC, 'Restoring Trust – FAQ' (n88); European Commission, 'EU Chief Negotiator says EU-US trade deal not about deregulation, as third round of talks end in Washington' IP(2013) 1306 final; European Commission, 'Independent study outlines benefits of EU-US trade Agreement' MEMO(2013) 211 final; European Commission, 'EU Trade Relationships: United States' (*europa.eu*, 2021); European Parliament, 'TTIP: Trade agreements must not undermine EU

2013 Trade in Services Agreement – The negotiations for an international Trade in Services Agreement (TiSA) were initiated in 2013 by 23 WTO members,[169] including the EU and the United States. TiSA aimed at increasing the trade in services by remedying trade barriers, including discriminatory rules. The United States lobbied to include and apply the "principle of free cross-border data flows to the entire agreement by placing it in the core text"[170] in order to prioritize the commercial flow of information, and, at least to a certain extent, nullify data protection and privacy concerns. The European Parliament took a firm stance against "the U.S. proposals on movement of information (and argued that they) should immediately and formally be opposed".[171,172] The EU also confirmed its position that data (privacy) protection is a fundamental right that is not negotiable. TiSA's negotiations were surrounded by secrecy and the criticism following the publication of secret documents on WikiLeaks may have contributed to eventually rejecting TiSA's proposal completely.[173]

2016 Umbrella Agreement – The 2016 EU-U.S. Data Protection Umbrella Agreement[174] entered into force in 2017 and aims to provide a "comprehensive high-level data protection framework for EU-U.S. law enforcement cooperation".[175] The Umbrella Agreement mainly concerns data protection in the context of the "prevention, investigation, detection or prosecution of criminal offences",[176] and aims to strengthen police and judicial cooperation, including the fight against terrorism. All personal data exchanges between the EU and the United States for these specific purposes, including personal data transferred by private entities

data protection laws, say Civil Liberties MEPs' *(europa.eu*, 31 Mar 2015); European Sources Online, *Information Guide EU-US Relations* (Cardiff University Press 2014) 10-11; Jussi Hanhimäki, *Pax Transatlantica* (OUP 2021) 69 and 91-92.

169 The 23 World Trade Organization (WTO) parties were: Australia, Canada, Chile, Colombia, Costa Rica, European Union (28), Hong Kong, Iceland, Israel, Japan, Liechtenstein, Mauritius, Mexico, New Zealand, Norway, Pakistan, Panama, Peru, South Korea, Switzerland, Taiwan, Turkey, and the United States.

170 Berka (n58) 180; 'Trade in Services Agreement (TiSA), Annex on Electronic Commerce, US-proposed Art. X.6: Movement of Information' (*WikiLeaks*, 3 Jun 2015).

171 Berka (n58) 181.

172 European Parliament, 'Report containing the European Parliament's recommendations to the Commission on the negotiations for the Trade in Services Agreement (TiSA)' (*europa.eu*, 25 Jan 2016).

173 Academic Library, 'Trade in Services Agreement' (*ebrary.net*, 2025); Berka (n58) 180-181; Rachel Fefer, *Trade in Services Agreement (TiSA) Negotiations* (CRS Report, 2017) 1-2; Office of the United States Trade Representative, 'Trade in Services Agreement' (*USTR Archives*, 2025).

174 Agreement between the United States of America and the European Union on the protection of personal information relating to the prevention, investigation, detection, and prosecution of criminal offences [2016] OJ L 336/3 (Umbrella Agreement).

175 Carmen-Cristina Cirlig, Conclusion of the EU-US data protection umbrella agreement (European Parliament Legislative Train, 2022) 1-2.

176 Article 1.1 Umbrella Agreement; Cirlig (n175) 1.

to law enforcement authorities, must comply with the provisions set out in the Umbrella Agreement. This agreement is, however, not a self-standing legal instrument as it is designed to supplement an already existing general EU-U.S. data transfer framework. The Umbrella Agreement does, consequently, not constitute a legal basis for EU-U.S. personal data transfers for law enforcement purposes, and requires the development of a separate agreement or adequacy decision that can serve as a legal basis for transatlantic data transfers.[177]

[177] Article 1.1-1.3 and 3.1 and 5.1 Umbrella Agreement; Berka (n58) 182-185; Cirlig (n175) 1-2; EC, 'Rebuilding Trust' (n92) 8; EC, 'Restoring Trust – FAQ' (n88) 5-6; EC, 'EU-US data transfers' (n132); European Commission, 'European Commission ready to start talks with US on personal data agreement to fight terrorism or crime' IP(2010) 1661 final; European Commission, 'Fact Sheet: Questions and Answers on the EU-U.S. Data Protection "Umbrella Agreement"' MEMO(2016) 4183 final; European Parliament, 'Parliamentary questions: Review of the EU-US data protection umbrella agreement' E-004472/2020; European Parliament, 'Parliamentary questions: Review of the EU-US data protection umbrella agreement: Answers given by Mr Reynders on behalf of the European Commission' E-004472/2020(ASW).

CHAPTER 2
METHODOLOGICAL APPROACH

The second chapter briefly explains the methodological approach that was taken to conduct the research on which this book is based.[178] This discussion includes why the EU and the United States were chosen for comparison, what the objectives and legal method of this book are, and which terminological choices were made. To this end, the main concepts used throughout this book are defined and the conceptual choices of the author are clarified.

§ 1. WHY THE UNITED STATES AND THE EU

The biggest companies involved in the smart device market and big tech, such as Google, Amazon, and Apple, are located in the United States, but sell their devices and offer their services also in the European Union.[179] European citizens' personal data is consequently collected and traded by U.S. companies, which results in an extensive data flow and an important economic relationship between the two sides of the Atlantic.[180] Many EU citizens rely on the services of U.S. companies, such as Google, Facebook, LinkedIn, WhatsApp, or Skype, on a daily basis for their work and communications, making their operationality an economic and social necessity. Many people are insufficiently informed and aware of which data about them is collected, for what purposes, and with whom this collected data is shared. With the emergence of 5G and artificial intelligence, data flows will only increase and become even more detailed. U.S.-designed consumer goods face, moreover, difficulties when entering the EU market, as both sides approach personal data collection and data privacy differently. The EU's focus on fundamental rights and the U.S. commercial approach reveal a transatlantic gap regarding data privacy. A clear understanding

178 For an extensive discussion of the methodological approach: Sylvia Lissens, *The U.S. and EU approach towards personal data protection: "A collision of tides or a convergence of waves?" A legal exploration of the differences and convergences between the United States and the European Union* (Doctoral Thesis KU Leuven, 2025) 41-53.

179 de Beer *et al.* (n2) 167-200.

180 Frederik Zuiderveen Borgesius, Dominique Hagenauw, and Hielke Hijmans, *Privacy Bridges: EU and US privacy experts in search of transatlantic privacy solutions* (37th International Privacy Conference Amsterdam, 2015) 11.

of the U.S. and EU approaches towards data privacy, commerce, and intelligence is necessary, because any protection that does not adequately deal with personal data transfers across jurisdictions will remain ineffective and endanger citizens' personal data. Setting hard lines on the European side does not protect consumers' rights nor commerce and disadvantages U.S. companies and EU citizens alike. Transatlantic differences cannot only be identified in the legal field but are also grounded in the cultural and historical context in which each region developed, and their discussion is included in this book through a three-level analysis explained in the next section. The literature is dominated by an EU perspective in the European Union and a U.S. perspective in the United States on transatlantic commercial data use, technology, and national security interests. Adding a cross-fertilized U.S.-EU perspective may enrich the already existing (regional) scientific literature in the field of data privacy. In a globalized world, countries and regions must after all cooperate to effectively protect citizens' personal data while ensuring personal data flows.

§ 2. OBJECTIVES AND LEGAL METHOD

The overarching objective of this book is to deepen the understanding of, and determine the differences and convergences between, the EU and U.S. legal approaches towards personal data protection, for the private sector, for civil society, and for government intelligence and law enforcement agencies. The coherence and convergences that can be identified on each of these levels play a fundamental role in facilitating the development of a roadmap for the U.S. and EU approaches towards data privacy to co-exist.

The first specific objective (*Chapter 3*) is to determine data privacy principles that transnational economic data privacy regulation and legal instruments have in common for the private sector. To this end, the general data privacy principles set out in the OECD Guidelines on the Protection of Privacy and Transborder Flows of Personal Data, the Council of Europe Convention (108) for the Protection of Individuals with Regard to Automatic Processing of Personal Data, the U.S. Privacy Act, the California Consumer Privacy Act, the Virginia Consumer Data Protection Act, and the EU GDPR are compared. This comparison results in an overarching framework with general data privacy principles for the United States and the EU to co-exist, securing data privacy and supporting commerce.

The second specific objective (*Chapter 4*) is to explain the importance of the historical, philosophical, and cultural context in which the U.S. and EU legal systems are rooted and in which they further developed for the formation of their respective legal frameworks on data privacy. Of particular importance to this discussion are the philosophical understanding of the concepts of privacy and property regarding personal data, the interplay between the right to privacy and freedom of speech in the downstream dissemination of lawfully obtained truthful information, and the distinct level of tolerance of government interference in citizens' private lives and the (liberal) market. This historical, philosophical, and cultural context partially explains why Americans and Europeans conceptualize and understand personal data and data privacy in a different way but also shows that both regions have more in common than would seem at first sight.

The third specific objective (*Chapter 5*) is to reveal that the regulatory balance struck by U.S. and EU intelligence and law enforcement agencies tends to prioritize national security over personal data privacy interests, even though both regions claim to respect the balance. Far-reaching U.S. surveillance laws were introduced after the terrorist attacks in New York on September 11, 2001, which were revealed by whistleblower Edward Snowden and led to public outrage. The duty to protect citizens' fundamental rights, even in the fight against terrorism, is embedded in the EU's policy on the fight against terrorism,[181] but the CJEU's case law in the aftermath of the Snowden revelations shows that EU Member States employ very similar data collection and processing practices. The U.S. national security exception is, consequently, not that different from national security exceptions employed by Member States of the European Union. Also, in this regard, both regions have more in common than would seem at first sight.

The functional comparative legal method was employed in this book, as it focuses on a specific social issue or an overarching factual problem in different legal systems, namely data privacy (U.S.) or personal data protection (EU), rather than to focus on norms and concepts which are specific for a certain legal system or region.[182] The focus on data privacy can be qualified as a micro comparison, but in order to adequately compare the U.S. and EU legal approaches towards data privacy, a macro comparative approach was also taken which focused on the specific way of thought and legal culture of the systems concerned.[183] A legal system cannot only be understood from 'the law in the books' and 'the law in action' as the system is often rooted in and reflects other important underlying social, philosophical, and historical values, which were taken into account in this book.[184]

§ 3. TERMINOLOGY

The concepts of 'personal data protection' and 'data privacy' are used as synonyms. The former concept is used in the European Union, while the latter concept is used in the United States, but both concepts cover the same idea, namely the

181 The Stockholm Programme – An open and secure Europe serving and protecting citizens [2010] OJ C 115/1.

182 Emmanouil Billis, 'On the Methodology of Comparative Criminal Law Research' (2017) 24 MJECL 864, 867; Lina Kestemont, *Handbook on Legal Methodology* (Intersentia 2018) 38-47.

183 Kestemont (n182) 37-38.

184 Mark van Hoecke, *Epistemology and Methodology of Comparative Law* (1st edn, Hart Publishing 2004) 167.

protection of someone's personal data as related to people's privacy. Personal data protection or data privacy is consequently considered to be narrowly intertwined with and a sub-category of privacy. Similarly, the concepts of 'personal data' and 'personal information' are used as synonyms, where the former is predominantly used in the European Union, and the latter in the United States. The concept of 'data processor' is, outside the EU discussion, used in a general way to refer to private entities and companies which engage in data collection and processing activities. The EU-specific distinction between 'data processors' and 'data controllers' is not maintained outside the EU discussion, qualifying all entities as 'data processors' and all activities relating to the handling, collection, use, and dissemination of people's data as 'data processing'.

The private sector concept refers to private companies and their commercial activities. The public sector or 'government' concept refers to the European government conceptualization as opposed to the American executive conceptualization. The former encompasses the people and the system (including institutions and departments) that officially control the country,[185] while the latter refers to the U.S. President, the advisors, departments, and agencies responsible for implementing and enforcing the laws enacted by Congress.[186] The concept of 'national security' is defined as "the safety of a nation and its people, institutions, etc., especially from military threat or from espionage, terrorism, etc.".[187] Countries, and in particular government intelligence and law enforcement agencies, rely on the 'national security exception' to justify limitations on their required compliance with certain rules and laws when necessary to safeguard national security purposes. 'National security laws' and 'surveillance laws' are, therefore, also used as synonyms. Finally, the concept 'States' with capital letter is used to reference U.S. States, EU Member States, and countries more generally.

185 Dictionary, 'Government' (*cambridge.org*, 2025).

186 The White House, 'The Executive Branch' (*archives.gov*, 2020); U.S. House of Representatives, 'Branches of Government' (*house.gov*, 2025).

187 Oxford English Dictionary, 'National Security' (*oed.com*, 2025).

CHAPTER 3

LEGAL-HISTORICAL DATA PRIVACY OVERVIEW

The third chapter provides a legal-historical overview of the evolution of personal data protection / data privacy legislation in the United States, EU, and selected international organizations. The discussed legal instruments cover the public (government) and private sector, with the exclusion of law enforcement and national security, which will be discussed in the fifth chapter. The legal instruments considered in this chapter are, to a large extent, inspired by or related to the 1973 Report of the U.S. Department of Health, Education, and Welfare (HEW), setting out Fair Information Practice Principles (FIPPs).[188] Therefore, U.S. data privacy legislation is chosen as starting point, followed by legal instruments developed by selected international organizations, an overview of EU personal data protection legislation, and a concluding analysis, structured in a geographical-chronological way.

§ 1. U.S. DATA PRIVACY LEGAL INSTRUMENTS

Public v. Private Sector – Personal data protection is framed as data privacy in the United States, linking it directly to the concept of privacy.[189] There is no comprehensive omnibus U.S. data privacy legislation encompassing both the public and private sector, as a sectoral approach and self-regulation are preferred, leading to the applicability of a 'patchwork' of federal, State, and sector regulations. Different sectors (e.g. health,[190] banking,[191] children's privacy,[192] …) have their own legal frameworks to regulate data privacy. U.S. data privacy regulations can be grouped into those governing data processing by the government, law enforcement specifically, and private actors engaging

---

188 Bygrave, *Data Privacy Law* (n37) 33; Heisenberg (n66) 32; Hoofnagle *et al.* (n11) 70-77; Solove, 'Introduction' (n43) 1882; Solove and Hartzog (n61) 592; Zuiderveen Borgesius *et al.* (n180) 16-20.

189 Shawn Boyne, 'Data Protection in the United States' (2018) 66 AJCL 299, 299.

190 1996 Health Insurance Portability and Accountability Act, 110 Stat. 1936.

191 1999 Gramm-Leach-Bliley Act, 113 Stat. 1338.

192 1998 Children's Online Privacy Protection Act, 15 U.S.C. 6501-6505.

in commercial activities.[193] The structure of this section follows this tripartite distinction. The first subsection discusses data privacy regulation for the U.S. public sector (government) at the federal level, where it is necessary (and at the outset legitimate) to collect personal data to make the government system operational (e.g. issue documents, provision of services, …).[194] Secondly, and discussed in the fifth chapter, data privacy regulation for law enforcement and intelligence purposes is considered where the (at the outset illegitimate) collection of citizens' personal data necessitates protective measures against government overreach.[195] Thirdly, selected data privacy regulation for the U.S. private sector (commerce) at the federal as well as the State level is scrutinized. U.S. States have the competence to regulate intra-State commerce, whereas the federal government has the competence to regulate interstate and foreign commerce.[196] With the fast-paced expansion of U.S. State consumer privacy acts (at the time of writing 20 out of 50 U.S. States)[197] in recent years, the 2018 California Consumer Privacy Act (CCPA) and the 2021 Virginia Consumer Data Protection Act (VCDPA) were selected for discussion. The CCPA and VCDPA were the first two State consumer privacy acts promulgated in the United States, with California being the first one of its kind,[198] and Virginia being California's first follower.

193 Philip Agre and Marc Rotenberg (eds), *Technology and Privacy* (MIT Press 1998) 5; Jeeyun (Sophia) Baik, 'Data Privacy against Innovation or against Discrimination?' (2020) 52 TelematInform 101431 1, 1-2; Bennett (n140) 137; Birnhack (n56) 509; Boyne (n189) 299; Bygrave, *Data Protection Law* (n17) 54; Bygrave, *Data Privacy Law* (n37) 103; Fred Cate, *Privacy in the information age* (Brookings Institution 1997) vii and 80-81 and 109; Wilson Freeman, *California Dreamin' of Privacy Regulation: The California Consumer Privacy Act and Congress* (CRS, 2018) 1; Fromholz (n74) 461-462; Gutwirth *et al.* (n32) 179-180; Ganka Hadjipetrova and Hannah Poteat, 'States Are Coming to the Force of Privacy in the Digital Era' (2014) 6 Landslide 13, 13-14; Heisenberg (n66) 9 and 27-40 and 80-84; Hoofnagle *et al.* (n11) 70; Lynskey, *The foundations* (n42) 4-24; Stephen Mulligan and Chris Linebaugh, *Data Protection and Privacy Law: An Introduction* (CRS, 2022) 1; Emmanuel Pernot-Leplay, 'EU Influence on Data Privacy Laws' (2019) 18 CTLJ 101, 102-112; Malavika Raghavan, 'Data protection regulation' in V. Sridhar (ed), *Data-centric Living* (1st edn, Routledge 2021) 229; Solove and Hartzog (n61) 587; Elizabeth Stainforth, 'Collective Memory or the Right to Be Forgotten?' (2022) 15 MemStud 257, 264; Jonathan Wiener, 'Whose Precaution After All?' (2003) 13 DJCIL 207, 246.

194 Zuiderveen Borgesius *et al.* (n180) 10.

195 *Ibid.*

196 Tenth Amendment to the U.S. Constitution, 15 Dec 1791; Article I, Sec.8, Cl.3 U.S.C.; Edward Barret, 'State Regulation of Commerce' (*encyclopedia.com*, 1986).

197 These are: California, Colorado, Connecticut, Delaware, Florida, Indiana, Iowa, Kentucky, Maryland, Minnesota, Montana, Nebraska, New Hampshire, New Jersey, Oregon, Tennessee, Texas, Utah, Vermont, and Virginia.: Brian Eckert, 'Data privacy laws in the United States (updated March 2025)' (*Didomi*, 2025).

198 Baik (n193) 1; Bloomberg Law, 'California Consumer Privacy Laws' (*Bloomberg Law*, 2024); Harrison Enright, 'What a Data Privacy Law Should Look like in West Virginia' (2022) 125 WVLR 263, 269; Hadjipetrova and Poteat (n193) 14; Mulligan and Linebaugh, *An Introduction* (n193) 1; Sanford Shatz and Paul Lysobey, 'Update on the California Consumer Privacy Act and Other States' Actions' (2022) 77 BusLaw 539, 539.

The principles set out in the U.S. State acts that followed California and Virginia can to a large extent be related to the two pioneering States, including specific California provisions and/or reflecting 'Virginia+' or 'Virginia-'[199] models.[200]

A. U.S. PUBLIC SECTOR

The (legal) relationship between U.S. citizens and the government regarding (data) privacy is in the first place regulated by the U.S. Constitution, and more specifically by the U.S. Fourth Amendment and its evolutionary interpretation by the U.S. courts, which is considered in *Chapter 4, § 1, A., i)*. Secondly, the 1973 Report by the U.S. Department of Health, Education, and Welfare (HEW) is discussed below, as it set out influential Fair Information Practice Principles, which were partially enshrined in, thirdly, the 1974 Privacy Act.

i) 1973 HEW Report

Digital revolution – The computer-based record-keeping system, and with it automated data processing, began to emerge in the 1970s, since "computers … (were) destined to become the principal medium for making, storing, and using records about people"[201] in the public as well as the private sector. Computers provide a time- and resource-saving means to aid governments to process large amounts of (personal) data in a much shorter time. The Secretary of the U.S. Department of Health, Education, and Welfare (HEW), Eliot Richardson, was aware of these innovations, and the possible risks they could bring about. Therefore, Richardson commissioned an 'Advisory Committee on Automated Personal Data Systems, Records, Computers, and the Rights of Citizens' to conduct a study on these innovations in 1972. Interestingly, the members of this Advisory Committee encompassed a broad spectrum of stakeholders and disciplines, including (but not limited to) public and private sector representatives, members of civil society, lawyers, social service providers, academics, researchers,

---

199 Libbie Canter uses the Virginia+ and Virginia- taxonomy.: Daniel Solove and Libbie Canter, 'Webinar U.S. State Privacy Law Developments' (*youtube.com*, 29 Aug 2023); Daniel Solove, Libbie Canter, and Jenna Zhang, 'Webinar U.S. State Privacy Law Developments 2024' (*youtube.com*, 3 Oct 2024).

200 Bloomberg Law, 'Virginia Consumer Data Protection Act (VCDPA)' (*Bloomberg Law*, 2024); Enright (n198) 286-297; Javier Garyiene, 'State Privacy Law Developments' (2021) 77 TBL 255, 255; Lars Lindgren, 'Virginia's New Consumer Data Protection Act' (*JOLT Harvard Law School*, 16 Mar 2021).

201 U.S. Department of Health, Education & Welfare, *Records, Computers, and the Rights of Citizens* (Report of the Secretary's Advisory Committee on Automated Personal Data Systems, 1973) DHEW Publication No. (OS) 73-94 (1973 HEW Report) v-vii.

and State legislators.[202] This diversity led to the inclusion of a broad range of, sometimes conflicting, opinions, which eventually converged towards a conclusive report. The Advisory Committee completed its task in July 1973, bringing its findings and recommendations together in the '1973 HEW Report on Records, Computers, and the Rights of Citizens', setting out the highly influential Fair Information Practice Principles (FIPPs).[203]

Findings and Recommendations – The main findings of the 1973 HEW Report are surprisingly similar to today's digital privacy concerns, even though they were drafted 50 years ago:

> "the net effect of computerization is that it is becoming much easier for record-keeping systems to affect people than for people to affect record-keeping systems. Even in non-governmental settings, an individual's control over the use that is made of personal data he gives to an organization, or that an organization obtains about him, is lessening. Concern about computer-based record-keeping usually centers on its implications for personal privacy, and understandably so if privacy is considered to entail control by an individual over the uses made of information about him. In many circumstances in modern life an individual must either surrender some of that control or forego the services that an organization provides. Although there is nothing inherently unfair in trading some measure of privacy for a benefit, both parties to the exchange should participate in setting the terms."[204]

The drafters of the 1973 HEW Report decided to focus on safeguarding (data) privacy and due process (setting the terms equally) in relation to (personal) data processing. 'Personal privacy' was defined as "the kind of disclosure and use made of identifiable information about (individuals) in a record" that directly affects them, including decisions about these individuals, which should be made based on accurate and up-to-date information held about them.[205] Due process safeguards were suggested in the form of concrete mechanisms which individuals could use in order to ensure that the (personal) data held about them in the records used to make decisions were accurate and adequately protected.[206] Important to notice is that Colin Bennett correctly observes that the FIPPs developed to protect these privacy and due process interests "are *procedural* safeguards, consistent with the American emphasis on due process rights".[207]

202 1973 HEW Report (n201) ix; Bennett (n140) 70-71.
203 1973 HEW Report (n201) v-xi; Bennett (n140) 70-71; Purtova, *Property Rights* (n31) 116-117.
204 1973 HEW Report (n201) xx.
205 1973 HEW Report (n201) vi and 40-41; Bennett (n140) 97.
206 1973 HEW Report (n201) vi-viii.
207 Bennett (n140) 98.

FIPPs – The most influential part of the 1973 HEW Report was undoubtedly the 'Code of Fair Information Practice for all automated personal data systems' or the 'Fair Information Practice Principles' (FIPPs). The five principles developed in this framework can, up until today, be found in international data protection legal frameworks as well as in the EU GDPR and its predecessor, the 1995 Directive.[208] These five principles are:

> "1) There must be no personal data record-keeping systems whose very existence is secret (*transparency*);
> 2) There must be a way for an individual to find out what information about him is in a record and how it is used (*right of access*);
> 3) There must be a way for an individual to prevent information about him that was obtained for one purpose from being used or made available for other purposes without his consent (*purpose limitation*);
> 4) There must be a way for an individual to correct or amend a record of identifiable information about him (*data accuracy*); and
> 5) Any organization creating, maintaining, using, or disseminating records of identifiable personal data must assure the reliability of the data for their intended use (*data quality*) and must take precautions to prevent misuse of the data (*data security*)".[209]

Enforcement – The HEW Advisory Committee did not encourage enforcement in the form of a specially dedicated ombudsperson or institution. Rather, the Committee looked at the courts for active enforcement of the FIPPs. An ombudsperson was considered remedial, requiring already established rights and procedures, while "a centralized, independent Federal agency ... would be extremely complicated, costly, and might (have) uselessly impede(d) desirable applications of computers to record keeping".[210] The fear of hampering innovation and possible positive applications of record-keeping by both the public and the private sector led the Advisory Committee to "recommend that institutions should be held legally responsible for unfair information practice and should be liable for actual and punitive damages to individuals".[211,212]

---

208 Bygrave, *Data Privacy Law* (n37) 13; FTC, *Privacy Online: Fair Information Practices in the Electronic Marketplace* (A Report to Congress, 2000) 3-4; Hoofnagle *et al.* (n11) 70-77; Solove, 'Introduction' (n43) 1882; Solove and Hartzog (n61) 592; Zuiderveen Borgesius *et al.* (n180) 16.

209 1973 HEW Report (n201) xx-xxi.

210 *Ibid.* 42-43.

211 *Ibid.* 44.

212 1973 HEW Report (n201) 42-44; Bennett (n140) 198-199.

ii) 1974 Privacy Act

Watergate Scandal – In 1972-1974, the Watergate Scandal took place in the United States, which was a catalyst for the passing of the 1974 Privacy Act.[213] The scandal started in 1972 with the arrest of five burglars at the Democratic National Committee headquarters in the Watergate Complex in Washington D.C. The Republican President Richard Nixon initially denied his involvement in this operation, but one of the burglars turned out to be part of Nixon's Committee to Re-elect the President. Judge John Sirica presided over the trial in 1973, where his persistent witness questioning led to information and revelations about the Nixon administration's involvement. Consequently, the Senate established a special Senate Investigation Committee that would be led by Samuel Ervin and hold televised hearings. During these hearings, corruption practices involving illegal financing of the spying operations and wiretapping practices of conversations held in the Oval Office were revealed. The tapes were subpoenaed, but President Nixon refused to hand them over. Pressured by the U.S. Supreme Court, the public, and an impeachment procedure, President Nixon finally handed over the tapes, which contained incriminating content, and resigned a few days later in August 1974.[214] The Watergate Scandal provided the perfect context for public as well as political endorsement "to open up the executive establishment and cleanse the government of the murky and conspiratorial influences of the Nixon White House".[215] Senator Samuel Ervin was serving his last term in Congress, and as a strong advocate of individuals' privacy rights, the (rapid) promulgation of the 1974 Privacy Act was considered a reward for his privacy efforts.[216]

FIPPs implementation – The 1974 Privacy Act provides "certain safeguards for an individual against an invasion of personal privacy by requiring Federal agencies"[217] to observe and comply with seven principles when

213 1974 Privacy Act (As Amended), 88 Stat. 1896, Public Law 93-579, as codified at 5 U.S.C. 552a.

214 Committee on Government Operations United States Senate and the Committee on Government Operations House of Representatives, *Legislative history of the Privacy Act of 1974, S. 3418 (Public Law 93-579) source book on privacy* (U.S. Government Printing Office 1976) 8-9; FBI, 'Watergate' (*fbi.gov*, 2024); Michael Genovese, *The Legacy of Watergate and the Nixon Presidency* (1st edn, Palgrave Macmillan 2023) 45-95; National Archives and Records Administration, 'American Originals' (*archives.gov*, Mar 1996); Rick Perlstein, 'Watergate scandal: United States history' (*Britannica*, 9 Nov 2024); The Editors of Encyclopaedia Britannica, 'Watergate scandal summary: Learn about the trial and aftermath of the Watergate Scandal' (*Britannica*, 2024).

215 Bennett (n140) 72.

216 *Ibid.* (n140) 69-74 and 232.

217 1974 Privacy Act, Section 2(b).

they engage in the processing and handling of personal data. Personal (data) privacy is "directly affected by the collection, maintenance, use, and dissemination of personal information by Federal agencies".[218] The Privacy Act's scope of application excludes, as a consequence, government authorities of the U.S. States. The principles enshrined in the 1974 Privacy Act were a codification and concretization of the five FIPPs set out in the 1973 HEW Report. The dual focus on privacy as well as due process rights was also maintained.[219] Principles (1), (2), (3), and (4) correspond to the five FIPPs, and provide that a Federal agency processing individuals' personal data has to:

> "(1) permit an individual to determine what records pertaining to him are collected, maintained, used, or disseminated by such agencies (*right of access*);
> (2) permit an individual to prevent records pertaining to him obtained by such agencies for a particular purpose from being used or made available for another purpose without his consent (*purpose limitation*);
> (3) permit an individual to gain access to information pertaining to him in Federal agency records, to have a copy made of all or any portion thereof, and to correct or amend such records (*data accuracy*); and
> (4) collect, maintain, use, or disseminate any record of identifiable personal information in a manner that assures that such action is for a necessary and lawful purpose (*legitimate processing*), that the information is current and accurate for its intended use (*data quality*), and that adequate safeguards are provided to prevent misuse of such information (*data security*)".[220]

Two additional principles relate to the possibility to "(5) permit exemptions from such requirements … only in those cases where there is an important public policy need for such exemption as has been determined by specific statutory authority, and (the responsibility of the courts for) (6) … civil suit(s) for any damages which occur as a result of willful or intentional action which violates any individual's rights under this Act (*enforcement*)".[221] Finally, a disclosure limitation (subject to exceptions) was included, prohibiting an "agency (to) disclose any record which is contained in a system of records by any means of communication to any person, or to another agency, except pursuant

218 *Ibid.*, Section 2(a)(1).
219 Bennett (n140) 71; Bygrave, *Data Privacy Law* (n37) 99; Committee on Government Operations (n214) 167-168; Raphael Gellert, 'Understanding Data Protection as Risk Regulation' (2015) 18 JInternetL 3, 7; Heisenberg (n66) 33-34 and 189-190; Hoofnagle *et al.* (n11) 70; Lynskey, *The foundations* (n42) 17; Pernot-Leplay (n193) 112; Zuiderveen Borgesius *et al.* (n180) 16.
220 1974 Privacy Act, Section 2(b)(1) (4).
221 *Ibid.*, Section 2(b)(5)-(6).

to a written request by, or with the prior written consent of, the individual to whom the record pertains (*transparency*)".[222,223]

Enforcement – The initial drafts of the 1974 Privacy Act appointed a Federal Privacy Board to enforce its provisions, but this provision was adjusted and deleted in the legislative process.[224] While the Senate approved of the Federal Privacy Board, the House was against it. A compromise was found by transforming the Privacy Board into a Privacy Protection Study Commission, which was of a more advisory and analytical nature. Centralized oversight was not foreseen; rather, reliance on the courts' enforcement was encouraged. Colin Bennett calls this "a typical (American) solution (which) rejected paternalism and left the onus where it had always been – with the individual".[225] The courts could, under this framework, only enforce the principles set out in the 1974 Privacy Act, but "they ha(d) no further powers to compel federal agencies to change their practices".[226] It was up to the federal agencies to enact internal guidelines and to implement the FIPPs into their policies. The due process component, consequently, prevailed over the privacy component as the 1974 Privacy Act was more "a records' management statute rather than a mechanism to protect individual rights",[227] rendering it a procedural rather than a rights-based document.[228]

B. U.S. PRIVATE SECTOR

i) Federal Level

Comprehensive legislative attempts – U.S. Congress' representatives and senators have attempted to propose comprehensive consumer data privacy bills regulating the private sector on several occasions but have so far not succeeded. The three topics causing most discussion center around the introduction (or not) of an individual right of action, the dedicated enforcement agency, and whether the federal act would preempt already existing State acts.[229]

---

222 *Ibid.*, Section 3(b).

223 Bennett (n140) 101-111; Committee on Government Operations (n214) 240-241; Heisenberg (n66) 33-34.

224 Bennett (n140) 71-74 and 170-175 and 198-199; Lynskey, *The foundations* (n42) 26-27.

225 Bennett (n140) 215.

226 Lynskey, *The foundations* (n42) 26-27.

227 Bennett (n140) 177.

228 Bennett (n140) 71-74 and 170-175 and 198-199; Lynskey, *The foundations* (n42) 17-26.

229 A Bill to establish protections for covered data of individuals, and for other purposes, MUR24230 L4H S.L.C., 118th Congress 2nd Session; Lauren Feiner, 'Lawmakers unveil new bipartisan digital privacy bill after years of impasse' (*The Verge*, 8 Apr 2024); Frederick Aspen Publishers Inc, 'Obama Administration Unveils Blueprint for a 'Privacy Bill of Rights' to Protect

The Congressional Research Service noticed that today's notion of 'personal data protection' encompasses both "*data privacy* (i.e. how to control the collection, use, and dissemination of personal information) and *data security* (i.e. how to protect personal information from unauthorized access or use and respond to such unauthorized access or use)".[230] The assumption in the U.S. system is that individuals are, in the first place, themselves responsible for monitoring and protecting their personal data (and privacy).[231] The discussion on preemption is divided between members of government that want the federal act to set basic minimum standards (allowing States to regulate higher minimum conduct standards above the federal minimum) versus members that want the federal act to set high minimum conduct standards (preempting State acts).[232] Pro-privacy movements and online privacy scandals[233] made U.S. citizens realize that their personal data was not adequately protected. Since comprehensive federal legislative attempts in the area of consumer data privacy consistently failed, the U.S. States decided to step in legislatively and promulgate their own State consumer privacy acts.[234] The preemption discussion seemed more timely in the past where States had not yet acted legislatively in the field of data privacy. It can be expected that in today's proliferation of State consumer privacy acts, the States will defend their legal position and oppose federal preemption. However, the multitude of States promulgating their own version of consumer privacy rights also contributes to a legislative patchwork which is difficult to navigate for the private sector, as companies often operate nationwide or even worldwide.[235]

Consumers Online' (2012) 29 CILW 21, 21-22; Jonathan Gaffney, *Watching the Watchers: A Comparison of Privacy Bills in the 116th Congress* (CRS, 2020) 1-5; Jonathan Gaffney, Chris Linebaugh, and Eric Holmes, *Overview of the American Data Privacy and Protection Act, H.R. 8152* (CRS, 2022) 1-5; Heisenberg (n66) 40; Lindgren (n200); Bryce Newell and others, 'Regulating The Data Market' (2024) 45 UPaJInt'lL 1055, 1058-1064; Pernot-Leplay (n193) 114-122; Solove and Hartzog (n61) 587; The White House, *Consumer Data Privacy in a Networked World: A Framework for Protecting Privacy and Promoting Innovation in the Global Digital Economy* (The White House Report, 2012) 1-52; U.S. Senate Committee on Commerce, Science, and Transportation, 'Committee Chairs Cantwell, McMorris Rodgers Unveil Historic Draft Comprehensive Data Privacy Legislation' (*senate.gov*, 7 Apr 2024).

230 Stephen Mulligan and Chris Linebaugh, *Data Protection Law: An Overview* (CRS, 2019) 54; Mulligan and Linebaugh, *An Introduction* (n193) 1.

231 Heisenberg (n66) 135-136; see *Chapter 4, § 1, A. and § 3, A.*

232 Article VI, Cl.2 U.S.C.; Bryan Adkins, Alexander Pepper, and Jay Sykes, *Federal Preemption: A Legal Primer* (CRS, 2023) ii; Freeman (n193) 4-5; Gaffney (n229) 4-5; Mulligan and Linebaugh, *An Overview* (n230) 62-63; Mulligan and Linebaugh, *An Introduction* (n193) 2; Pernot-Leplay (n193) 120-122.

233 See *Chapter 4, § 3, A., ii), a).*

234 Heisenberg (n66) 27.

235 Gaffney (n229) 4; Heisenberg (n66) 35 and 117; Mulligan and Linebaugh, *An Overview* (n230) 62-63; Pernot-Leplay (n193) 120-122; Paul Schwartz, 'Preemption and Privacy' (2009) 118 YLJ 902, 902.

Consumer privacy right – The data privacy discussion in the private sector (commerce) area is in the United States mainly focused on the rights of individuals vis-à-vis powerful big tech companies that use their users' personal data to develop innovative algorithms and digital services. Data privacy rights are therefore qualified as consumer (privacy) rights, which can be retrieved in State consumer privacy acts promulgated in the different U.S. States. These acts aim to protect consumers' data privacy interests without inhibiting innovation and personal data usage by businesses.[236] Unlike in the European Union, where personal data protection achieved the status of a fundamental right,[237] the (consumer) right to data privacy has to compete and be balanced with other conflicting rights and (economic) interests, such as commerce and freedom of speech.[238] Self-regulation was initially preferred over top-down federal regulation as the latter could stifle innovation. The FTC was tasked to ensure and enforce that companies apply their own rules.[239] As the liberal market prevailed over the later-introduced consumer privacy rights, the preference for an opt-out system of personal data collection can be situated in the U.S. approach where individuals primarily have to take active steps to protect their privacy if they do not wish that private companies use their data to develop business models and techniques.[240]

FTC enforcement – The Federal Trade Commission (FTC) is a U.S. federal administrative agency, established by the 1914 Federal Trade Commission Act,[241] and responsible for "protecting the public from deceptive or unfair business practices, consumer protection, (with) competition jurisdiction in broad sectors of the economy".[242,243] While in the U.S. sectoral approach a specific enforcing agency is responsible for each sector separately, the FTC is often looked at for nationwide antitrust and federal consumer law enforcement.[244] The latter is based on the prohibition of unfair and deceptive trade practices set out in

236 Enright (n198) 263.

237 See *Chapter 3, § 3, B., ii).*

238 See *Chapter 4, § 2, A., i) and ii).*

239 Solove and Hartzog (n61) 598.

240 Woodrow Hartzog and Neil Richards, 'The Surprising Virtues of Data Loyalty' (2022) 71 Emory LJ 985, 1005; Heisenberg (n66) 35 and 159; Newell *et al.* (n229) 1063; Richard Peltz-Steele, 'The New American Privacy' (2013) 44 GJIL 365, 378; Pernot-Leplay (n193) 111; U.S. Senate Committee (n229).

241 1914 FTC Act, 15 U.S.C., § § 41-58 (Sec.1-Sec.27).

242 FTC, 'About the FTC' (*ftc.gov*, 2024).

243 1914 FTC Act, § 45 (Sec.5) (a); Bygrave, *Data Privacy Law* (n37) 114-177; Freeman (n193) 1-2; Hadjipetrova and Poteat (n193) 14; Hoofnagle *et al.* (n11) 7; Mulligan and Linebaugh, *An Overview* (n230) 30-32; Mulligan and Linebaugh, *An Introduction* (n193) 1; Solove and Hartzog (n61) 598-599; Zuiderveen Borgesius *et al.* (n180) 16-17.

244 Hadjipetrova and Poteat (n193) 13-14; Mulligan and Linebaugh, *An Overview* (n230) 57; Mulligan and Linebaugh, *An Introduction* (n193) 2; Zuiderveen Borgesius *et al.* (n180) 22-29.

Section 5 of the FTC Act,[245] which the FTC interpreted extensively to include the enforcement of compliance with private companies' privacy policies. In addition to the FTC's experience with (regular) consumer privacy infringement cases, the FTC broadened its enforcement in the digital age to also encompass consumer data privacy cases involving the collection and dissemination of personal data resulting from the growing use of mobile internet-connected devices.[246] In *1998 Privacy Online: A Report to Congress*,[247] updated in 2000,[248] the FTC identified five fair information practice principles:

"1) **Notice** – data collectors must disclose their information practices before collecting personal information from consumers (*transparency*);
2) **Choice** – consumers must be given options with respect to whether and how personal information collected from them may be used for purposes beyond those for which the information was provided (*purpose limitation & legitimate processing*);
3) **Access** – consumers should be able to view and contest the accuracy and completeness of data collected about them (*data accuracy*);
4) **Security** – data collectors must take reasonable steps to assure that information collected from consumers is accurate (*data accuracy*) and secure from unauthorized use (*data security*); and
5) **Enforcement** – the use of a reliable mechanism to impose sanctions for noncompliance with these fair information practices (*enforcement*)".[249,250]

The FTC formulated additional principles in its litigations, and more specifically in the settlements of these litigations, which contribute to the development of a 'common law of privacy'.[251] These principles include, among others, that companies are bound by their (data) privacy policies, have to respect their promises towards the consumers regarding data security, cannot apply their changed policies retroactively, nor collect personal data for other purposes than they really intend.[252] 'Personally identifiable data' is,

245 1914 FTC Act, § 45 (Sec.5).

246 FTC, *Privacy Online* 2000 (n208) 33; FTC, *Mobile Privacy Disclosures* (n2) i; Mike Hintze, 'In Defense of the Long Privacy Statement' (2017) 76 MdLRev 1044, 1080; Justin Hurwitz, 'Data Security and the FTC's Uncommon Law' (2016) 101 Iowa LRev 955, 957-964; Karsenti (n2) 55-56; Pałka, 'Data Management' (n44) 603-604; Solove and Hartzog (n61) 583-590.

247 FTC, *Privacy Online* (A Report to Congress, 1998) 63p.

248 FTC, *Privacy Online* 2000 (n208) 56p.

249 *Ibid.* 4.

250 FTC, *Privacy Online* 1998 (n247) 7-11.

251 Cate (n193) 111-121; Hurwitz (n246) 955-971; Mulligan and Linebaugh, *An Overview* (n230) 32; Pałka, 'Data Management' (n44) 604-607; Solove and Hartzog (n61) 583-585 and 606-622.

252 *FTC v Sun Spectrum Communications Organization Inc. et al.*, FTC Matter/File Number 032 3032 (24 Oct 2005); *FTC v Frostwire LLC and Angel Leon*, FTC Matter/File Number 112 3041 (12 Oct 2011); *FTC v In the Matter of Sears Holdings Management Corporation*, FTC Matter/File Number 082 3099/C-4264 (28 Feb 2018); Bygrave, *Data Privacy Law* (n37) 114; Mulligan

according to the FTC, "data (which) can be reasonably linked to a particular person, computer, or device".[253] The broadening to 'reasonably linked' was necessary as anonymization and de-identification of collected personal data by private companies often do not prevent that the data can still be traced back to the individual it was collected from.[254] Important to notice is that the FTC cannot impose fines for first-time breaches (only for subsequent breaches of FTC settlements) and can only bring a collective action in the public interest in case of (data) privacy breaches. A private right of action for an individual complainant and individual redress is not provided.[255] Given the FTC's responsibility for consumer (data) privacy protection, and the similarity between the compliance principles,[256] this agency was chosen to enforce the legal framework on transatlantic personal data flows[257] on the U.S. side. The reluctance to create a new federal enforcement body,[258] and the (data) privacy expertise and norms that the FTC has developed make the FTC (in cooperation with the Attorney General for the public sector) a "de facto federal Data Protection Authority for the United States"[259] for collective action in the public interest, even though the FTC's main responsibility remains the enforcement of antitrust and federal consumer law through civil suits, with privacy policy compliance being only an extended interpretation of its responsibilities.

ii) 2018 California Consumer Privacy Act

Background – The State of California was among the first States to enshrine the right to privacy in its constitution and enact a data breach notification law.[260] The 2003 California Online Privacy Protection Act (CalOPPA),[261] which

and Linebaugh, *An Overview* (n230) 32-34; Mulligan and Linebaugh, *An Introduction* (n193) 1; Solove and Hartzog (n61) 628-643.

253 Fox and Grubbs Hoy (n24) 415; FTC, *Self-Regulatory Principles For Online Behavioral Advertising* (FTC Staff Report, 2009) ii-iii and 25; FTC, *Protecting Consumer Privacy in an Era of Rapid Change: Recommendations for Businesses and Policymakers* (FTC Report, 2012) vii and 15-22.

254 FTC, *Self-Regulatory Principles* (n253) 25; FTC, *Protecting Consumer Privacy* (n253) 18-22; Scassa and Sattler (n13) 115-116 and 130.

255 Bygrave, *Data Privacy Law* (n37) 114; Gutwirth *et al.* (n32) 180; Hadjipetrova and Poteat (n193) 14; Mulligan and Linebaugh, *An Overview* (n230) 34-35 and 57; Mulligan and Linebaugh, *An Introduction* (n193) 2; Solove and Hartzog (n61) 610.

256 Solove and Hartzog (n61) 604 and 643.

257 Namely, the 2000 Safe Harbour and 2016 Privacy Shield adequacy decisions; see *Chapter 1, § 2., A. and B.*

258 See *Chapter 3, § 1, A., ii).*

259 Bygrave, *Data Privacy Law* (n37) 177; Solove and Hartzog (n61) 600 and 676.

260 Baik (n193) 3; Hadjipetrova and Poteat (n193) 14; Pernot-Leplay (n193) 116.

261 California Business and Professions Code, Division 8. Special business regulations [18400-22949.92.2], added by Stats. 1941, Ch.44., Chapter 22. Internet Privacy Requirements [22575-22579], added by Stats. 2003, Ch.829, Sec.3.

came into effect in 2004 and was amended in 2013, was also the first of its kind to require "an operator of a commercial Web site or online service that collects personally identifiable information through the Internet about individual consumers residing in California who use or visit its commercial Web site or online service (to) post its privacy policy on its Web site".[262,263] Consequently, the 2018 California Consumer Privacy Act (CCPA)[264] was created as a response to the European GDPR, and came into force in 2020.[265] The CCPA aims to provide Californians with data privacy rights and give (to a certain extent) the control over Californians' personal data back to the consumers, as opposed to the businesses.[266] In 2020, the CCPA was updated and amended by the California Privacy Rights Act (CPRA),[267] which came into force in 2023.[268] Given the presence of major big tech companies, such as Google or Meta, and given California's pioneering initiative, the CCPA was expected to set the standard for other U.S. States that would follow. Within the States' regulatory initiatives, the CCPA has, however, become an outlier.[269]

Definition personal data – Personal information is, in the CCPA, defined as "information that identifies, relates to, describes, is capable of being associated with, or could reasonably be linked, directly or indirectly, with a particular consumer or household".[270] This definition also encompasses "inferences drawn from any of the (personal) information identified … to create a profile about a consumer reflecting the consumer's preferences, characteristics, psychological trends, predispositions, behavior, attitudes, intelligence, abilities, and aptitudes".[271,272]

---

262 *Ibid.* § 22575(a).

263 John Delaney and Christine Lyon, 'Does Your Privacy Policy Comply with the California Online Privacy Protection Act?' (2005) 24 BFSP Report 7, 7; Hadjipetrova and Poteat (n193) 14; Kamala Harris, *Making Your Privacy Practices Public: Recommendations On Developing A Meaningful Privacy Policy* (California Department of Justice, 2014) 1-6; Hintze (n246) 1046-1048.

264 Title 1.81.5. California Consumer Privacy Act of 2018 (CCPA), Cal.Civ.Code § § 1798.100–1798.199.

265 CCPA § 1798.198.(a); Baik (n193) 1-2; Freeman (n193) 1.

266 Woodrow Hartzog, 'The case against idealising control' (2018) 4 EDPL 423, 425; Pernot-Leplay (n193) 117.

267 2020 California Privacy Rights Act, Assembly Bill No.1194 Ch.567, An Act To Amend Sections 1798.99.31, 1798.145, and 1798.185 of the Civil Code, Relating to Privacy, Approved By Governor Oct 8, 2023, Filed With Secretary of State Oct 8, 2023 (CPRA).

268 CPRA Sec.31(a); Bloomberg Law, 'California' (n198); Enright (n198) 269; Garyiene (n200) 255; Shatz and Lysobey (n198) 539.

269 Baik (n193) 1; Newell *et al.* (n229) 1062; Pernot-Leplay (n193) 116-119; Solove, 'Data Is What Data Does' (n16) 1092; Solove and Canter (n199).

270 CCPA § 1798.140.(v)(1).

271 CCPA § 1798.140.(v)(1)(K).

272 Baik (n193) 3; Bloomberg Law, 'California' (n198); Enright (n198) 269-270; Freeman (n193) 2; Mulligan and Linebaugh, *An Overview* (n230) 38; Pernot-Leplay (n193) 118; Sanford Shatz and Susan Chylik, 'The California Consumer Privacy Act of 2018' (2020) 75 BusLaw 1917, 1919.

Scope of application – The CCPA protects consumers who are "a natural person who is a California resident (i.e. "every individual who is in this State for other than a temporary or transitory purpose"[273] and "every individual domiciled in this State who is outside the State for a temporary or transitory purpose"[274]), however identified, including by any unique identifier".[275] The CCPA applies to any business "organized or operated for the profit or financial benefit of its shareholders or other owners, that collects consumers' personal information, or on the behalf of which such information is collected and that alone, or jointly with others, determines the purposes and means of the processing of consumers' personal information, that does business in the State of California, and that ... (A) had annual gross revenues in excess of twenty-five million dollars ($25,000,000) in the preceding calendar year, or (B) alone or in combination, annually buys, sells, or shares the personal information of 100,000 or more consumers or households, or (C) derives 50 percent or more of its annual revenues from selling or sharing consumers' personal information".[276] The CCPA's scope of application also extends to any service provider, contractor or third party acting on behalf of or in cooperation with the formerly defined business. Additionally, the CCPA covers "any entity that controls or is controlled by (such) a business ..., and that shares common branding with the business and with whom the business shares consumers' personal information",[277] "a joint venture or partnership composed of businesses in which each business has at least a 40 percent interest",[278] and "a person that does business in California, ... and that voluntarily certifies to the California Privacy Protection Agency that it is in compliance with, and agrees to be bound by, (the CCPA)".[279,280]

Data privacy principles – The safeguards foreseen in the CCPA are similar to and expand those enshrined in the 1974 Privacy Act, namely:

(1) "a business ... shall, at or before the point of collection, inform consumers of (specified practices)",[281] including a consumer's right to know what personal information is being collected,[282] a consumer's right to know what personal information is sold or shared and to whom[283] (*transparency*);

---

273 California Code of Regulations (CCR), Title 18, § 17014.(a)(1).
274 CCR § 17014.(a)(2).
275 CCPA § 1798.140.(i).
276 CCPA § 1798.140.(d)(1).
277 CCPA § 1798.140.(d)(2).
278 CCPA § 1798.140.(d)(3).
279 CCPA § 1798.140.(d)(4).
280 Bloomberg Law, 'California' (n198); Enright (n198) 271-272; Freeman (n193) 2; Mulligan and Linebaugh, *An Overview* (n230) 38; Mulligan and Linebaugh, *An Introduction* (n193) 2; Pernot-Leplay (n193) 117; Shatz and Chylik (n272) 1918.
281 CCPA § 1798.100.(a).
282 CCPA § 1798.110.
283 CCPA § 1798.115.

(2) "a business shall not retain a consumer's personal information or sensitive personal information ... for longer than is reasonably necessary for that disclosed purpose"[284] (*storage and time limitation*);
(3) "a business' collection, use, retention, and sharing of a consumer's personal information shall be reasonably necessary and proportionate to achieve the purposes for which the personal information was collected or processed, or for another disclosed purpose that is compatible with the context in which the personal information was collected ..."[285] (*data quality & purpose limitation*);
(4) "a business that collects a consumer's personal information shall implement reasonable security procedures and practices ... to protect the personal information from unauthorized or illegal access, destruction, use, modification, or disclosure ..."[286] (*data security*);
(5) a consumer's right to delete personal information,[287] a consumer's right to correct inaccurate personal information,[288] and a consumer's right to access personal information[289] (*data accuracy & right of access*);
(6) a consumer's right to opt out of sale or sharing of personal information[290] and a consumer's right of no retaliation following opt out or exercise of other rights[291] (*legitimate processing*);
(7) and a consumer's right to limit use and disclosure of sensitive personal information[292] and a special category of 'sensitive data'[293] (*sensitive data*).[294]

Exemptions – Within the U.S. sectoral approach, the CCPA is only applicable as a supplementary regulation to areas that have not yet been regulated, excluding already regulated subjects, such as health or bank-related data, from its scope of application.[295] Collection, processing, retention, sharing, selling, and use of personal information that complies with "federal, State, or local laws or comply with a court order or subpoena"[296] or with "a civil, criminal, or regulatory inquiry,

---

284 CCPA § 1798.100.(a)(3).
285 CCPA § 1798.100.(c).
286 CCPA § 1798.100.(e).
287 CCPA § 1798.105.
288 CCPA § 1798.106.
289 CCPA § 1798.110.
290 CCPA § 1798.120.
291 CCPA § 1798.125.
292 CCPA § 1798.121.
293 CCPA § 1798.140.(ae).
294 Baik (n193) 3; Bloomberg Law, 'California' (n198); Enright (n198) 271; Freeman (n193) 3; Mulligan and Linebaugh, *An Overview* (n230) 38-39; Mulligan and Linebaugh, *An Introduction* (n193) 2; Pernot-Leplay (n193) 117-118; Shatz and Chylik (n272) 1919-1923; Solove, 'Data Is What Data Does' (n16) 1083 1092.
295 CCPA § 1798.145.(c)-(g) and § 1798.146.(a).
296 CCPA § 1798.145.(a)(1)(A).

investigation, subpoena, or summons by federal, State, or local authorities",[297] or is in cooperation with a law enforcement[298] or government agency's emergency request[299] is excluded from the CCPA's scope of application. Other excluded areas encompass "deidentified or aggregate consumer information",[300] "a consumer's personal information if every aspect of that commercial conduct takes place wholly outside of California",[301] "household data",[302] and the possibility to refuse a consumer's personal data deletion request if necessary "to exercise free speech",[303] or "to engage in public or peer-reviewed scientific, historical, or statistical research that conforms or adheres to all other applicable ethics and privacy laws".[304,305]

Sanctions – The CCPA foresees two types of corrective measures, civil and administrative, in the case of *Personal Information Security Breaches*. These cybersecurity breaches encompass situations where "any consumer whose non-encrypted and nonredacted personal information ..., or whose email address in combination with a password or security question and answer that would permit access to the account is subject to an unauthorized access and exfiltration, theft, or disclosure as a result of the business's violation of the duty to implement and maintain reasonable security procedures and practices".[306] Firstly, the CCPA provides consumers with relief in the form of a "civil action (A) to recover damages in an amount not less than one hundred dollars ($100) and not greater than seven hundred and fifty ($750) per consumer per incident or actual damages, whichever is greater; (B) injunctive or declaratory relief; or (C) any other relief the court deems proper".[307] Before initiating a civil action, the consumer is required to notify the concerned business 30 days in advance in writing, in order to provide the latter with the possibility to remedy the violation. If the business succeeds in remedying the violation and gives written notice of it to the consumer, the latter will not anymore be able to bring a civil action.[308] Additionally, the Attorney General can bring a civil action "in the name of the people of the State of California" for a violation of the CCPA's requirements in

297 CCPA § 1798.145.(a)(1)(B).
298 CCPA § 1798.145.(a)(1)(C).
299 CCPA § 1798.145.(a)(1)(D)(i).
300 CCPA § 1798.145.(a)(1)(F).
301 CCPA § 1798.145.(a)(1)(G).
302 CCPA § 1798.145.(p).
303 CCPA § 1798.105.(d)(4).
304 CCPA § 1798.105.(d)(6).
305 Enright (n198) 270; Freeman (n193) 2-3; Shatz and Chylik (n272) 1922-1923.
306 CCPA § 1798.150.(a)(1).
307 *Ibid.*
308 CCPA § 1798.150.(b); Bloomberg Law, 'California' (n198); Enright (n198) 272-273; Freeman (n193) 4; Mulligan and Linebaugh, *An Overview* (n230) 39; Shatz and Chylik (n272) 1923.

the form of "an injunction and ... a civil penalty of not more than two thousand five hundred dollars ($2,500) for each violation or seven thousand five hundred dollars ($7,500) for each intentional violation and each violation involving the personal information of minor consumers".[309] In this case, a 30-day notification and remediation period also has to be observed.[310] Secondly, the CCPA foresees the possibility of administrative enforcement by the California Privacy Protection Agency in the form of "an administrative fine of not more than two thousand five hundred dollars ($2,500) for each violation or seven thousand five hundred dollars ($7,500) for each intentional violation or violations involving the personal information of consumers whom the business, service provider, contractor, or other person has actual knowledge are under 16 years of age".[311] In case the Attorney General decides to bring a civil action, which is successful, the California Privacy Protection Agency's administrative action will lapse, giving priority to the civil action over the administrative one.[312] In case the California Privacy Protection Agency has already administratively sanctioned (or decided not to sanction) a business for a violation of the CCPA's requirements before the Attorney General initiates a civil action for the same violation, the latter action will likewise not be permissible.[313]

Enforcement body – The CCPA's two types of corrective measures correspond with two types of enforcement bodies, namely administrative and civil. Similar to the more centralized enforcement in the EU by the EDPB or on a U.S. federal level by the FTC, the CCPA establishes "in State government the California Privacy Protection Agency ... vested with full administrative power, authority, and jurisdiction to implement and enforce the (CCPA)".[314] The California Privacy Protection Agency consists of "a five-member board, including the chairperson, (and) Californians with expertise in the areas of privacy, technology, and consumer rights".[315] The California Privacy Protection Agency and the Attorney General[316] can act respectively administratively and civilly to compel businesses to comply with the provisions set out in the CCPA. Additionally, a right of civil

309 CCPA § 1798.199.90.(a).
310 Bloomberg Law, 'California' (n198); Freeman (n193) 4; Garyiene (n200) 255-261; Mulligan and Linebaugh, *An Overview* (n230) 39; Shatz and Chylik (n272) 1923.
311 CCPA § 1798.155.(a).
312 CCPA § 1798.199.90.(c) and § 1798.199.100; Bloomberg Law, 'California' (n198).
313 CCPA § 1798.199.90.(d) and § 1798.199.100.
314 CCPA § 1798.199.10.(a).
315 *Ibid.*
316 CCPA § 1798.199.90; Bloomberg Law, 'California' (n198); Enright (n198) 273; Freeman (n193) 4; Mulligan and Linebaugh, *An Overview* (n230) 39; Mulligan and Linebaugh, *An Introduction* (n193) 2; Shatz and Chylik (n272) 1923.

action is provided for injured consumers in case of personal information security breaches at the California State level.[317]

iii) 2021 Virginia Consumer Data Protection Act

Background – The State of Virginia was the second U.S. State to promulgate consumer data privacy legislation, which came into force in 2023.[318] As the CCPA's follower, the 2021 Virginia Consumer Data Protection Act (VCDPA)[319] has become an anchor point for successive State consumer privacy acts.[320] A noticeable distinction between the CCPA and the VCDPA is the strong business lobbying that occurred in the adoption process of the latter act.[321] Due to this lobbying, the VCDPA is considered more 'business-friendly' than the CCPA. One example is the inclusion of the provision that "obligations imposed on controllers or processors (by the VCDPA) shall not restrict a controller's or processor's ability to collect, use, or retain data to conduct internal research to develop, improve, or repair products, services, or technology".[322]

Definition personal data – Personal data protected by the VCDPA encompasses broadly "any information that is linked or reasonably linkable to an identified or identifiable natural person".[323,324]

Scope of application – The VCDPA protects 'consumers' which are "natural person(s) … resident of (Virginia) acting only in an individual or household context", not when "acting in a commercial or employment context".[325] Personal data 'controllers' and 'processors' have to comply with the requirements set out in the VCDPA when they "conduct business in (Virginia) or produce products or services that are targeted to residents of (Virginia)", and if they control or process personal data "of at least 100,000 consumers during a calendar year, or of at least 25,000 consumers and derive over 50 percent of gross revenue from

---

317 CCPA § 1798.150.(a)(1) and § 1798.199.90.(e); Baik (n193) 3; Bloomberg Law, 'California' (n198); Enright (n198) 272-273; Freeman (n193) 4; Garyiene (n200) 255-261; Mulligan and Linebaugh, *An Overview* (n230) 39; Shatz and Chylik (n272) 1923.

318 Bloomberg Law, 'Virginia' (n200); Enright (n198) 273; Garyiene (n200) 255-261; Lindgren (n200); Newell *et al.* (n229) 1058; Michael Young and Dorian Simmons, 'New Virginia Privacy Law Promises Big Impacts' (2021) 38 Comp&InternetLaw 3, 3.

319 Code of Virginia, Chapter 53. Consumer Data Protection Act, § 59.1-575–§ 59.1-585 (VCDPA).

320 Bloomberg Law, 'Virginia' (n200); Solove and Canter (n199).

321 Lindgren (n200); Newell *et al.* (n229) 1063.

322 VCDPA § 59.1-582.B.1.

323 VCDPA § 59.1-575.

324 Bloomberg Law, 'Virginia' (n200); Enright (n198) 274-275; Lindgren (n200).

325 VCDPA § 59.1-575.

the sale of personal data".[326] 'Controllers' are "natural or legal person(s) that, alone or jointly with others, determine the purpose and means of processing personal data".[327] 'Processors' are "a natural or legal entity (acting) on behalf of a controller",[328] reflecting the terminology used in the EU GDPR.[329,330]

Data privacy principles – The VCDPA provides consumers with the possibility (and right) to request certain information from the personal data processors, to which the latter have 45 days (extendable by 45 days) to reply. Consumers have the right to request the following information regarding their personal data:

"1. to confirm whether or not a controller is processing the consumer's personal data and to access such personal data (right of access);
2. to correct inaccuracies in the consumer's personal data, taking into account the nature of the personal data and the purposes of the processing ... (*data accuracy*);
3. to delete personal data provided by or obtained about the consumer (*deletion rights*);
4. to obtain a copy of the consumer's personal data that the consumer previously provided to the controller ... that allows the consumer to transmit the data to another controller without hindrance ... (*data portability*); and
5. to opt out of the processing of the personal data for purposes of (i) targeted advertising, (ii) the sale of personal data, or (iii) profiling in furtherance of decisions that produce legal or similarly significant effects concerning the consumer (*legitimate processing*)".[331]

Data controllers, on their side, have a duty to "provide consumers with a reasonably accessible, clear, and meaningful privacy notice ..."[332] (*transparency*), and the responsibility to:

"1. limit the collection of personal data to what is adequate, relevant, and reasonably necessary in relation to the purposes (of processing), as disclosed to the consumer (*data quality & purpose limitation*);

326 VCDPA § 59.1-576.
327 VCDPA § 59.1-575.
328 *Ibid.*
329 See *Chapter 3, § 3, B., iv), b).*
330 Bloomberg Law, 'Virginia' (n200); Enright (n198) 276; Garyiene (n200) 255-261; Lindgren (n200); Jeffrey Mann, 'What Virginia's New Consumer Data Protection Act Means for You and Your Data Collection' (2021) 38 Comp&InternetLaw 17, 17; Shatz and Lysobey (n198) 539-547; Young and Simmons (n318) 3.
331 VCDPA § 59.1-577.A.
332 VCDPA § 59.1-578.C.

2. (subject to exceptions), not process personal data for purposes that are neither reasonably necessary to nor compatible with the disclosed purposes (of processing), as disclosed to the consumer, unless the controller obtains the consumer's consent (*purpose limitation & legitimate processing*);
3. establish, implement, and maintain reasonable administrative, technical, and physical data security practices to protect the confidentiality, integrity, and accessibility of personal data ... (*data security*);
4. not process personal data in violation of State and federal laws that prohibit unlawful discrimination against consumers (*non-discrimination & legitimate processing*); and
5. not process sensitive data concerning a consumer without obtaining the consumer's consent ... (*sensitive data & legitimate processing*)".[333]

Additionally, a data controller has a duty to "clearly and conspicuously disclose (the sale to third parties or the processing of personal data for targeted advertising), as well as the manner in which a consumer may exercise the right to opt out of such processing",[334] and "establish ... one or more secure and reliable means for consumers to submit a request to exercise their consumer rights ... (*transparency*)".[335] A time limitation requirement is only foreseen for the processing of "any personal data collected from a known child, (which should occur no) longer than is reasonably necessary to provide the online service, product, or feature (*storage and time limitation*)".[336,337]

Exemptions – Similar to the CCPA, the VCDPA does not apply to already regulated areas, such as health or bank related data.[338] Likewise, the collection, processing, retention, sharing, selling, and use of personal information in compliance with "federal, State, or local laws, rules, or regulations"[339] or within "a civil, criminal, or regulatory inquiry, investigation, subpoena, or summons by federal, State, local, or other governmental authorities"[340] or in cooperation with law enforcement agencies,[341] an emergency request,[342] or scientific research,[343] is excluded from the VCDPA's scope of application. "Any body, authority,

333 VCDPA § 59.1-578.A.
334 VCDPA § 59.1-578.D.
335 VCDPA § 59.1-578.E.
336 VCDPA § 59.1-578.F.1.d.
337 Bloomberg Law, 'Virginia' (n200); Enright (n198) 274-277; Garyiene (n200) 255-261; Lindgren (n200); Mann (n330) 17-18; Shatz and Lysobey (n198) 539-547; Young and Simmons (n318) 4-6.
338 VCDPA § 59.1-576.B.-C.
339 VCDPA § 59.1-582.A.1.
340 VCDPA § 59.1-582.A.2.
341 VCDPA § 59.1-582.A.3.
342 VCDPA § 59.1-582.A.6.
343 VCDPA § 59.1-582.A.8.

board, bureau, commission, district, or agency of (the State of Virginia) or of any political subdivision of (the State of Virginia), ... nonprofit organization, or institution of higher education"[344] is excluded from the VCDPA's scope of application, as well as "de-identified data or publicly available information",[345] and "personal data (processing) by a person in the course of a purely personal or household activity".[346] Finally, "the rights or freedoms of any persons, such as exercising the right of free speech pursuant to the First Amendment ..."[347] cannot be adversely affected by observing the VCDPA's principles.[348]

Sanctions – In the case of a (suspected) violation of the VCDPA's principles, the Attorney General has to notify the concerned controller or processor in writing of this violation, "identifying the specific provisions (that allegedly) have been or are being violated",[349] and provide the concerned controller or processor with a timeframe of 30 days to remedy the situation. If an express written statement is provided to the Attorney General within this timeframe that the situation has been remedied and no future violations will occur, the situation is considered remedied, requiring no further action. In case no remediation takes place, "the Attorney General may initiate an action in the name of (the State of Virginia) and may seek an injunction to restrain any violations of (the VCDPA's principles) and civil penalties of up to $7,500 for each violation".[350] The VCDPA does not explicitly provide a private right of action[351] for violations of its requirements.[352]

Enforcement body – The Attorney General is empowered by the VCDPA, and has exclusive authority, to issue a civil investigative demand if there is reasonable cause that a violation of the VCDPA's requirements has occurred or is about to occur.[353] There is no separate administrative enforcement body and no private right of action such as foreseen in the EU or as established by the CCPA in California.

---

344 VCDPA § 59.1-576.B.

345 VCDPA § 59.1-575.

346 VCDPA § 59.1-582.E.

347 *Ibid.*

348 Bloomberg Law, 'Virginia' (n200); Enright (n198) 274-275; Garyiene (n200) 255-261; Lindgren (n200); Mann (n330) 18; Shatz and Lysobey (n198) 539-547; Young and Simmons (n318) 3.

349 VCDPA § 59.1-584.B.

350 VCDPA § 59.1-584.C.

351 VCDPA § 59.1-584.E.

352 Bloomberg Law, 'Virginia' (n200); Enright (n198) 277; Garyiene (n200) 255-261; Lindgren (n200); Mann (n330) 18; Shatz and Lysobey (n198) 539-547; Young and Simmons (n318) 3-4.

353 VCDPA § 59.1-583 and § 59.1-584.A.; Bloomberg Law, 'Virginia' (n200); Enright (n198) 277; Lindgren (n200); Mann (n330) 18; Shatz and Lysobey (n198) 539-547, Young and Simmons (n318) 3-4.

Table 1. Common Fair Information Principles: U.S. Government and U.S. State Laws

	U.S. Government			U.S. State Laws	
	HEW Report	Privacy Act	FTC	CCPA § 1798.	VCDPA § 59.1-
1. Data Quality	✓	✓	✓	✓	✓
Purpose Limitation	3	S2.b.2	2	100(c)	578.A.2
Data Minimization	5	S2.b.4	/	100(c)	578.A.1
Time and Storage Limitation	/	/	/	100(a)(3)	/
2. Legitimate processing	✓	✓	✓	✓	✓
Lawful / Consent / Opt-in / Opt-out	3	S2.b.2 S2.b.4	2	120	577.A.5 578.A.2
Non-discrimination (incl. sensitive data)	/	/	/	121	578.A.4 578.A.5
Right to object	/	/	/	125	577.C. 578.A.4
3. Notification and Transparency	✓	✓	✓	✓	✓
Processing information / Privacy Policy	1	S2.b.1	1	100(a)	578.C.
Disclosure to 3rd parties	/	S3.b	/	100(a)(1) 115	578.C.4-5
Right of access	2	S2.b.3	3	110	577.A.1
Data breach notification	/	/	/	29(a)** 82(a)**	§ 18.2- 186.6***
4. Data Accuracy	✓	✓	✓	✓	✓
Accurate, up-to-date	5	S2.b.4	4	/	/
Correction rights	4	S2.b.3	3	106	577.A.2
Deletion rights	/	/	/	105	577.A.3
Notification to 3rd parties	/	/	/	105(c)(1)	/
5. Data Security	✓ 5	✓ S2.b.4	✓ 4	✓ 100(e)	✓ 578.A.3

(continued)

Table 1. *continued*

	U.S. Government			U.S. State Laws	
	HEW Report	Privacy Act	FTC	CCPA § 1798.	VCDPA § 59.1-
6. Enforcement	x	✓	✓	✓	✓
Administrative body	/	/	5	155(a)	/
Court	/	S2.b.6	/	150(a)* 199.90(a)	583 584
Remedies	/	/	5	150(a)* 155(a) 199.90(a)	584.C
Private right of action	/	S2.b.6	/	150*	584.E (no PRoA)

* only for personal information security breaches

** not part of CCPA (§ 1798.100–§ 1798.199.100); separate legal provisions of the Civil Code

*** not part of VCDPA (Title 59.1: Trade and Commerce); separate legal provisions of the Code of Virginia

§ 2. INTERNATIONAL DATA PRIVACY PROTECTION LEGAL INSTRUMENTS

The awareness of the importance of electronic privacy and data protection has been apparent since the 1970s, as the data processing industry began to emerge, occupying a central place in global economic structures.[354] The two institutions whose legal instruments in the area of personal data protection are most influential in the international landscape, and specifically for the United States and the European Union, are the Organization for Economic Cooperation and Development (OECD) and the Council of Europe (CoE).[355] The OECD Guidelines on the Protection of Privacy and Transborder Flows of Personal Data and the interpretation of Article 8 ECHR together with CoE Convention 108(+) for the Protection of Individuals with Regard to Automatic Processing of Personal Data had an extensive impact on States that had not (yet) acted legislatively by the time these documents were adopted.[356]

354 Explanatory Memorandum 1980 OECD Guidelines, I.1.; OECD, *OECD Declaration on Transborder Data Flows* (OECD Digital Economy Papers No.1, 1985); OECD, *Ministerial Declaration on the Protection of Privacy on Global Networks* (OECD Legal Instruments, 2024) 3.

355 Meg Ambrose and Jef Ausloos, 'The Right To Be Forgotten Across The Pond' (2013) 3 JInfPolicy 1, 9; Bennett (n140) 139; Heisenberg (n66) 25; Joy Liddicoat, *Human Rights and the Internet* (Intersentia 2021) 72; Lynskey, *The foundations* (n42) 47-48; Pernot-Leplay (n193) 103; Solove, 'Data Is What Data Does' (n16) 1088.

356 Bennett (n140) 139.

A. ORGANIZATION FOR ECONOMIC COOPERATION AND DEVELOPMENT

Background – The Organization for Economic Cooperation and Development (OECD) is an international organization that has been stimulating greater well-being, world trade, and economic progress since 1961, and advises governments on growth policies that focus on resilience, inclusivity, and sustainability.[357] The OECD has at the time of writing 38 signatory States,[358] which include the United States and 22[359] of the 27[360] EU Member States. The European Union is not a member, but participates in the work of the OECD.[361] In 1980, the OECD mandated an expert committee, consisting of lawyers familiar with the capabilities of new technologies and national/regional data protection laws (in as far as these laws existed), to develop guidelines for privacy protection and transborder personal data flows.[362] These guidelines were based on common concerns regarding personal data processing and/or the identification of similar personal data protection principles in different countries.[363] The (mainly economic) aim of these non-binding guidelines was to facilitate cross-border personal data transfers by ensuring an equal level of protection through compliance with common principles.[364] The OECD had no enforcement power as the guidelines were formulated as a recommendation, and

[357] OECD, 'Our history' (*oecd.org*, 2025); The Editors of Encyclopaedia Britannica, 'Organisation for Economic Co-operation and Development' (*Britannica*, 9 Apr 2025).

[358] Namely, Australia, Austria, Belgium, Canada, Chile, Colombia, Costa Rica, Czech Republic, Denmark, Estonia, Finland, France, Germany, Greece, Hungary, Iceland, Ireland, Israel, Italy, Japan, South Korea, Latvia, Lithuania, Luxembourg, Mexico, Netherlands, New Zealand, Norway, Poland, Portugal, Slovakia, Slovenia, Spain, Sweden, Switzerland, Turkey, United Kingdom, and United States.

[359] Namely, Austria, Belgium, Czech Republic, Denmark, Estonia, Finland, France, Germany, Greece, Hungary, Ireland, Italy, Latvia, Lithuania, Luxembourg, Netherlands, Poland, Portugal, Slovakia, Slovenia, Spain, and Sweden.

[360] Namely, Austria, Belgium, Bulgaria, Croatia, Cyprus, Czech Republic, Denmark, Estonia, Finland, France, Germany, Greece, Hungary, Ireland, Italy, Latvia, Lithuania, Luxembourg, Malta, Netherlands, Poland, Portugal, Romania, Slovakia, Slovenia, Spain, and Sweden.

[361] OECD, 'Members and partners' (*oecd.org*, 2025).

[362] Explanatory Memorandum 1980 OECD Guidelines, Introduction, 1; Cate (n193) 34; Fred Cate and Viktor Mayer-Schönberger, 'Tomorrow's privacy' (2013) 3 IDPL 67, 67; Fromholz (n74) 466; Heisenberg (n66) 52; A.C.M. Nugter, *Transborder Flow of Personal Data within the EC* (Kluwer 1990) 22.

[363] Explanatory Memorandum 1980 OECD Guidelines, I.5.; Bennett (n140) 95-96.

[364] Explanatory Memorandum 1980 OECD Guidelines, II.1.25.; Bennett (n140) 138; Bygrave, *Data Protection Law* (n17) 32; Bygrave, *Data Privacy Law* (n37) 43; Fred Cate, 'The EU data protection directive, information privacy, and the public interest' (1995) 80 IowaLRev 431, 431; Cate (n193) 34; Christofi and Verdoodt (n107) 32-33; Fromholz (n74) 466; Gutwirth *et al.* (n32) 276-277; Nugter (n362) 22; OECD, *OECD Declaration* (n354); Pernot-Leplay (n193) 103; Judith Rauhofer, 'Privacy is dead, get over it!' (2008) 17 ICT Law 185, 189.

relied on its signatories' voluntary cooperation.[365] The 1980 OECD Guidelines were in the first place addressed to 'Member countries', which included the United States and the majority of EU Member States, but also non-member countries, international organizations, industry, and businesses were encouraged to take the 'Recommendation Concerning Guidelines Governing the Protection of Privacy and Transborder Flows of Personal Data'[366] and the 'Declaration on the Protection of Privacy on Global Networks'[367] into account.[368]

1980 OECD Guidelines – The 1980 OECD Guidelines on the Protection of Privacy and Transborder Flows of Personal Data[369] identify eight principles that the public and private sectors of the signatory States have to comply with when manually or automatically (computerized) processing personal data;[370]

1) collection limitation: including obtaining the data "by lawful and fair means and, where appropriate, with the knowledge or consent of the data subject";
2) data quality: the collected data has to be relevant and necessary for "the purposes for which they are to be used" and "should be accurate, complete, and kept up-to-date";
3) purpose specification: should occur "not later than at the time of data collection and the subsequent use limited to the fulfillment of those purposes";
4) use limitation: the collected personal data can only be used, disclosed, or made available for purposes other than those indicated "with the consent of the data subject, or by the authority of law";
5) security safeguards: should be employed to protect the collected personal data "against such risks as loss or unauthorized access, destruction, use, modification or disclosure";
6) openness: includes a transparency requirement "about developments, practices and policies with respect to (the collected) personal data, ..., as well as the identity and usual residence of the data controller";

365 OECD Guidelines on the Protection of Privacy and Transborder Flows of Personal Data [1980] Preface, 7; Bennett (n140) 138; Fromholz (n74) 467; Heisenberg (n66) 54; Nugter (n362) 22.

366 OECD Guidelines [1980] Recommendation of the Council concerning Guidelines Governing the Protection of Privacy and Transborder Flows of Personal Data, 11-18.

367 OECD Guidelines [1980] Declaration on the Protection of Privacy on Global Networks, 59-62.

368 *Ibid.*, 62; Bennett (n140) 136-140; Bygrave, *Data Protection Law* (n17) 32-33; Heisenberg (n66) 8-9.

369 OECD Guidelines on the Protection of Privacy and Transborder Flows of Personal Data [1980] C(80)58/FINAL.

370 1980 OECD Guidelines, Part One, 2; Bygrave, *Data Privacy Law* (n37) 43; Nugter (n362) 22.

7) individual participation: includes the right to obtain information regarding whether a controller has a data subject's personal data, regarding the data held by the controller "within a reasonable time ... and in a form that is readily intelligible", regarding the reasons for denying the former request from a consumer, and a right "to challenge data relating to (the data subject) and, if the challenge is successful to have the data erased, rectified, completed or amended"; and
8) accountability principle: requiring data controllers to comply with the former principles.[371,372]

Personal data is defined as "any information relating to an identified or identifiable individual (data subject)".[373] Specific safeguards for sensitive data were not included in the Guidelines. The expert committee struggled to reach consensus on the protected categories, as they believed that the protection of sensitive data is more dependent on the context in which the data is used rather than protecting the data for its own sake.[374] The United States agrees with this approach, while the EU disagrees.[375] Additionally, the OECD recognized the added value of privacy policies provided by companies on their websites to facilitate transparency and comparison in the trade market. In its supplementary documents, the OECD noticed, however, that the lengthy and complicated wording of contemporary privacy policies impedes their potential added value.[376] Finally, an exception to the applicability of the rules was included for "national sovereignty, national security and public policy ('*ordre public*'), (which) should be as few as possible, and made known to the public".[377]

2013 OECD Guidelines – The 1980 OECD Guidelines on the Protection of Privacy and Transborder Flows of Personal Data were updated in 2013.[378] The eight data protection principles themselves have remained unchanged.

371 1980 OECD Guidelines, Part Two, 14-16.

372 Ambrose and Ausloos (n355) 9-10; Bennett (n140) 100; Christofi and Verdoodt (n107) 32-33; Gutwirth *et al.* (n32) 182 and 276-277; Nugter (n362) 22-23; Pernot-Leplay (n193) 103.

373 1980 OECD Guidelines, Part One, 1.b).

374 Explanatory Memorandum 1980 OECD Guidelines, I.19.a) and II.B.; Bygrave, *Data Protection Law* (n17) 69; Bygrave, *Data Privacy Law* (n37) 46; Quinn and Malgieri (n36) 1587-1588; Solove, 'Data Is What Data Does' (n16) 1088-1089.

375 Pernot-Leplay (n193) 103.

376 Gutwirth *et al.* (n32) 277-278; OECD, *Privacy Online: OECD Guidance on Policy and Practice* (OECD, 2003) 13-17; OECD, *Making Privacy Notices Simple: An OECD Report and Recommendations* (OECD Digital Economy Papers No.120, 2006).

377 1980 OECD Guidelines, Part One, 4.

378 OECD Guidelines on the Protection of Privacy and Transborder Flows of Personal Data (updated 2013) [2013].

The 2013 update mainly concerns an elaboration of the accountability principle through the introduction of measures aimed at strengthening the accountability of signatory States for their compliance with the data protection principles. Four new elements were introduced for this purpose; a privacy management program, a security breach notification, the establishment of privacy enforcement authorities, and possibilities for interoperability. The first element, the privacy management program, requires data controllers to set up "appropriate safeguards based on privacy risk assessment, (including) plans for responding to inquiries and incidents".[379] The second security breach notification requirement mandates data controllers to notify "privacy enforcement authorities or other relevant authorities where there has been a significant security breach affecting personal data, (and also the affected data subjects) where the breach is likely to adversely affect"[380] the latter. The third element recommends signatory States to "establish and maintain privacy enforcement authorities with the governance, resources and technical expertise necessary to exercise their powers effectively and to make decisions on an objective, impartial and consistent basis".[381] The fourth element promotes international cooperation and interoperability "among (national) privacy frameworks that give practical effect to these Guidelines".[382,383]

B. COUNCIL OF EUROPE

Pre-1981 initiatives – The Council of Europe (CoE) was set up in 1949 in the aftermath of the Second World War as an intergovernmental organization to preserve and ensure respect for human rights, democracy, and the rule of law, and has at the time of writing 46 Member States,[384] and 6 observer States[385]

379 2013 OECD Guidelines, Part Three, 15.

380 2013 OECD Guidelines, Part Three, 15.c).

381 2013 OECD Guidelines, Part Five, 19.c).

382 2013 OECD Guidelines, Part Six, 21.

383 Bygrave, *Data Privacy Law* (n37) 44-51; Cécile de Terwangne, 'Council of Europe convention 108+' (2021) 40 CLSR 105497 1, 1; Pernot-Leplay (n193) 103.

384 Namely, Albania, Andorra, Armenia, Austria, Azerbaijan, Belgium, Bosnia and Herzegovina, Bulgaria, Croatia, Cyprus, Czech Republic, Denmark, Estonia, Finland, France, Georgia, Germany, Greece, Hungary, Iceland, Ireland, Italy, Latvia, Liechtenstein, Lithuania, Luxembourg, Malta, Republic of Moldova, Monaco, Montenegro, Netherlands, North Macedonia, Norway, Poland, Portugal, Romania, San Marino, Serbia, Slovakia, Slovenia, Spain, Sweden, Switzerland, Turkey, Ukraine, and United Kingdom.

385 Namely, Canada, Holy See, Israel, Japan, Mexico, and the United States.

of which the United States is one.[386] The CoE has been an important player in the data protection and electronic privacy arena by adopting resolutions and recommendations to raise awareness and address possible issues resulting from the collection and processing of personal data since the 1970s.[387] Fifty years later, many of those issues and core principles regarding personal data collection, storage, and access can still be found in the EU GDPR.[388] The CoE identified significant differences between the Member States in their level of industrialization and in their national laws (or their absence) regarding data privacy. Already in the 1970s, Article 8 ECHR right to privacy was explicitly mentioned[389] in the CoE's legislative documents and linked to the concept of personal data protection in the ECtHR's case law.[390]

i) Article 8 ECHR: Right to Privacy

1950 European Convention on Human Rights – On the 4th of November 1950, the CoE adopted the European Convention for the Protection of Human Rights and Fundamental Freedoms (ECHR)[391] to ensure that people's human rights are respected. The adoption of the ECHR was a reaction to the Jewish persecution during the Second World War, and personal data protection was subsequently categorized within the ambit of the right to privacy enshrined in Article 8.[392] Up until today, the ECHR has been one of the most influential human rights conventions. In 1959, the European Court of Human Rights (ECtHR) was created to enforce States' compliance with the ECHR's

386 Bennett (n140) 133; Klaus Brummer, 'Uniting Europe' (2012) 20 EurRev 403, 404-410; Council of Europe, 'Our member States' (*coe.int*, 2025); Council of Europe, 'The Council of Europe at a glance' (*coe.int*, 2025); Fromholz (n74) 467; Pałka, 'Data Management' (n44) 617.

387 Council of Europe [1973] Resolution (73) 22 and Explanatory Report on the Protection of the Privacy of Individuals vis-à-vis Electronic Data Banks in the Private Sector; Council of Europe [1973] Resolution (73) 23 on harmonisation measures in the field of legal data processing in the member States of the Council of Europe; Council of Europe [1974] Resolution (74) 29 on the protection of individuals vis-à-vis electronic data banks in the public sector.

388 See *Chapter 3, § 3, B., iv).*

389 CoE, Resolution (74) 29 (n387).

390 CoE, Resolution (73) 22 (n387); CoE, Resolution (74) 29 (n387); Council of Europe [1980] Recommendation No. R(80) 13 on Exchange of Legal Information relating to Data Protection; Council of Europe [1981] Recommendation No. R(81) 19 on Access to Information held by Public Authorities; Bennett (n140) 133-136; Centre for Intellectual Property and Information Law, 'European Data Protection and e-Privacy – Transnational Resources' (*Cambridge University*, 2025); Nugter (n362) 24-25.

391 Council of Europe [1950] European Convention for the Protection of Human Rights and Fundamental Freedoms (ECHR).

392 CoE, Resolution (73) 22 (n387); CoE, Resolution (74) 29 (n387); Robert Kagan, *Of Paradise and Power* (2nd edn, Vintage Books 2004) 58-62; James Whitman, 'The Two Western Cultures of Privacy' (2004) 113 YLJ 1151, 1164-1171; See *Chapter 4, § 1, B., i).*

provisions.[393] Only States can be held liable before the ECtHR. The ECHR's provisions extend, through their horizontal effect, however also to infringements by individuals vis-à-vis individuals as the State should prevent infringements from occurring. Indirectly, the ECHR's influence consequently affects private parties, as they can rely on the ECtHR's case law in national proceedings.[394]

Right to Privacy – Of particular importance for the personal data protection discussion is Article 8 ECHR, which ensures that "everyone has the right to respect for his private and family life, his home and his correspondence",[395] and encompasses informational privacy, personal development, and individual autonomy.[396] Exceptions to this right are only allowed when "by a public authority … in accordance with the law and necessary in a democratic society in the interests of national security, public safety or the economic well-being of the country, for the prevention of disorder or crime, for the protection of health or morals, or for the protection of the rights and freedoms of others".[397] Article 8 ECHR right to privacy was initially a negative right aimed at preventing States from interfering with people's private and family life. In the evolution of the ECtHR's jurisprudence, a positive obligation for the States to promote and protect someone's private and family life was read into the scope of application of Article 8 ECHR.[398] The European Court of Human Rights has further concretized the interpretation of Article 8 ECHR in the area of personal data protection in its case law, since the ECHR should be applied as a "living instrument

---

393 Ed Bates, *The Evolution of the European Convention on Human Rights* (OUP 2010) 180; Gutwirth *et al.* (n32) 280; Pałka, 'Data Management' (n44) 618.

394 *X. and Y. v Netherlands* App no 8978/80 (ECtHR, 26 Mar 1985) para 23; *I. v Finland* App no 20511/03 (ECtHR, 17 Jul 2008) para 36; *K.U. v Finland* App no 2872/02 (ECtHR, 2 Dec 2008) para 43; Lucas Bergkamp, 'EU Data Protection Policy: The Privacy Fallacy' (2002) 18 CLSR 31, 33; Bygrave, *Data Privacy Law* (n37) 87-88; Gutwirth *et al.* (n32) 17 and 65-66; Lynskey, *The foundations* (n42) 113-115; Purtova, *Property Rights* (n31) 227-240.

395 Article 8.1 ECHR.

396 Bygrave, *Data Privacy Law* (n37) 96; Gutwirth *et al.* (n32) 69; Lynskey, *The foundations* (n42) 108; Purtova, *Property Rights* (n31) 229; Nadezhda Purtova, 'The illusion of personal data as no one's property' (2015) 7 LIT 83, 94.

397 Article 8.2 ECHR.

398 *Johnston and Others v Ireland* App no 9697/82 (ECtHR, 18 Dec 1986) para 55(c); *Gaskin v United Kingdom* App no 10454/83 (ECtHR, 7 Jul 1989) para 41; *McGinley and Egan v United Kingdom* App nos 21825/93 and 23414/94 (ECtHR, 9 Jun 1998) para 98; *Odièvre v France* App no 42326/98 (ECtHR, 13 Feb 2003) para 40; *I. v Finland* (n394) para 36; *K.U. v Finland* (n394) para 42; Bergkamp (n394) 33; Bygrave, *Data Privacy Law* (n37) 87-88; Christofi and Verdoodt (n107) 44-45; Gutwirth *et al.* (n32) 17 and 65-66; Uta Kohl, 'The Right To Be Forgotten in Data Protection Law and Two Western Cultures of Privacy' (2023) 72 ICLQ 737, 759; Lynskey, *The foundations* (n42) 106-107; Purtova, *Property Rights* (n31) 231-240; Daniel Solove, 'Conceptualizing Privacy' (2002) 90 CLR 1087, 1120.

which … must be interpreted in the light of present-day conditions",[399] including technological novelties.[400]

ECtHR data processing case law – The ECtHR extended the scope of application of Article 8 ECHR to include the protection of individuals' personal data, as well as certain specific aspects of personal data protection.[401] Article 8 ECHR is not an absolute right, and interferences can be justified when in accordance with the law, pursuing a legitimate aim, and necessary in a democratic society based on Article 8.2 ECHR. Firstly, the practice of collecting, storing, and using personal data was included in the scope of application of Article 8 ECHR. In 2006 *Segerstedt-Wiberg and others v Sweden*,[402] 2011 *Shimovolos v Russia*,[403] 2020 *Trajkovski and Chipovski v North Macedonia*,[404] and 2020 *Gaughran v United Kingdom*,[405] the ECtHR stated that "the collection and storage of (personal) information … amount(s) to interference with the applicants' right to respect for private life as secured by (Article 8.1 ECHR)",[406] which can be justified if the storage is necessary[407] and/or if sufficient safeguards are foreseen against blanket and indiscriminate retention powers.[408,409] In 2012 *M.M. v United Kingdom*,[410] the Court explained that "as long as (someone's) data are retained and capable of being disclosed, (he/she) remains a victim of any potential violation of article 8 arising from retention or disclosure".[411,412]

399 *Tyrer v UK* App no 5856/72 (ECtHR, 25 Apr 1978) para 31.

400 Bygrave, *Data Privacy Law* (n37) 87; Plixavra Vogiatzoglou and Peggy Valcke, 'Two Decades of Article 8 CFR' in Eleni Kosta, Ronald Leenes, and Irene Kamara (eds), *Research Handbook on EU Data Protection* (Edward Elgar 2022) 14.

401 *Leander v Sweden* App no 9248/81 (ECtHR, 17 May 1985) para 54; *Lundvall v Sweden* App nos 10473 and 10473/83 (ECtHR, 1 Dec 1985) p.130; *Gaskin* (n398) paras 37-41; *Z. v Finland* App no 22009/93 (ECtHR, 25 Feb 1997) para 95; *M.S. v Sweden* App no 20837/92 (ECtHR, 27 Aug 1997) para 41; *McGinley and Egan* (n398) para 97; *Amann v Switzerland* App no 27798/95 (ECtHR, 16 Feb 2000) para 65; *Rotaru v Romania* App no 28341/95 (ECtHR, 4 May 2000) paras 43-44; Magdalena Brewczynska, *Policing via banks: The question of legitimacy of personal data sharing* (Doctoral Thesis Tilburg University, 2024) 13; Christofi and Verdoodt (n107) 28-44; EU Agency for Fundamental Rights, *Handbook on European data protection law* (EU Publications Office 2018) 17; Gutwirth *et al.* (n32) 18; Kohl (n398) 757-761; Purtova, 'The illusion' (n396) 94; Zuiderveen Borgesius *et al.* (n180) 14.

402 *Segerstedt-Wiberg and others v Sweden* App no 62332/00 (ECtHR, 6 Jun 2006).

403 *Shimovolos v Russia* App no 30194/09 (ECtHR, 21 Jun 2011) paras 58-71.

404 *Trajkovski and Chipovski v North Macedonia* App nos 53205/13 and 63320/13 (ECtHR, 13 Feb 2020) paras 37-55.

405 *Gaughran v United Kingdom* App no 45245/15 (ECtHR, 13 Feb 2020) paras 58-98.

406 *Segerstedt-Wiberg* (n402) para 73; *Shimovolos* (n403) para 66.

407 *Segerstedt-Wiberg* (n402) paras 69-92.

408 *Trajkovski and Chipovski* (n404) para 54; *Gaughran* (n405) para 96.

409 Lynskey, *The foundations* (n42) 108.

410 *M.M. v United Kingdom* App no 24029/07 (ECtHR, 13 Nov 2012) paras 149-207.

411 *M.M. v United Kingdom* (n410) para 159.

412 Bygrave, *Data Privacy Law* (n37) 111.

In 2021 *Zoltán Varga v Slovakia*,[413] the ECtHR added that also "processing and use of personal data … fall within the scope of the notion of private life for the purposes of article 8 (ECHR)".[414] The ECtHR interpreted two specific types of data, namely fingerprints and banking documents, as consisting of personal data. In 2008 *S. and Marper v United Kingdom*[415] and 2013 *M.K. v France*,[416] the Court specified that "the retention of fingerprints (on the national authorities' records in connection with an identified or identifiable individual) constitutes an interference with the right to respect for private life".[417,418] In 2015 *M.N. and Others v San Marino*[419] and 2015 *G.S.B. v Switzerland*,[420] the ECtHR added that "information retrieved from banking documents undoubtedly amounts to personal data concerning an individual, irrespective of it being sensitive information or not, (and that) bank accounts are to be considered as personal data protected by article 8 (ECHR)".[421]

ECtHR sensitive data case law – Secondly, the ECtHR has specified certain special categories of sensitive data that require additional protection. In 2008 S. and *Marper v United Kingdom*,[422] 2019 *Catt v United Kingdom*,[423] and 2023 *Glukhin v Russia*,[424] the Court expressed its opinion that "personal data revealing ethnic origin"[425] as well as "personal data revealing political opinion"[426] fall within "the special categories of sensitive data attracting a heightened level of protection".[427] In 2016 *Y.Y. v Russia*[428] and 2018 *Mockutė v Lithuania*,[429] the ECtHR added "that the disclosure – without a patient's consent – of medical records containing highly personal and sensitive data about a patient … constituted an interference with the patient's right to respect for private life".[430]

---

413 *Zoltán Varga v Slovakia* App nos 58361/12, 25592/16, and 27176/16 (ECtHR, 20 Jul 2021) paras 95-174.

414 *Zoltán Varga* (n413) para 144.

415 *S. and Marper v United Kingdom* App nos 30562/04 and 30566/04 (ECtHR, 4 Dec 2008) paras 58-126.

416 *M.K. v France* App no 19522/09 (ECtHR, 18 Apr 2013) paras 20-47.

417 *S. and Marper* (n415) para 86; *M.K. v France* (n416) para 29.

418 Bygrave, *Data Privacy Law* (n37) 128; Lynskey, *The foundations* (n42) 108.

419 *M.N. and Others v San Marino* App no 28005/12 (ECtHR, 7 Jul 2015) paras 24-85.

420 *G.S.B. v Switzerland* App no 28601/11 (ECtHR, 22 Dec 2015) paras 44-98.

421 *M.N. and Others* (n419) para 51; *G.S.B. v Switzerland* (n420) para 51.

422 *S. and Marper* (n415).

423 *Catt v United Kingdom* App no 43514/15 (ECtHR, 24 Jan 2019) paras 72-128.

424 *Glukhin v Russia* App no 11519/20 (ECtHR, 4 Jul 2023) paras 58-91.

425 *S. and Marper* (n415) para 76.

426 *Catt* (n423) para 112; *Glukhin* (n424) para 76.

427 *S. and Marper* (n415) para 76; *Catt* (n423) para 112; *Glukhin* (n424) para 76.

428 *Y.Y. v Russia* App no 40378/06 (ECtHR, 23 Feb 2016) paras 32-60.

429 *Mockutė v Lithuania* App no 66490/09 (ECtHR, 27 Feb 2018) paras 78-106.

430 *Y.Y. v Russia* (n428) para 39; *Mockutė* (n429) para 95.

ECtHR data protection case law – Thirdly, certain personal data protection principles were already at an early stage recognized by the ECtHR, such as data access, data correction, data security, and purpose limitation. In 1989 *Gaskin v United Kingdom*,[431] the Court stressed that its finding of a violation of Mr. Gaskin's right to access personal information relating to him "is reached without expressing any opinion on whether general rights of access to personal data and information may be derived from (article 8.1 ECHR)".[432,433] In 2002 *M.G. v United Kingdom*,[434] 2005 *Roche v United Kingdom*,[435] and 2017 *Yonchev v Bulgaria*,[436] the ECtHR confirmed, however, that denying applicants' access to their medical/social service records and/or providing "no appeal (possibilities) against a refusal of access to any independent body"[437] constituted "a failure to fulfill the positive obligation to protect the applicant's private and family life"[438] and "to provide an effective and accessible procedure enabling the applicant(s) to have access to all relevant and appropriate information"[439] violating Article 8.1 ECHR.[440] In 2000 *Rotaru v Romania*,[441] the Court read a right to correction of wrongful personal data into the scope of application of Article 8 ECHR.[442] In 2008 *Cemalettin Canlı v Turkey*,[443] the ECtHR explained that "the keeping and forwarding to the ... court of (an) inaccurate police report (containing inaccurate personal data of which rectification was requested but denied) constitute(s) an interference with the applicant's right to respect for his private life".[444] In 2008 *I. v Finland*,[445] the Court held for the first time that "a failure on the part of the hospital to guarantee the security of (applicant's) data against unauthorised access ... (constitutes) a breach of the State's positive obligation to secure respect for her private life by means of a system of data protection rules and safeguards".[446] In 2013 *Avilkina and others v Russia*,[447] the ECtHR confirmed that "placing no specific limits on the prosecutor's authority to obtain a person's medical records ... (is) sufficient for the Court to conclude that ... (no sufficient safeguards are provided) to

---

431 *Gaskin* (n398) paras 41-63.
432 *Ibid.* para 37.
433 Bygrave, *Data Privacy Law* (n37) 96-97; Purtova, *Property Rights* (n31) 230.
434 *M.G. v United Kingdom* App no 39393/98 (ECtHR, 24 Sep 2002).
435 *Roche v United Kingdom* App no 32555/96 (ECtHR, 19 Oct 2005).
436 *Yonchev v Bulgaria* App no 12504/09 (ECtHR, 7 Dec 2017) paras 32-63.
437 *M.G. v United Kingdom* (n434) para 30.
438 *Ibid.* para 31.
439 *Roche* (n435) para 167; *Yonchev* (n436) para 50.
440 Bygrave, *Data Privacy Law* (n37) 171.
441 *Rotaru* (n401).
442 *Ibid.* para 46.
443 *Cemalettin Canlı v Turkey* App no 22427/04 (ECtHR, 18 Nov 2008) paras 18-44.
444 *Ibid.* para 37.
445 *I. v Finland* (n394) paras 26-49.
446 *Ibid.* paras 37 and 48.
447 *Avilkina and others v Russia* App no 1585/09 (ECtHR, 6 Jun 2013) paras 25-54.

prevent disclosure inconsistent with the respect for the applicants' private life guaranteed under (article 8 ECHR)".[448] In 1997 *M.S. v Sweden*,[449] 1997 *Z. v Finland*,[450] 2005 *Sciacca v Italy*,[451] 2012 *P. and S. v Poland*,[452] and 2022 *M.K. v Ukraine*,[453] the Court assessed whether the disclosure of applicants' (health) data, contrary to the initial purposes for which that data was collected, complied with Article 8 ECHR right to privacy. The Court found an interference for the disclosure of this data to the public,[454] but justified the interference on other accounts.[455,456]

ECtHR data to be forgotten case law – Finally, in 2018 *M.L. and W.W. v Germany*,[457] the ECtHR cited, and to some extent confirmed, the CJEU's 2014 *Google Spain*[458] decision establishing a right to be forgotten.[459] The ECtHR agreed with the CJEU regarding the prevalence of freedom of speech (including the right to information of the public) over the applicants' right to privacy in this situation, but did not engage in an analysis of the distinction between search engines (to which the CJEU's right to be forgotten was applicable) and media outlets (to which the CJEU's right to be forgotten was not applicable). The ECtHR did not have to conduct the latter analysis, since "the material at issue … could no longer be found on the Internet using search engines … (even though) two articles published by Spiegel online could … still be found … the applicants' names were not included in full",[460] and moreover "subject to additional restrictions, (such as) paid access (or) subscriber-only access".[461] During the 2018 modernization of 1981 Convention 108 to Convention 108+ (*both discussed below*), it was also decided not to include an explicit right to be forgotten.[462] Lee Bygrave,[463] Paul De Hert and Serge Gutwirth conclude, therefore, that the ECtHR allows Member State authorities to process personal data to a large extent, and intervenes only in cases of "flagrant abuse or

448 *Ibid.* paras 49 and 53.
449 *M.S. v Sweden* (n401) paras 28-44.
450 *Z. v Finland* (n401) paras 71-114.
451 *Sciacca v Italy* App no 50774/99 (ECtHR, 11 Jan 2005) paras 22-31.
452 *P. and S. v Poland* App no 57375/08 (ECtHR, 30 Oct 2012) paras 113-137.
453 *M.K. v Ukraine* App no 24867/13 (ECtHR, 15 Sep 2022) paras 27-61.
454 *Z. v Finland* (n401) paras 111-113; *Sciacca* (n451) para 28; *P. and S. v Poland* (n452) para 134; *M.K. v Ukraine* (n453) paras 44-61.
455 *Z. v Finland* (n401) paras 102-110; *M.S. v Sweden* (n401) para 44.
456 Bygrave, *Data Privacy Law* (n37) 154; Lynskey, *The foundations* (n42) 109; Purtova, *Property Rights* (n31) 230-231.
457 *M.L. and W.W. v Germany* App nos 60798/10 and 65599/10 (ECtHR, 28 Jun 2018) paras 65-116.
458 See *Chapter 3, § 3, C., i)*.
459 *M.L. and W.W. v Germany* (n457) para 97; Kohl (n398) 757.
460 *M.L. and W.W. v Germany* (n457) para 85.
461 *Ibid.* para 113.
462 de Terwangne, 'Convention 108+' (n383) 14.
463 Bygrave, *Data Privacy Law* (n37) 92.

risky use of data".[464] This case law overview confirms their observation, as initial interferences with Article 8.1 ECHR are often justified in the subsequent three-step justification test foreseen in Article 8.2 ECHR. Moreover, the principles of time and storage limitation, categories of sensitive data, disclosure to third parties, legitimate processing, right of access, enforcement/compliance control by an independent body, correction rights, data security, and purpose limitation were also read into the scope of application of Article 8 ECHR by the ECtHR as shown in the case law overview above.

ii) Convention 108(+) for the Protection of Individuals with Regard to Automatic Processing of Personal Data

1981 Convention 108 – The 1981 Council of Europe Convention (108) for the Protection of Individuals with Regard to Automatic Processing of Personal Data,[465] which took effect in 1985, was the first binding Convention enacted in Europe to address cross-border personal data protection problems in the private as well as the public sector.[466] Convention 108 was open for signature by the CoE Member States, and had to be subsequently ratified, accepted, or approved.[467] The Convention entered officially into force "on the first day of the month following the expiration of a period of three months after the date on which five Member States of the Council of Europe ha(d) expressed their consent to be bound by the Convention in accordance with the (procedure set out before)".[468] Non-Member States could also accede to Convention 108 after its entry into force, and upon invitation by "the Committee of Ministers of the Council of Europe by a decision taken by the (required) majority (and procedure)".[469] Convention 108 was proposed in 1980 and developed in coordination with the Organization for Economic Cooperation and Development (OECD, *see above*) to avoid discrepancies between these two legal instruments on personal data protection that were drafted at the time.[470] Convention 108 stressed from the very beginning "that it is necessary to reconcile the fundamental values of respect for privacy and the free flow of

464 Gutwirth *et al.* (n32) 23.
465 Council of Europe [1981] Convention for the Protection of Individuals with regard to Automatic Processing of Personal Data, *European Treaty Series – No.108* (Convention 108).
466 Article 3 Convention 108; Cate (n193) 34; Christofi and Verdoodt (n107) 33; Nugter (n362) 25-26; Rauhofer (n364) 189.
467 Article 22.1 Convention 108.
468 Article 22.2 Convention 108.
469 Article 23.1 Convention 108.
470 Explanatory Memorandum 1980 OECD Guidelines, I.20.; Bennett (n140) 137; Bygrave, *Data Privacy Law* (n37) 43.

information between peoples".[471] Both documents were inspired by the 1973 U.S. HEW Report on Records, Computers, and the Rights of Citizens.[472,473] Convention 108 included the principles of data minimization, purpose and retention period limitations, special protected categories of data, data security, data accuracy, users' access to their own information, and a national security exception.[474] Interestingly, Article 12 mentioned that "a Party shall not, for the sole purpose of the protection of privacy, prohibit or subject to special authorization transborder flows of personal data going to the territory of another Party",[475] even though Articles 3.2, 9, and 24 provided for significant derogations of the general principles. The possibility of derogations led to different implementations of Convention 108 by the Member States. The Convention also included cooperation and mutual assistance clauses[476] for Member States, but without addressing issues of data flows to non-Member States. The principles enshrined in this Convention were binding on the Member States, but the ratification of this Convention was not successful and not mandatory, which hampered its practical influence.[477] Businesses were, moreover, excluded from the Convention negotiations, which led to the prevalence of privacy interests.[478] The ECtHR subsequently implemented and enforced the requirements set out in Convention 108 through compliance with Article 8 ECHR in its case law.[479]

---

471 Preamble Convention 108; Gutwirth *et al.* (n32) 182.

472 See *Chapter 3, § 1, A., i).*

473 Pałka, 'Data Management' (n44) 578-584.

474 Article 5-9 Convention 108.

475 Article 12 Convention 108.

476 Article 13-17 Convention 108.

477 By 1995, 21 Member States had signed and 16 Member States had ratified Convention 108. By 2025, 46 Member States had signed, and 46 Member States and 9 non-Member States had ratified Convention 108.: Council of Europe, 'Chart of signatures and ratifications of Treaty 108' (*coe.int*, 2025).

478 Convention 108; Article 29 WP, 'The Future of Privacy: Joint contribution to the Consultation of the European Commission on the legal framework for the fundamental right to protection of personal data' (WP168, 1 Dec 2009) 5; Article 29 WP, 'Opinion 01/2014' (n631) 3; Bennett (n140) 133-136; Bygrave, *Data Privacy Law* (n37) 31-43; Joseph Cannataci and Jeanne Mifsud-Bonnici, 'Data Protection Comes of Age' (2005) 14 ICT Law 5, 6; Cate, 'EU data protection directive' (n364) 431-432; Cate (n193) 34-35; EU Agency for Fundamental Rights (n401) 17; Fromholz (n74) 467; Gutwirth *et al.* (n32) 68-79 and 182; Heisenberg (n66) 25 and 52-54; Lynskey, *The foundations* (n42) 48; Nugter (n362) 26-28 and 225-261; Pałka, 'Data Management' (n44) 619; Pernot-Leplay (n193) 108; Solove, 'Data Is What Data Does' (n16) 1088.

479 For example: *Z. v Finland* (n401) para 95; *Rotaru* (n401) para 43; *Cemalettin Canli* (n443) para 34; *S. and Marper* (n415) paras 41-44 and 103-104; *M.M. v United Kingdom* (n410) paras 122-141 and 188; *Breyer v Germany* App no 50001/12 (ECtHR, 30 Jan 2020) paras 57 and 74; *L.D. v Hungary* App no 36345/16 (ECtHR, 9 Mar 2023) paras 42-43 and 123; Bygrave, *Data Protection Law* (n17) 35 and 123; Zuiderveen Borgesius *et al.* (n180) 14.

2018 Convention 108+ – The CoE adopted an amending protocol[480] in 2018 to update Convention 108 to a renewed Convention 108+,[481] which came into force in 2023.[482,483] Similar to its predecessor, Convention 108+ was open for signature by the CoE Member States, and had to be subsequently ratified, accepted, or approved.[484] The Convention entered officially into force "on the first day of the month following the expiration of a period of three months after the date on which five Member States of the Council of Europe ha(d) expressed their consent to be bound by the Convention in accordance with the (procedure set out before)".[485] The possibility for non-Member States to accede to Convention 108+ after its entry into force was also maintained to a large extent, upon invitation by "the Committee of Ministers of the Council of Europe … by a decision taken by the (required) majority (and procedure)".[486] The 9-page document became a 35-page document, containing 31 Articles instead of the initial 27, which aimed at adjusting the Convention to the new digital world. Article 5, for example, introduced the requirements that "data processing shall … reflect … a fair balance between all interests concerned, whether public or private, and the rights and freedoms at stake".[487] The concept of the 'right to data protection' is in Convention 108+ used together with the concept of the right to privacy, which may suggest that it is evolving to become a separate right from the (general) right to privacy (such as in the EU Charter[488]). The choice of wording in former Article 12 ("A Party shall not, *for the sole purpose of the protection of privacy*, prohibit or subject to special authorisation transborder flows of personal data going to the territory of another Party"[489]) was also replaced by "*for the sole purpose of the protection of personal data*"[490] in new Article 14. This Article further resonates with the EU GDPR, requiring that "the transfer of personal data may only take place where *an appropriate level of protection* based on the provisions of this Convention is secured".[491] The newly added Article 7.2 Convention 108+ introduced a security breach notification

480 Council of Europe [2018] Protocol amending the Convention for the Protection of Individuals with regard to Automatic Processing of Personal Data (ETS No.108) CM(2018)2-final.

481 Council of Europe [2018] Protocol amending the Convention for the Protection of Individuals with regard to Automatic Processing of Personal Data (CETS No.223) CM/Inf(2018)15-final (Convention 108+).

482 By 2025, 40 Member States and 6 non-Member States had signed, and 28 Member States and 3 non-Member States had ratified Convention 108+.: Council of Europe, 'Chart of signatures and ratifications of Treaty 223' (*coe.int*, 2025).

483 de Terwangne, 'Convention 108+' (n383) 1-2.

484 Article 26.1 Convention 108+.

485 Article 26.2 Convention 108+.

486 Article 27.1 Convention 108+.

487 Article 5 Convention 108+.

488 See *Chapter 3, § 3, B., ii).*

489 Article 12 Convention 108.

490 Article 14 Convention 108+.

491 *Ibid.*

requirement,[492] and Article 8.1 introduced an (active) information obligation on the data controller as opposed to the previous possibility for the person concerned to request this information.[493,494]

Table 2. Common Fair Information Principles: OECD and Council of Europe

	OECD		Council of Europe	
	1980 Guidelines	2013 Guidelines	Convention 108	Convention 108+
1. Data Quality	✓	✓	✓	✓
Purpose Limitation	3	3	5.b	5.4.b
Data Minimization	1	1	5.c	5.1 & 5.4.c
Time and Storage Limitation	/	/	5.e	5.4.e
2. Legitimate processing	✓	✓	✓	✓
Lawful / Consent / Opt-in / Opt-out	1 & 4	1 & 4	5.a	5.2-5.3
Non-discrimination (incl. sensitive data)	/	/	6	6
Right to object	7.c	7.c	8.d	9.1.d
3. Notification and Transparency	✓	✓	✓	✓
Processing information / Privacy Policy	3 & 6	3 & 6	8.a	8.1
Disclosure to 3rd parties	/	/	/	8.1.d
Right of access	7.a	7.a	8.b	9.1.b
Data breach notification	/	Part.3.15.c	/	7.2
4. Data Accuracy	✓	✓	✓	✓
Accurate, up-to-date	2	2	5.d	5.4.d
Correction rights	7.d	7.d	8.c	9.1.e
Deletion rights	7.d	7.d	8.c	9.1.e
Notification to 3rd parties	/	/	/	/

(continued)

492 Article 7.2 Convention 108+.
493 Article 8.1 Convention 108+.
494 Convention 108+; Colin Bennett, *The Council of Europe's Modernized Convention on Personal Data Protection* (Centre for International Governance Innovation, 2020) 3-6; de Terwangne, 'Convention 108+' (n383) 6-16; Pernot-Leplay (n193) 108.

Table 2. *continued*

	OECD		Council of Europe	
	1980 Guidelines	2013 Guidelines	Convention 108	Convention 108+
5. Data Security	✓ 5	✓ 5	✓ 7	✓ 7.1
6. Enforcement	?	✓	x	✓
Administrative body	8?*	Part.5.19.c	/	15
Court	8?*	/	/	15.2.d
Remedies	/	/	10	12
Private right of action	/	/	/	/

* principle 8 OECD Guidelines requires accountability of a data controller for compliance with measures implementing the principles set out in the Guidelines, without further specification

§ 3. EU PERSONAL DATA PROTECTION LEGAL INSTRUMENTS

The European Union is a supranational economic and political organization consisting of 27 European Member States.[495,496] One of the EU's main founding ideas was the creation of an internal market by eliminating tariff and non-tariff barriers for intra-European trade, and was operationalized through the introduction of common standards and rules.[497] Similarly, when computerization began to develop in the 1970s, different regulatory regimes for personal data flows were perceived as potential trade barriers for the emerging European data processing industry. This section provides an overview of the European Union's legislative initiatives in the area of the protection and free flow of personal data, together with an overview of relevant case law of the Court of Justice of the European Union. The Center for Intellectual Property and Information Law of Cambridge University provides a concise historical overview of European[498] legal initiatives in the area of

495 Namely, Austria, Belgium, Bulgaria, Croatia, Cyprus, Czech Republic, Denmark, Estonia, Finland, France, Germany, Greece, Hungary, Ireland, Italy, Latvia, Lithuania, Luxemburg, Malta, Netherlands, Poland, Portugal, Romania, Slovakia, Slovenia, Spain, and Sweden.: European Union, 'EU countries' (*europa.eu*, 2025).

496 Publications Office of the European Union, 'A short guide to the EU' (*europa.eu*, 2023).

497 Heisenberg (n66) 2; Agata Ludera-Ruszel, 'Free movement of workers as an instrument of creation of the European common market' (2015) 9 EurIntegrStud 161, 162.

498 These legal resources include initiatives by the European Union as well as by the Council of Europe; the latter were already discussed above in *Chapter 3, § 2, B*.

personal data protection and electronic privacy,[499] which is used as the basis for the discussion in this section.

A. PRE-1995 LEGISLATIVE INITIATIVES

1975 European Parliament Resolution – The European Parliament issued its first resolution on individuals' rights and data processing[500] in 1975 as a response to the increasing developments in technology and the need to adequately protect individuals' personal data in these circumstances. The European Commission shared the Parliament's concerns on this matter but was of the opinion that the Member States were better suited to protect their citizens' rights at the State level in the upcoming digital era.[501]

1979 European Parliament Resolution – Four years later, the European Parliament reiterated the "legitimate concern of the general public over the risks of mistaken or improper use of the data stored in data banks, whether local, regional, national or international"[502] in its 1979 resolution on individuals' rights and data processing.[503] The Parliament voiced in this resolution its "conscious(ness) of the need to guarantee the free movement of information within the Community without prejudice to the restrictions justified by considerations of national security",[504] better known as the national security exception,[505] which would become one of the main problematic features identified in the *Schrems* cases.[506] The Parliament called again "on the Commission to prepare a proposal for a Directive on the harmonization of legislation on data protection to provide citizens of the Community with the maximum protection"[507] and to introduce "an independent body … to monitor the application in its territory of the Community norms".[508,509]

1981 European Commission Recommendation – Two years after the 1979 Parliament resolution, the European Commission issued a

499 Centre for Intellectual Property and Information Law (n390).
500 European Parliament, Resolution on the Protection of the Rights of Individuals in the Face of Developing Technical Progress in the Field of Automatic Data Processing [1975] OJ C 60/48.
501 Lynskey, *The foundations* (n42) 50; Rauhofer (n364) 189.
502 European Parliament (n503) 35.
503 European Parliament, Resolution on the Protection of the Rights of the Individual in the face of Technical Developments in Data Processing [1979] OJ C 140/34.
504 *Ibid.* 35.
505 See *Chapter 5.*
506 See *Chapter 1, § 2, A. and B.*
507 European Parliament (n503) 35.
508 *Ibid.* 38.
509 European Parliament (n503); Heisenberg (n66) 15 and 53.

recommendation[510] encouraging Member States to sign and ratify Council of Europe Convention 108[511] before the end of 1982. The Commission expressed its concern that "data processing (may) increase the danger that data will be misused (and that) individuals' privacy demands comprehensive protection in this field".[512] Therefore, the "Commission reserved the right to propose that the Council adopt an instrument on the basis of the EEC Treaty, if all the Member States do not ... sign and ratify (CoE Convention 108)".[513,514]

1982 European Parliament Resolution – The European Parliament reacted to the Commission's initiative with a new resolution,[515] noting that "it is not clear when all the Member States of the Community will finally have signed and ratified (CoE Convention 108) (as) a number of Community countries do not yet have laws protecting the citizen from the misuse of data files and data processing".[516] To remedy this issue, the Parliament stressed the need for a harmonized approach to personal data protection where "consideration should be given to a draft Directive",[517] which would eventually be adopted in 1995.[518]

B. 1995–2024 LEGISLATIVE INITIATIVES

i) 1995 EU Personal Data Protection Directive

a) Background

1995 Directive – The EU adopted the 1995 Personal Data Protection Directive[519] as the first binding legal instrument in the area of personal

---

510 European Commission, Recommendation of 29 Jul 1981 relating to the Council of Europe Convention for the Protection of Individuals with regard to Automated Processing of Personal Data [1981] OJ L 246/31.

511 See *Chapter 3, § 2, B., ii)*.

512 European Commission (n510).

513 *Ibid.*

514 Bygrave, *Data Privacy Law* (n37) 55; Lynskey, *The foundations* (n42) 48.

515 European Parliament, Resolution on the Protection of the Rights of the Individual in the Face of Technical Developments in Data Processing [1982] OJ C 87/39.

516 *Ibid.* 40.

517 *Ibid.*

518 Heisenberg (n66) 15.

519 Directive 95/46/EC of 24 Oct 1995 on the protection of individuals with regard to the processing of personal data and on the free movement of such data [1995] OJ L 281/31. *See also:* Amended proposal for a Council Directive on the protection of individuals with regard to the processing of personal data and on the free movement of such data [1992] OJ C 311/30, 30-61.

data protection at the EU level, which was largely based on the principles enshrined in CoE Convention 108.[520,521] A directive is a binding EU instrument "as to the result to be achieved, ... but (leaves) to the national authorities the choice of form and methods".[522] The 1995 Directive was drafted by DG Internal Market, situating it within the subject matter of the internal market, and ensured that "Member States shall protect ... natural persons' ... right to privacy with respect to the processing of personal data, (without restricting or prohibiting) the free flow of personal data between Member States"[523] through a harmonization of "the different existing standards of (personal) data protection in Europe".[524, 525] The increase in personal data transfers and commerce was facing problems in a fragmented landscape with countries like Germany, Sweden, and France having one of the most comprehensive data protection laws, while other EU Member States had little or none.[526] Article 29 of the 1995 Directive set up a Working Party (Article 29 WP, *see below*) where national data protection commissioners could meet, and which was responsible for determining whether third countries fulfilled an adequate level of protection for European personal data to be exported to.[527] The Member States had three years to implement the provisions of the 1995 Directive into their national law, upon which the Directive's provisions became directly enforceable on 24 October 1998 and the EU gained authority to assess and adjudicate cases relating to personal data protection, even though some Member States had still not implemented the Directive by that time.[528]

---

520 See *Chapter 3, § 2, B., ii)*.

521 Article 31 Directive 95/46/EC was amended by Regulation (EC) No 1882/2003 of 29 Sep 2003 (OJ L 284/18) but will not be discussed further in this book.

522 Article 288.3 TFEU. *See also:* Sacha Prechal, *Directives in EC Law* (2nd edn, OUP 2005) 349p.

523 Article 1 Directive 95/46/EC.

524 Heisenberg (n66) 27.

525 Article 29 WP, 'The Future of Privacy' (n478) 6; Bygrave, *Data Privacy Law* (n37) 55; Cate, 'EU data protection directive' (n364) 432; Sybe de Vries and others (eds), *The EU Charter of Fundamental Rights as a binding instrument* (Hart Publishing 2015) 263; Fromholz (n74) 468; Gutwirth *et al.* (n32) 8-9 and 278; Heisenberg (n66) 16-27 and 54; Lynskey, *The foundations* (n42) 50.

526 Case no 89-78 of 11 Jul 1989, Commission Nationale de l'Informatique et des Libertés (CNIL); Bennett (n140) 60-82; Cannataci and Mifsud-Bonnici (n478) 6; Cate, 'EU data protection directive' (n364) 431; Cate (n193) 32-35; Christofi and Verdoodt (n107) 29-32; de Vries *et al.* (n525) 236-237; Gloria González Fuster, *The Emergence of Personal Data Protection as a Fundamental Right of the EU* (1st edn, Springer 2014) 56-65; Heisenberg (n66) 15-16; Lynskey, *The foundations* (n42) 49; Rauhofer (n364) 188; Maria Tzanou, 'Data Protection as a Fundamental Right next to Privacy?' (2013) 3 IDPL 88, 90; Vogiatzoglou and Valcke (n400) 13-16.

527 Heisenberg (n66) 27.

528 Article 32.1 Directive 95/46/EC; Article 29 WP, 'Recommendation 3/99 on the preservation of traffic data by Internet Service Providers for law enforcement purposes' (WP25, 7 Sep 1999) 3; Article 29 WP, 'The Future of Privacy' (n478) 5 and 17; Article 29 WP,

Privacy and commerce – Similarly to CoE Convention 108's grounding in Article 8 ECHR right to privacy,[529] the recitals and Article 1 of the 1995 Directive reiterated the importance for respect for the right to privacy (a fundamental right) on the one hand and the facilitation of trade in and free flow of personal data in the EU on the other hand.[530] Harmonizing Member States' national data protection laws had to ensure equal protection throughout the EU, which in its turn had to facilitate the free flow of and trade in personal data between the Member States as no objections could be made regarding shortcomings in the applicable national laws. The objectives of privacy and commerce have consequently been narrowly intertwined since the beginning, which resonates with Sjaak Nouwt's conclusion[531] that a dual economic and human rights approach should be adopted for meaningful personal data protection.[532] Some critics point out that the economic approach was in fact predominant in the creation of the 1995 Directive (harmonization and abolishing trade barriers), and that the human rights approach was only subsidiary (and added afterward) to justify the inclusion of the right to personal data protection in the EU Charter of Fundamental Rights.[533] This statement is true when one considers only the legal basis established by EU law, but the intertwinement with Article 8 ECHR's right to privacy cannot be denied. The 1995 Directive was legally based on the EU competence to adopt harmonization measures to establish the internal market enshrined in Article 95 EC (now Article 114.1 TFEU), as the EU did not have the competence to enact legislation concerning fundamental rights.[534] However, the Directive also indicated its grounding in "the respect for the right to privacy" as enshrined in Article 8 ECHR and resulted from the unsuccessful implementation of CoE Convention 108.[535]

'Opinion 01/2014' (n631) 3; Peter Blume, 'It Is Time for Tomorrow' (2015) 18 JInternetL 3, 3; J C Hans Buitelaar, 'Privacy: Back to the Roots' (2012) 13 GerLawJ 171, 174-175; Bygrave, *Data Protection Law* (n17) 30; Cannataci and Mifsud-Bonnici (n478) 6-7; Cate (n193) 36; EU Agency for Fundamental Rights (n401) 17; Fromholz (n74) 462; Gutwirth *et al.* (n32) 79; Heisenberg (n66) 78; Pałka, 'Data Management' (n44) 617; Rauhofer (n364) 189.

529 See *Chapter 3, § 2, B.*

530 Recitals 2-3 and 10-11 and Article 1.2 Directive 95/46/EC; Bygrave, *Data Privacy Law* (n37) 57; Gutwirth *et al.* (n32) 8; Lynskey, *The foundations* (n42) 9.

531 Gutwirth *et al.* (n32) 291.

532 Blume (n528) 6; Buitelaar (n528) 174-175; Bygrave, *Data Protection Law* (n17) 40; Bygrave, *Data Privacy Law* (n37) 191; Cate, 'EU data protection directive' (n364) 432; Christofi and Verdoodt (n107) 34-35; de Vries *et al.* (n525) 237; Fromholz (n74) 462; Lynskey, *The foundations* (n42) 8-10 and 46 and 76-77; Purtova, *Property Rights* (n31) 208.

533 Bygrave, *Data Privacy Law* (n37) 58; Lucie Guibault and P Bernt Hugenholtz (eds), *The Future of the Public Domain* (Kluwer 2006) 243-244; Lynskey, *The foundations* (n42) 47-58 and 87; Nugter (n362) 29.

534 Bygrave, *Data Protection Law* (n17) 40; de Vries *et al.* (n525) 237; Heisenberg (n66) 55; Orla Lynskey, 'Deconstructing data protection' (2014) 63 ICLQ 569, 570-571; Lynskey, *The foundations* (n42) 9 and 47 and 76-87; Purtova, *Property Rights* (n31) 208.

535 See *Chapter 3, § 2, B., ii).*

The same legal bases are indicated in the explanatory memorandum to Article 8 EU Charter (*see below*).[536] Other critics counter the former argument by tilting to the other side of the spectrum where "the outcome … is best explained by looking at the role of interest groups during the negotiations (where a) detailed history of the negotiations shows that in the EU businesses were not consulted at all during the drafting of the Directive (and) the principle designers of the (1995 Directive) were national data privacy authorities, many of whom considered data privacy a fundamental human right",[537] resulting in "little scope for traditional negotiations based on economic interests (as) privacy cannot be bartered for economic interests".[538] One of these dominant voices was Germany's (Hessian) data protection commissioner, Spiros Simitis. Given that Germany was one of the countries with the strictest data protection laws, Spiros Simitis emphasized the importance of defining personal data protection as a fundamental human right. A fundamental human rights qualification results, after all, in its ability to trump non-fundamental human rights interests, such as those of businesses or commerce.[539] Interestingly, the 1995 Directive did not exclude the possibility for self-regulation, even encouraging "the drawing up of codes of conduct intended to contribute to the proper implementation of the national provisions adopted by the Member States pursuant to this Directive, taking account of the specific features of the various sectors".[540] In this way, the EU was putting a mix forward of general personal data protection rules established at the State level together with a more detailed implementation of these rules in sector-specific regulation.[541]

Omnibus regime? – The EU approach to personal data protection is often portrayed as an omnibus regime encompassing the private and public sectors alike, following the example of CoE Convention 108.[542,543] The initial refusal of the European Commission to act legislatively in the area of personal data protection on the Parliament's request in the 1980s was, however, based on the reasoning "that data protection was primarily a public sector concern regarding the regulation of government databanks and that (the Commission) did not have jurisdiction to regulate such public sector issues".[544] In the first draft of the 1995 Directive, the public and private sectors were regulated separately

536 Article 29 WP, 'Working Document 01/2016' (n642) 4-5; Blume (n528) 3; Gutwirth *et al.* (n32) 70; Lynskey, *The foundations* (n42) 268; Tzanou (n526) 91.

537 Heisenberg (n66) 41.

538 Gutwirth *et al.* (n32) 125.

539 Heisenberg (n66) 10 and 41-63; Lynskey, *The foundations* (n42) 16; David Vogel, *The Politics of Precaution* (PUP 2012) 286.

540 Article 27.1 Directive 95/46/EC.

541 Cannataci and Mifsud-Bonnici (n478) 13; Cate (n193) 32-33.

542 See *Chapter 3, § 2, B., ii)*.

543 Recital 55 Directive 95/46/EC; Recital 122 and Article 55.2 GDPR; Cate (n193) 32-33; Christofi and Verdoodt (n107) 36; Lynskey, *The foundations* (n42) 15-17.

544 Lynskey, *The foundations* (n42) 16.

and differently, but this distinction in treatment was subsequently removed by the European Parliament and merged into an 'omnibus regime'.[545] Orla Lynskey[546] disagrees with this 'omnibus' portrayal, as many (public sector) areas were (and still are) to a large extent excluded from the EU personal data protection legislation's scope of application (1995 Directive as well as its 2016 GDPR successor, *see below*).[547] National security and law enforcement are one of the excluded areas situated in the public sector, with "less stringent rules applicable to data processing for law enforcement purposes",[548] which will be discussed in *Chapter 5*.

b) Content

Definition personal data – The 1995 Directive defined 'personal data' as "any information relating to an identified or identifiable natural person ('data subject')".[549] 'An identifiable person' was someone "who can be identified, directly or indirectly, in particular by reference to an identification number or to one or more factors specific to his physical, physiological, mental, economic, cultural or social identity".[550,551]

Scope of application – The principles set out in the 1995 Directive were applicable "to the processing of personal data wholly or partly by automatic means, and to the processing otherwise than by automatic means of personal data which form part of a filing system (i.e. "any structured set of personal data which are accessible according to specific criteria, whether centralized, decentralized or dispersed on a functional or geographical basis"[552]) or are intended to form part of a filing system".[553]

Data protection principles – The 1995 Directive set the following 'General rules on the lawfulness of the processing of personal data' out in its Chapter II,[554] which can be situated in 8 categories:[555]

---

545 Heisenberg (n66) 10 and 41-63; Lynskey, *The foundations* (n42) 16; Vogel (n539) 286.
546 Lynskey, *The foundations* (n42) 18-23.
547 Article 29 WP, 'Working Document on surveillance of electronic communications for intelligence and national security purposes' (WP228, 5 Dec 2014) 30; Gutwirth *et al.* (n32) 227-228.
548 Lynskey, *The foundations* (n42) 19.
549 Article 2(a) Directive 95/46/EC.
550 *Ibid.*
551 Cate, 'EU data protection directive' (n364) 433; de Vries *et al.* (n525) 306.
552 Article 2(c) Directive 95/46/EC.
553 Article 3.1 Directive 95/46/EC.
554 Cate, 'EU data protection directive' (n364) 433-436; Christofi and Verdoodt (n107) 36-37; Gutwirth *et al.* (n32) 132; Treacy and Bapat (n3) 12.
555 The choice and definition of categories is explained in *§ 4. Interim analysis*.

1) Data quality: is improved through purpose specification, purpose limitation, data minimization (i.e. "adequate, relevant and not excessive in relation to the purposes for which (the personal data) are collected and/or further processed"[556]), data accuracy, time and storage limitation;[557]
2) Legitimate processing: consisting of fair and lawful processing[558] and requiring data subjects to provide their unambiguous consent to the processing or that the processing is necessary for one of the legalizing bases specified in the 1995 Directive; in the case of non-compliance, data subjects have a right to object to the illegitimate processing;[559]
3) Sensitive data: consisting of the prohibition, to which exemptions are possible, to process certain special categories of data, namely "data revealing racial or ethnic origin, political opinions, religious or philosophical beliefs, trade-union membership, someone's health or sex life";[560,561]
4) Notification and transparency: consisting of an obligation for the data controller to provide data subjects with information relating to the data controller's identity, the purpose of the processing, whether the data will be disclosed to third parties, whether data subjects can or must reply to questions (and the consequences of non-compliance), and whether the data subjects have a right of access and a right to rectification regarding data held on them;[562]
5) Right of access: granting data subjects (a.o.) the right to request information regarding whether, which, and how data relating to them is processed;[563]
6) Correction rights: granting data subjects the right to request rectification, erasure, or blocking of personal data that were not processed in conformity with the requirements set out in the 1995 Directive, and of personal data that are incomplete or inaccurate, with a requirement to share these corrections with third parties to whom the data were disclosed, unless this would involve a disproportionate or impossible effort;[564]
7) Data security: consisting of the obligation for data controllers to take appropriate technical and organizational measures to maintain security and prevent unauthorized processing and access, accidental or unlawful destruction, accidental loss, alteration, and other unlawful forms of processing;[565]

---

556 Article 6.1(c) Directive 95/46/EC.
557 Article 6(b)-(e) Directive 95/46/EC.
558 Article 6(a) Directive 95/46/EC.
559 Article 7 and 14 Directive 95/46/EC.
560 Article 8.1 Directive 95/46/EC.
561 Article 8 Directive 95/46/EC.
562 Article 10 Directive 95/46/EC.
563 Article 12(a) Directive 95/46/EC.
564 Article 12(b)-(c) Directive 95/46/EC.
565 Recital 46 and Article 17.1 Directive 95/46/EC.

8) Enforcement:[566] mandating Member States to establish a public supervisory authority (or Data Protection Authority; DPA) to monitor the national application and implementation of the 1995 Directive through an independent approach with two types of powers, investigative powers and effective powers of intervention, where individuals as well as representing associations can seek relief.[567]

Article 29 Working Party – Article 29 of the 1995 Directive established the Working Party on the Protection of Individuals with regard to the Processing of Personal Data (Article 29 WP), consisting of a representative of each of the independent supervisory agencies of the Member States, a representative of the Community institutions' authorities, and a representative of the European Commission. Article 29 WP took decisions by simple majority and was tasked to independently advise the Commission on the level of personal data protection in Member States as well as third countries, and to ensure a uniform application of national rules implementing the 1995 Directive.[568]

Exemptions – The 1995 Directive specified certain categories of personal data that were exempted from its scope of application. These encompassed personal data collected or processed for an activity outside the scope of community (EU) law, processing operations concerning public security, defense, State security, the economic well-being of the State when related to State security, State activities in areas of criminal law, personal data collection or processing by a natural person for a purely personal or household activity, and personal data collected and processed for purposes of journalism or artistic or literary expression.[569] The latter exception was considered necessary to find a balance between privacy and freedom of expression interests.[570]

Accountability – Article 23 of the 1995 Directive contained a liability clause, requiring data controllers to provide compensation to data subjects that had suffered damage which resulted from acts that were incompatible with the requirements set out in the 1995 Directive. Data controllers did not have to provide compensation if they could prove that they were not responsible for the acts and events that resulted in the sustained damage. The specific amount of

566 The enforcement requirements are set out in Chapter VI Supervisory Authority and Working Party on the Protection of Individuals with Regard to the Processing of Personal Data of Directive 95/46/EC.

567 Recital 62 and Article 28 Directive 95/46/EC.

568 Recital 65 and Article 29-30.1 Directive 95/46/EC; Bygrave, *Data Privacy Law* (n37) 174-175; Heisenberg (n66) 16-29; Lynskey, 'Deconstructing' (n534) 571; Richard Peltz-Steele, 'The pond betwixt' (2015) 19 JInternetL 15, 16; Purtova, *Property Rights* (n31) 170.

569 Recitals 12-17 and 37-44 and Article 3.2 and 9 and 13.1 Directive 95/46/EC.

570 Article 9 Directive 95/46/EC; Bygrave, *Data Privacy Law* (n37) 143-144; Heisenberg (n66) 28-30; Lynskey, *The foundations* (n42) 20.

compensation or the way to calculate this amount were, however, not provided in the 1995 Directive, and left to the Member States to determine.[571]

Adequacy Decision – The most innovative, but also controversial, component introduced by the 1995 Directive was an extraterritorial application. Chapter IV was dedicated to the "Transfer of personal data to third countries" and stated that such a "transfer may take place only if … the third country in question ensures an adequate level of protection",[572] which would be assessed by the European Commission. Criteria to assess this 'adequacy requirement' were "the nature of the data, the purpose and duration of processing, the country of origin and country of final destination, and the rules of law, professional rules and security measures in force in the third country".[573] If a third country did not pass the 'adequacy test', the "Member States (had to) take the measures necessary to prevent any transfer of data"[574] to that country. Ever since, this requirement has caused difficulties for personal data flows between the EU and third countries, and more specifically the United States.[575] Colin Bennett defines this approach as "convergence through penetration",[576] since other States are forced to conform to the standards set by, in this case, the European Union.

Standard Contractual Clauses (SCCs) – An alternative to the adequacy decision was set forth in Article 26 of the 1995 Directive, allowing Member States to transfer personal data to a third country that did not ensure adequate protection if the data controller implemented adequate safeguards to protect individuals' privacy, which could be provided by appropriate contractual clauses. In this way, the data exporter and importer committed themselves contractually to observing and guaranteeing the requirements of the 1995 Directive.[577]

ii) 2000–2009 EU Treaties

Article 16 TFEU – The 2007 Lisbon Treaty, consolidating the (amended) TEU and TFEU, entered into force in 2009.[578] A new right to personal data protection

---

571 Article 23-24 Directive 95/46/EC; Cate, 'EU data protection directive' (n364) 436.

572 Article 25 Directive 95/46/EC.

573 Article 25.2 Directive 95/46/EC.

574 Article 25.4 Directive 95/46/EC.

575 Article 25 Directive 95/46/EC; Article 29 WP, 'The Future of Privacy' (n478) 9 and 23; Bygrave, *Data Protection Law* (n17) 31; Bygrave, *Data Privacy Law* (n37) 190-193; Cate (n193) 41; Cate, 'EU data protection directive' (n364) 437; EC, 'Restoring Trust – FAQ' (n88); Fromholz (n74) 462; Gutwirth *et al.* (n32) 263-273; Heisenberg (n66) 1 and 27-31; Lynskey, *The foundations* (n42) 41-43; Peltz-Steele, 'The pond betwixt' (n568) 1 and 16.

576 Bennett (n140) 140-143.

577 Article 26 Directive 95/46/EC; Bygrave, *Data Privacy Law* (n37) 194; Heisenberg (n66) 75.

578 Article 6 Treaty of Lisbon amending the Treaty on the European Union and the Treaty establishing the European Community [2007] OJ C 306/1.

was introduced in Article 16 TFEU, which provided a legal basis for the EU to enact legislation in this area:

1. Everyone has the right to the protection of personal data concerning them.
2. The European Parliament and the Council ... shall lay down the rules relating to the protection of individuals with regard to the processing of personal data by Union institutions, bodies, offices and agencies, and by the Member States when carrying out activities which fall within the scope of Union law, and the rules relating to the free movement of such data. Compliance with these rules shall be subject to the control of independent authorities. ...

In 2010 *Schecke and Eifert*,[579] the CJEU pointed out that the right to personal data protection is not absolute and interferences are possible in relation to this right's function in society. The EU institutions decided to use this new Article 16 TFEU as the legal basis to adopt the 1995 Directive's successor, the 2016 General Data Protection Regulation, shifting the predominant legal grounding from the previous 'internal market' to the 'fundamental right to personal data protection'.[580]

EU Charter of Fundamental Rights – Even though the EU Charter of Fundamental Rights[581] (EU Charter) is not a part of the founding Treaties, Article 6.1 TEU states that "the rights, freedoms and principles set out in the Charter of Fundamental Rights of the European Union of 7 December 2000 ... shall have the same legal value as the Treaties"[582] from the entry into force of the Lisbon Treaty (and the TEU) in 2009.[583] The fundamental right to personal data protection is enshrined in Article 8 of the EU Charter and provides that:

1. Everyone has the right to the protection of personal data concerning him or her.
2. Such data must be processed fairly for specified purposes and on the basis of the consent of the person concerned or some other legitimate basis laid down by law. Everyone has the right of access to data which has been collected concerning him or her, and the right to have it rectified. 3. Compliance with these rules shall be subject to control by an independent authority.

---

579 Joined Cases C-92/09 and C-93/09 *Volker und Markus Schecke GbR and Hartmut Eifert v Land Hessen* [2010] para 48; see *Chapter 3, § 3, C., i).*

580 Preamble 12 GDPR; Article 29 WP, 'The Future of Privacy' (n478) 5; Article 29 WP, 'Working Document WP228' (n547) 27; Blume (n528) 5; Bygrave, *Data Privacy Law* (n37) 59; de Vries *et al.* (n525) 238 and 256-267; EU Agency for Fundamental Rights (n401) 17; Lynskey, *The foundations* (n42) 7-14 and 61-66 and 87 and 119; Purtova, *Property Rights* (n31) 223.

581 Charter of Fundamental Rights of the European Union [2012] OJ C 326/391 (EU Charter).

582 Article 6 TEU.

583 Blume (n528) 5; Christofi and Verdoodt (n107) 15; de Vries *et al.* (n525) 1; Gutwirth *et al.* (n32) 8; Lynskey, *The foundations* (n42) 61; Pernot-Leplay (n193) 108-109; Purtova, *Property Rights* (n31) 223.

The explanatory memorandum clarifies that Article 8 EU Charter "has been based on article 286 (EC Treaty; now replaced by article 16 TFEU and article 39 TEU) and Directive 95/46/EC ... as well as on article 8 of the ECHR and on (CoE Convention 108), which has been ratified by all the Member States".[584] Recital 4 of the GDPR (*see below*) explains that even though personal data protection has the status of a fundamental right, it has to be "balanced against other fundamental rights, in accordance with the principle of proportionality".[585,586]

Limited scope of application – The (fundamental) right to personal data protection is, in its post-Lisbon version, enshrined in two legal provisions, namely Article 16 TFEU and Article 8 EU Charter. Both Article 16.2 TFEU and Article 51.1 EU Charter limit the scope of application of these provisions to personal data processing activities carried out by Union institutions, bodies, offices and agencies ... and by the Member States when carrying out activities within the scope of Union law or implementing Union law only.[587]

Ambiguous legal basis – The legal basis of the EU Charter provision proclaiming the fundamental right to personal data protection as set out in the explanatory documents is ambiguous. The explanatory memorandum to the EU Charter states that "this article (8) has been based on article 286 (EC Treaty) and Directive 95/46/EC ... and on the free movement of such data ... as well as on article 8 of the ECHR and on the (CoE Convention 108), which has been ratified by all the Member States".[588] In particular, Directive 95/46/EC is problematic as a legal basis, as it would imply that a primary EU law provision is based on secondary EU law, which is not a solid and convincing ground. This criticism was also formulated by Orla Lynskey, as she observed that "although the 1995 Directive predates the EU Charter, the Charter indicates that the Directive enshrines a fundamental right (and) viewed from this perspective, the Charter merely codifies the right to data protection which was first given expression

---

584 Explanations relating to the Charter of Fundamental Rights [2007] OJ C 303/20.

585 Recital 4 GDPR.

586 Cannataci and Mifsud-Bonnici (n478) 7; Christofi and Verdoodt (n107) 39; de Vries *et al.* (n525) 303; Vogiatzoglou and Valcke (n400) 17.

587 Article 16.2 TFEU; Article 51.1 EU Charter; Article 29 WP, 'The Future of Privacy' (n478) 5; Article 29 WP, 'Working Document WP228' (n547) 27-30; Bergkamp (n394) 33; Blume (n528) 5; Bygrave, *Data Privacy Law* (n37) 58-59; Cannataci and Mifsud-Bonnici (n478) 7; de Vries *et al.* (n525) 237-250 and 266-267 and 299-300; EU Agency for Fundamental Rights (n401) 17; Gutwirth *et al.* (n32) 71-77; Heisenberg (n66) 2; Christopher Kuner and others, 'An unstoppable force and an immoveable object?' (2018) 8 IDPL 1, 1; Lynskey, 'Deconstructing' (n534) 570; Lynskey, *The foundations* (n42) 7 and 89-90; Pałka, 'Data Management' (n44) 619-620; Tzanou (n526) 90.

588 Explanations relating to the Charter of Fundamental Rights [2007] OJ C 303/20; Cannataci and Mifsud-Bonnici (n478) 10; European Parliament, 'Annotated Draft Charter of Fundamental Rights of the European Union' (*europa.eu*, 11 Oct 2000) 11.

in the EU legal order by the Directive".[589,590] This interpretation would even imply that a primary EU law provision was not only based on, but also codified, secondary EU law.

iii) 1997–2016 Article 29 WP Opinions and Recommendations

Article 29 WP advisory documents – After its establishment, the Article 29 WP[591] became very active in advising the European Commission on personal data protection matters through the issuance of Opinions, Recommendations, and Working Documents, and continued up until it was replaced by the EDPB in 2016 (*see below*).[592] The documents issued by the Article 29 WP between 1997 and 2016 were consolidated and archived on the European Commission's website.[593] A non-exhaustive selection of the Article 29 WP's advisory work related to EU-U.S. data privacy, smart devices, the interests of private companies, civil society, and law enforcement, and the characteristics of the U.S. system in this regard, is briefly presented in this section.

Opinion 1/99 –The Article 29 WP issued its first Opinion 1/99[594] on the level of personal data protection in the United States in 1999. The Article 29 WP stated that the proposals regarding the level of personal data protection were "intended to be discussed by representatives of U.S. companies with the Federal Department of Commerce",[595] as in the United States this subject matter was situated within the commerce sector. The EU, on the contrary, stressed that these "fundamental principles and rights (are) based on a common culture of respect for privacy and other values that are inherent in the human being",[596] bringing them within the scope of fundamental human rights (as opposed to commerce). The Opinion points out that the principles included in the 1995 Directive are to a large extent an implementation of "the principles set out in the 1980 OECD Privacy Guidelines,[597] signed, among others, by the United States".[598]

589 Lynskey, *The foundations* (n42) 39.
590 Lynskey, 'Deconstructing' (n534) 571.
591 See *Chapter 3, § 3, B., i), b).*
592 Bygrave, *Data Privacy Law* (n37) 174-175.
593 European Commission, 'Justice: Data Protection: Article 29 archives 1997-2016, Opinions and recommendations' (*europa.eu*, 2025).
594 Article 29 WP, 'Opinion 1/99 Concerning the level of data protection in the United States and the ongoing discussions between the European Commission and the United States Government' (WP15, 26 Jan 1999).
595 *Ibid.* 2.
596 *Ibid.*
597 See *Chapter 3, § 2, A.*
598 Article 29 WP, 'Opinion 1/99' (n594) 3; as confirmed in Article 29 WP, 'Opinion 4/99 on The Frequently Asked Questions to be issued by the U.S. Department of Commerce in relation to the proposed "Safe Harbor Principles"' (WP21, 7 Jun 1999) 5.

The Article 29 WP was from the beginning aware that "privacy and data protection in the United States is found in a complex fabric of sectoral regulation"[599] as opposed to the EU approach where the 1995 Directive aimed at horizontally harmonizing personal data protection in the EU Member States. Therefore, the Article 29 WP concluded already in 1999 that "the current (U.S.) patchwork of narrowly-focused sectoral laws and voluntary self-regulation cannot ... provide adequate protection in all cases for personal data transferred from the European Union".[600]

Recommendation 3/99 – In order to combat computer-related crime, the G8 countries[601] adopted a 10-point action plan in 1999, of which one point was "the preservation of historical and future traffic data by Internet Service Providers for law enforcement purposes and disclosure of such data to law enforcement authorities".[602] As a response, the Article 29 WP issued Recommendation 3/99[603] on the preservation of traffic data by Internet Service Providers for law enforcement purposes, where a three-month retention period was put forward based on the Article 29 WP's analysis. The Article 29 WP acknowledged the importance of "traffic data ... in the context of the investigation of crimes perpetrated over the Internet", but reminded national governments also "about the principles on the protection of the fundamental rights and freedoms of natural persons, and in particular of their privacy and the secrecy of their correspondence, which need to be taken into account in this context".[604]

Recommendation 4/99 – When the EU Charter was drafted, The Article 29 WP issued Recommendation 4/99[605] on the inclusion of the fundamental right to personal data protection in the European catalogue of fundamental rights. The Article 29 WP had noticed that in some EU Member States the right to personal data protection had acquired constitutional force, and that the European Commission and the ECtHR had constructed "a fundamental right based on various human rights which relate to the protection of personal data".[606] The inclusion of a fundamental right to personal data protection would, moreover,

599 Article 29 WP, 'Opinion 1/99' (n594) 2.

600 Article 29 WP, 'Opinion 1/99' (n594) 2; as confirmed in Article 29 WP, 'Opinion 2/99 on the Adequacy of the "International Safe Harbor Principles" issued by the U.S. Department of Commerce on 19th April 1999' (WP19, 3 May 1999) 2.

601 The G8 or "Group of Eight (is an) intergovernmental organization that originated in 1975 through informal summit meetings of the leaders of the world's leading industrialized countries, (namely) the United States, the United Kingdom, France, West Germany, Italy, Canada, Japan", and Russia (1997-2014).: Karen Mingst, 'Group of Eight' (*Brittanica*, 2024).

602 Article 29 WP, 'Recommendation 3/99' (n528) 2.

603 Article 29 WP, 'Recommendation 3/99' (n528).

604 *Ibid.* 2.

605 Article 29 WP, 'Recommendation 4/99 on the inclusion of the fundamental right to data protection in the European catalogue of fundamental rights' (WP26, 7 Sep 1999).

606 *Ibid.* 2.

"make such protection a legal requirement throughout the Union and reflect its increasing importance in the information society".[607]

Opinion 7/99 – In Opinion 7/99[608] on the Level of Data Protection provided by the Safe Harbor Principles, the Article 29 WP raised attention to the addition of 'publicly available data' to the list of categories of personal data that were excluded from the scope of application of data privacy rules in the United States, as publicly available data (and publicly available information in general) is not considered to be protected by the U.S. Fourth Amendment.[609]

Opinion 10/2001 – In the aftermath of the 9/11 terrorist attacks in New York in 2001, the Article 29 WP issued Opinion 10/2001[610] on the need for a balanced approach in the fight against terrorism. Article 29 WP stressed that while it was necessary "for democratic societies to engage in a fight against terrorism",[611] it was similarly important to observe "the commitment of our democratic societies to ensure respect for the fundamental rights and freedoms of the individual",[612] of which the right to personal data protection was part. Given that "terrorism is not a new phenomenon and cannot be qualified as a temporary phenomenon",[613] the Article 29 WP reiterated that "the long-term impact of (rapidly implemented) urgent policies"[614] should be taken into account and that "the obligation to respect the principle of proportionality"[615] should in particular be observed. Opinion 10/2001 stated in conclusion that "a key element of the fight against terrorism involves ensuring that we preserve the fundamental values which are the basis of our democratic societies and the very values that those advocating the use of violence seek to destroy".[616]

Opinion 13/2011 – In 2011, the Article 29 WP noticed the development of "a whole new category of location-based services"[617] capable of providing an "intimate overview of habits and patterns of the owner of such a device".[618]

---

607 *Ibid.*

608 Article 29 WP, 'Opinion 7/99 on the Level of Data Protection provided by the "Safe Harbor" Principles as published together with the Frequently Asked Questions (FAQs) and other related documents on 15 and 16 November 1999 by the U.S. Department of Commerce' (WP27, 3 Dec 1999).

609 *Ibid.* 5-6; see *Chapter 4, § 2, A., i).*

610 Article 29 WP, 'Opinion 10/2001 on the need for a balanced approach in the fight against terrorism' (WP53, 14 Dec 2001).

611 *Ibid.* 2.

612 *Ibid.* 3.

613 *Ibid.*

614 *Ibid.*

615 *Ibid.*

616 *Ibid.* 4.

617 Article 29 WP, 'Opinion 13/2011' (n620) 3.

618 *Ibid.* 7.

The innovative dimension of geolocation services embedded in smart devices raised many concerns. When someone uses a smart device equipped with geolocation, the device will automatically connect to an antenna base station covering a certain geographical area. Based on this information, it is possible to determine the device's, and hence the person's, location.[619] The more sophisticated geolocation services become, such as GPS or Wi-Fi nowadays, the more accurate the device's location will be. As a response, Opinion 13/2011[620] on geolocation services on smart devices required data subjects' "prior, express and informed consent"[621] to make use of these services. Moreover, "data subjects (had to) be able to withdraw their consent ... without any negative consequences for the use of the device",[622] as is currently often still the case. Finally, the Opinion suggested that geolocation services should be switched off by default.[623]

Opinion 2/2013 – In 2013, the Article 29 WP followed suit by addressing the applications or 'apps'[624] on smart devices. In Opinion 2/2013[625] on apps on smart devices, the Article 29 WP provided guidance on privacy issues resulting from the emerging use of apps on smart devices. One of the risks highlighted was the security of the collected, processed, and shared personal data. Due to a high "degree of fragmentation between the many players in the app development landscape",[626] it was important that all players uphold a high level of security as "the chain of multiple actors is only as strong as its weakest link".[627,628] Opinion 2/2013 reiterated that users' consent for data processing should be obtained before the installation of an app, that the purpose limitation and data minimization principles should be observed, and that users should correctly be informed about data processing practices.[629] Finally, Opinion 2/2013 emphasized that these requirements apply to every entity offering 'apps' in the European Economic Area, regardless of where the service provider is located.[630]

---

619 See, for example, the *Carpenter* case discussed in *Chapter 4, § 2, A., i).*

620 Article 29 WP, 'Opinion 13/2011 on Geolocation services on smart mobile devices' (WP185, 16 May 2011).

621 *Ibid.* 15.

622 *Ibid.*

623 Article 29 WP, 'Opinion 13/2011' (n620) 13; Farmer (n15) 115; Scassa and Sattler (n13) 103-105 and 118-119.

624 See the explanation of 'apps' in *Chapter 1, § 1, A.*

625 Article 29 WP, 'Opinion 02/2013 on apps on smart devices' (WP202, 27 Feb 2013).

626 *Ibid.* 2.

627 *Ibid.*

628 Article 29 WP, 'Opinion 02/2013' (n625) 18-21.

629 *Ibid.* 5 and 14-24.

630 *Ibid.* 7-8; Rooney (n1) 8-10.

Opinion 1/2014 – Opinion 1/2014[631] on the application of necessity and proportionality concepts and data protection within the law enforcement sector was issued by the Article 29 WP in 2014. The necessity and proportionality concepts were also highly relevant in both *Schrems* cases.[632] The Article 29 WP explained that these concepts were developed by the ECtHR in its Article 8 ECHR case law, as personal data protection was perceived as part of someone's privacy.[633] "An examination of past, present and future data protection legislation reveals that the protection of personal data evolved from the right to private life as provided for in Article 8 of the ECHR of 1950. With the increase of new technologies and surveillance possibilities, both in the public and in the private sector, it became apparent that there needed to be further protection for individuals from third parties (particularly the State) in addition to 'defensive' rights recognised under Article 8 ECHR by ensuring that the individual had the right to control his/her own personal data."[634] For the *necessity* concept, the Article 29 WP concluded that it "should not be interpreted too broadly, (n)or too literally",[635] through the application of a three-step test; "1) Does the interference correspond to a pressing social need?, 2) Is the interference caused by the measure proportionate to the legitimate aim being pursued?, and 3) Were the reasons given to justify the interference relevant and sufficient?".[636] For the *proportionality* concept, the Article 29 WP concluded that it "essentially requires that a measure which interferes with an ECHR right should go no further than needed to fulfill the legitimate aim being pursued".[637]

Opinion 8/2014 – With the emergence of the Internet of Things[638] (IoT) in 2014 and the privacy risks related to it, the Article 29 WP issued Opinion 8/2014[639] on the Recent Developments on the Internet of Things. The identified privacy risks included a lack of transparency due to the involvement of various stakeholders, a loss of control over personal data due to complex data flows, non-compliance with the data minimization requirement, and security risks when smart devices were not equipped with proper security features. The latter privacy risk had already been identified by the Article 29 WP in Opinion 2/2013

631 Article 29 WP, 'Opinion 01/2014 on the application of necessity and proportionality concepts and data protection within the law enforcement sector' (WP211, 27 Feb 2014).
632 See *Chapter 1, § 2, A. and B.*
633 Article 29 WP, 'Opinion 01/2014' (n631) 2-3.
634 *Ibid.* 3.
635 *Ibid.* 6.
636 *Ibid.* 7.
637 *Ibid.* 9.
638 See *Chapter 1, § 1, A.*
639 Article 29 WP, 'Opinion 8/2014' (n2).

(*see above*). The Article 29 WP formulated recommendations to remedy some of these privacy issues, such as performing Privacy Impact Assessments before new IoT applications are launched, applying a Privacy by Design approach to minimize the personal data collected, and ensuring that service users will not face negative (financial or denial of access) consequences when exercising their privacy rights.[640]

Working Document 01/2016 – In the aftermath of the 2015 *Schrems I* case,[641] The Article 29 WP issued Working Document 01/2016 on the justification of interferences with the fundamental rights to privacy and data protection through surveillance measures when transferring personal data.[642] This Document set out four 'European Essential Guarantees' "based on the jurisprudence of the CJEU and the ECtHR",[643] which had to be observed when interfering with fundamental rights for surveillance purposes. The first guarantee stated that "processing (of personal data) should be based on clear, precise and accessible rules"[644] in accordance with the law. The second guarantee ensured that the requirements of "necessity and proportionality with regard to the legitimate objectives pursued need(ed) to be demonstrated"[645] when processing personal data. The third guarantee stated that "an independent oversight mechanism should exist"[646] to ensure the lawful processing of personal data. The CJEU expressed its preference for "a court or … an independent administrative body",[647] while the ECtHR was of the opinion that "it is in principle desirable to entrust supervisory control to a judge",[648] but did not exclude other possible bodies as long as they are "independent of the authorities carrying out the surveillance, and vested with sufficient powers and competence to exercise an effective and continuous control".[649] The fourth and final guarantee ensured that "effective remedies need to be available to the individual"[650] in case of unlawful access to or a request for rectification of his/her personal data. The last guarantee resonates with

640 *Ibid.* 21-23; Limpert (n3) 2; Salgado (n3) 12-14.

641 See *Chapter 1, § 2, A*.

642 Article 29 WP, 'Working Document 01/2016 on the justification of interferences with the fundamental rights to privacy and data protection through surveillance measures when transferring personal data (European Essential Guarantees)' (WP237, 13 Apr 2016).

643 *Ibid.* 4.

644 *Ibid.* 7.

645 *Ibid.* 7-9.

646 *Ibid.* 9-10.

647 Joined Cases C-293/12 and C-594/12 *Digital Rights Ireland Ltd v Minister for Communications* [2014] para 62.

648 *Klass and others v Germany* App no 5029/71 (ECtHR, 6 Sep 1978) para 56.

649 *Ibid.*

650 Article 29 WP, 'Working Document 01/2016' (n642) 11-12.

Article 47 EU Charter, which provides that "everyone whose rights and freedoms guaranteed by (EU) law are violated has the right to an effective remedy before a tribunal".[651,652]

iv) 2016 General Data Protection Regulation

a) Background

GDPR – The 2016 General Data Protection Regulation (GDPR)[653] became applicable in May 2018 and repealed the 1995 Directive[654] as it had become outdated in the quickly developing technological world.[655] The GDPR aims to strengthen the protection of personal data and to regulate the use of personal data by the private as well as, although more limited, by the public sector (*see below*). The EU decided to replace the 1995 Directive with a Regulation, as the fragmented implementation of the 1995 Directive had led to different levels of protection in the Member States. Contrary to a Directive which is only binding as to the result that has to be achieved, a Regulation is "binding in its entirety and directly applicable in all Member States",[656] and a stronger instrument to enforce and unify personal data protection in the European Union (and beyond).[657]

Privacy and commerce – The interaction between the right to privacy and the free movement of personal data was a central element in the 1995 Directive, but in the GDPR almost all references to 'privacy' have been replaced by 'personal data protection', as the latter had acquired the status of a fundamental right in the EU.[658] Orla Lynskey concludes, therefore, that both the 1995 Directive and the 2016 GDPR have a "dual economic and rights-based objective".[659] Sjaak Nouwt disagrees as the 1995 Directive was enacted based on the internal market competence of the EU, being more economic than rights-based, and was corrected by the inclusion of a human rights approach in the GDPR.[660] The dual

651 Article 47 EU Charter.

652 Article 29 WP, 'Working Document 01/2016' (n642).

653 Regulation (EU) 2016/679 of 27 Apr 2016 on the protection of natural persons with regard to the processing of personal data and on the free movement of such data, and repealing Directive 95/46/EC [2016] OJ L 119/1 (GDPR).

654 See *Chapter 3, § 3, B., i).*

655 Article 94 and 99.2 GDPR.

656 Article 288.2 TFEU.

657 Recitals 9 and 13 and Article 94 GDPR; Blume (n528) 5; Buitelaar (n528) 181; de Vries *et al.* (n525) 256; EU Agency for Fundamental Rights (n401) 17; Eur-Lex, 'Summaries of EU legislation: GDPR' (*europa.eu*, 2025); Lynskey, *The foundations* (n42) 8; Pałka, 'Data Management' (n44) 614; Peltz-Steele, 'American Privacy' (n240) 373-374.

658 Lynskey, *The foundations* (n42) 10.

659 *Ibid.* 8.

660 Gutwirth *et al.* (n32) 285-286.

economic and rights-based objective might not have been equally divided in the 1995 Directive as the economic objective prevailed indeed. The importance of the protection of the right to privacy has, however, also been stressed on multiple occasions in the 1995 Directive and related documents.[661] As for personal data transfers to third countries, the GDPR states that, on the one hand, they "are necessary for the expansion of international trade and international cooperation",[662] but that they also "raise new challenges and concerns with regard to the protection of personal data".[663,664]

Fundamental right – The first sentence of the GDPR sets out that "the protection of natural persons in relation to the processing of personal data is a fundamental right",[665] a unique elevation of status globally.[666] The fundamental rights' aspect is also emphasized in the first Article of the GDPR, as "this Regulation protects fundamental rights and freedoms of natural persons and in particular their right to the protection of personal data".[667] As a fundamental right, personal data protection is guaranteed for every human being "whatever their nationality or place of residence".[668]

b) Content

Definition personal data – The GDPR defines personal data as "any information relating to an identified or identifiable natural person (the 'data subject')".[669] "An identifiable natural person is (someone) who can be identified, directly or indirectly, (by a characteristic) such as a name, an identification number, location data, an online identifier or to one or more factors specific to the physical, physiological, genetic, mental, economic, cultural or social identity of that natural person".[670] Recital 14 excludes legal persons from the GDPR's scope of application, as it only applies to natural persons.[671] Anonymous information and personal data of deceased persons is also excluded from the GDPR's scope of application.[672]

---

661 See *Chapter 3, § 3, B., i) and iii).*
662 Recital 101 GDPR.
663 *Ibid.*
664 Recitals 2-5 GDPR.
665 Recital 1 GDPR.
666 Bygrave, *Data Privacy Law* (n37) 59.
667 Article 1.3 GDPR.
668 Recitals 2 and 14 GDPR.
669 Recital 26 and Article 4.1 GDPR.
670 Article 4.1 GDPR.
671 Recital 14 GDPR.
672 Recitals 26-27 GDPR.

Scope of application – The GDPR is applicable to "activities of … *a controller* (i.e. "the natural or legal person, public authority, agency or other body which determines the purposes and means of the processing of personal data"[673]) *or a processor* (i.e. "the natural or legal person, public authority, agency or other body which processes personal data on behalf of the controller"[674]) *in the Union*, regardless of whether the processing takes place in the Union or not"[675] *and* is also applicable "to the processing of personal data of *data subjects who are in the Union* by a controller or processor not established in the Union, where the processing activities are related to: (a) the offering of goods or services …; or (b) the monitoring of their behaviour as far as their behaviour takes place within the Union".[676] The processing of personal data has to occur "wholly or partly by automated means (or) … by other than automated means which (are intended to) form part of a filing system, which is a structured set of personal data accessible according to specific criteria, whether centralised, decentralised or dispersed on a functional or geographical basis",[677] and includes the "collection, recording, organisation, structuring, storage, adaptation or alteration, retrieval, consultation, use, disclosure by transmission, dissemination or otherwise making available, alignment or combination, restriction, erasure or destruction"[678] of this data, in order to be situated within the GDPR's scope of application.

Data protection principles – The GDPR sets out the following Principles, Rights of the data subject, and Obligations for controllers and processors in Chapters II-IV, which can be situated into 8 categories:[679]

1) Data quality: is improved through purpose specification, purpose limitation, data minimization (i.e. "adequate, relevant and limited to what is necessary in relation to the purposes for which (the personal data) are processed"[680]), data accuracy, time and storage limitation;[681]
2) Legitimate processing: consisting of lawful, fair, and transparent processing[682] and requiring data subjects to provide their freely given, specific, informed, and unambiguous consent to the processing or that

673 Article 4.7 GDPR.
674 Article 4.8 GDPR.
675 Article 3.1 GDPR.
676 Recitals 23-24 and Article 3.2 GDPR.
677 Article 2.1 and 4.6 GDPR.
678 Article 4.2 GDPR.
679 The choice and definition of categories is explained in § 4. *Interim analysis*.
680 Article 5.1(c) GDPR.
681 Article 5.1(b)-(e) GDPR.
682 Article 5.1(a) GDPR.

the processing is necessary for one of the purposes specified in the GDPR; in the case of non-compliance, data subjects have a right to object to the illegitimate processing;[683]

3) Sensitive data: consisting of the prohibition, to which exemptions are possible, to the processing of certain special categories of personal data, namely "personal data revealing racial or ethnic origin, political opinions, religious or philosophical beliefs, or trade union membership, and the processing of genetic data, biometric data for the purpose of uniquely identifying a natural person, data concerning health or data concerning a natural person's sex life or sexual orientation";[684,685]
4) Notification and transparency: consisting of an obligation for the data controller to provide data subjects with information relating to the data controller's identity and contact details, the contact details of the data protection officer, the purposes of the processing and its legal basis, including any intent to change the purposes at a later stage, the recipients of the personal data, whether the data will be transferred to a third country or international organization and the related safeguards to this transfer, information relating to fair and transparent processing, and, in case applicable, the legitimate interests;[686]
5) Right of access: granting data subjects (a.o.) the right to request and access information regarding whether, which, and how data relating to them is being processed;[687]
6) Correction rights: granting data subjects the right, to which exemptions are possible, to request rectification, erasure, and restriction of the processing of personal data that were not processed in conformity with the requirements set out in the GDPR, and of data that are incomplete or inaccurate, with a requirement to share these corrections (including erasure and processing restriction requests) with third parties to whom the data were disclosed;[688]
7) Data security: consisting of the obligation for data controllers to take appropriate technical and organizational measures to ensure the security of personal data, and protect the data against unauthorized and unlawful processing, accidental loss, destruction, and damage;[689]

683 Recital 32 and Article 6-7 and 21 GDPR.
684 Recital 51 and Article 9.1 GDPR.
685 Article 9 GDPR.
686 Article 13 GDPR.
687 Article 15 GDPR.
688 Article 16-19 GDPR.
689 Article 5.1(f) GDPR.

8) Enforcement:[690] mandating Member States to establish an independent public authority (or national supervisory authority; DPA) to monitor the GDPR's application through four types of powers; investigative powers (to investigate complaints by data subjects), corrective powers (to issue warnings and sanctions), authorization powers, and advisory powers.[691]

Information duty data breach – One of the new features introduced by the GDPR, and originating in California,[692] is a personal data breach information duty for data processors and controllers to inform the competent supervisory authority within 75 hours and the data subjects without undue delay of a data breach which "is likely to result in a high risk".[693] A personal data breach occurs when "a security breach leading to the accidental or unlawful destruction, loss, alteration, unauthorised disclosure of, or access to, personal data transmitted, stored or otherwise processed"[694] has taken place.[695] The Article 29 WP urged the EU legislators already in its 2009 Future of Privacy statement to include a privacy breach notification provision in its personal data protection legislation.[696]

European Data Protection Board replaces Article 29 WP – With the GDPR replacing the 1995 Directive, the Article 29 WP was also replaced by the European Data Protection Board (EDPB). Similar to its Article 29 WP predecessor, the EDPB has to monitor and ensure the uniform application of the GDPR by the EU Member States and "provide the Commission with an opinion for the assessment of the adequacy of the level of protection in a third country or international organization".[697] The EDPB is an independent body with legal personality, consisting of each Member States' supervisory authority and the European Data Protection Supervisor, and takes decisions by simple majority, unless otherwise provided for by the GDPR.[698]

Exemptions – The GDPR excludes certain categories of personal data from its scope of application, such as the processing of personal data for an activity outside the scope of EU law, for activities related to the EU common foreign and security policy, for a purely personal or household activity by a natural person,

690 The enforcement requirements are set out in Chapter VI Independent supervisory authorities of the GDPR.
691 Recitals 117-129 and Article 51-59 GDPR.
692 See *Chapter 3, § 1, B., ii)*.
693 Article 34.1 GDPR.
694 Article 4.12 GDPR.
695 Recital 86 and Article 33-34 GDPR.
696 Article 29 WP, 'The Future of Privacy' (n478) 16.
697 Article 70.1(s) GDPR.
698 Recital 139 and Article 68-72 GDPR; Lynskey, *The foundations* (n42) 68-69; Peltz-Steele, 'American Privacy' (n240) 377.

and for State activities in areas of criminal law and national security.[699] Similar to the 1995 Directive, the GDPR includes derogations and exemptions when personal data processing occurs for journalistic, academic, artistic, or literary expression purposes, and safeguards when personal data processing occurs for scientific, historical research or statistical purposes, and archiving purposes in the public interest, as in these cases the right to personal data protection has to be reconciled with the right to freedom of expression and information.[700]

Accountability – Where the 1995 Directive included a liability clause and left the specification of fines to the Member States,[701] the GDPR stipulates explicitly that non-compliance with its principles can result in high fines[702] of up to €20 million or 4% of a company's total worldwide annual turnover.[703] Data subjects can file a complaint with the supervisory authority when they deem that their right to personal data protection was violated. The Article 29 WP urged the EU legislators already in its 2009 Future of Privacy statement to include "the power to impose financial sanctions on (data) controllers and processors".[704]

Adequacy Decision – The requirement for an adequate level of personal data protection to the level provided in the EU for data transfers to non-EU or third countries is upheld in Article 45 GDPR. The EU Commission retains the power to decide if "a third country, a territory or specified sector within a third country, or an international organization, offers an adequate level of data protection".[705] Elements to be taken into account by the Commission are "whether the third country respects the rule of law, access to justice as well as international human rights norms and standards and its general and sectoral law, including legislation concerning public security, defence and national security as well as public order and criminal law".[706] Additional guarantees that should be provided by a third country are effective independent supervision of the compliance, effective administrative and judicial redress mechanisms, and effective and enforceable rights for data subjects. Obtaining an adequacy

699 Recitals 16-19 and Article 2.2 GDPR.

700 Recitals 153-156 and Article 85 GDPR; Peltz-Steele, 'American Privacy' (n240) 379.

701 Article 23-24 Directive 95/46/EC.

702 Meta was fined a record amount of €1.2 billion on the 22nd of May 2023 for transferring Europeans' personal data to the United States, where "Meta is subject to U.S. surveillance laws".: NOYB, 'NOYB win: €1.2 billion fine against Meta over EU-US data transfers' (*noyb.eu*, 22 May 2023).

703 Article 77 and 79 and 83 GDPR; Pałka, 'Data Management' (n44) 620; Peltz-Steele, 'American Privacy' (n240) 377.

704 Article 29 WP, 'The Future of Privacy' (n178) 22.

705 Preamble 103 GDPR.

706 Recital 104 GDPR.

decision results in free transfers of personal data without the necessity of any other type of authorization. If a third country ceases to fulfill the personal data requirements, the adequacy decision will be revoked.[707]

Standard Contractual Clauses – In the absence of an adequacy finding, the GDPR upholds the alternative use of Standard Contractual Clauses (SCCs) provided for in the 1995 Directive for personal data transfers to a third country. The data importer and exporter commit themselves in the SCCs to comply with and be accountable for respecting the GDPR's rules and principles. The CJEU provided, however, a stricter interpretation of Article 46 GDPR SCCs by requiring 'a level of protection essentially equivalent to that guaranteed in the EU' similar to Article 45 GDPR adequacy in the *Schrems II*[708] case, shifting the responsibility for an 'adequacy' determination of a third country system from the national Data Protection Authorities to the data importers/exporters, as was explained in *Chapter 1, § 2, C.*

Binding Corporate Rules – A second alternative for personal data transfers to countries that have not obtained an adequacy decision consists of Binding Corporate Rules (BCRs). BCRs were introduced in 2003 by the Article 29 WP and "are legally binding and apply to and are enforced by every member concerned of the group of undertakings, or group of enterprises engaged in a joint economic activity".[709] This specific mechanism is suitable for "international data transfers within the same corporate group (and) must first be approved by the national Data Protection Authorities".[710] BCRs provide flexibility to companies as they can be drafted in accordance with companies' needs, but their specific application within a corporate group limits their wider international applicability.[711]

C. CJEU CASE LAW

CJEU – The Court of Justice of the European Union (CJEU) was established in 1952 and is the highest authority to ensure that EU law is observed when interpreting and applying the EU Treaties.[712] This section provides a

---

707 Recitals 103-107 and Article 44-45 GDPR; Berka (n58) 176-177; Bradford *et al.* (n139) 34; Lynskey, *The foundations* (n42) 43-44; Pałka, 'Data Management' (n44) 620; Peltz-Steele, 'American Privacy' (n240) 376.

708 See *Chapter 1, § 2, B.*

709 Article 47.1(a) GDPR.

710 Olivier Proust and Emmanuelle Bartoli, 'Binding Corporate Rules' (2012) 2 IDPL 35, 35.

711 Recital 108 GDPR; Article 29 WP, 'The Future of Privacy' (n478) 11; Proust and Bartoli (n710) 36.

712 Court of Justice of the European Union, 'The Institution: General Presentation' (*europa.eu*, 2025); Gutwirth *et al.* (n32) 29-33; Hoofnagle *et al.* (n11) 71.

non-exhaustive overview of the CJEU's case law in the area of personal data protection and data privacy.

i) *Case Law Overview*

Personal data protection – In 2003 *Österreichischer Rundfunk*,[713] the CJEU applied the ECtHR's Article 8 case law[714] to determine whether the communication of employees' salaries, where this information had not been anonymized, to public authorities as well as to the public in general, interfered with someone's private life, but left the decision on the necessity and proportionality of the measure to the Member State courts.[715] It is interesting that the CJEU made reference to Article 8 ECHR instead of Article 8 EU Charter, which already enshrined the fundamental right to personal data protection.[716] Possibly the Court reasoned that the EU Charter had not yet acquired constitutional status, as this only occurred in 2009 with the entry into force of the Lisbon Treaty. In 2003 *Lindqvist*,[717] the Court decided that the publication of parish members' data (personal information, contact details, work, hobbies, ...)[718] on the parish's website constituted personal data processing covered by the 1995 Directive and did not fall within one of the exempted categories.[719] In both 2003 *Österreichischer Rundfunk* and 2003 *Lindqvist*, the CJEU confirmed the dual economic and human rights approach of the 1995 Directive.[720] In 2010 *Schecke and Eifert*,[721] after the entry into force of the Lisbon Treaty, the Court invalidated secondary EU law provisions in the form of regulations, for their interference with Articles 7 and 8 EU Charter.[722] The CJEU conflated both rights, moreover, as it stated that "the right to respect for private life with regard to the processing of personal data, recognised by articles 7 and 8 of the (EU) Charter ..., concerns any information relating to an identified or identifiable individual".[723,724] In 2010

713 Joined Cases C-465/00, C-138/01, and C-139/01 *Rechnungshof v Österreichischer Rundfunk and Others and Christa Neukomm and Joseph Lauermann v Österreichischer Rundfunk* [2003].
714 *Ibid.* paras 71-72.
715 *Ibid.* para 90; Purtova, 'The illusion' (n396) 90-91.
716 Gutwirth *et al.* (n32) 29-33.
717 C-101/01 *Criminal proceedings against Bodil Lindqvist* [2003].
718 *Ibid.* para 13.
719 *Ibid.* paras 27 and 48.
720 *Rundfunk* (n713) para 70; *Lindqvist* (n717) para 79.
721 *Schecke and Eifert* (n579).
722 *Ibid.* paras 64 and 92; de Vries *et al.* (n525) 304-305.
723 *Schecke and Eifert* (n579) para 1.
724 Christofi and Verdoodt (n107) 49; Gloria González Fuster, *Study on the essence of the fundamental rights to privacy and to protection of personal data* (EDPS, 2022) 33; Lynskey, 'Deconstructing' (n534) 569-581; Purtova, 'The illusion' (n396) 91; Vogiatzoglou and Valcke (n400) 31-37.

Commission v Germany,[725] the Court held that subjecting data protection authorities to State scrutiny interferes with the requirement that these authorities be completely independent, as set forth in Article 28.1 of the 1995 Directive.[726] In 2010 *Bavarian Lager*,[727] the CJEU (partially) disconnected EU personal data protection legislation from Article 8 ECHR by deciding that Article 8 ECHR cannot limit the scope of application of EU personal data protection regulation.[728] In 2011 *ASNEF*,[729] the Court referred to Articles 7 and 8 of the EU Charter in its analysis regarding personal data protection, as opposed to its previous reference to Article 8 ECHR.[730] In 2011 *Deutsche Telekom*,[731] the CJEU considered the second question referred in this case based on the individual's consent requirement and purpose specification and limitation principles as part of Article 8.2 EU Charter.[732] In 2014 *Google Spain*,[733] the Court attempted to find a balance between the right to personal data privacy and freedom of information/speech, referring to Articles 7 and 8 EU Charter in tandem.[734] Finally, in 2022 *SpaceNet and Telekom*,[735] the CJEU stated that "it should be borne in mind that the protection of the fundamental right to privacy requires, according to the settled case law of the Court, that derogations from and limitations on the protection of personal data must apply only in so far as is strictly necessary".[736]

Personal data privacy – The brief overview of personal data protection case law of the CJEU shows the evolution of the relationship between Article 8 ECHR and Articles 7 (privacy) and 8 (personal data protection) EU Charter. The Court initially referred to Article 8 ECHR in its case law analysis, but after the EU Charter gained constitutional status with the entry into force of the Lisbon Treaty in 2009, the Court shifted this reference to the equivalent provisions of the EU Charter. While the right to privacy and the right to personal data protection are included separately in the EU Charter, the CJEU refers in its case law to both Articles together, even conflating them. This consistent dual use

---

725 C-518/07 *European Commission v Federal Republic of Germany* [2010].

726 *Ibid.* para 56.

727 C-28/08 P. *European Commission v The Bavarian Lager Co. Ltd.* [2010].

728 *Ibid.* paras 58-62.

729 Joined Cases C-468/10 and C-469/10 *Asociación Nacional de Establecimientos Financieros de Crédito, Federación de Comercio Electrónico y Marketing Directo v Administración del Estado* [2011].

730 *Ibid.* paras 40-42.

731 C-543/09 *Deutsche Telekom AG v Bundesrepublik Deutschland* [2011].

732 *Ibid.* paras 51-67.

733 C-131/12 *Google Spain SL and Google Inc. v Agencia Española de Protección de Datos and Mario Costeja González* [2014].

734 *Ibid.* paras 97-99.

735 Joined Cases C-793/19 and C-794/19 *Bundesrepublik Deutschland v SpaceNet AG and Telekom Deutschland GmbH* [2022]; see *Chapter 5, § 3, B.*

736 *Ibid.* para 67.

can refer to the origins of the right to personal data protection in the right to privacy as part of the latter, but also to the expansion of the scope of application of the right to privacy when combined with its personal data protection sister right.[737]

ii) Right to Personal Data Protection 'Essence'

Infringement essence – In *Schrems I* and *Schrems II*,[738] the CJEU found an infringement of 'the essence' of the fundamental right to privacy and effective judicial protection, which is considered a severe infringement as it touches upon the core or very substance of a right, severely hindering the right's exercise and existence.[739] Article 23 GDPR and Article 52.1 EU Charter provide possibilities to restrict or limit the GDPR's and EU Charter's scope of application, as long as these restrictions have a legal basis and "respect the essence of those (fundamental) rights and freedoms".[740,741] The CJEU has not specified what 'the essence' of the fundamental right to privacy, and more importantly of the right to personal data protection, exactly is.[742] Some of the theories identified in the literature will try to shed light on the 'essence' of the right to personal data protection in this section.

Privacy – The dominant theory that follows from the CJEU's case law (*see above*), joined by Orla Lynskey,[743] is that the right to privacy constitutes the essence of the fundamental right to personal data protection. J C (Hans) Buitelaar draws a similar conclusion from the German Constitutional court's 1983 *Census* case,[744] where the court warned for the depersonalization of people if they are reduced to mere sources of information pointing to "the essence of the basic principles ... at stake in protecting privacy in the information society".[745] This reasoning is, however, problematic, because if the right to privacy constitutes the 'essence' of the right to personal data protection, then what is the added

737 Article 29 WP, 'Opinion 01/2014' (n631) 4; de Vries *et al.* (n525) 268; Lynskey, *The foundations* (n42) 89-90; Tzanou (n526) 96-97; Vogiatzoglou and Valcke (n400) 12; Plixavra Vogiatzoglou, *The Era of Pre-Crime* (Doctoral Thesis KU Leuven, 2023) 208-209.

738 See *Chapter 1, § 2, A. and B.*

739 *Schrems I* (n96) paras 94-95; *Schrems II* (n119) para 187; Article 29 WP, 'Working Document 01/2016' (n642) 9; Maja Brkan, 'The Essence of the Fundamental Rights to Privacy and Data Protection' (2019) 20 GerLawJ 864, 866-869; Christofi and Verdoodt (n107) 21; González Fuster (n724) 10-16; Vogiatzoglou (n737) 189-191.

740 Article 52.1 EU Charter; Article 23.1 GDPR.

741 Article 29 WP, 'Working Document 01/2016' (n642) 5; Brkan (n739) 867; de Vries *et al.* (n525) 242.

742 Lynskey, *The foundations* (n42) 173; Vogiatzoglou and Valcke (n400) 33.

743 *Ibid.* 172 and 271.

744 German Bundesverfassungsgericht, Census Judgment of the First Senate of 15 Dec 1983, 1 BvR 209, 269, 362, 420, 440, 484/83; see *Chapter 4, § 1, B., i).*

745 Buitelaar (n528) 193.

value of creating this new fundamental right? The right to privacy's history in the Council of Europe goes back to the 1950s and is grounded in the protection of people's human dignity.[746] Instead of introducing a new fundamental right to personal data protection to safeguard, in essence, the right to privacy, an evolutionary interpretation of the latter could have reached the same goal. While the intertwinement between the right to personal data protection and the right to privacy cannot be denied, the right to privacy alone cannot be the 'essence' of the right to personal data protection.

Data security – The second theory identified in the literature is that data security constitutes the 'essence' of the fundamental right to personal data protection.[747] If organizational and technical measures preventing unauthorized access, alteration, loss, or destruction (data security[748]) are in place, the collected personal data can be (adequately) protected against the respective risks. Jean-Marc Dinant specifies that these security measures should relate to (1) who can access which kind of information (availability), (2) who cannot access which kind of information (confidentiality), and (3) who can modify which kind of information in which circumstances (integrity).[749] The obligation to implement adequate security measures contributes, moreover, to the accountability of personal data controllers and processors.[750] Even the CJEU seemed to imply in its 2014 *Digital Rights Ireland*[751] reasoning, that "the essence of the fundamental right to the protection of personal data enshrined in article 8 of the Charter ... (is not affected since) certain principles of data protection and data security must be respected by providers, (such as) appropriate technical and organisational measures ... adopted against accidental or unlawful destruction, accidental loss or alteration of the data".[752] Given the quickly evolving technological landscape, Peter Blume favors the inclusion of general standards in the law as opposed to specific technical measures which may become outdated rapidly.[753] Data security is an essential component to ensure personal data protection, but the requirement for adequate technical measures can

746 See *Chapter 4, § 1, B., i).*
747 Blume (n528) 7-8; Brkan (n739) 878; Cate and Mayer-Schönberger (n362) 69; Gutwirth *et al.* (n32) 111-112 and 181; Lynskey, *The foundations* (n42) 172; Tzanou (n526) 91; Vogiatzoglou (n737) 225; World Summit on the Information Society, *Declaration of Principles – Building the Information Society: a global challenge in the new Millennium* (Document WSIS-03/GENEVA/DOC/4-E, 2003) B.5), 35.
748 Article 17.1 Directive 95/46/EC; Article 5.1(f) GDPR.
749 Gutwirth *et al.* (n32) 111-112.
750 Purtova, 'The illusion' (n396) 96.
751 *Digital Rights* (n647); see *Chapter 5, § 3, A.*
752 *Ibid.* para 40.
753 Blume (n528) 7.

questionably be the only 'essence' of this new fundamental right as this would reduce the right to procedural requirements.

Data quality – A third theory for the 'essence' conceptualization of the right to personal data protection, advocated by Maria Tzanou,[754] consists of data quality[755] requirements. These requirements can be found in Article 8.2 EU Charter and encompass fair data processing, purpose specification, legitimate basis for processing (consent or legal provisions), data access, and rectification rights. Maria Tzanou adds the prohibition to process sensitive data to this list[756] as it is essential to protect the principle of non-discrimination, and further identifies "the 'hard core' of data protection (which protects) what needs to be protected, so that the final values that data protection pursues such as individual autonomy, dignity, and personal identity are safeguarded",[757] echoing the interests protected by the right to privacy. This circular reasoning brings the analysis back to the dominant theory where personal data protection safeguards, in essence, the right to privacy.

More complex? – Article 8.3 EU Charter adds yet another constitutional element, or 'essence', to the right to personal data protection, consisting of "compliance ... control by an independent authority",[758] which role has been conferred upon the Data Protection Authorities.[759] Where the right to privacy is closer related to preserving people's personal space and human dignity, the right to personal data protection seems to focus more on limitations and conditions for personal data processing.[760] Consequently, the right to personal data protection "does not protect us from data processing but from unlawful and/or disproportionate data processing".[761] This brings the analysis back to the conclusion reached on the data security aspect, that personal data protection seems, in essence, to be of a procedural nature. When the procedural rules set out by (first the 1995 Directive and now) the GDPR are fulfilled, the right to personal data protection will not be infringed. However, if the right to personal data protection consists in the essence of procedural rules, what do these procedural rules aim to protect? A logical answer would be the right to human dignity, personal identity, individual autonomy, and hence privacy. Maria Tzanou reached the same conclusion above.

---

754 Tzanou (n526) 91-98.

755 Article 6 Directive 95/46/EC; Article 5.1(a)-(e) GDPR; see *§ 4. Interim analysis* for an explanation of the definition and conceptualization of this category.

756 Tzanou (n526) 97-98.

757 *Ibid.* 98.

758 Article 8.3 EU Charter.

759 Gutwirth *et al.* (n32) 131-133; Lynskey, *The foundations* (n42) 267-268.

760 Zuiderveen Borgesius *et al.* (n180) 14.

761 Gutwirth *et al.* (n32) 3.

Data privacy – It is understandable that a new fundamental right, to personal data protection, should protect a fundamental interest other than privacy, as there is otherwise no added value in creating a new separate right. The intertwinement between both interests can, however, not be denied. The 1995 Directive was explicitly rooted in the right to privacy and Article 8 ECHR. The ECtHR interprets Article 8 ECHR right to privacy as encompassing personal

Table 3. Common Fair Information Principles: EU

	European Union	
	1995 Directive	GDPR
1. Data Quality	✓	✓
Purpose Limitation	6.1.b	5.1.b
Data Minimization	6.1.c	5.1.c
Time and Storage Limitation	6.1.e	5.1.e
2. Legitimate processing	✓	✓
Lawful / Consent / Opt-in / Opt-out	6.1.a 7	5.1.a 6
Non-discrimination (incl. sensitive data)	8	9
Right to object	14	21
3. Notification and Transparency	✓	✓
Processing information / Privacy Policy	10	12 & 13
Disclosure to 3rd parties	10.c	13.1.a
Right of access	12.a	15
Data breach notification	/	33-34
4. Data Accuracy	✓	✓
Accurate, up-to-date	6.1.d	5.1.d
Correction rights	12.b	16
Deletion rights	12.b	17
Notification to 3rd parties	12.c	19
5. Data Security	✓ 17	✓ 5.1.f & 32
6. Enforcement	✓	✓
Administrative body	28	51
Court	22	79
Remedies	23-24	82-84
Private right of action	22	77-79

data protection in its case law, and the CJEU conflates both rights in its own case law as shown above. Forcing this newly created right to have 'an essence' of its own distinguishable from the right to privacy is, therefore, an artificial endeavor. Lee Bygrave[762] and Federico Fabbrini[763] have a suggestion in the form of a new concept; data privacy. This concept is broadly used in the United States and consists of a contraction between the concepts of 'privacy' and 'personal data protection'. The concept of data privacy shows that it concerns a different type of privacy (namely that of personal data) but retains the link with its privacy roots. One of the main elements protected by the right to privacy is someone's home. To enter someone's home, one needs an invitation from the owner (consent) or a search warrant (legitimate interest). In a similar way, someone's personal data can be processed when the data controller obtains consent of the person concerned or acts with one of the legitimate aims set out in the law. The right to personal data protection is in this interpretation a digital evolution of the right to privacy and does not require a separate fundamental right to be created, but rather an evolutionary interpretation to be adopted.

§ 4. INTERIM COMPARATIVE EU-U.S. ANALYSIS

Private v. public sector – The main distinction between the U.S. and the EU approach towards personal data privacy is situated in their scope of application. Where a separate regulation is in place for U.S. federal agencies, namely the 1974 Privacy Act, and (certain) private sectors operating in the United States, complemented by recently increasing U.S. State consumer privacy acts for the private sector, the EU proclaims to have one comprehensive data privacy approach, which can be found in the GDPR. The broad exemptions in the GDPR for public sector activities, such as law enforcement and national security discussed in *Chapter 5, § 3 and § 5*, contradict, however, its comprehensiveness. The OECD and CoE embrace an all-encompassing approach by setting out minimum personal data protection standards that have to be observed by both the public and the private sector. Przemysław Pałka advocates a sectoral approach over a one-fits-all format for personal data protection legislation as the stakes and values involved differ significantly (private versus public sector and/or different private sectors).[764] The current evolution in the United States to adopt comprehensive U.S. State consumer privacy acts contradicts the

762 Bygrave, *Data Privacy Law* (n37) 26.
763 de Vries *et al.* (n525) 261-262.
764 Pałka, 'Data Management' (n44) 634-635.

preference for a sectoral approach within the private sector, and brings it closer to the EU comprehensive approach. Orla Lynskey's observation that the EU comprehensive approach is actually not that all-encompassing as many exemptions (and separate laws) are dedicated to the public sector (government agencies and law enforcement) supports, on the contrary, the preference for a sectoral approach for data privacy, namely a separate legal framework for the public and private sector.

Convergence private sector commerce – A core distinction between the EU and the U.S. approach towards data privacy can be found in the qualification of the right to personal data protection. In the EU, personal data protection is qualified as a fundamental right, which "might (only) be balanced against other human (or fundamental) rights, but not against interests like economic efficiency or innovation".[765,766] The EU fundamental rights approach has already caused (severe) issues in the EU-U.S. adequacy negotiations due to the EU's strong stance on non-negotiability. In the United States, "the protection of personal data is always balanced against other interests such as commerce or free speech",[767] as it is qualified as a consumer (privacy) right[768] correlating with businesses' duty not to mislead or deceive consumers, which can result in different prices/services being charged/offered to different people, depending on whether consumers opted-in/out of the collection/sharing/ sale of their personal data. U.S. State consumer privacy acts are applicable to private companies active in the State concerned, and complement the sectoral approach where certain sectors have their own sector-specific data privacy legislation that they have to observe. The CCPA and VCDPA explicitly exclude State and governmental authorities from their scope of application. The discussion of the legal frameworks shows, however, that also in the EU a balancing exercise takes place. Before the Lisbon Treaty elevated the EU Charter (which codifies the fundamental right to personal data protection) to a treaty with constitutional value, this balancing exercise could explicitly be found in the 1995 Directive's aim to facilitate intra-EU free flow of (and commerce in) personal data. The 2016 GDPR embraced the fundamental right status of personal data protection, but the commerce dimension is still present. The privacy-commerce balance is also enshrined in the U.S. State consumer privacy acts discussed in this book, as well as in the OECD Guidelines and CoE Convention 108(+). The OECD is more commerce-oriented while the CoE is more privacy-oriented, but both organizations strive to find a balance between

765 *Ibid.* 616.
766 Bygrave, *Data Privacy Law* (n37) 110; Pernot-Leplay (n193) 111.
767 Pernot-Leplay (n193) 115.
768 *Ibid.* 111.

both interests. Orla Lynskey and Sjaak Nouwt pointed already to the dual economic and human rights-based approach which is necessary to effectively protect and enhance personal data flows. The same logic can, therefore, be found behind the development of common personal data protection principles by the OECD, the CoE, and the EU, as they all aimed at introducing the same minimum standards of protection to allow personal data transfers between their Member States. Certain common data privacy principles can also be identified in the U.S. (State) acts selected for discussion.

General data privacy principles – The adoption of common data privacy principles may not only facilitate the free flow of personal data within the Member States of the OECD, CoE, EU, and in the future probably the United States, but broadly accepted principles can facilitate the global free flow of personal data while protecting people's privacy interests. The typical EU distinction between data controllers and data processors is not maintained, as the increasingly growing data processing chain complicates the identification of controllers and processors, preferring the use of 'data processors' for all the actors involved in data processing activities. Several attempts have been made to develop universal data privacy principles based on different legal frameworks.[769] Based on the (evolution of the) legal documents discussed in this chapter, the following six general personal data protection (or data privacy) categories can be formulated, which can provide an example of a global common data privacy standard, even though their interpretation and use may differ between the country/region/ organization involved:

1) a data quality requirement: the quality of the data is enhanced when the collected data is adequate, accurate, and up-to-date for its intended use, and limited to the information needed for the data processing purposes.[770] Consequently, this principle encompasses the requirements for the collected personal data to be only used for the purposes it was initially collected for and as was communicated to the individual at the time of collection (*purpose limitation & purpose specification*), the requirement

---

769 Article 29 WP, 'The Future of Privacy' (n478) 10; Bennett (n140) 101-111; Data Protection and Privacy Commissioners, *Montreux Declaration: The protection of personal data and privacy in a globalized world: a universal right respecting diversities* (27th International Conference of Data Protection and Privacy Commissioners, 2005); Data Protection and Privacy Commissioners, *Madrid Resolution: International Standards on the Protection of Personal Data and Privacy* (International Conference of Data Protection and Privacy Commissioners, 2009); Gutwirth *et al.* (n32) 175-188.

770 Laura Sebastian-Coleman, *Measuring Data Quality for Ongoing Improvement* (1st edn, Elsevier 2013) 39-41.

for the collected personal data to be relevant for and limited to what is necessary for the stated and intended use of the data (*data minimization*), and the requirement for the collected personal data not to be retained for longer than necessary to fulfill the stated or intended purposes, as this impedes its accuracy and correctness (*time and storage limitation*);

2) a **legitimate processing** requirement: personal data can only be collected in a *lawful* way, which requires a legal basis or legitimate aim, people whose personal data are collected must be provided with *opt-in/opt-out* options for the data collection, and people's *consent* is required for certain specific types of processing (such as but not limited to: when the individual can be adversely affected or when the processing could not be foreseen based on the information provided), data processors have to ensure that their data processing practices do not result in discriminatory practices (*non-discrimination*), finally people should have a *right to object* to illegitimate forms of processing and should not be discriminated for exercising their data privacy rights;
3) a **notification and transparency** requirement: data processors must provide individuals with certain information regarding the data processing, possibly in a *privacy policy* (such as but not limited to: information relating to data processing practices (quality, legitimate, accuracy, rights), information relating to the data processor (address, contact details), and information relating to appeal bodies (administrative and/or courts)), data processors must inform individuals about possible *disclosure* of their personal data *to third parties*, individuals must have a right to access personal data held on them (*right of access*), and data processors have a duty to notify the person concerned in case of a data breach involving their personal data (*data breach notification*);
4) a **data accuracy** requirement: the collected data has to be *accurate* and kept *up-to-date*, which includes *correction rights* for individuals in case of incomplete or inaccurate personal data and the possibility to request erasure (*deletion rights*) of personal data (subject to a balancing exercise with other competing rights), data processors should also *notify third parties* with whom the data was shared to comply with these requests (if reasonably possible);
5) a **data security** requirement: the collected personal data must be kept safe from unauthorized access and destruction through the implementation of technical and/or practical measures;
6) an **effective enforcement** requirement: individuals must have access to an effective *remedy* (remediation or sanction) enforced by an *administrative body* or a *court* in case of non-compliance with the data privacy principles.

The exact content of these principles should be further developed on an international level by multidisciplinary working groups consisting of businesses, privacy lawyers, civil society representatives, government officials etc. to determine standards that are feasible and desirable by the stakeholders involved.

International cooperation and influence – Any protection that does not adequately deal with personal data transfers across jurisdictions will eventually remain ineffective and endanger citizens' personal data and privacy on a global level. The Article 29 WP "support(ed) the development of a global instrument providing for enforceable, high-level privacy and data protection principles"[771] in Opinion 04/2014,[772] and emphasized that "cooperation between international (big data) regulators needs to be firmly based on the different applicable legal frameworks"[773] in Statement WP221.[774] The 1995 Directive stimulated self-regulation for the private sector, which was better suited to address the specific features of different sectors, supplementing the general data protection rules as set out in the 1995 Directive.[775] The 2016 GDPR encourages international cooperation and the development of an international framework for personal data protection to facilitate the free flow of personal data.[776] There is a broadly accepted feeling that a fragmented landscape for personal data transfers is undesirable and calls for an international legal framework for personal data protection and data privacy have already been made.[777] The legal-historical overview in this chapter shows a legislative cascade starting with the Fair Information Practice Principles developed in the 1973 HEW Report, followed by the 1980 OECD Guidelines and the 1981 Council of Europe Convention 108, and ending in enforceable EU data protection legislation, going from a softer directive in 1995 to a strict regulation in 2016.[778] The gradual evolution of some requirements has become evident in the overview of the different legal documents drafted in the United States, the EU, and by the international organizations OECD and CoE.

---

771 Article 29 WP, 'Opinion 04/2014' (n16) 16.

772 Article 29 WP, 'Opinion 04/2014' (n16).

773 Article 29 WP, 'Statement WP221' (n774) 3.

774 Article 29 WP, 'Statement of the WP29 on the impact of the development of big data on the protection of individuals with regard to the processing of their personal data in the EU' (WP221, 16 Sep 2014).

775 Article 27.1 Directive 95/46/EC; Cannataci and Mifsud-Bonnici (n478) 13.

776 Article 50 GDPR.

777 Article 29 WP, 'The Future of Privacy' (n478) 10; Bygrave, *Data Privacy Law* (n37) 205; Cate (n193) 128-132; Gutwirth *et al.* (n32) 175-176 and 286; Christopher Kuner, 'An International Legal Framework for Data Protection' (2009) 25 CLSR 307, 307-309; Purtova, *Property Rights* (n31) 31-32.

778 Bygrave, *Data Privacy Law* (n37) 33.

Selected legal instruments – The updated versions of the legal instruments discussed in this book remedied identified issues and added other elements that had become important in the quickly evolving digital world. In the first data quality category, the requirements of purpose limitation and data minimization can be found in almost all the legal documents. The time and storage limitation requirement is less universal, as it is included in the CoE Convention(s), EU law, and California State legislation, but excluded from the OECD Guidelines, U.S. governmental acts, and Virginia State legislation. In the second legitimate processing category, the requirements for lawful processing and the need to obtain consent can also be found in all the legal documents discussed. Besides the legal documents applicable to the U.S. government, all the other documents include a right to object. A lot of discussion occurred regarding whether to include the category of sensitive data. The U.S. States of California and Virginia followed the EU's inclusive example, but the OECD and U.S. government were reluctant. The discussion on sensitive data also suggests that the focus should not be that much on the data itself, but rather on the context in which this data is used, in particular when this use can lead to discriminatory practices.[779] In the third notification and transparency category, the duty for data processors to provide information on their activities to individuals and people's right to access the personal data held on them can be found in all legal documents discussed. In the updated versions, a data breach notification requirement was also included. In the fourth data accuracy category, all the legal documents provide individuals with correction rights, but deletion rights are not provided by the legal documents applicable to the U.S. government, and the U.S. State acts of California and Virginia are the only ones not requiring personal data to be kept up-to-date and accurate. Interestingly, it is not broadly required to inform third parties with whom the data were shared of correction and deletion rights exercised by the person concerned. The fifth data security category has been present since the early beginning and is included in all the legal documents discussed. The sixth and final enforcement provision was not included in the early legal documents, but as its importance became clear over the years, it was included in all the recent provisions. Some legal systems have a preference for administrative authorities, others for courts, and yet others grant both institutions enforcement authority. Concrete remedies are enshrined in the FTC Act, the U.S. State legislation of California and Virginia, the Council of Europe Convention, and EU law. A private right of action can be found in EU law but is very limited or non-existent in the selected legal

[779] See *Chapter 4, § 2, C.*

documents from the United States at a federal as well as State level. When taking a broader perspective, the main requirements in the EU and the United States are not that different. The EU rejects the U.S. sectoral approach and FTC enforcement but also refuses to take a closer look at its content as opposed to its format. The United States rejects the EU's strong data protection principles but also refuses to acknowledge their similarities with the OECD Guidelines to which the United States is a party and has already agreed to comply with. It is necessary that both parties adopt an open attitude and listen attentively to each other's arguments. The common elements that they share are, after all, often overshadowed by minor formal differences resulting from misunderstandings and national pride.

Enforcement – The EU criticized the United States for a lack of an effective enforcement mechanism to safeguard individuals' data privacy interests, but the EU GDPR's enforcement was also found to be defective.[780] A closer look shows that a different type of enforcement is in place in the United States, stimulating active consumer participation in safeguarding their personal data,[781] which could also be interesting for the European Union. The cure period foreseen by the FTC, CCPA, and VCDPA is a welcoming enforcement mechanism balancing consumer and business interests. Consumers must be informed by businesses about how to exercise their rights, and in case of a violation, a consumer can notify the business involved, which will have a certain amount of time to remedy the situation before further action is taken. This approach is advantageous for the consumer as well as the business, as consumers can obtain rapid relief, while businesses can avoid high fines. By July 2021, the California Attorney General announced a 75% compliance rate within the foreseen 30-day cure period by businesses that were notified of breaches.[782] Unwilling businesses will still face high fines if they refuse to comply with the requirements. This two-level enforcement, consisting of firstly a cure period, and secondly enforcement through an administrative authority or court, should therefore be welcomed. Colin Bennett observed that "self-help and judicial enforcement, while ineffectual in practice, (were) perceived as the natural American solution … preventing the creation of a separate, nonjudicial institution to mediate between citizens and their government".[783]

---

[780] Giulia Gentile and Orla Lynskey, 'Deficient By Design? The Transnational Enforcement of the GDPR' (2022) 71 ICLQ 799, 799-801; Publications Office of the European Union, *The Future of Data Protection: Effective enforcement in the digital world* (EDPS Conference Report, 2022) 14.

[781] Enright (n198) 271.

[782] Enright (n198) 296; Shatz and Lysobey (n198) 541-542.

[783] Bennett (n140) 199.

The FTC expanded its regulatory competences by not only verifying whether businesses comply with the promises they make in their privacy policies, but also to take into account consumers' expectations.[784] Even though this expansion is contested in court,[785] the consumers' expectations approach could provide a solution for the different EU-U.S. data privacy approaches as consumer expectations are converging on both sides of the Atlantic. The commonly accepted data privacy principles set out in the CCPA, the VCDPA, and the FTC Report are to a large extent aligned with the main principles of the EU GDPR. Instead of forcing the promulgation of comprehensive federal data privacy legislation in the United States, the observation of these principles could be accepted as common practice and reasonable expectation by consumers in the digital era, and enforced by the U.S. FTC.[786] This expansion of the FTC's enforcement competences would, however, have to go in tandem with the implementation of a private right of action for consumers to judicially enforce their data privacy rights adequately. The current practice of collective action in the public interest has shown to rather protect companies' interests instead of effectively protecting consumers. In the context of internet data scraping practices, it was predominantly private companies that complained about their competitors for violations of data privacy rights and non-compliance with privacy policies.[787] Introducing a private right of action would empower consumers and allow the United States to comply with the main EU requirements regarding personal data protection, facilitating transatlantic data flows, while a clear codification of the FTC's principles would remedy the U.S. courts' criticisms[788] that these principles are arbitrary and unclear. This approach would also require an effort from the EU to familiarize itself with the FTC's practices, and would contribute to mutual understanding as 'adequate protection' requires similar (protective) practices, not identical legislative wording. The FTC could, therefore, adequately be considered as the U.S. federal counterpart for EU Member States' DPAs, albeit complemented by judicial enforcement.

Procedural right – The introduction in the EU legal order of a new fundamental right to personal data protection, next to the already existing

---

784 Solove and Hartzog (n61) 667-672.

785 *FTC v Wyndham Worldwide Corporation*, No.13-1887, 10 F.Supp.3d 602 (D.N.J. 2014); *LabMd Inc. v FTC*, No.14-12144, 776 F.3d 1275 (11th Cir. 2015); Hurwitz (n246) 1018-1019.

786 Solove and Hartzog (n61) 675-676.

787 Louise Matsakis, 'Scraping the Web Is a Powerful Tool. Clearview AI Abused It' (*Wired*, 25 Jan 2020).

788 *FTC v Wyndham Worldwide Corp*, No.14-3514 (3d Cir. 2015); *LabMd Inc. v FTC*, No.16-16270, 894 F.3d 1221 (11th Cir. 2018); Hurwitz (n246) 963-987.

fundamental right to privacy, is a controversial novelty. While it is true that the fundamental right to personal data protection encompasses certain elements that cannot be qualified under the right to privacy, the two rights cannot completely be disconnected. The 'essence' discussion in *§ 3, C., ii)* above provided different interpretations for what this new fundamental right may protect and require; safeguarding people's privacy interests, personal data's security or enhancing personal data's quality, or even introducing independent authorities (in the form of DPAs) to ensure compliance control. Even the CJEU provided different interpretations of the conceptualization of 'the essence' of this new fundamental right, focusing on the requirement of data security and conflating personal data protection with safeguarding privacy. Consequently, the EU fundamental right to personal data protection can be considered a procedural right, as its 'essence' seems to consist of data security safeguards to protect privacy interests, rendering the U.S. concept 'data privacy' more adequate as it reflects the privacy origins of the right to personal data protection and the delineation that the protected privacy interests are limited to people's personal data. The necessity to create a new fundamental right to protect privacy in the digital era can, therefore, be considered redundant, as an evolutionary interpretation can achieve the same objective. The dual focus on privacy and security, and hence the procedural nature of 'data privacy' can also be identified on the U.S. side. The 1973 HEW Report set out procedural safeguards to protect privacy and due process interests alike. The procedural component also prevailed in the 1974 Privacy Act, as it was more "a records' management statute … than a mechanism to protect individual rights".[789] The Congressional Research Service joined this observation in 2019 when it noticed that today's notion of 'personal data protection' encompasses both "*data privacy* and *data security*".[790] Are the EU and the U.S. approach towards data privacy consequently that different? The distinction seems to be situated more in terminology (fundamental versus consumer right) than in the actual understanding of the concept (protecting privacy interests by procedural safeguards).

Distinct approach – In certain areas, the EU and U.S. approach towards personal data privacy differs significantly. Firstly, banking documents were, by the ECtHR,[791] considered to be personal data, protected by Article 8 ECHR, whereas the U.S. Supreme Court[792] held that people cannot expect

---

[789] Bennett (n140) 177.

[790] Mulligan and Linebaugh, *An Overview* (n230) 54; Mulligan and Linebaugh, *An Introduction* (n193) 1.

[791] *M.N. and Others* (n419) paras 24-85; *G.S.B. v Switzerland* (n420) paras 44-98.

[792] *United States v Miller* [1976] 425 U.S. 435; see *Chapter 4, § 2, A., i).*

banking information to be private, as private information has to be actively secreted, and because they decided to share this information with a third party, namely the bank employee, they lost their privacy interests in this information. Secondly, a journalistic exception is enshrined in EU data protection legislation, while this is not the case in the United States. The EU decision to include and the U.S. decision to exclude a journalistic exception from their respective data privacy laws is partially related to the distinct privacy versus freedom of speech approach (discussed in *Chapter 4, § 2, A.*), and partially to the active versus passive government perception (discussed in *Chapter 4, § 3, A., i) and B., i)*). Jane Kirtley explains that the inclusion of a journalistic exception in a legislative act "invites (the) government to define journalism (or art or literature)"[793] and what is in- and excluded from this exception, constituting "a principle anathema in the United States for its resemblance to colonial press licensing".[794,795] This practice may rather undermine than preserve the necessary checks and balances if journalists are expected to scrutinize the government.[796] Article 85.3 GDPR includes a safeguard for these situations as "each Member State (is required to) notify to the (EU) Commission the provisions of its law which it has adopted pursuant to (the journalistic, academic, artistic, and literary exception)".[797] Whether this remedy is sufficient and adequate to protect journalistic freedom is, of course, another question. The scope of this book does not extend to a detailed discussion of freedom of the press or related areas, but for the upcoming discussion in *Chapter 4, § 2, A.* on the interplay between the right to privacy and freedom of speech, this is an interesting observation worth mentioning. Thirdly, criminal convictions and "arrest records are open to public inspection and copying, even (when) the suspect (was) never charged or not convicted"[798] in the United States, whereas personal data and information from criminal convictions can only be processed by dedicated official authorities, like law enforcement or national security agencies, in the EU. This observation invites the reader to further explore these briefly mentioned subjects, as a detailed discussion falls outside the scope of this book.

---

793 Peltz-Steele, 'American Privacy' (n240) 379-380.
794 *Ibid.* 380.
795 Jane Kirtley, 'The EU Data Protection Directive and the First Amendment' (1995) 80 IowaLRev 639, 648-649.
796 Bergkamp (n394) 35; Kirtley (n795) 639-649.
797 Article 85.3 GDPR.
798 Hoofnagle *et al.* (n11) 83.

Table 4. General Data Privacy Principles

	U.S. Government			U.S. State Laws		OECD		Council of Europe		European Union	
	HEW Report	Privacy Act	FTC	CCPA § 1798.	VCDPA § 59.1-	1980 Guidelines	2013 Guidelines	Convention 108	Convention 108+	1995 Directive	GDPR
1. Data Quality	✓	✓	✓	✓	✓	✓	✓	✓	✓	✓	✓
Purpose Limitation	3	S2.b.2	2	100(c)	578.A.2	3	3	5.b	5.4.b	6.1.b	5.1.b
Data Minimization	5	S2.b.4	/	100(c)	578.A.1	1	1	5.c	5.1 & 5.4.c	6.1.c	5.1.c
Time and Storage Limitation	/	/	/	100(a)(3)	/	/	/	5.e	5.4.e	6.1.e	5.1.e
2. Legitimate processing	✓	✓	✓	✓	✓	✓	✓	✓	✓	✓	✓
Lawful / Consent / Opt-in / Opt-out	3	S2.b.2 S2.b.4	2	120	577.A.5 578.A.2	1 & 4	1 & 4	5.a	5.2-5.3	6.1.a 7	5.1.a 6
Non-discrimination	/	/	/	121	578.A.4 578.A.5	/	/	6	6	8	9
Right to object	/	/	/	125	577.C. 578.A.4	7.c	7.c	8.d	9.1.d	14	21
3. Notification & Transparency	✓	✓	✓	✓	✓	✓	✓	✓	✓	✓	✓
Processing information / Privacy Policy	1	S2.b.1	1	100(a)	578.C.	3 & 6	3 & 6	8.a	8.1	10	12 & 13
Disclosure to 3rd parties	/	S3.b	/	100(a)(1) 115	578.C.4-5	/	/	/	8.1.d	10.c	13.1.a
Right of access	2	S2.b.3	3	110	577.A.1	7.a	7.a	8.b	9.1.b	12.a	15
Data breach notification	/	/	/	29(a)** 82(a)**	§ 18.2- 186.6***	/	Part.3.15.c	/	7.2	/	33-34

(continued)

Table 4. *continued*

	U.S. Government			U.S. State Laws		OECD		Council of Europe		European Union	
	HEW Report	Privacy Act	FTC	CCPA § 1798.	VCDPA § 59.1-	1980 Guidelines	2013 Guidelines	Convention 108	Convention 108+	1995 Directive	GDPR
4. Data Accuracy	✓	✓	✓	✓	✓	✓	✓	✓	✓	✓	✓
Accurate, up-to-date	5	S2.b.4	4	/	/	2	2	5.d	5.4.d	6.1.d	5.1.d
Correction rights	4	S2.b.3	3	106	577.A.2	7.d	7.d	8.c	9.1.e	12.b	16
Deletion rights	/	/	/	105	577.A.3	7.d	7.d	8.c	9.1.e	12.b	17
Notification to 3rd parties	/	/	/	105(c)(1)	/	/	/	/	/	12.c	19
5. Data Security	✓ 5	✓ S2.b.4	✓ 4	✓ 100(e)	✓ 578.A.3	✓ 5	✓ 5	✓ 7	✓ 7.1	✓ 17	✓ 5.1.f & 32
6. Enforcement	x	✓	✓	✓	✓	?	✓	x	✓	✓	✓
Administrative body	/	/	5	155(a)	/	8?****	Part.5.19.c	/	15	28	51
Court	/	S2.b.6	/	150(a)* 199.90(a)	583 584	8?****	/	/	15.2.d	22	79
Remedies	/	/	5	150(a)* 155(a) 199.90(a)	584.C	/	/	10	12	23-24	82-84
Private right of action	/	S2.b.6	/	150*	584.E (no PRoA)	/	/	/	/	22	77-79

* only for personal information security breaches

** not part of CCPA (§ 1798.100–1798.199.100); separate legal provisions of the Civil Code

*** not part of VCDPA (Title 59.1: Trade and Commerce); separate legal provisions of the Code of Virginia

**** principle 8 OECD Guidelines requires accountability of a data controller for compliance with measures implementing the principles set out in the Guidelines, without further specification

§ 5. INTERIM CONCLUSION

This chapter provided an overview of the legal-historical evolution of data privacy rules developed in the United States, in the EU, and within the international organizations of the OECD and the Council of Europe. The EU and the United States are often portrayed as having a fundamentally different approach towards personal data protection, but a more detailed overview shows that they have more in common than may seem at first sight. The discussion and quest for the 'essence' of the newly created EU fundamental right to personal data protection revealed that the core interests protected by this fundamental right consist of a combination of data security and people's privacy, which comes close to the U.S. concept of data privacy, where procedural safeguards (such as technical and organizational security measures) aim at safeguarding individuals' (digital) privacy. The sectoral approach with a different regulatory framework for the public and the private sector is present in both the United States and the EU. Even though the EU claims to have an omnibus regime, many public sector (government, law enforcement, national security, ...) exemptions can be found in the EU legal framework. The so-called 'omnibus' personal data protection approach preferred by the EU is, as a consequence, not that different from the U.S. approach (although much less explicit). The U.S. sectoral approach within the private sector has shown to be ineffective as comprehensive State consumer privacy acts keep emerging. A convergence can, hence, be detected between both sides of the Atlantic towards an 'omnibus' data privacy regime for the private sector. Based on the legal documents discussed in this chapter, it was possible to identify common data privacy elements which were present from the early beginning, or which were added later during updating works. These elements are brought together in six main data privacy categories, comprising several related data privacy principles, consisting of data quality, legitimate processing, transparency, data accuracy, data security, and effective enforcement. Effective enforcement of these principles has shown to be necessary, which resulted in the adoption of enforcement mechanisms in legal instruments that had not foreseen such mechanisms in their first versions. The findings in this book suggest that a two-level approach, constituting of, firstly, a cure period where injured individuals can notify the business concerned to remedy the irregularity within a limited period of time, and, secondly, enforcement by a designated court or administrative authority in case of non-remediation, can provide an effective remedy for both individuals (to obtain quick relief) and businesses (to avoid high fines). The six identified data privacy categories with their related data privacy principles can provide the basis for an international framework for personal data protection, focusing on the private sector, to enhance and facilitate transborder flows and trade in personal data, while respecting the privacy interests of the people concerned.

CHAPTER 4
HISTORICAL-PHILOSOPHICAL DATA PRIVACY OVERVIEW

The fourth chapter provides a historical-philosophical contextualization of the U.S. data privacy and EU personal data protection frameworks discussed in the previous chapter. The first section goes back to the historical roots of privacy legislation in both the United States and the European Union to show how the privacy concept, as developed in an analogue world, has evolved to be applicable in a digital world. The second section continues with a discussion of the interplay between the right to privacy on the one hand, and freedom of speech and the prohibition of discrimination on the other hand, and how these approaches differ (and show similarities) between the United States and the European Union. The third section delves into the stereotypical characteristics of both systems and discusses whether these stereotypes are accurate, and if so, under which conditions. Finally, the comparative findings are brought together in the interim conclusion at the end of this chapter.

§ 1. BACK TO THE ROOTS

An analysis and discussion of the origins of the legal frameworks discussed in the previous chapter can provide a better understanding of where these conceptualizations come from and what they represent. The U.S. approach towards data privacy originates in a property protection context but has gradually evolved to also recognize people's privacy expectations in situations unrelated to someone's property. The EU approach towards personal data protection is rooted in safeguarding privacy and human dignity interests but recognizes the importance of commercial activities regarding personal data for the private sector. The United States as well as the EU balance privacy and commercial interests in their personal data protection approaches. This overview aims at clarifying why one side is more prone to tilt to one side of the balance as opposed to the other, and where these differences in approach may come from.

A. U.S. APPROACH TOWARDS DATA PRIVACY

Privacy versus Property – Data privacy is, in the United States, approached from a dual perspective; privacy and property. On the one hand, the right to privacy originates in an evolutionary interpretation of the U.S. Fourth Amendment's prohibition of unlawful interference with a person's home by the State, which was extended in U.S. tort law to interferences with people's lives and solitude in interpersonal relations, while on the other hand, personal data is perceived as a commodity, someone's property, that can be traded in commercial settings. The section below sheds some light on this two-tier conceptualization that can be identified in the U.S. approach towards (data) privacy.

i) Non-Interference

U.S. roots – The Bill of Rights to the U.S. Constitution,[799] and more specifically the Fourth Amendment safeguarding "the right of the people to be secure in their persons, houses, papers, and effects, against unreasonable searches and seizures ...",[800] provides a starting point for the discussion on the origins of privacy in the United States. As a consequential product of the American republican revolution, the drafters of the U.S. Constitution phrased this legal document as a liberty-oriented basis for the pursuit of happiness, with provisions for non-interference by the State in private affairs.[801] The "American right to privacy still takes much the form that it took in the eighteenth century: it is the right to freedom from intrusions by the State, especially in one's own home"[802] with a focus on "the physical space surrounding an individual".[803,804] The U.S. Supreme Court's 'State action doctrine' prescribes that "the U.S. Constitution in general, and its individual rights in particular, apply only to State action, not to private action(:) State action, as a matter of principle, is all government action, (i.e.) action by the executive, legislature, and judiciary at the State and federal level; private action is all non-government action".[805,806] Consequently, when computerization

799 Bill of Rights to the U.S. Constitution, 15 Dec 1791.

800 Fourth Amendment to the U.S. Constitution, 15 Dec 1791.

801 Bygrave, *Data Privacy Law* (n37) 112; Cate (n193) 99; Kohl (n398) 741-743; Vance Packard, *The Naked Society* (Penguin books 1966) 261-262; Pernot-Leplay (n193) 111; Purtova, *Property Rights* (n31) 106-113; Priscilla Regan, 'Legislating privacy' in Bart van der Sloot and Aviva de Groot (eds), *The Handbook of Privacy Studies* (Amsterdam University Press 2018) 59; Zuiderveen Borgesius *et al.* (n180) 16; see *Chapter 4, § 3, A., i)*.

802 Whitman (n392) 1161.

803 Cate (n193) 20.

804 Bygrave, *Data Privacy Law* (n37) 112; Cate (n193) 57; Kohl (n398) 741-742; Mulligan and Linebaugh, *An Overview* (n230) 1-5.

805 Stephan Jaggi, 'State Action Doctrine' (*Oxford Constitutional OUP Law*, 2025).

806 *Denver Area Ed. Telecom. Consort., Inc. v FCC* [1996] 518 U.S. 727, 737; *Manhattan Community Access Corp. v Halleck* [2019] No.17-1702, 587 U.S. _; Cate (n193) 50-65 and 99; Purtova, *Property Rights* (n31) 108.

and digital record-keeping was emerging in the 1960s, "Americans … exercised … concern for (their privacy) in relation to State activities (leading to) … 'privacy' (being) essentially (conceived) as a form of information control"[807] to prevent the government from having too much personal information on its citizens and from using this information (against them), resulting in separate legal instruments to protect data privacy in the form of the 1973 HEW Report and the 1974 Privacy Act.[808] Louis Brandeis reiterated in his dissent to 1928 *Olmstead v United States*[809] that "the protection guaranteed by the Amendments … (and by) … the makers of our Constitution … conferred, as against the Government, the right to be let alone – the most comprehensive of rights, and the right most valued by civilized men".[810,811] It was not until the 1967 *Katz v United States*[812] case that the U.S. Supreme Court detached the Fourth Amendment's (privacy) protection from specific places, namely the home, and proclaimed that "the Fourth Amendment protects people, not places".[813,814] "In *Katz* (SCOTUS) moved towards an understanding of privacy as a right to engage in private activities whether in a public or a private place",[815] as observed by Judith Rauhofer. Justice Harlan set a twofold requirement forth in his concurring opinion for the Fourth Amendment's protection against an unreasonable search; "first that a person have exhibited an actual (subjective) expectation of privacy and, second, that the expectation be one that society is prepared to recognize as 'reasonable'",[816] hence the 'reasonable expectation of privacy' requirement.[817] Rauhofer concludes that "this shift from a location-based to an expectation-based definition has underpinned American privacy laws ever since".[818] Additionally, the U.S. Supreme Court clarified in the landmark 1965 *Griswold v Connecticut*[819] case that "specific guarantees in the Bill of Rights have penumbras, formed by emanations from those guarantees that help give them life and substance (and which constitute) various guarantees (that) create zones of privacy".[820] In order to enjoy and exercise the rights enshrined in several amendments, a zone or right to privacy has to be observed to a certain extent.[821] The concept of privacy consists not just of situations where

807 Bygrave, *Data Privacy Law* (n37) 24.
808 Bennett (n140) 67-68; Fromholz (n74) 470; see *Chapter 3, § 1, A.*
809 *Olmstead v United States* [1928] 277 U.S. 438.
810 *Ibid.* para 478.
811 Cate (n193) 57; Greenwald, *No Place to Hide* (n16) 172.
812 *Katz v United States* [1967] 389 U.S. 347.
813 *Ibid.* para 351.
814 Mulligan and Linebaugh, *An Overview* (n230) 5.
815 Rauhofer (n364) 187.
816 *Katz* (n812) para 361.
817 Agre (n193) 7; Jonathan Bard, 'Unpacking the Dirtbox' (2016) 57 BCLR 731, 736-737; Bygrave, *Data Privacy Law* (n37) 181; Cate (n193) 57-58; Gutwirth *et al.* (n32) 47; Kohl (n398) 763.
818 Rauhofer (n364) 187.
819 *Griswold v Connecticut* [1965] 381 U.S. 479.
820 *Ibid.* para 484.
821 Bennett (n140) 66-67; Kohl (n398) 743; Zuiderveen Borgesius *et al.* (n180) 16.

people want to hide certain information, and which are often countered by the 'nothing-to-hide' argument, but consists also of other (active) elements which are necessary to enable the exercise of other constitutionally protected rights.[822] For example, some aspects of the right to privacy go in tandem with the freedom of speech enshrined in the First Amendment, because the ability for people's seclusion enables their freedom of speech.[823] Other aspects of privacy, such as withholding (embarrassing) personal facts or the right to be forgotten, can be at odds with the freedom of speech and the freedom of information.[824] When discussing the privacy concept, it is therefore important to take all its different aspects into account.

Extension to interpersonal relations – The initial focus on the protection of property (someone's home) did not entail an explicit right to privacy, but was in people-to-people relations interpreted as such by Samuel Warren and Louis Brandeis in their highly influential 1890 Harvard Law Review article *The Right to Privacy*,[825] and defined as 'the right to be let alone'.[826] "Fearing the encroachment of advancing civilization ... new advances in photography and the intrusive press, the authors posited that the individual had to be able to retreat from the world into solitude"[827] or seclusion, according to Dorothee Heisenberg. This seclusion is not only necessary from government interference, but also from unwanted interference by other people. Warren and Brandeis' innovative interpretation still left some loopholes in the evolving world, which William Prosser attempted to fill in his 1960 *Privacy*[828] article by founding a privacy law in U.S. tort law. In Prosser's definition, which was included in the *Restatement (Second) of Torts*[829] replacing its first version that only included a "single privacy right",[830] privacy consisted of four different elements or torts, namely "(1) intrusion upon the plaintiff's seclusion or solitude, or into his private affairs, (2) public disclosure of embarrassing private facts about the plaintiff, (3) publicity which places the plaintiff in a false light in the public eye, (and) (4) appropriation, for the defendant's advantage, of the plaintiff's name or likeness".[831,832] In the 1977

822 Daniel Solove, 'Why Privacy Matters Even If You Have 'Nothing to Hide'' (2011) 57 CHE 1, 1-4.
823 See *Chapter 4, § 2, A.*
824 *Ibid.*
825 Samuel Warren and Louis Brandeis, 'The Right to Privacy' (1890) 4 HarvLRev 193, 193-220.
826 Bennett (n140) 65-66; Bygrave, *Data Privacy Law* (n37) 24; Cate (n193) 57 and 89; Greenwald, *No Place to Hide* (n16) 172-173; Heisenberg (n66) 33; Paul Ohm, 'Sensitive Information' (2015) 88 SCalLRev 1125, 1162; Pernot-Leplay (n193) 112; Warren and Brandeis (n825) 193-205; Zuiderveen Borgesius *et al.* (n180) 16.
827 Heisenberg (n66) 33.
828 William Prosser, 'Privacy' (1960) 48 CLR 383, 383-423.
829 Restatement (Second) of Torts (1997) § 652.A.-E.
830 Cate (n193) 89.
831 Prosser (n828) 389.
832 Bennett (n140) 66; Cate (n193) 89-90; Heisenberg (n66) 33; Mulligan and Linebaugh, *An Overview* (n230) 4; Richard Murphy, 'Property Rights in Personal Information' (1996)

Whalen v Roe[833] case, the U.S. Supreme Court held, albeit in a Fourteenth Amendment situation, that "cases … characterized as protecting 'privacy' have in fact involved at least two different kinds of interests: (one) is the individual interest in avoiding disclosure of personal matters, and another is the interest in independence in making certain kinds of important decisions".[834,835] According to Stephen Mulligan and Chris Linebaugh, "the first of the interests listed in *Whalen* could potentially relate to data protection (as) … the right to avoid certain disclosures has come to be known as the right to 'informational privacy'".[836] Information privacy or information control is defined by Alan Westin as "the claim of individuals, groups, or institutions to determine for themselves when, how, and to what extent information about them is communicated to others".[837,838] When applied to data privacy, Mulligan and Linebaugh point out that the restricted "common law privacy (torts) focus on public disclosure of private facts"[839] combined with the State action doctrine hampers its application to personal data, as it cannot encompass requirements such as data security or purpose limitation nor the private sector. The inability to provide a clearcut definition of the concept of privacy, and, by extension, data privacy, as it is often "determined almost entirely by the context in which it is derived and applied",[840] and the difficulty to balance this interest against other constitutionally protected rights impede public policy intervention in the area of (data) privacy up until today.[841] Lee Bygrave identifies "the enhanced potential for large organizations to amass data on individuals and thereby subject the latter to excessive control"[842] as the fundamental danger to someone's data privacy, which can be extended to also include State entities, and can explain the necessity to promulgate State consumer privacy acts to protect citizens' privacy interests against powerful big tech companies. Similarly, Prosser's "State tort actions are the principal source today of adjudicated legal rights concerning privacy, (but) they offer little protection for information privacy".[843] As Prosser's "torts have proven difficult to

84 GeoLJ 2381, 2390-2393; Ohm (n826) 1162-1163; Purtova, *Property Rights* (n31) 100; Zuiderveen Borgesius *et al.* (n180) 16.

833 *Whalen v Roe* [1977] 429 U.S. 589.

834 *Ibid.* paras 598-600.

835 Mulligan and Linebaugh, *An Overview* (n230) 6; Purtova, *Property Rights* (n31) 110.

836 Mulligan and Linebaugh, *An Overview* (n230) 6.

837 Alan Westin, *Privacy and Freedom* (Athenaeum 1967) 7.

838 Bennett (n140) 70; Cate (n193) 22.

839 Mulligan and Linebaugh, *An Overview* (n230) 7.

840 Cate (n193) 22.

841 Agre (n193) 6; Bennett (n140) 66; Bygrave, *Data Protection Law* (n17) 126-127; Bygrave, *Data Privacy Law* (n37) 28; Cate (n193) 3 and 19; Christofi and Verdoodt (n107) 41-42; Cohen (n38) 1380; Heisenberg (n66) 13-14 and 35-36; Arthur Miller, *The assault on privacy* (University of Michigan Press 1971) 25; Solove, 'Conceptualizing Privacy' (n398) 1088-1089; Zuiderveen Borgesius *et al.* (n180) 12.

842 Bygrave, *Data Privacy Law* (n37) 24.

843 Cate (n193) 90.

apply to data privacy",[844] Daniel Solove expands Prosser's privacy taxonomy by focusing on privacy harmful activities.[845] In Solove's privacy conceptualization, there is not one all-encompassing definition, but there are rather family resemblances between the different privacy aspects that can be placed under the bigger 'umbrella' of privacy.[846] Solove explains in his 2008 *Understanding Privacy*[847] book how attempts to find one common definition for the concept of privacy are either too broad or too narrow.[848] Alternatively, four basic groups of (privacy) harmful activities are suggested, namely: (1) Information Collection, (2) Information Processing, (3) Information Dissemination, and (4) Invasion. Within each of these groups, different but related subgroups are identified, which are discussed below.

Evolutionary interpretation – The American tension between a property and privacy approach cannot only be noticed in the data privacy discussion, but also in the U.S. Supreme Court's jurisprudence on the Fourth Amendment, and more specifically in the *Katz v United States* case. Initially, the Fourth Amendment was perceived as property protection, namely the protection of someone's home against unlawful State intrusions, but was extended in *Katz* to include private activities regardless of the location where these activities take place. Warren and Brandeis observe in this regard that "the common law secures to each individual the right of determining, ordinarily, to what extent his thoughts, sentiments, and emotions shall be communicated to others".[849] This expression initially took place within the confines of someone's home, but expanded to telephone conversations, and all sorts of internet-enabled communication nowadays, which do not only occur in someone's home, but also in public places. Justice Harlan's 'reasonable expectation of privacy' requirement developed in the *Katz* case with regard to people-to-government relations can also be observed in the people-to-people-trade relations context, where the FTC held that private companies have to respect and comply with their consumers' expectations regarding privacy policies and personal data management standards.[850] In the previous chapter it was already critically pointed out that consumers' expectations change and are not always possible to predict. Consequently, a codification of these expectations was suggested to provide clarification for businesses.[851] William Prosser remarks

844 Zuiderveen Borgesius *et al.* (n180) 16.
845 Ann Bartow, 'A Feeling of Unease about Privacy Law' (2006) 155 UPaLRev 52, 52.
846 Solove, *Understanding Privacy* (n194) 45; Solove, 'Why Privacy Matters' (n822) 2-3.
847 Solove, *Understanding Privacy* (n194).
848 Solove, 'Conceptualizing Privacy' (n398) 1090-1094; Solove, *Understanding Privacy* (n194) 12-38.
849 Warren and Brandeis (n825) 198.
850 See *Chapter 3, § 1, B., i).*
851 *Ibid.*

accurately in his *Privacy*[852] article that people's privacy expectations are also subjective, and that they differ "between public and private figures",[853] and even within these more and less publicly known categories of people.[854] Corien Prins uses celebrities' property and privacy interests "in their name and fame"[855] as example; "the magazine Hello! published without permission photographs of the wedding of celebrities Michael Douglas and Catherine Zeta-Jones ... their anger was, however, fueled not so much by the fact that they felt their privacy had been violated ... rather, the couple had entered into an exclusive publication contract with another magazine OK! and had made ... their wedding into a commercial transaction ... by publishing the pictures, Hello! had deprived them of their right to exploit their celebrity status for profit".[856] Consequently, Prins suggests "Why not extend such a property interest to the personal data of ordinary individuals? For, with the advent of digital technologies, hasn't personal data of us all become an asset that is worth real money?"[857] Some celebrities may prefer to exploit their lives and personal information for financial gain, but others, like Samuel Warren, may prefer to keep this information private. It is, therefore, not surprising that judges prefer to grant compensation in cases where objective 'bodily injury' or at least quantifiable injury can be proven, as opposed to subjective hurt feelings.[858] Warren and Brandeis observed in 1890 already that "modern enterprise and invention have, through invasions upon (people's) privacy, subjected (them) to mental pain and distress, far greater than could be inflicted by mere bodily injury",[859] but up until today it is still very difficult to quantify this 'mental pain and distress'. Prosser holds onto the focus on concretely sustained harm, albeit acknowledging that this is difficult to define and often revolves around conceptualizations and interpretations of 'mores'.[860] Solove shifts the focus to privacy harmful activities, not requiring concrete proof of harm. Ann Bartow criticizes Solove's expansion which "fail(s) to sufficiently identify and animate the compelling ways that privacy violations can negatively impact the lives of living, breathing human beings beyond simply provoking feelings of unease",[861] but this interpretation fails in its turn to acknowledge that 'mental pain and distress' can indeed result in far greater harm to the people concerned than 'mere bodily injury'.

---

852 Prosser (n828) 383-423.
853 *Ibid.* 385.
854 *Ibid.* 410-415.
855 Guibault and Bernt Hugenholtz (n533) 224.
856 *Ibid.* 237.
857 *Ibid.* 224.
858 See *Chapter 4, § 3, A., ii), b).*
859 Warren and Brandeis (n825) 196.
860 Prosser (n828) 397-400 and 419-423.
861 Bartow (n845) 52.

Privacy conceptualization – Solove's umbrella conceptualization of privacy has been chosen in this book as the basis for defining the concept of privacy and its relationship with personal data protection in a modern (digital) interpretation. More specifically, the first, second, and third principal groups of privacy harmful activities from Solove's Taxonomy of Privacy are discussed: (1) Information Collection (Surveillance), (2) Information Processing (Aggregation, Identification, and Secondary use), and (3) Information Dissemination (Disclosure). *Information Collection (Surveillance)* consists of the "watching, listening to, or recording of an individual's activities".[862] To this end, the personal data collection practices of private[863] as well as State entities[864] are discussed in this book. *Information Processing* comprises "the way information is stored, manipulated, and used".[865] The *Information Processing* principal group of (privacy) harmful activities is further divided into subgroups, of which three are dealt with in this book. Firstly, the privacy harmful sub-activity of (data) *Aggregation* occurs when different types of data (usually also from different sources) about the same person are collected and put together, revealing information that cannot be deducted from the separate information sets individually.[866] Secondly, the privacy harmful sub-activity of *Identification* occurs when the collected (anonymized) data is reconnected to their original owners, identifying them. Thirdly, the privacy harmful sub-activity of *Secondary Use* is related to the purpose limitation requirement and occurs when the collected data is used for different unrelated purposes than the ones they were collected for, without the owner's consent. *Information Dissemination (Disclosure)* consists of "the revelation of truthful information about a person that affects the way others judge her reputation".[867,868] Each of these (sub-)groups cover (data) privacy-related elements, and the occurrence of each element can endanger people's (data) privacy interests by harming their reputation, their feelings, their public image, their level of control over their personal information available (and to whom), and the way in which they eventually behave.

ii) Property, Self-Determination, and Individual Control

Liberal market – The predominantly liberty-focused and liberal market approach of the U.S. Bill of Rights gives extensive responsibility to the people to pursue their own happiness, protect their private property, and make their own choices

---

862 Solove, *Understanding Privacy* (n194) 104.
863 See *Chapter 3*.
864 See *Chapter 5*.
865 Solove, *Understanding Privacy* (n194) 104.
866 *Ibid.*; Solove, 'Why Privacy Matters' (n822) 4.
867 Solove, *Understanding Privacy* (n194) 105.
868 *Ibid.* 103-105.

of which they will bear the consequences.[869] As a result, "U.S. scholars were the first to propose that personal information should be formally recognized as an object of property rights (in the early 1970s)".[870] Chris Hoofnagle *et al.* point to the people's responsibility "to read and critically evaluate privacy notices, and make choices in the marketplace based on this careful study".[871] If they disagree, "individuals are expected to rationally opt out of undesirable platforms and implement privacy-protecting tools when necessary".[872] The opt-out system places the burden on individuals, as opposed to businesses, to actively engage in privacy settings that reflect their preferences. People can exercise individual control over their personal data when they do not wish for businesses providing services to use this data by actively opting out of the companies' data collection and processing practices.[873] In consumer relations with businesses, the 'Notice and Choice' principle provides the requested balance, at least in theory. Businesses must provide information about their data collection and processing practices ('Notice'), which enables consumers to make informed decisions about whether to engage with the business concerned ('Choice').[874] Today's digital world impedes, however, in practice the "withdraw(al) from these platforms when the digital service has become a public infrastructure everyone widely needs and uses … (shifting the) framing of privacy … from 'privacy as dignity' to 'privacy as commodity' over the past decades".[875]

Whose property? – The individual whose personal data is concerned is, logically, the main proprietor of this data. Lucas Bergkamp advocates, however, the 'labor-desert theory'[876] where "the person that collects and manipulates the data has made the investments to create a valuable resource: the (individual to whom the data relates) has not in any significant way contributed to that value creation".[877] The added value created by data processing activities, and hence by the effort of the data processor, is remunerated "under (the) commodity frame, (where) the creator of data – a user – is not necessarily equal to the monetary beneficiary of the data – a digital platform".[878] Bergkamp's statement is controversial, as the processing activities are enabled by people's personal data, and processing would not be possible without first collecting the unique personal data.

---

869 See *Chapter 4, § 3, A., i)*.
870 Purtova, *Property Rights* (n31) 2.
871 Hoofnagle *et al.* (n11) 73.
872 Baik (n193) 2.
873 Heisenberg (n66) 159; Lynskey, *The foundations* (n42) 234.
874 Hartzog and Richards (n240) 1001; Hoofnagle *et al.* (n11) 79; Lynskey, *The foundations* (n42) 233; Newell *et al.* (n229) 1066-1067; Pałka, 'Data Management' (n44) 602-604; Solove, 'Introduction' (n43) 1880-1891.
875 Baik (n193) 2.
876 Cohen (n38) 1381.
877 Bergkamp (n394) 39.
878 Baik (n193) 2.

"The most vital resource for the Information Industry is the user"[879] and "at least some property rights in personal data should be given to people whose data are feeding the ... information economy"[880] as they are eventually the owners and creators of their own personal data, according to Nadezhda Purtova. The CJEU tilted the balance to the other extreme in the 2004 *Fixtures Marketing Ltd.*[881] case where it stated that "in determining whether a database owner has made the necessary substantial investment in obtaining, presenting or verifying information, courts must disregard any investment in the creation of the information so obtained, presented or verified ... (the CJEU) clearly rejected the proposition that 'obtaining' information includes creating information".[882] Daniel Solove finds a middle ground between both statements where the importance of the involvement of both parties, the individual and the data processor, is acknowledged; "the market value of information is not created exclusively by the labor of the individual to whom it relates but in part by the third party that compiles the information".[883] Purtova places this 'propertization' movement around the time when "behavioural marketing and (processed) personal data (became) the 'new oil' of the modern economy, (while also being) a means of giving back to the individual control over data pertaining to him".[884] Personal data cannot just be qualified as a commodity or 'thing' where "one person's use of the data makes the information less useful for others".[885] If, after all, person A is the proprietor of a car, his use will impede person B's use of the same car as person B can only use the car when person A is not driving and gives person B permission to drive ... Commercial models using personal data have shown, on the contrary, that there is economic value to be extracted from personal data, and that this "data may be replicated many times over without losing any of its utility".[886] Daniel Solove concurs that "information can be easily transmitted, and once known by others, cannot be eradicated from their minds ... unlike physical objects, information can be possessed simultaneously within the minds (and arguably databases) of millions".[887] Julie Cohen provides in her 2000 *Examined Lives: Informational Privacy and the Subject as Object*[888] article a linguistic analysis of "property talk about privacy in general, and data privacy in particular ... 'private' ... means 'not public' in the sense that a secret is not publicly known ... 'private' also means 'not common-owned' and set apart from that which is common

879 Purtova, 'The illusion' (n396) 104.
880 *Ibid.* 86.
881 C-444/02 *Fixtures Marketing Ltd v Oy Veikkaus Ab* [2004] para 53.
882 Guibault and Bernt Hugenholtz (n533) 171.
883 Solove, 'Conceptualizing Privacy' (n398) 1113.
884 Purtova, 'The illusion' (n396) 84.
885 Fromholz (n74) 464.
886 *Ibid.*
887 Solove, 'Conceptualizing Privacy' (n398) 1113.
888 Cohen (n38) 1373-1438.

or owned by others".[889] Cohen concludes that "we lack a word for describing control over things without legal or beneficial ownership of them – a word that signifies that the thing described is both not common and not owned".[890] From a European fundamental rights perspective, personal data is inalienable, as it is narrowly related to the core of people's personhood and their human dignity. From an American liberal market perspective, personal data is an alienable good that can be sold or given to someone else, including to a private company. Orla Lynskey warns that the latter approach may entail the risk that "people (will) treat their personal data more like their car than their soul".[891] To view personal data only through a property lens is to lose "the intermediate value of data protection as an instrument aimed at fostering the autonomic capabilities of individuals and therefore not something they may dispose of or trade on the market of personal information".[892] Valorization in a data privacy discussion cannot only be expressed in terms of monetary gains or finances; people's thoughts, ideas, and reputations also have an intrinsic personal value and reflect who they are, contributing to self-development and eventually a democratic society. Nadezhda Purtova stressed that legislative "inaction (would) effectively amount to legitimization of property rights 'grabbed' by the Information Industry, rendering the individual defenceless in the face of corporate power eroding his/her autonomy, privacy and right to informational self-determination",[893] referencing the Californian Gold Rush. According to *Umbeck's theory of emerging property rights and the data rush*,[894] it was possible to equally divide property rights among all the gold miners as they could be considered equal. The situation is different in the case of personal data, where individuals do not have equal power to contest powerful private entities' establishment of property rights in the personal data of the former.[895] Paul Schwartz concurs with Purtova that "a privacy statute in this area is needed to provide for government enforcement of privacy standards and promises"[896] as the trading mechanisms are set out unilaterally by the private sector. The promulgation of State consumer data privacy acts in the United States, and, by extension, the EU data protection initiatives, became the remedy to provide individual control over 'not-common and not-owned' personal information.

Individual control – The focus on people's active engagement in protecting and handling their personal data as they wish, combined with the default 'Notice and

889 *Ibid.* 1379.
890 *Ibid.*
891 Lynskey, *The foundations* (n42) 238.
892 Gutwirth *et al.* (n32) 50.
893 Purtova, 'The illusion' (n396) 84.
894 John Umbeck, *A Theory of Property Rights* (1st edn, Iowa State University Press 1981) 158p.
895 Cohen (n38) 1375; Purtova, 'The illusion' (n396) 87-88.
896 Paul Schwartz, 'Property, Privacy, and Personal Data' (2004) 117 HarvLRev 2056, 2120.

Choice' principle, which is grounded in people's consent, leads several authors[897] to link personal data's property conceptualization with people's ability to exercise individual control over their data. Alan Westin's definition of information control as set out above is interpreted as entailing "a sort of 'intangible property right' held by each individual over his or her personal data and that individuals (can) legally 'sell' their personal information on the market and, in that way, 'choose their optimal mix of privacy without parental intervention from the State'".[898] From a liberal market perspective, people have full control and power of disposition over their personal data. If they decide to transfer, whether through a private agreement, their personal data to a private company, they lose their power of disposition over this data, their property rights are terminated and conveyed to someone else. The buyer can, in its turn, "freely transfer to third parties whatever interest the buyer acquired from (the) initial seller".[899] Paul Schwartz warns that if personal data protection is left completely to the trade market and businesses, "people (will) trade away too much of their propertized data and thereby erode existing levels of privacy".[900,901] The possibility to transfer or share personal data is in today's digital world indeed somewhat unfortunately translated into a binary framework of 'yes I share my personal data' or 'no I do not make use of the service or product'.[902] Mark Lemley admits that "we must be willing to accept ... that there is no good 'market solution' and endorse some government regulation of the behavior of data collectors".[903] In this case, "property rights (in personal data) are limited by data protection requirements".[904] Westin's information control/privacy conceptualization "led naturally to a set of (these) procedural guarantees to assist individuals to determine for themselves when, how and to what extent information about them is communicated to others".[905]

B. EU APPROACH TOWARDS DATA PRIVACY

Three situations – The right to privacy, and, by extension, the concept of privacy, encompasses, broadly speaking, three types of situations; privacy as seclusion in a people-to-people relationship, privacy as non-interference in a

---

897 Bergkamp (n394) 38; Buitelaar (n528) 176-177 and 193-194; Fromholz (n74) 464; Lynskey, *The foundations* (n42) 231 and 252; Purtova, 'The illusion' (n396) 84.

898 Gutwirth *et al.* (n32) 69.

899 Pamela Samuelson, 'Privacy as Intellectual Property?' (2000) 52 SLR 1125, 1138.

900 Schwartz, 'Property' (n896) 2077.

901 Cohen (n38) 1391; Schwartz, 'Property' (n896) 2082 and 2101.

902 Buitelaar (n528) 176-177; Cate and Mayer-Schönberger (n362) 67; Cohen (n38) 1397; Guibault and Bernt Hugenholtz (n533) 246-247; Hoofnagle *et al.* (n11) 79; Pałka, 'Data Management' (n44) 603; Purtova, *Property Rights* (n31) 179.

903 Mark Lemley, 'Private Property' (2000) 52 SLR 1545, 1554.

904 Purtova, *Property Rights* (n31) 195.

905 Bennett (n140) 96-97.

people-to-government relationship, and privacy as individual control.[906] Privacy as *seclusion* in a people-to-people relationship enables personal development by protecting people's communication (such as letters or emails) and by allowing people to express their ideas and opinions freely in their personal space. People need a certain level of secrecy in their lives in order to discuss, confront and try out certain ideas or beliefs that they might have. These confrontations shape people's opinions as they stimulate engagement in discussions where arguments can be confirmed or rebutted, and contribute to the establishment of democratic societies.[907] Similarly, "the strong protection of personal data continues to be a 'necessary utopia' (S. Simitis) if one wishes to safeguard the democratic nature of our political systems".[908] Privacy as *non-interference* in a people-to-government relationship provides people with the liberty to live and organize their lives according to their plans and beliefs without interference from the State, such as unlawfully entering someone's private home or unlawful interferences with people's lives and bodies.[909] Finally, privacy as *individual control* empowers people to make decisions for and about themselves, such as which information they are willing to share and with whom. In a personal data protection context, individual control can be "associated with the ideal of self-determination"[910] as it aims to restore, to a certain extent, the decisional power of the people over their personal data in people-to-government and people-to-private-companies relations.

i) *Human Dignity, Self-Determination, and Personal Identity*

EU roots – Human dignity has traditionally been the source of human rights protection in EU and international human rights law.[911] Lee Bygrave observes that "in much of Europe … protection of privacy tends to be intimately tied to protection of dignity and honour".[912] Several authors[913] trace the roots of the

---

906 Bennett (n140) 13; Buitelaar (n528) 185; Gutwirth *et al.* (n32) 61-67; Jerry Kang, 'Information Privacy in Cyberspace Transactions' (1998) 50 SLR 1193, 1202-1203; Lynskey, *The foundations* (n42) 101-103; Solove, 'Conceptualizing Privacy' (n398) 1088-1092.

907 Buitelaar (n528) 184-186; J C Hans Buitelaar, 'Post-mortem privacy and informational self-determination' (2017) 19 EthicsInfTechnol 129, 134; Cohen (n38) 1425-1426; Charles Fried, 'Privacy' (1968) 77 YLJ 475, 483-484; Fromholz (n74) 465; Poullet, 'Data protection' (n45) 213-216; Solove, 'Conceptualizing Privacy' (n398) 1102-1109; Westin (n837) 24-34.

908 Gutwirth *et al.* (n32) 78.

909 Miller (n841) 204; Rauhofer (n364) 187; Solove, 'Conceptualizing Privacy' (n398) 1099-1102.

910 Bygrave, *Data Protection Law* (n17) 130.

911 Article 1 EU Charter; Article 1 Universal Declaration of Human Rights, United Nations, 10 Dec 1948.

912 Bygrave, *Data Privacy Law* (n37) 112.

913 Bennett (n140) 30; Bergkamp (n394) 32-36; Buitelaar (n528) 174; Cate (n193) 43-44; Hoofnagle *et al.* (n11) 82; Rauhofer (n364) 193; Whitman (n392) 1164-1171; Zuiderveen Borgesius *et al.* (n180) 14.

privacy-human dignity link back to the Second World War, when personal data from Jewish citizens was (ab)used by the government to track and detain them. The cruelties and inhumane treatment of human beings during that time are considered a low point in European history. The enshrining of human dignity in the German constitution, but also in other international legal documents, is the cornerstone to ensuring that these cruelties will 'never again' occur and that personal data will not be (ab)used by the government. The European Convention on Human Rights (ECHR) was created in 1950 as a reaction to the cruelties of the Second World War.[914] Subsequently, the protection of personal data was categorized within the right to privacy enshrined in Article 8.[915] The EU Charter is a younger legal instrument created in 2000 and qualifies personal data protection as a fundamental right in itself,[916] given the confrontation since the 1970s with the "dehumanizing qualities of automated record keeping (and automatic data processing), where the individual is no longer a living, breathing person but a file with a name, number and label".[917] Stefano Rodotà understands "data protection (therefore) as an expression of human dignity".[918] James Whitman explains that the Nazi cruelties were only a catalyst for the elevation of human dignity, but that the core idea of human dignity and its link with privacy had emerged in Europe in the 17th century. In the strictly hierarchical and monarchical society of Louis XIV's France, the right to privacy was already entrenched with the right to human dignity, albeit only for the wealthy aristocrats, where "public humiliation was used as a tool of disempowerment".[919] As these prominent societal figures had an image and social status to uphold, infringements of their wealthy image were penalized, though rather under a form of 'disrespect' instead of privacy as we know it today. Alan Westin provides a continuation of this evolution as "demands for legal protection of a right to personal privacy (were) made by elite groups in modern democracies: by political and cultural dissenters, by celebrities seeking some respite from intrusive cameramen and reporters, and by intellectual elements".[920] The fascist movement was a catalyst for the spread of this upper-class protection of social status and image, and hence the idea of privacy protection, to a broader group of (certain) citizens. "Fascist politics involved precisely the promise that all members of the nation-state would be equal in 'honor' – that all racial Germans, for example, would be

---

914 Bergkamp (n394) 33; Christofi and Verdoodt (n107) 27-28; Pałka, 'Data Management' (n44) 618.

915 See *Chapter 3, § 2, B., i).*

916 See *Chapter 3, § 3, B., ii).*

917 Ruth Cohen, *Whose File Is It Anyway? How open records can improve record-keeping* (National Council for Civil Liberties 1982) 10.

918 Gutwirth *et al.* (n32) 82.

919 Kohl (n398) 745.

920 Alan Westin, 'Entering the Era of Databank Regulation and How We Got There' in OECD, *Policy Issues in Data Protection and Privacy* (OECD 1976) 95.

'masters'".[921,922] Socialist and communist politics also sought to establish that everyone is considered 'equal'. The emergence of hate speech and anti-discrimination laws to "intervene in practices of public humiliation"[923] can, according to Uta Kohl, be situated within the same trend. Whitman concludes that it was a combination of, firstly, the differences between the upper and lower classes, secondly, the spread of 'upper class rights' to the whole of society, and thirdly, the Nazi cruelties that established the notion that everyone's dignity had to be respected.[924] The fundamental rights' protection afforded by the EU legal framework differs, consequently, between natural and legal persons as it is related to safeguarding human dignity. Peter Oliver quotes Lord Thurlow[925] to explain why legal persons are often excluded from the EU legal framework on personal data protection[926] by referring to the practice of public humiliation as punishment: "Did you ever expect a corporation to have a conscience, when it has no soul to be damned and no body to be kicked?".[927] More recently, in 2006, ECtHR Advocate General Leendert Geelhoed shared a similar opinion that "it is not possible simply to transpose the findings of the European Court of Human Rights (for natural persons) without more to legal persons or undertakings".[928,929] The ECtHR confirmed in the 2011 *Uj v Hungary*[930] case that "there is a difference between the commercial reputational interests of a company and the reputation of an individual concerning his or her social status (whereas) the latter might have repercussions on one's dignity, for the Court interests of commercial reputation are devoid of that moral dimension".[931,932] The elevated qualification of the right to personal data protection as a separate and self-standing fundamental right in Article 8 EU Charter might lead to its privacy and human dignity roots being forgotten.[933] This link is made in Article 88 GDPR, which explicitly includes "rules … to safeguard the data subject's human dignity".[934] The European Data Protection Supervisor (EDPS) also stated in Opinion 4/2015 that "respect for, and the safeguarding of, human dignity could be the counterweight to the pervasive surveillance and asymmetry of power which now confronts the

---

921 Whitman (n392) 1166.
922 Kohl (n398) 745-746; Westin (n837) 28-40; Whitman (n392) 1166.
923 Kohl (n398) 745.
924 *Ibid.*; Whitman (n392) 1165-1189.
925 "Lord Thurlow was a Lord Chancellor of the late eighteenth century".: de Vries *et al.* (n525) 288.
926 See *Chapter 3, § 3, B., iv), b).*
927 de Vries *et al.* (n525) 288.
928 Opinion of Advocate General Geelhoed delivered on 19 Jan 2006 *Commission of the European Communities v SGL Carbon* App no C-301/04 P para 63.
929 de Vries *et al.* (n525) 294.
930 *Uj v Hungary* App no 23954/10 (ECtHR, 19 Oct 2011).
931 *Ibid.* para 22.
932 de Vries *et al.* (n525) 314.
933 Gutwirth *et al.* (n32) 50 and 71-75; Tzanou (n526) 93-94.
934 Article 88 GDPR.

individual ... privacy is an integral part of human dignity, and the right to data protection was originally conceived in the 1970s and 1980s as a way of compensating the potential for the erosion of privacy and dignity through large scale personal data processing".[935]

Personal identity and (informational) self-determination – Other authors[936] make a similar link between human dignity, privacy, and personal data protection "by arguing in favour of the interpretation of the protection of privacy as protection of personal identity".[937] "The basic attribute of an effective right of privacy is the individual's ability to control the circulation of information relating to himself",[938] as people's identity is reflected in the personal image that they uphold in society.[939] Translated to the digital age, this encompasses people's digital identity and their online personal image, since "personal information plays a constitutive role of who I am and can become".[940] This personal image also differs depending on the circumstances in which people find themselves, such as at home or at work, while "personal data processing erodes the ability of the individual to self-present in different ways in different circumstances, thereby encouraging individuals to abandon their multiple selves and behave in one way in all circumstances".[941] Uta Kohl explains that "in the Continental European culture of privacy, privacy is ... preoccupied with one's public image as the foundation for self-authorship (and) about controlling one's image in the public realm".[942] When, on the contrary, a person's digital "profile (is) drawn up without one's influence providing a wrongful picture of oneself, (this) gives rise to irritation or distress, (as) it (prevents people) from being able to present (their) self-identity to others in the manner (they) see fit".[943,944] In this understanding, personal data protection functions as a means to an end, not an end in itself.[945] "It is not "data" that is in need of protection; it is the individual

935 EDPS, 'Opinion 4/2015 Towards a New Digital Ethics: Data, Dignity and Technology' (*europa.eu*, 11 Sep 2015) 12.

936 Buitelaar (n528) 182-187; Bygrave, *Data Protection Law* (n17) 166-168; Guibault and Bernt Hugenholtz (n533) 238; Kohl (n398) 745-747; Solove, 'Conceptualizing Privacy' (n398) 1116-1119; Westin (n837) 33-34.

937 Luciano Floridi, 'On Human Dignity as a Foundation for the Right to Privacy' (2016) 29 PhilosTechnol 307, 308.

938 Miller (n841) 25.

939 Buitelaar (n528) 188.

940 Floridi (n937) 308.

941 Lynskey, *The foundations* (n42) 215.

942 Kohl (n398) 744.

943 Buitelaar (n528) 185.

944 Agre (n193) 7-8; Vogiatzoglou (n737) 206.

945 Bennett (n140) 33-34; Cohen (n38) 1386-1387; Gutwirth *et al.* (n32) 45-76; Solove, 'Conceptualizing Privacy' (n398) 1148-1149; Tzanou (n526) 93; Vogiatzoglou (n737) 216; Westin (n837) 39.

to whom the data relates",[946] according to Viktor Mayer-Schönberger. A similar interpretation was given in the December 1983 *Census*[947] case where the German Federal Constitutional Court acknowledged that "the protection of personal data (is) not an end in itself or a final or primary value but 'merely' a tool (though an essential one), making possible the *exercise* of the fundamental and basic individual 'right' to self-development, while being itself distinct from autonomy, self-determination or self-development (depending on how one calls the primary values sustaining privacy)".[948,949] Luciano Floridi explains that human dignity is grounded in human exceptionalism, which exists in modern philosophy of the human ability to self-determination and rational autonomy.[950] Lee Bygrave brings all the formerly mentioned elements together and concludes that "data protection laws are essentially about safeguarding privacy and/or informational autonomy/self-determination",[951] which is confirmed in ECtHR jurisprudence.[952] Julie Cohen similarly links the 'liberty of self-determination' directly to personal data protection as "the power (for the individual) to define oneself to the world in the way one wishes".[953] Consumer profiling practices and police surveillance at public events inhibit people's self-determination and autonomy to choose freely, as in the first case their freedom of choice is limited and in the second case influenced by potential (negative) consequences, impacting their human dignity and the existence of a free and democratic society.[954]

Criticisms – It was illustrated above that both the right to privacy and the right to personal data protection are grounded in the protection of human dignity and aim to uphold it. These fundamental rights are exercised through people's ability to (informational) self-determination and the construction of their personal

---

946 Agre (n193) 219.

947 German BVerfG, Census Judgment (n744).

948 Gutwirth *et al.* (n32) 52.

949 German BVerfG, Census Judgment (n744); Bennett (n140) 41-42 and 76; Buitelaar (n528) 184; Bygrave, *Data Protection Law* (n17) 108; Bygrave, *Data Privacy Law* (n37) 28 and 179-180; Christofi and Verdoodt (n107) 30-31; Gutwirth *et al.* (n32) 50-54 and 69-79; Lynskey, 'Deconstructing' (n534) 572 and 591-592; Lynskey, *The foundations* (n42) 178-179; Poullet, 'Data protection' (n45) 215-216; Rauhofer (n364) 187-193; Tzanou (n526) 89-90; Vogiatzoglou and Valcke (n400) 14.

950 Floridi (n937) 309.

951 Bygrave, *Data Protection Law* (n17) 168.

952 *Daróczy v Hungary* App no 44378/05 (ECtHR, 1 Jul 2008) paras 32-33; *Satakunnan Markkinapörssi Oy and Satamedia Oy v Finland* App no 931/13 (ECtHR, 27 Jun 2017) para 137; de Terwangne, 'Convention 108+' (n383) 3.

953 Cohen (n38) 1400.

954 Article 29 WP, 'Opinion 1/2008 on data protection issues related to search engines' (WP148, 4 Apr 2008) 7-8; Buitelaar (n528) 175; Bygrave, *Data Privacy Law* (n37) 112; Cohen (n38) 1423-1424; Floridi (n937) 307-312; Gutwirth *et al.* (n32) 46-70; Kosta and Kamara (n37) 473-480; Lynskey, *The foundations* (n42) 215; Rauhofer (n364) 193; Schwartz, 'Property' (n896) 2087-2088.

(digital) identity where they present their image to society and the (digital) world. The right to personal data protection can, in this interpretation, indeed be considered as a 'tool' or 'a means to an end' to protect people's human dignity, personal identity, self-determination, and autonomy, and hence their privacy, in an evolving digital world. Orla Lynskey criticizes this conceptualization in four ways.[955] Firstly, there is no conclusive "consensus in the EU as to the precise content of the right to human dignity"[956] and what it exactly encompasses. While not aiming to provide a definition or clearcut conceptualization of human dignity, the discussion above has provided an overview of the protected interests and their relationship with human dignity as interpreted in the context of personal data protection. Secondly, if personal data protection law safeguards people's human dignity, people "*must* be allowed to waive (their) rights as such a waiver constitutes an exercise of (their) rights (and) any prohibition in data protection legislation would constitute a breach of human dignity, as it would entail the delegation of power over the data subject's rights from the data subject to the legislature".[957] Julie Cohen[958] and Corien Prins[959] concur with this observation. There are, however, examples of already existing situations where government regulation limits people's ability to waive certain protections in order to protect their human dignity. Some people may consider certain allowed behavior as inhumane, such as tattoos or sadomasochism. Even though tattoos are nowadays largely accepted as long as people give their permission, the Nazi detainees who had their numbers tattooed on their arms against their will perceived this as inhumane and degrading treatment. The line between allowed and inhumane practices can be more difficult to draw in the case of certain (sadomasochistic) practices, but the sole fact that someone 'agrees' to certain practices does not always mean that everything is allowed, and the government should and does intervene when situations become too violent or go too far. While, understandably, not everyone will agree with this statement, certain governmental interventions do seem necessary to protect people and safeguard their human dignity. Limitations on people's ability to choose freely or to agree to waive their (fundamental) rights, giving priority to the protection of these rights by the State or legislature, are already incorporated in many European legal systems where the State has an active duty to protect people's rights, including safeguarding their human dignity.[960] Thirdly, the provisions on the fundamental rights to personal data protection and to privacy can be found in the Chapter on

---

955 Lynskey, *The foundations* (n42) 99-101.

956 *Ibid.* 99.

957 *Ibid.* 100.

958 Cohen (n38) 1391-1392.

959 Guibault and Bernt Hugenholtz (n533) 241-242.

960 See *Chapter 4, § 3, B., i).*

'freedoms' as opposed to the Chapter on 'human dignity' in the EU Charter.[961] The discussion in this book takes a broader perspective than the EU Charter and includes the ECHR as well as secondary EU law. An analysis of the exact positioning of the rights to personal data protection and privacy within the EU Charter and the reasons for this positioning are, therefore, outside the scope of this discussion. Fourthly, if personal data protection aims at safeguarding human dignity, there is a "fundamental tension between the assertion that human dignity is an essential element which underpins data protection and the ostensible desire on the part of the EU to commodify personal data and to develop an EU market for its trade".[962] The right to personal data protection has only obtained a fundamental right status in the European Union. Not all EU Member States necessarily agree with this status elevation, as Orla Lynskey observed that "while this inclusion of a right to data protection in (Article 8 of the EU) Charter reflects the recognition of such an independent right in several EU Member States, it cannot be said that there is a 'common constitutional tradition' vis-à-vis data protection across EU Member States ... several Member States, including the Netherlands, Spain, and Finland treat the right to data protection as a subset of the right to privacy",[963] which can consequently be balanced with other rights and (economic) interests. The sole act of trading personal data does not infringe on people's human dignity, as it is, again, a means to an end. It is rather the way in which this data is traded and processed that can harm people's dignity. The emphasis should, therefore, be placed on the purposes of data processing instead of on protecting the data as such. The use of personal data for the improvement of medical research or data security serves, for example, a beneficial societal purpose.[964] Enhanced education and awareness campaigns can equip people with the ability to make more conscious choices about whether to share their personal data without endangering their human dignity. It is important to not only focus on the protection of personal data as such, but to also take into account the broader context in which this processing is taking place.

Related or different? – The relationship between the right to personal data protection and the right to privacy can be categorized in three ways: "(i) data protection and privacy are separate but complementary rights[965] (data protection ≠ privacy); (ii) data protection is a subset of the right to privacy[966] (data protection ≤ privacy); and (iii) data protection is an independent right which serves a multitude of functions including, but not limited to, the protection of

961 Lynskey, *The foundations* (n42) 100.
962 *Ibid.* 101.
963 *Ibid.* 89.
964 Cate and Mayer-Schönberger (n362) 72; Pałka, 'Data Management' (n44) 630; Solove, 'Introduction' (n43) 1893-1896.
965 Lynskey, *The foundations* (n42) 94-101.
966 *Ibid.* 101-103.

privacy[967] (data protection > privacy)".[968] The last model is often employed in the EU as both rights are separately enshrined in the EU Charter (privacy in Article 7 and personal data protection in Article 8), and a separate right for personal data protection was created in Article 16 TFEU.[969] Even though scholars agree on the origins of the right to personal data protection as it is rooted in Article 8 ECHR right to privacy, they disagree on whether both rights can still be equaled.[970] "Some (may) argue that privacy protection ... and personal data protection ... have evolved into two highly distinct concepts, whereby personal data protection nowadays has nothing to do with fundamental freedoms",[971] but in Corien Prins' understanding both rights are "all about controlling information power".[972] While Lee Bygrave shares the opinion that "data protection laws typically express as one of their primary aims the safeguarding of an individual person's right to privacy",[973] Orla Lynskey observes that "the (EU) Charter's inclusion of an independent right to data protection differentiates it from other international human rights documents which treat data protection as a subset of the right to privacy".[974] Moreover, the right to personal data protection grants individuals proactive rights to ensure compliance as opposed to the right to privacy.[975] Lynskey continues that "the right to privacy clearly applies in situations when data protection legislation does not ... what distinguishes data protection from so-called 'informational privacy' is that data protection applies to a broader range of personal data processing activities and grants individuals more rights over this broader range of data (and hence) more control over more personal data than privacy".[976] Bygrave concurs with Lynskey regarding the latter remark, but explains that this will depend on which definition of 'privacy' is chosen to compare with.[977] This book advocates the second model, accepted by the majority of scholars,[978] where personal data protection is not only a facet of the right to privacy but also a digital evolutionary interpretation and application of this right. The 1995 Directive as well as the Article 29 WP advisory documents include many references to the right to privacy as the foundation of the right

---

967 *Ibid.* 103-104.
968 *Ibid.* 90.
969 See *Chapter 3, § 3, B., ii).*
970 Kohl (n398) 738.
971 Guibault and Bernt Hugenholtz (n533) 227.
972 *Ibid.* 228.
973 Bygrave, *Data Protection Law* (n17) 37.
974 Lynskey, 'Deconstructing' (n534) 569-570.
975 *Ibid.* 592.
976 Lynskey, *The foundations* (n42) 11.
977 Bygrave, *Data Privacy Law* (n37) 3 and 28-29.
978 E.g.: Agre (n193) 2-3; Lynskey, *The foundations* (n42) 101-103; Poullet, 'Data protection' (n45) 214; Daniel Solove, *The Digital Person* (NYU Press 2004) 93-123; Westin (n837) 158.

to personal data protection.[979] In Recommendation 3/99, the Article 29 WP stated that "(the 1995) Directive harmonises the conditions of the protection of the right to privacy".[980] Article 29 WP's Opinion 10/2001 reiterated that "these Directives aim to ensure ... the right to privacy with regard to the processing of personal data and ... the respect of the (ECHR), in particular article 8 thereof".[981] On the 1st European Data Protection Day in 2007, the Article 29 WP proclaimed that "fundamental rights (and) in particular the fundamental right to privacy is best defended by an independent data protection authority".[982] When the Treaty of Lisbon was adopted in 2007, and with it the revised TEU and TFEU together with the EU Charter, personal data protection became a (fundamental) right in itself. Even though personal data protection was elevated to a separate (fundamental) right, the Article 29 WP recalled its origins as "references to the right to privacy in article 1 of Convention 108 and article 1 of the 1995 Directive show that the right to data protection inter-relate(s) with the right to privacy, (even though) the right to protection of personal data has evolved as a separate right in the subsequent (EU Charter), which as well as providing for the right to a private and family life under (Article) 7, also provides an explicit right to the protection of personal data under (Article) 8".[983] Maria Tzanou stated in her 2013 article on *Data protection as a fundamental right next to privacy?* that "the way in which data protection has been drafted obstructs the right itself to operate independently from privacy ... data protection is not 'mature' enough, as it currently stands, to operate alone".[984] Consequently, she endorses Daniel Solove's conceptualization where "privacy is an umbrella notion for a plurality of things that covers aspects of data protection in any case".[985] J C (Hans) Buitelaar perceives that "(information privacy) is not a new kind of privacy but, in a sense, a subcategory of the concept".[986] Uta Kohl concludes that "although data protection law is framed in seemingly technical concepts and language (e.g. 'data' instead of 'information' ...) and present(ed) as a form of data management, it is clearly an expanded version of privacy ... with its focus on (the protection of) 'personal' rather than 'private' information".[987] The findings in this book support the opinion of these authors.

---

979 See *Chapter 3, § 3, B., i), a), and iii).*
980 Article 29 WP, 'Recommendation 3/99' (n528) 3.
981 Article 29 WP, 'Opinion 10/2001' (n610) 3.
982 Article 29 WP, 'Resolution by the Article 29 Working Party on the 1st European Data Protection Day' (WP130, 24 Jan 2007) 2.
983 Article 29 WP, 'Opinion 01/2014' (n631) 3-4.
984 Tzanou (n526) 97.
985 *Ibid.* 96.
986 Buitelaar (n528) 187.
987 Kohl (n398) 749.

ii) *Individual Control*

Decisional or informational privacy – (Data) privacy as self-determination is closely linked to individual control, which is also conceptualized as decisional or informational privacy. "Ensuring individual control over personal data is widely perceived as the goal of data protection and is often highlighted as such (not only by scholars but also) by political leaders and commentators",[988] as well as by "the entire tech industry (which concurs) that privacy is, in fact, all about control".[989] Recital 7 of the EU GDPR explicitly states that "natural persons should have control of their own personal data".[990] The exercise of individual control is grounded in safeguarding human dignity as "it respects peoples' choices"[991] and enables (informational) autonomy.[992] Consequently, Orla Lynskey and Stefano Rodotà share the observation that "enhanced individual control is … one of the objectives underpinning EU data protection law (which in its turn) is a necessary element of this enhanced control".[993,994] Privacy as individual control was the third situation discussed above which privacy encompassed. This conceptualization can also be brought in relation to the first, privacy as seclusion, and second, privacy as non-interference situations. For the first, people-to-people, and by extension people-to-private-companies, situation, the prohibition for private companies to unduly interfere with people's decisional rights aims at ensuring that people can engage in free decision-making, which can be hampered by consumer profiling. "Usage of personal data has vital importance for the privacy of citizens in the information society where the role of personal data can be compared with the role played by oil in the industrial society … how personal data is processed and accordingly the level of privacy is determined by the legal boundaries creating fences in defense of intruders aiming at violating privacy",[995] according to Peter Blume. "The data privacy debate is a debate about freedom of choice"[996] and "empowering individuals",[997] since private actors had become too strong to negotiate with, resulting in a loss of control and autonomy for individuals.[998] This interpretation supports government intervention in the private sector to actively protect people's rights in interpersonal and commercial relations. For the second people-to-government situation, surveillance at public

[988] Cate and Mayer-Schönberger (n362) 68.
[989] Hartzog (n266) 424.
[990] Recital 7 GDPR.
[991] Hartzog (n266) 426.
[992] Buitelaar (n528) 175; Tzanou (n526) 89.
[993] Lynskey, *The foundations* (n42) 11.
[994] Christofi and Verdoodt (n107) 5; Gutwirth *et al.* (n32) 79.
[995] Blume (n528) 4.
[996] Cohen (n38) 1391.
[997] *Ibid.* 1396.
[998] Bennett (n140) 26.

events using facial recognition or biometric identification technologies, where people cannot control how the collected data will be used or affect them, hampers people's exercise of their freedoms and expression of their ideas and thoughts, which does not only limit their free development as a person in a way they desire, but also a free and democratic society at large.[999]

Consent – The EU legal framework for personal data protection aims at restoring people's ability to exercise individual control over their data by the provision of detailed (micro-)rights. These consist, among others, of data rectification rights, erasure rights, and access rights.[1000] The most important micro-right is situated in the requirement for legitimate processing, where six non-hierarchical justifying grounds of equal status are provided, of which people's consent is one. Recently, the predominant emphasis on consent as acceptable legal basis for data processing activities has been noticed in decisions by the CJEU[1001] and the EDPB,[1002] which led to a decrease in acceptance of the other possible legal bases for legitimate processing set out in Article 6 of the GDPR.[1003] "Where a data protection regime is underwritten by an ethic of rights and where … the ethic is based on a choice (or will) theory of rights … consent must be central to that regime"[1004] as it enables the people to decide whether and which information, in the form of their personal data, they want to share with private companies.[1005] The GDPR does not just require consent for data processing activities, this consent has to be 'granular', meaning that it has to be given for each type of processing separately.[1006] The paradoxical consequence of this requirement is that private companies draw up detailed terms and conditions, to which individuals have to consent if they want to make use of the service, which then become too long and detailed for the average person to read and understand.[1007] However, it is also not

---

999 Buitelaar (n528) 187-189; de Vries *et al.* (n525) 237-238; Fromholz (n74) 465; Gutwirth *et al.* (n32) 78; Rauhofer (n364) 188; Solove, 'Conceptualizing Privacy' (n398) 1109-1115; Westin (n837) 32.

1000 See *Chapter 3, § 3, B., iv), b).*

1001 C-252/21 *Meta Platforms Inc and Others v Bundeskartellamt* [2023].

1002 EDPB, 'Binding Decision 3/2022 on the dispute submitted by the Irish SA on Meta Platforms Ireland Limited and its Facebook service (Art. 65 GDPR)' (*europa.eu*, 5 Dec 2022).

1003 Centre for Information Policy Leadership, *The Limitations of Consent as a Legal Basis for Data Processing in the Digital Society* (CIPL, 2024) 6-8.

1004 Gutwirth *et al.* (n32) 87.

1005 Buitelaar (n528) 176; Gutwirth *et al.* (n32) 88-89; Lynskey, *The foundations* (n42) 180-189; Poullet, 'Data protection' (n45) 224-225; Purtova, *Property Rights* (n31) 201-202; Purtova, 'The illusion' (n396) 91-92; Solove, 'Introduction' (n43) 1880.

1006 Article 7(a) Directive 95/46/EC; Recital 32 and Article 4.11 GDPR; Article 29 WP, 'Opinion 02/2013' (n625) 15; Rooney (n1) 9-10.

1007 de Beer *et al.* (n2) 161-163 and 185-200; Forbrukerradet, *#Toyfail: An analysis of consumer and privacy issues in three internet-connected toys* (Forbrukerradet, 2016) 9-12; Forbrukerradet, 'Norway consumer body stages live app terms reading' (*BBC News*, 25 May 2016); FTC, *Mobile Privacy Disclosures* (n2) 10; Option consommateurs, *Enfants sous écoute: La protection de la vie privée dans l'environnement des jouets intelligents* (Rapport de recherche, 2018) 21-22;

possible to simplify the detailed terms and conditions as this would carry the risk to omitting necessary information which has to be provided by EU law.[1008] Peter Blume questions, therefore, "whether the European mode of data protection with its many and detailed rules is at all suitable to ensure the protection of citizens in the modern digital world in which personal data is processed everywhere in immense quantities".[1009] The inclusion of the consent requirement, and more in particular granular consent, is theoretically positive in the context of individual control, but impractical in today's digital world.[1010] Not only average people but even experts have difficulties "assess(ing) how their personal information will be used"[1011] (cognitive problems in Daniel Solove's definition) and to imagine how big and interconnected the chain of personal data traders is (structural problems in Daniel Solove's definition).[1012] The former problems relate to the difficulty in estimation which personal data is collected and to what extent that data will be shared with third parties. People cannot fairly estimate the costs and benefits of consenting (or disagreeing) with data processing, which leads to the inability of individuals "at the time of transacting ... to assess what value (they) should receive for any transfer of the same data".[1013,1014] The latter problems relate to "the scale of personal data processing ... (where) there are simply too many entities that collect, use, and disclose people's data for the rational person to handle"[1015] as more and more data controllers, processors, and third parties are involved in the processing chain.[1016] Yves Poullet warns that this chain will only proliferate in the future with the development of the Internet of Things.[1017] As the upscaling of personal data collection is getting beyond people's ability to understand, and consent to data processing is often provided for convenience reasons (e.g. to access a website's content or use a service) instead of for informed-consent reasons, "regulatory flanking measures"[1018] are indeed needed.[1019] People may well prefer to 'trade' their personal data for the access to a product or service, but for this decision to be valid in a world of power imbalances, it requires a

Przemysław Pałka and others, 'Make privacy policies longer and appoint LLM readers' (2025) 4 ArtifIntellLaw 1, 1-2; Scassa and Sattler (n13) 118-120; Solove, 'Introduction' (n43) 1885-1886; 'Canadians want user-friendly information about privacy policies' (*DM Magazine*, 25 Jan 2018).

1008 Hartzog (n266) 430; Pałka, 'Data Management' (n44) 622; Solove, 'Introduction' (n43) 1885.

1009 Blume (n528) 3.

1010 Buitelaar (n528) 191; Solove, 'Introduction' (n43) 1880-1893.

1011 Cohen (n38) 1397.

1012 Solove, 'Introduction' (n43) 1880-1893.

1013 Samuelson (n899) 1138.

1014 Article 29 WP, 'The Future of Privacy' (n478) 17; Cate and Mayer-Schönberger (n362) 67-68; Schwartz, 'Property' (n896) 2091; Zuiderveen Borgesius *et al.* (n180) 25.

1015 Lynskey, *The foundations* (n42) 247-248.

1016 Article 29 WP, 'The Future of Privacy' (n478) 17; Solove, 'Introduction' (n43) 1888.

1017 Poullet, 'Data protection' (n45) 211-212; see *Chapter 1, § 1, A.*

1018 Lynskey, *The foundations* (n42) 257.

1019 Buitelaar (n528) 175 and 194; Hartzog (n266) 432; Poullet, 'Data protection' (n45) 216.

technically well-informed and knowledgeable society.[1020] The currently required lengthy legal terms and conditions embedded in privacy policies do not achieve their goal. Private companies have fulfilled their duty to inform consumers by using hyperlinks to the terms and conditions. These hyperlinks lead to complex legal terms and conditions which are (1) never accessed by consumers since they do not click on the hyperlinks, or (2) accessed by consumers but not read due to their length, or (3) accessed and read by consumers but not understood due to their complexity. The terms and conditions are, additionally, often of a general nature instead of product- or service-specific, making it difficult to distinguish which specific rules are applicable to the individual's situation. When people agree to these general and complex terms and conditions without being able to fully understand them, this can hardly be considered 'informed consent' as "the requirement that consent has to be informed starts from the assumption that it needs to be fully understandable to the data subject what will happen if he decides to consent to the processing of his data".[1021,1022] Orla Lynskey concludes that "given misgivings regarding the robustness of individual consent, such an approach (can)not be accepted".[1023]

C. INTERIM COMPARATIVE EU-U.S. ANALYSIS

Data Privacy – The U.S. roots of (data) privacy originate in the Bill of Rights' Fourth Amendment, which protects people against unlawful State interferences with their private property, and more specifically, their home. Similarly, although qualified differently, the EU roots of (data) privacy can be traced back to the atrocities of the Second World War which were a consequence of State abuse of personal data. Privacy protection was in the United States extended by SCOTUS from places (someone's home) to people (when they expect to have privacy) in the *Katz* case. The reasonable expectation of privacy principle that followed from this case requires that people must have a subjective expectation of privacy in the situation that they find themselves in, but also that this expectation of privacy is objectively accepted as reasonable by society at large. The protection of the Fourth Amendment was in this way adjusted from location-based to expectation-based. Based on the EU's history, the protection of personal data was grounded in the protection of people's human dignity, which was enshrined

1020 Rauhofer (n364) 186.

1021 Article 29 WP, 'The Future of Privacy' (n478) 17.

1022 de Beer *et al.* (n2) 161-163 and 185-200; Forbrukerradet, *#Toyfail* (n1007) 9-12; Forbrukerradet, 'Norway' (n1007); FTC, *Mobile Privacy Disclosures* (n2) 10; Option consommateurs (n1007) 21-22; Scassa and Sattler (n13) 118-120; Solove, 'Introduction' (n43) 1885-1886; 'Canadians want user-friendly information' (n1007).

1023 Lynskey, *The foundations* (n42) 86.

in several legal documents. This conceptualization encompasses in the (data) privacy area the ability to determine for oneself, through the exercise of individual control over one's personal information, how their personal image and identity, or reputation, is presented to the world. As the EU initially did not have the competence to enact fundamental rights legislation, the protection of personal data was grounded in the internal (trade) market and the facilitation of its 'free flow', which comes close to the U.S. property conceptualization of personal data discussed below. The U.S. expectation-based privacy conceptualization was gradually extended to people-to-people relations through Warren and Brandeis' right to be let alone in the form of seclusion and extended by Prosser's four-tier privacy torts. When applied in the data privacy area, attention should be drawn to the conceptualization of 'information privacy', which concerns people's control over how their private information is communicated to others, and Daniel Solove's extension of Prosser's conceptualization to a general four category group of privacy harmful activities, divided into subgroups. The aim and origins of personal data protection legislation in both the EU and the United States were, and are, to prevent the State as well as private companies from exercising (abusive) control over people based on the extensive amount of (their personal) information in the State's and companies' possession, and the latter's data processing activities which reveal even more detailed information based on the initially collected pieces of personal data. The tools through which this aim is achieved are restoring the power imbalance and enabling people to control the information that is circulated about them in order to uphold their personal image and identity (reputation) in the public sphere, which is 'constitutive of who I am and can become', and necessary for self-authorship. The ability to become who and what people want through self-authorship is shared by the EU and the United States. Personal data protection serves in the EU as a (procedural) means to achieve an (fundamental rights) end, where 'it is not the data as such that need(s) to be protected but the people to whom that data relates'. Regulatory initiatives should, therefore, concern the purposes of data processing, by prohibiting discriminatory practices or activities which inhibit people's freedom of choice, as opposed to procedural elements to solely 'tick the boxes'. Orla Lynskey's tripartite European relationship between the right to personal data protection and privacy (data protection ≠ / ≤ / > privacy) can be interpreted as different sides of the same coin which are all inherently correct and able to co-exist. Given that the concept of privacy has a long history and evolved into an ambiguous term as it had to adapt over time and space, 'privacy' encompasses a broad range of aspects. The newer European concept of personal data protection enabled its tailoring to the specific privacy needs of people in the digital age, given its explicit roots in the right to privacy. The protection of personal data can, consequently, be situated within the broad notion that the right to privacy encompasses through an evolutionary interpretation of this right in a modern digital world.[1024] Instead of a new concept for this particular situation, Stefano Rodotà suggests that in the United States personal data protection "is actually the endpoint of a long evolutionary process experienced by the privacy concept – from its original definition as the right to be left alone, up to the right to keep control over one's information and determine how one's private sphere is to be built up".[1025] The two highest European courts share this opinion to a certain extent as both the CJEU, which conflates both rights, and the ECtHR, which included the protection of personal data in Article 8 ECHR right to privacy's scope of application, use the concepts of privacy and personal data protection interchangeably. Chris Hoofnagle *et al.*[1026] concurs with Uta Kohl's observation that the EU and the United States "are broadly concerned with self-authorship but localise its flourishing in different realms; … whilst Anglo-American privacy limits protection to the private sphere and personal confidential information … (carving) out the body, the home, and implicitly the family, as the space for self-sovereignty; … in Continental European culture privacy is neither confined to intimate or personal confidential information nor necessarily limited to an a priori private sphere … (and) fixes its attention on the public realm as the arena for personal self-determination under conditions of respect and dignity".[1027] People's ability to seclude themselves from the State as well as from other people is necessary to enable their personal development and a democratic society. Alan Westin's U.S. definition of information privacy, encompassing "the claim of individuals, groups, or institutions to determine for themselves when, how, and to what extent information about them is communicated to others",[1028] shares common elements with Luciano Floridi's European "interpretation of the protection of privacy as protection of personal identity".[1029] In conclusion, self-determination and individual control are "the essential element(s) of both market-based and dignity-based privacy regimes".[1030]

Personal Data as Property – Given the U.S. roots of data privacy in the Fourth Amendment's property protection, it is not surprising that the idea of providing people with property rights over their personal data emerged in the United States. Enshrining property rights in personal data enables people to actively protect and exercise individual control over their data in accordance with their preferences for self-determination. Consequently, individuals are required to opt out of private companies' data collection and data processing activities in

1024 Buitelaar (n528) 201-202; Solove, 'Conceptualizing Privacy' (n398) 1093 and 1146-1147.
1025 Gutwirth *et al.* (n32) 80.
1026 Hoofnagle *et al.* (n11) 69-70.
1027 Kohl (n398) 747-748.
1028 Westin (n837) 7.
1029 Floridi (n937) 308.
1030 Buitelaar (n528) 195.

the U.S. system if they do not wish their data to be used for those purposes. The ECHR does not as such preclude a property conceptualization of personal data under Article 1 of Protocol No. 1 ECHR which purports that "Every natural or legal person is entitled to the peaceful enjoyment of his possessions. ... The preceding provisions shall not, however, in any way impair the right of a State to enforce such laws as it deems necessary to control the use of property in accordance with the general interest ...".[1031] The ECtHR has clarified that "the concept of 'possessions' referred to in the first part of (this Article) has an autonomous meaning which is not limited to ownership of physical goods and is independent of the formal classification in domestic law: certain other rights and interests constituting assets can also be regarded as 'property rights', and thus as "possessions", for the purposes of this provision".[1032,1033] The ECHR's interpretation can, consequently, be "altered to meet human needs and reflect human values",[1034] which includes the possibility to qualify an asset such as personal data as someone's property. The EU's historical entanglement between the protection of personal data and human dignity, though, leads "the majority of contributors to the debate, especially in Europe, (to) reject property rights doctrines as a desirable basis for data privacy law"[1035] given that "the right to data protection has to do with protecting one's personality – not one's property".[1036] In a similar way, intellectual 'property' rights are qualified as such, but Warren and Brandeis observed already in 1890 that "the principle which protects personal writings and all other personal productions ... against publication in any form, is in reality not the principle of private property, but that of an inviolate personality".[1037] Unlike intellectual property, people are not 'just' the creators of their personal data, they are the subject of it. The trend shifted in the United States initially from 'privacy as dignity to privacy as commodity' through the 'Notice & Choice' system that was set up, but as it soon became apparent that people did not have that much 'choice' in practice, the adoption of U.S. State consumer privacy acts shifted this approach again by providing consumers with certain rights over their personal data to prohibit abusive processing practices and restore the power imbalance that had emerged between consumers (data subjects) and private companies (data processors). Orla Lynskey remarks that the pre-GDPR EU legal framework supported a property rights approach[1038] as

---

1031 Article 1 Prot. No. 1 ECHR.

1032 *Gasus Dosier- und Fördertechnik GmbH v the Netherlands* App no 15375/89 (ECtHR, 23 Feb 1995) para 53; *Anheuser-Busch Inc v Portugal* App no 73049/01 (ECtHR, 11 Jan 2007) para 63.

1033 Guibault and Bernt Hugenholtz (n533) 236; Lynskey, *The foundations* (n42) 231-241.

1034 Hanoch Dagan, 'The Craft of Property' (2003) 91 CLR 1517, 1532.

1035 Bygrave, *Data Privacy Law* (n37) 14.

1036 Gutwirth *et al.* (n32) 81.

1037 Warren and Brandeis (n825) 205.

1038 Lynskey, *The foundations* (n42) 253.

the 1995 Directive was an internal market document with a focus on free flow of personal data, bringing this conceptualization closer to the U.S. trade and property approach. The 2016 GDPR shifted the focus to a fundamental rights approach, which has become too strict and detailed to be labeled as 'just' enabling free flow of personal data in the EU internal market (and beyond). The EU and U.S. regulatory systems approach personal data from a dual privacy (dignity) and property (trade/commerce) perspective. In their legislative evolution, each region tilted first too much to one side but was subsequently corrected to be more balanced again. The U.S. approach tilted towards the property conceptualization, but "without developed data protection legislation, information industries (... tended to be ...) 'free-riding' and, controlled only by market forces ... able to collect (personal) data without limitations",[1039] which was corrected by the adoption of State consumer privacy acts. The EU approach tilted towards the privacy conceptualization, but criticisms about the rigid structure of the GDPR hampering and burdening the EU trade market and competitiveness,[1040] and the ignorance of "the benefits of data use to data subjects",[1041] lead to reconsideration whether the current approach is indeed the right one. When compared to the United States, the EU tends to prefer "to err on the side of caution and to forego any potential benefit the data could have in the future or another context"[1042] by restricting and reducing the amount of personal data that can be collected, stored, shared or sold, which may seriously limit future valuable uses of this data.[1043] U.S.-based big tech companies, such as Meta or Google, were enabled to grow and become successful by collecting (and processing) their users' personal data, which was available to them directly on their platforms. Small and medium-sized companies are often reliant on the personal data collected by these big tech companies for their own activities. Chris Hoofnagle *et al.* express criticism that "viewed negatively, the GDPR appears to be a big data business killer",[1044] and Mark Lemley concludes that "the lesson of the European (1995) Directive ... (is that) ... unless it is intelligently done and narrowly tailored to important interests, increased privacy regulation could interfere with many valuable economic activities".[1045] These criticisms were confirmed in the 2024 Draghi Report,[1046] where "access to health data (was found to be) one of the preconditions for the development of AI in the pharma industry but (was found to be) constrained by fragmentation (and) in particular, although GDPR contains

1039 Purtova, *Property Rights* (n31) 216-217.
1040 Mario Draghi, *The future of European competitiveness* (European Commission Report, 2024); Pałka, 'Data Management' (n44) 626.
1041 Bergkamp (n394) 35.
1042 Heisenberg (n66) 14.
1043 Bergkamp (n394) 42.
1044 Hoofnagle *et al.* (n11) 76.
1045 Lemley (n903) 1556-1557.
1046 Draghi (n1040).

options to use patient data for health research … (it) … prevent(s) the industry from tapping into a wealth of available electronic data",[1047] disadvantaging the EU economically.[1048]

Legislative intervention – The trade market did not succeed (through self-regulation) to restore the power imbalance between businesses and consumers, resulting in legislative interventions taken by EU and U.S. (State) governments in commercial as well as people-to-government relations to enable people to effectively exercise individual control over their personal data through 'partial privacy self-management'.[1049,1050] One specific feature which is important to mention in the distinctive EU and U.S. approaches towards data privacy in commercial relations is the option to opt in/out of data collection and data processing activities. The EU GDPR employs a default opt-out system, where individuals have "the right not to be subject to a decision based solely on automated processing, including profiling, which produces legal effects concerning (them) or similarly significantly affects (them)",[1051] unless people provide their active opt-in consent, which must be "freely given, specific, informed and unambiguous".[1052] The California (CCPA) and Virginia (VCDPA) State consumer acts employ, on the contrary, a default opt-in system, where individuals are provided with the possibility to opt out of data collection and data processing activities. The CCPA requires that "a page or setting view that the consumer accesses to set the opt-out preference signal … should (include) up to three choices …: (I) Global opt-out from sale and sharing of personal information, including a direction to limit the use of sensitive personal information; (II) Choice to 'Limit the use of my sensitive personal information'; (III) Choice titled 'Do not sell/do not share my personal information for cross-context behavioral advertising'",[1053] which is defined as "the targeting of advertising to a consumer based on the consumer's personal information obtained from the consumer's activity across businesses, distinctly-branded websites, applications, or (other) services … with which the consumer intentionally interacts".[1054] The VCDPA similarly provides individuals with the possibility "to opt out of the processing of the personal data for purposes of (i) targeted advertising, (ii) the sale of personal data, or (iii) profiling in furtherance of decisions that produce legal or similarly significant effects concerning the consumer".[1055] The EU adopts a default opt-out system whereas the selected U.S. State acts adopt a default opt-in system. The California and

1047 *Ibid.* 32.
1048 Bergkamp (n394) 31-32.
1049 Solove, 'Introduction' (n43) 1902.
1050 Schwartz, 'Property' (n896) 2080-2083.
1051 Article 22 GDPR.
1052 Article 4(11) GDPR.
1053 CCPA § 1798.185.(a)(18)(A)(vi).
1054 CCPA § 1798.140.(k).
1055 VCDPA § 59.1-577.A.5.

Virginia acts came into force in the economic sphere as consumer privacy acts, balancing business interests, through allowing default personal data collection and processing, with personal privacy interests, through the possibility to opt out of these practices. The legislative initiatives of the EU result from the historical context of government abuse of citizens' personal data and the subsequent protection of individuals' human dignity and privacy interests, where a default opt-out system requires affirmative action from the individual to opt in to data collection and processing activities if one wishes to allow these practices.[1056] Both approaches allow people to exercise individual control over their personal data, and while it is true that the burden of action is placed on different stakeholders, respectively the people or the businesses, the decisional autonomy is guaranteed in both systems. If someone values the protection of their data, they will engage in opting out of data processing, whether this question is asked to them directly in an opt-in system or whether a search for a page with an opt-out request for data collection and processing practices is required. The U.S. 'Notice and Choice' model and the EU's emphasis on consent as legitimizing basis for data processing are the same tools, as was acknowledged in the Safe Harbor adequacy decision;[1057] in both cases the individual has to agree or disagree to businesses' data collection and processing activities based on the information that the latter provides.[1058] The EU protective (and paternalistic) legal framework aims to ensure that people cannot 'contract away' or hollow out their (guaranteed) personal data rights when entering into private agreements or contracts,[1059] while facilitating businesses' international operations through the application of one standard instead of multiple ones, but the current regulatory framework has become too strict and procedural in relation to its initial aim to protect individuals' human dignity and privacy interests.[1060] The focus should, therefore, be brought back to the purposes (as opposed to the procedural aspects) of data collection and processing, to protect the people behind the data instead of the data as such. A certain degree of State intervention is, consequently, necessary to remedy "the most objectionable personal data processing practices",[1061] but the intervention should also be limited to these practices only. The Article 29 WP shared a similar opinion already in 1998 that EU "privacy protection ... must be applied within the context of a framework of enforceable data protection rules, which provide a minimum and non-negotiable level of privacy protection for all individuals",[1062]

1056 Buitelaar (n528) 175; Cohen (n38) 1391; Gutwirth *et al.* (n32) 79; Hartzog (n266) 426; Lynskey, *The foundations* (n42) 11; Tzanou (n526) 89.

1057 Decision 2000/520/EC, 11.

1058 Gutwirth *et al.* (n32) 184; Solove, 'Introduction' (n43) 1880-1891.

1059 Lynskey, *The foundations* (n42) 40.

1060 Blume (n528) 5; Bygrave, *Data Protection Law* (n17) 364; Guibault and Bernt Hugenholtz (n533) 227.

1061 Lynskey, *The foundations* (n42) 237.

1062 Article 29 WP, 'Opinion 1/98 Platform for Privacy Preferences (P3P) and the Open Profiling Standard (OPS)' (WP11, 16 Jun 1998) 2; Lynskey, *The foundations* (n42) 40.

which corresponded more to the rules enshrined in the 1995 Directive than those in the 2016 GDPR. "Together with the EU's direct effect doctrine, (the GDPR in its current form) results in an extremely rigid governance framework, difficult to comply with by corporations collecting data as a part of their business model, as many of the tech companies do",[1063] and provides them with a competitional disadvantage. The current practice where people are offered the (only) choice between 'yes I share my personal data' or 'no I do not use the service or product' cannot render their 'consent' to be an effective empowerment tool. A change of approach in the EU system is required, as the current form of 'consent' cannot be considered informed nor meaningful. "Self-management and paternalism should be viewed as complementary tools to facilitate effective control",[1064] but "the law (should be able to) override people's ability to consent when the individual or social harms ... clearly outweigh the benefits".[1065,1066] Legislative intervention is needed, but should be effective, limited to what is strictly necessary, and balance people's privacy interests and businesses' commercial interests. This balance is also recognized in the EU as well as U.S. regulatory approaches towards data privacy, which demonstrates that a legal framework cannot only focus on one aspect, be it the protection of human dignity and privacy or the propertization of personal data.

§ 2. INTERPLAY WITH FREEDOM OF SPEECH AND PROHIBITION OF DISCRIMINATION

Personal data protection is not only closely related to the right to privacy, as shown in the previous section, but is also related to freedom of speech and aims to protect against discriminatory practices. This section discusses the interplay between the right to privacy and freedom of speech in the United States as well as in the EU in more detail, through an analysis of the interplay between the U.S. Fourth and First Amendment, and Articles 8 and 10 of the ECHR, since the equivalent Articles in the EU Charter were drafted following the example of the ECHR.[1067] The additional level of protection provided for personal data categorized as 'sensitive' can be understood in the context of the prohibition of discrimination. The fast-paced advancements in big data analytics threaten this conceptualization though by making it redundant, and encourage a rethinking of the differentiation in levels of personal data protection.

1063 Pałka, 'Data Management' (n44) 616.
1064 Lynskey, *The foundations* (n42) 272.
1065 Solove, 'Introduction' (n43) 1896.
1066 *Ibid.* 1895-1896.
1067 Explanations relating to the Charter of Fundamental Rights [2007] OJ C 303/20-21.

A. RIGHT TO PRIVACY VERSUS FREEDOM OF SPEECH

The core value protected by freedom of speech is the ability to express one's opinion freely, enabling debates and confrontation, and eventually the establishment of a democratic society.[1068] There is a discrepancy in approach between the United States and the EU with regard to the possibilities for downstream dissemination of lawfully obtained truthful personal data. In the United States, someone's freedom of speech and the ability to share this information will often prevail, while in the EU the balance will more likely tilt towards the protection of someone's privacy.[1069]

i) U.S. Fourth Amendment versus First Amendment

Reasonable expectation of privacy – In the U.S. discussion on privacy law, a distinction has to be made again between people-to-government relations and people-to-private-sector-commerce relations.[1070] The first category of people-to-government relations falls within the scope of application of the Bill of Rights, containing the amendments to the U.S. Constitution, and builds on the discussion of the Fourth Amendment and the 1967 *Katz v United States*[1071] case provided in *Chapter 4, § 1, A., i)*. In *Katz*, SCOTUS stated that "what a person knowingly exposes to the public, even in his own home or office, is not a subject of Fourth Amendment protection".[1072] The U.S. 'secrecy paradigm' or 'third party doctrine' requires that secret or private information has to be actively secreted. Private information that is voluntarily shared with a third party loses its protection, giving prevalence to freedom of speech.[1073] The U.S. Supreme Court interpreted the third party doctrine extensively in its case law. In 1976 *United States v Miller*,[1074] SCOTUS held that there is "no legitimate 'expectation of privacy' in ... documents ... (that)

1068 Jack Balkin, 'Free Speech in the Algorithmic Society' (2018) 51 UCDLR 1149, 1151.

1069 Bennett (n140) 137; Bergkamp (n394) 35; Cate (n193) 89-100; Heisenberg (n66) 35-36; Hoofnagle *et al.* (n11) 75; Ronald Krotoszynski Jr., 'A Comparative Perspective on the First Amendment' (2004) 78 Tulane LRev 1549, 1577-1579; Peltz-Steele, 'American Privacy' (n240) 367-368; Zuiderveen Borgesius *et al.* (n180) 19.

1070 Birnhack (n56) 509.

1071 *Katz* (n812).

1072 *Ibid.* 351.

1073 *California v Greenwood* [1988] 486 U.S. 35, paras 43-44; Bard (n817) 737; Woodrow Hartzog, 'The Public Information Fallacy' (2019) 99 BULRev 459, 461-475; William Heffernan, 'Fourth Amendment Privacy Interests' (2001) 92 JCLRC 1, 32-38; Kohl (n398) 742; Emma Marshall and others, 'Police Surveillance of Cell Phone Location Data' (2019) 37 BehavSciLaw 751, 753; Peltz-Steele, 'American Privacy' (n240) 407; Paul Rosenzweig, 'Civil Liberty and the Response to Terrorism' (2004) 42 DuqLRev 663, 675; Solove, *Understanding Privacy* (n194) 103-111 and 140-146; Warren and Brandeis (n825) 199-200; Matthew Wasserman, 'First Amendment limitations on police surveillance' (2015) 90 NYUnivLRev 1786, 1810-1811.

1074 *United States v Miller* (n792).

contain only information voluntarily conveyed to the banks and exposed to their employees in the ordinary course of business ... the depositor takes the risk, in revealing his affairs to another, that the information will be conveyed by that person to the Government ... the Fourth Amendment does not prohibit the obtaining of information revealed to a third party and conveyed by him to Government authorities, even if the information is revealed on the assumption that it will be used only for a limited purpose and the confidence placed in the third party will not be betrayed".[1075,1076] Similarly, in 1979 *Smith v Maryland*,[1077] the U.S. Supreme Court explained that "telephone users (must) realize that they must 'convey' phone numbers to the telephone company, since it is through telephone company switching equipment that their calls are completed ... it is too much to believe that telephone subscribers, under these circumstances, harbor any general expectation that the numbers they dial will remain secret".[1078,1079] In 1983 *United States v Knotts*,[1080] SCOTUS stated that "a person traveling in an automobile on public thoroughfares has no reasonable expectation of privacy in his movements from one place to another".[1081,1082] Advances in technological equipment have restrained the U.S. Supreme Court's interpretation of the third party doctrine to a certain extent. In 2001 *Kyllo v United States*,[1083] SCOTUS decided that "obtaining by sense-enhancing technology (*in casu* a thermal imager) any information regarding the interior of the home that could not otherwise have been obtained without physical 'intrusion into a constitutionally protected area' ... constitutes a search, at least where (as here) the technology in question is not in general public use".[1084] Similarly, in the landmark 2018 *Carpenter v United States*[1085] case, the U.S. Supreme Court considered the application of the Fourth Amendment and the third party doctrine to cell-site location information (CSLI), which provides "the ability to chronicle a person's past movements through the record of his cell phone signals".[1086,1087] The Court held that "given the unique nature of cell phone location records, the fact that the information is held by a third party does not by itself overcome the user's claim to Fourth Amendment

1075 *Ibid.* 442-443.

1076 Bennett (n140) 174; Marshall *et al.* (n1073) 753; Purtova, *Property Rights* (n31) 115; Tzanou (n526) 98.

1077 *Smith v Maryland* [1979] 442 U.S. 735.

1078 *Ibid.* 742-743.

1079 Marshall *et al.* (n1073) 753; Purtova, *Property Rights* (n31) 115; Solove, 'Data Is What Data Does' (n16) 1117.

1080 *United States v Knotts* [1983] 460 U.S. 276.

1081 *Ibid.* 281.

1082 Solove, 'Data Is What Data Does' (n16) 1118.

1083 *Kyllo v United States* [2001] 533 U.S. 27.

1084 *Ibid.* 34.

1085 *Carpenter v United States* [2018] 585 U.S. __.

1086 *Ibid.*, Chief Justice Roberts' opinion of the Court.

1087 Packard (n801) 282; Solove, 'Data Is What Data Does' (n16) 1118.

protection ... an individual maintains a legitimate expectation of privacy in the record of his physical movements as captured through CSLI".[1088,1089] In today's digital times, we are constantly 'sharing' information with internet and social media providers (third parties) without necessarily having the intention of making this information publicly available.[1090] The Court specified in *Carpenter* that "our decision today is a narrow one ... we do not express a view on matters not before us ... our opinion does not consider other collection techniques involving foreign affairs or national security".[1091] Consequently, it remains to be seen how the U.S. Supreme Court will expand or restrict its interpretation of the third party doctrine and the reasonable expectation of privacy in a digital world where all information is by definition shared with digital platforms hosted by third parties, whether these are public or private actors.

Lawfully obtained truthful information – The freedom to disseminate lawfully obtained truthful information is a near absolute right in the United States.[1092] The U.S. First Amendment ensures that "Congress shall make no law ... abridging the freedom of speech, or of the press",[1093] referring to the negative or passive role of government not to interfere with people's affairs.[1094] The U.S. Supreme Court confirmed in the landmark 1964 *New York Times Co. v Sullivan*[1095] case that "to sustain a claim of defamation or libel, the First Amendment requires that the plaintiff show that the defendant knew that a statement was false or was reckless in deciding to publish the information without investigating whether it was accurate".[1096,1097] Similarly, in 1967 *Curtis Publishing Co. v Butts*,[1098] SCOTUS confirmed that "a defamation cause of action may accrue when the media is reckless in publishing allegations about public figures without checking their accuracy".[1099] The latter decision was mitigated in 1968 *St. Amant v Thompson*,[1100] where the Court refined that "the reckless disregard for truth element in defamation claims requires a plaintiff to show that the defendant had serious

---

1088 *Ibid.*
1089 Mulligan and Linebaugh, *An Overview* (n230) 5-6.
1090 Hartzog, 'Public Information Fallacy' (n1073) 459-522; Heffernan (n1073) 82-87; Peltz-Steele, 'The pond betwixt' (n568) 18-22; Solove, *Understanding Privacy* (n194) 139-140.
1091 *Carpenter* (n1085) 17-18.
1092 Cohen (n38) 1429; Newell *et al.* (n229) 1107; Peltz-Steele, 'American Privacy' (n240) 368 and 383; Jeffrey Rosen, 'The Right to Be Forgotten' (2012) 64 SLR Online 88, 91.
1093 First Amendment to the U.S. Constitution, 15 Dec 1791.
1094 Cate (n193) 51; 'Free Speech Supreme Court Cases' (*Justia: U.S. Supreme Court*, 2024).
1095 *New York Times Co. v Sullivan* [1964] 376 U.S. 254.
1096 *Ibid.*
1097 Hartzog, 'Public Information Fallacy' (n1073) 506; Peltz-Steele, 'American Privacy' (n240) 383.
1098 *Curtis Publishing Co. v Butts* [1967] 388 U.S. 130.
1099 *Ibid.*
1100 *St. Amant v Thompson* [1968] 390 U.S. 727.

doubts about the accuracy of the material".[1101] In 1986 *Philadelphia Newspapers v Hepps*,[1102] the U.S. Supreme Court upheld that "where a newspaper publishes speech of public concern, a private-figure plaintiff cannot recover damages without also showing that the statements at issue are false",[1103] because "to do otherwise could 'only result in a deterrence of speech which the Constitution makes free'".[1104] William Prosser identified in the same 1960 Article where he conceptualized the four-tier privacy torts, discussed in the previous section, that the problematic case of "the effect of lapse of time, and the extent to which forgotten records … can be revived as still a matter of legitimate public interest"[1105] is unresolved in U.S. law. Two cases may shed some light on what a U.S. version of the European 'right to be forgotten'[1106] could entail. In 1931 *Melvin v Reid*,[1107] the Court of Appeal of California "held that the unnecessary use of the plaintiff's name, and the revelation of her history (as a prostitute) to new friends and associates, introduced an element which was in itself a transgression of her right of privacy".[1108] In 1968 *Schneider v Smith*,[1109] the U.S. Supreme Court held that an "Act (authorizing) a type of screening program directed at 'membership' or 'sympathetic association' …. (touches) on First Amendment rights … (and) that an unlimited and indiscriminate search of the employee's past which interferes with his associational freedom is unconstitutional".[1110,1111] However, the U.S. courts reversed this approach in their subsequent case law. In 1975 *Cox Broadcasting Corp. v Cohn*,[1112] the U.S. Supreme Court decided that "State(s) may not, consistently with the First and Fourteenth Amendments, impose sanctions on the accurate publication of a rape victim's name obtained from judicial records that are maintained in connection with a public prosecution and that themselves are open to public inspection".[1113,1114] In 1979 *Smith v Daily Mail Pub. Co.*,[1115] SCOTUS reaffirmed that "the State cannot … punish the truthful publication of an alleged juvenile delinquent's name lawfully obtained by a newspaper (even when this aims to protect) the anonymity of the juvenile offender (and) to

1101 *Ibid.*
1102 *Philadelphia Newspapers v Hepps* [1986] 475 U.S. 767.
1103 *Ibid.* 768-769.
1104 *Ibid.* 777.
1105 Prosser (n828) 396.
1106 See *Chapter 4, § 2, A., iii).*
1107 *Melvin v Reid* [1931] 112 Cal.App. 285, 297 P. 91.
1108 Prosser (n828) 396.
1109 *Schneider v Smith* [1968] 390 U.S. 17.
1110 *Ibid.* 24.
1111 Miller (n841) 203.
1112 *Cox Broadcasting Corp. v Cohn* [1975] 420 U.S. 469.
1113 *Ibid.* 470.
1114 Kohl (n398) 756.
1115 *Smith v Daily Mail Pub. Co.* [1979] 443 U.S. 97.

further his rehabilitation".[1116,1117] In 2004 *Gates v Discovery Communications*, the same Court of Appeal of California held that "the producers and presenters of a television documentary program may (not) be held liable in tort for publishing therein information they gathered from public official court records concerning a person who many years previously served a prison term for a felony conviction but who has since lived an obscure, lawful life and become a respected member of the community",[1118] which was confirmed by the Supreme Court of California.[1119] The filtering or blocking of information disseminated by private companies qualifies also as an infringement of this right. The decisive criterion for lawful publication and dissemination of information consists in the United States, consequently, of the determination of whether the disseminated information is true. Privacy rights are to a large extent confined to someone's (private) home in the United States, because "securing one person's privacy may infringe on another person's freedom of expression and information",[1120] and consequently, privacy rights gradually diminish when leaving the confines of the home and entering the public sphere, where the First Amendment's freedom of speech will prevail.[1121] This interpretation explains why public persons' privacy rights are less protected in the United States than non-public person's rights. A public person or figure "who by his own voluntary efforts has succeeded in placing himself in the public eye ... by his accomplishments, fame, or mode of living, or by adopting a profession ... gives the public a legitimate interest in his doings, his affairs, and his character ... (and) the press ... a privilege, guaranteed by the Constitution, to inform the public about those who have become legitimate matters of public interest".[1122,1123] This understanding is in line with the 'reasonable expectation of privacy' principle as public figures cannot expect the same level of privacy as their non-public counterparts on the subjective level, and this equation between the level of privacy granted to public and non-public figures would not be accepted by society as 'reasonable' on the objective level. SCOTUS confirmed in 1986 *Philadelphia Newspapers v Hepps*[1124] that "when the speech is of public concern and the plaintiff is a public official or public figure, the Constitution clearly requires the plaintiff to surmount a much higher barrier before recovering damages from a media defendant".[1125] The ascendancy

1116 *Ibid.*
1117 Peltz-Steele, 'American Privacy' (n240) 383-391.
1118 *Gates v Discovery Communications, Inc.* [Cal. 2004] 34 Cal.4th 679, 680.
1119 Kohl (n398) 756.
1120 Bergkamp (n394) 35.
1121 Joel Feinberg, 'Autonomy, Sovereignty, and Privacy' (1983) 58 NDLR 445, 453-454; Hoofnagle *et al.* (n11) 69-70; Kohl (n398) 743 and 767.
1122 Prosser (n828) 410-411.
1123 Peltz-Steele, 'American Privacy' (n240) 379; Prosser (n828) 410-412; Warren and Brandeis (n825) 215 216.
1124 *Philadelphia Newspapers* (n1102).
1125 *Ibid.* 775.

of the dissemination of truthful information over personal privacy interests is enshrined in § 652.D. of the *Restatement (Second) of Torts*,[1126] which states that "one who gives publicity to a matter concerning the private life of another is subject to liability to the other for invasion of his privacy, if the matter publicized is of a kind that (a) would be highly offensive to a reasonable person, and (b) is not of legitimate concern to the public".[1127,1128]

ii) U.S. State Consumer Privacy Acts

Maintained – The second category of people-to-private-sector-commerce relations is situated within the scope of application of U.S. State consumer privacy acts. The strong First Amendment protection of downward disseminated lawfully obtained truthful information is maintained in the U.S. State consumer privacy acts discussed in this book, namely those of California and Virginia. The California Consumer Privacy Act (CCPA) and the Virginia Consumer Data Protection Act (VCDPA) exclude publicly available personal information from their scope of application. The CCPA states in § 1798.140.(v)(2) that "'Personal information' does not include publicly available information or lawfully obtained, truthful information that is a matter of public concern … 'publicly available' means: information that is lawfully made available from federal, State, or local government records, or information that a business has a reasonable basis to believe is lawfully made available to the general public by the consumer or from widely distributed media; or information made available by a person to whom the consumer has disclosed the information if the consumer has not restricted the information to a specific audience …".[1129] The VCDPA specifies in § 59.1-575 that "'Personal data' does not include … publicly available information … 'Publicly available information' means information that is lawfully made available through federal, State, or local government records, or information that a business has a reasonable basis to believe is lawfully made available to the general public through widely distributed media, by the consumer, or by a person to whom the consumer has disclosed the information, unless the consumer has restricted the information to a specific audience".[1130] This reasoning is in line with U.S. Fourth Amendment jurisprudence, which requires that private information has to be actively secreted to be protected. By participating in a public event, for example, people cannot invoke privacy rights in this information.

1126 Restatement (Second) of Torts (1997) § 652.A.-E.
1127 Restatement (Second) of Torts (1997) § 652.D.
1128 Cate (n193) 90; Peltz-Steele, 'American Privacy' (n240) 385-386.
1129 CCPA § 1798.140.(v)(2).
1130 VCDPA § 59.1-575.

iii) *Article 8 versus 10 ECHR*

ECHR – EU personal data protection legislation is founded on the European Convention on Human Rights (ECHR),[1131] and more specifically on the balance between the right to privacy (Article 8) and freedom of speech (Article 10).[1132] According to Article 8 ECHR, "everyone has the right to respect for his private and family life, his home and his correspondence".[1133] An interference with this right can only occur by a public authority "in accordance with the law and (when) necessary in a democratic society in the interests of national security, public safety or the economic well-being of the country, for the prevention of disorder or crime, for the protection of health or morals, or for the protection of the rights and freedoms of others".[1134] Article 10 ECHR ensures that "everyone has the right to freedom of expression … this right shall include freedom to hold opinions and to receive and impart information and ideas without interference by public authority and regardless of frontiers …".[1135] Restrictions to this right are possible if they "are prescribed by law and are necessary in a democratic society, in the interests of national security, territorial integrity or public safety, for the prevention of disorder or crime, for the protection of health or morals, for the protection of the reputation or rights of others, for preventing the disclosure of information received in confidence, or for maintaining the authority and impartiality of the judiciary".[1136] EU personal data protection law includes 'public' personal information in addition to 'private' information, extending the protection to any personal information, whether publicly available, private, or actively 'secreted'.[1137]

ECtHR – The ECtHR takes generally a more restrictive approach than the EU as the Court only extends the scope of application of Article 8 ECHR to situations which are closely related to someone's 'private life', and to disclosures of publicly available information by the press which "can be shown as harming the person's 'physical or psychological integrity'".[1138,1139] Consequently, Peter Oliver observes

1131 Article 29 WP stated in its 'Working Document 01/2016' that "the fundamental rights protection offered to personal data in Europe not only relies on EU law, but also on the protection offered by the ECHR", and more in particular, "the fundamental right to a private life".: Article 29 WP, 'Working Document 01/2016' (n642) 4-5; Blume (n528) 3; Gutwirth *et al.* (n32) 71; Lynskey, *The foundations* (n42) 268; Tzanou (n526) 91.

1132 Article 29 WP, 'Opinion 1/2008' (n954) 8-13; Bygrave, *Data Protection Law* (n17) 40; Bygrave, *Data Privacy Law* (n37) 34; Cannataci and Mifsud-Bonnici (n478) 6; Cohen (n38) 1408.

1133 Article 8.1 ECHR.

1134 Article 8.2 ECHR.

1135 Article 10.1 ECHR.

1136 Article 10.2 ECHR.

1137 Purtova, *Property Rights* (n31) 225-229.

1138 Bygrave, *Data Privacy Law* (n37) 89.

1139 *Botta v Italy* App no 21439/93 (ECtHR, 24 Feb 1998) para 32; *Gillberg v Sweden* App no 41723/06 (ECtHR, 3 Apr 2012) para 66; *Nicolae Virgiliu Tănase v Romania* App no 41720/13 (ECtHR, 25 Jun 2019) para 126.

that "individuals who have been defamed are entitled, by virtue of Article 8 ECHR, to vindicate their reputation in judicial proceedings, at least where the attack on their reputation is so serious as to affect their personal integrity",[1140] even if the information intended to be disseminated is true. "The publication of a person's photograph (was found) to fall within the scope of his or her private life, even where the person concerned is a public figure"[1141] in the 2014 *Ion Cârstea v Romania*[1142] case. The Court held that "the decisive factor in balancing the protection of private life against freedom of expression should lie in the contribution that the published (information) make(s) to a debate of general interest".[1143] In this regard "a fundamental distinction needs to be made between reporting (factual matters) capable of contributing to (a) debate in a democratic society … relating to politicians in the exercise of their (official) functions …, and reporting details of the private life of an individual who … does not exercise (such) functions (with the sole aim of satisfying public curiosity)".[1144] The ECtHR has already held in the 2012 *Von Hannover v Germany (No. 2)*[1145] case that "although in certain special circumstances the public's right to be informed can even extend to aspects of the private life of public figures, particularly where politicians are concerned, this will not be the case – despite the person concerned being well known to the public – where the (information) relate(s) exclusively to details of the person's private life and ha(s) the sole aim of satisfying public curiosity in that respect".[1146] If, on the other hand, the considered information is truthful, contributes to a debate in a democratic society, and "the content of the article (is) balanced, informing on facts and not only intended to satisfy public curiosity",[1147] the Court has justified the information's dissemination and publication. The situation is more complicated when one family member reveals information about another family member through the media, as in that case both parties' privacy and freedom of speech are involved, and "one individual's privacy interests may conflict with another's, with the interests of society, or even with others of his own interests".[1148,1149] In the 2020 *Rodina v Latvia*[1150] case, the ECtHR emphasized that journalists should engage in 'responsible journalism' by providing both parties with equal opportunities to react to the facts in order to strike a fair balance between the interests involved, and by taking precautions,

1140 de Vries *et al.* (n525) 313.
1141 *Ion Cârstea* (n1142) para 29.
1142 *Ion Cârstea v Romania* App no 20531/06 (ECtHR, 28 Oct 2014).
1143 *Von Hannover v Germany* App no 59320/00 (ECtHR, 24 Jun 2004) para 76.
1144 *Ibid.* para 63; *Someşan and Butiuc v Romania* App no 45543/04 (ECtHR, 19 Nov 2013) para 27; *Ion Cârstea* (n1142) para 36; *Kajganić v Serbia* App no 27958/16 (ECtHR, 8 Oct 2024) para 65.
1145 *Von Hannover v Germany (No. 2)* App nos 40660/08 and 60641/08 (ECtHR, 7 Feb 2012).
1146 *Ibid.* para 110.
1147 *Fürst-Pfeifer v Austria* App nos 33677/10 and 52340/10 (ECtHR, 17 May 2016) para 44.
1148 Cate (n193) 31.
1149 Fromholz (n74) 465.
1150 *Rodina v Latvia* App nos 48534/10 and 19532/15 (ECtHR, 14 May 2020).

such as de-identifying or blurring, when publishing information supplied by one of the parties which involves identifiable information about the other party.[1151] Article 82 of the GDPR states that "Member States shall provide for exemptions or derogations … for (data) processing (activities) carried out for journalistic purposes or the purposes of academic, artistic or literary expression … if … necessary to reconcile the right to the protection of personal data with the freedom of expression and information".[1152,1153] Additionally, the European Court of Human Rights introduced a reasonable or legitimate expectation of protection and respect for someone's privacy or private life into its case law,[1154] but, like in the United States, the interpretation of the words 'reasonable' and 'expectation' is not always straightforward.[1155] Similarly to SCOTUS' case law set out above regarding public versus private figures, the ECtHR held in 2012 *Von Hannover v Germany (No. 2)*[1156] that "a distinction has to be made between private individuals and persons acting in a public context, as political figures or public figures … whilst a private individual unknown to the public may claim particular protection of his or her right to private life, the same is not true of public figures …".[1157] People that "inevitably and knowingly (expose themselves) to (public) scrutiny … should (display) a (greater) degree of tolerance (than an ordinary private individual)".[1158] The Court added in the 2016 *Fürst-Pfeifer v Austria*[1159] case that "members of the judiciary should not be treated on an equal footing with politicians … civil servants acting in an official capacity may nevertheless be subject to wider limits of acceptable criticism than ordinary citizens".[1160]

Privacy limits Freedom of Speech – Personal data protection can be interpreted as a limitation of the data processors' and controllers' freedom of speech. The ability to "receive and impart information without public authority interference and regardless of frontiers"[1161] is part of Article 10 ECHR freedom of expression. This provision seems to encompass data processors and controllers, as they

---

1151 *Ibid.* paras 123-125 and 130-135.

1152 Article 85.2 GDPR.

1153 Bergkamp (n394) 35.

1154 *Halford v United Kingdom* App no 20605/92 (ECtHR, 25 Jun 1997) para 45; *Von Hannover* (n1143) paras 51 and 69 and 78; *Bărbulescu v Romania* App no 61496/08 (ECtHR, 5 Sep 2017) paras 1 and 56 and 73; *Faludy-Kovács v Hungary* App no 20487/13 (ECtHR, 23 Jan 2018) para 31; *López Ribalda and Others v Spain* App nos 1874/13 and 8567/13 (ECtHR, 17 Oct 2019) paras 89 and 93 and 125.

1155 Bygrave, *Data Privacy Law* (n37) 89-90; Gutwirth *et al.* (n32) 24-25.

1156 *Von Hannover (No. 2)* (n1145).

1157 *Ibid.* para 110.

1158 *Lingens v Austria* App no 9815/82 (ECtHR, 8 Jul 1986) para 42; *Oberschlick v Austria* App no 20834/92 (ECtHR, 1 Jul 1997) para 29; *Faludy-Kovács* (n1154) para 30; *Kajganić* (n1144) para 65.

1159 *Fürst-Pfeifer* (n1147).

1160 *Ibid.* para 46.

1161 Article 10 ECHR.

lawfully obtain and collect truthful data, which they can share with third parties for, for example, profiling purposes.[1162] Personal data protection rights, which are grounded in the right to privacy and the protection of people's human dignity, may hamper this practice as illustrated by the following European case law.[1163] The German Constitutional Court decided in the 1981 *Mephisto*[1164] case that the preservation of the good reputation (or dignity) of a deceased actor prevailed over the publication of a novel where the deceased actor's reputation was defamed, resulting in an injunction against the novel's publication.[1165] The ECtHR decided in the 2008 *K.U. v Finland*[1166] case that "although freedom of expression and confidentiality of communications are primary considerations ..., such guarantee cannot be absolute and must yield on occasion to other legitimate imperatives, such as the prevention of disorder or crime or the protection of the rights and freedoms of others",[1167] which in this case was the right to privacy of the injured party.[1168] The CJEU decided in the 2014 *Google Spain*[1169] case that the right to privacy and the right to personal data protection prevail "not only (over) the economic interest of the operator of the search engine but also (over) the interest of the general public in finding that information upon a search relating to the data subject's name",[1170] and would become known as 'the right to be forgotten'.[1171] The right to be forgotten, also called 'the right to erasure',[1172] provides individuals with a right to request erasure of their personal data, and was enshrined in Article 17 GDPR in 2016, which further limited the possibilities for downstream dissemination of lawfully obtained truthful information.[1173] Uta Kohl nuances that "the right to be forgotten envisages that the relevant personal information is, and will, remain in the public domain, but should not be so easily traceable to the data subject".[1174] Peter Blume prefers to speak of "the right to be remembered with difficulty", as it is "a right to have links removed (which) does not imply that the data disappears ... the data is still out there ... it is just more difficult to find".[1175,1176] The Court decided indeed that personal data and

1162 Bygrave, *Data Protection Law* (n17) 40; Bygrave, *Data Privacy Law* (n37) 34; Cohen (n38) 1375 and 1409.
1163 Krotoszynski Jr. (n1069) 1573.
1164 German BVerfG, Mephisto Judgement of 24 Feb 1971, 1 BvR 435/68.
1165 Buitelaar (n528) 183-184; Krotoszynski Jr. (n1069) 1566-1569.
1166 *K.U. v. Finland* (n394).
1167 *Ibid.* para 49.
1168 Purtova, *Property Rights* (n31) 238-239.
1169 *Google Spain* (n733).
1170 *Ibid.* para 97.
1171 Balkin (n1068) 1201-1202; de Vries *et al.* (n525) 258.
1172 Kohl (n398) 739-750.
1173 Jef Ausloos, *The Right to Erasure in EU Data Protection Law* (OUP 2020) 196-274; Kohl (n398) 739-750.
1174 Kohl (n398) 762.
1175 Blume (n528) 10-11.
1176 *Ibid.*; Peltz-Steele, 'American Privacy' (n240) 368-370.

information remain available on the primary platforms; it is merely the links to these pages produced by Google (or another search engine) that have to be deleted following a request 'to be forgotten'.[1177] A request for the deletion of information from one Google subsidiary's website (for example, Spain) does also not result in the deletion of the same information from other Google subsidiaries' websites, let alone from the websites of all Google subsidiaries worldwide, which leads to flaws in the practical application of this approach.[1178]

Privacy enables Freedom of Speech – The right to privacy provides the opportunity for people to withdraw themselves from the public domain to express their thoughts and experiment with different ideas without negative repercussions, enabling freedom of speech. The ECtHR has confirmed that "there is ... a zone of interaction of a person with others, even in a public context, which may fall within the scope of 'private life'".[1179] In particular, individuals holding dissenting opinions are protected from the government to avert the development of authoritarian States where governments collect personal data to exercise control over their population. Where previously State entities had an important role in preserving freedom of speech and democracy, this has now shifted to also include "large private enterprises that ... have the technical and bureaucratic capacity to regulate and govern speech, through blocking, filtering, and removing content",[1180] and eventually to decide which information is shared with whom. A more concerning version of this phenomenon is the emergence of 'echo chambers' or 'filter bubbles', which consist of polarized groups 'echoing' the same ideas as the user holds. Social media providers allow people to choose which content they want to see, and the algorithm will further determine which content is relevant based on users' online behavior. In this way, private companies exercise control over their users by showing them only one side of the (political) discussion, leading to their eventual alignment with and strengthening of certain ideas due to the lack of confrontation with other and different opinions.[1181] This 'echoing' of one dominant opinion can endanger civil society's freedom of speech and ultimately democracy.[1182] Similarly, private

---

1177 *Google Spain* (n733) paras 80 and 88.

1178 Stainforth (n193) 265.

1179 *P.G. and J.H. v United Kingdom* App no 44787/98 (ECtHR, 25 Sep 2001) para 56; *Peck v United Kingdom* App no 44647/98 (ECtHR, 28 Jan 2003) para 57; *Von Hannover* (n1143) para 50; *Sciacca* (n451) para 29; *Denisov v Ukraine* App no 76639/11 (ECtHR, 25 Sep 2018) para 100; *López Ribalda* (n1154) para 88; *Glukhin* (n424) para 64; *Hurbain v Belgium* App no 57292/16 (ECtHR, 4 Jul 2023) para 188.

1180 Balkin (n1068) 1175.

1181 Bygrave, *Data Protection Law* (n17) 312; Cohen (n38) 1397-1408; Poullet, 'Data protection' (n45) 218-219; Purtova, *Property Rights* (n31) 50-51.

1182 Muhammad Al Atiqi, *Echo Chamber and Polarization in Social Media* (Springer 2023) 1; Alessandro Bessi and others, 'Users polarization on Facebook and YouTube' (2016) 11 PLOS One e0159641, e0159641; Matteo Cinelli and others, 'The echo chamber effect on social companies' profiling practices can result in behavior manipulation. Individuals have, in these situations, the feeling that they are deciding, while algorithmic selections actually define the content that is shown to users, which in turn leads users to make a preferential pre-designed decision. A specific advertisement can, for example, only be shown to a certain group of people, excluding others.[1183] Przemysław Pałka and Yves Poullet[1184] warn that "these harms (may) go beyond privacy and include … discrimination, preference (or behavior) manipulation, and even social exclusion".[1185] Woodrow Hartzog concludes that "the control we are given online is mediated, which means it cannot help but be engineered to produce particular results".[1186] To a certain extent, this is also necessary as it is impossible for individuals to exercise granular consent for each specific item that can be displayed in today's proliferation of digital entities and services. It is important to realize that people are making selected choices within pre-designed options, which limits their actual freedom of choice.[1187] Not only State entities but also private companies should, therefore, respect people's right to seclusion or privacy so they can safely express their opinion to contribute to discussions and a democratic society where personalities and ideas can develop and flourish.[1188]

B. SENSITIVE DATA AND THE PROHIBITION OF DISCRIMINATION

The connection between the protection of personal data (privacy) and the prohibition of discrimination can be found in the additional level of protection foreseen for 'sensitive personal data'. This 'special' category of personal data aims at providing safeguards against discriminatory practices, as shown in

media' (2021) 118 PNAS e2023301118 1, 1-2 and 5; Geschke *et al.* (n52) 130-133; Grusauskaite *et al.* (n52) 1-2; Lei Guo, Jacob Rohde, and Denis Wu, 'Who is responsible for Twitter's echo chamber problem?' (2020) 23 InfCommunSoc 234, 234-236; Kitchens *et al.* (n50) 1619-1622; Petrić Howe (n48).

1183 Bygrave, *Data Protection Law* (n17) 302-312; Gutwirth *et al.* (n32) 78; Eleanor Novek, Nikhil Sinha, and Oscar Gandy, 'The value of your name' (1990) 12 MediaCultSoc 525, 533-535; Purtova, *Property Rights* (n31) 50-51.

1184 Poullet, 'Data protection' (n45) 214.

1185 Pałka, 'Data Management' (n44) 559.

1186 Hartzog (n266) 426.

1187 *Ibid.* 426-429; Edward Janger and Paul Schwartz, 'The Gramm-Leach-Bliley act, information privacy, and the limits of default rules' (2002) 86 Minnesota LRev 1219, 1242; Newell *et al.* (n229) 1067-1072; Neil Richards and Woodrow Hartzog, 'A Duty of Loyalty for Privacy Law' (2021) 99 WashU LRev 961, 967; Schwartz, 'Property' (n896) 2083.

1188 Bygrave, *Data Protection Law* (n17) 136; Cate (n193) 20; Fromholz (n74) 471; Gutwirth *et al.* (n32) 79; Kosta and Kamara (n37) 484; Packard (n801) 264; Poullet, 'Data protection' (n45) 216; Purtova, *Property Rights* (n31) 46-47; Regan (n801) 59; Paul Schwartz, 'Privacy and Participation' (1995) 80 IowaLRev 553, 559-563; Solove, 'Why Privacy Matters' (n822) 3; Zuiderveen Borgesius *et al.* (n180) 16.

the previous chapter, but this categorization was not included in all the legal instruments discussed; partly due to unnecessity and partly due to discrepancies in opinion on which types of data should and should not be included in this category.[1189] This section provides an overview of the relationship between the additional level of protection provided for sensitive data and the prohibition of discrimination in the United States and the EU, and argues why the distinction in the level of protection of 'regular' and 'sensitive' data is becoming outdated.

i) U.S. Sensitive Personal Information

Federal level – The prohibition of discrimination is, at the U.S. federal level, enshrined in the U.S. Fourteenth Amendment, which states that "all persons born or naturalized in the United States, and subject to the jurisdiction thereof, are citizens of the United States and of the State wherein they reside. No State shall make or enforce any law which shall ... deprive any person of life, liberty, or property, without due process of law; nor deny to any person within its jurisdiction the equal protection of the laws".[1190] U.S. legislation on employment discrimination is left out of the scope of this book. The 1973 HEW Report as well as the 1974 Privacy Act, and the 1998 FTC Report do not afford an additional level of protection to sensitive personal data.[1191] Consequently, the discussion will focus below on the U.S. State consumer privacy acts.

State level – In contrast to the federal level, the State consumer privacy acts of California as well as Virginia, the two U.S. States explored in this book, include a provision for the additional level of protection of sensitive personal data. The CCPA defines sensitive personal information as "Personal information that reveals: a consumer's social security, driver's license, state identification card, or passport number, a consumer's account log-in, financial account, debit card, or credit card number in combination with any required security or access code, password, or credentials allowing access to an account, a consumer's precise geolocation, a consumer's racial or ethnic origin, citizenship or immigration status, religious or philosophical beliefs, or union membership, the contents of a consumer's mail, email, and text messages unless the business is the intended recipient of the communication, a consumer's genetic data, a consumer's neural data ..., the processing of biometric information for the purpose of uniquely identifying a consumer, personal information collected and analyzed concerning a consumer's health ... sex life or sexual orientation".[1192,1193]

1189 See *Chapter 3, § 2, A.*
1190 Fourteenth Amendment to the U.S. Constitution, 9 Jul 1868.
1191 See *Chapter 3, § 1, A. and B., i).*
1192 CCPA § 1798.140.(ae).
1193 Newell *et al.* (n229) 1081.

When sensitive personal information "is collected or processed without the purpose of inferring characteristics about a consumer",[1194] it is considered as regular 'personal information' according to the CCPA, which does not enjoy an additional level of protection. The collection and processing of sensitive personal data is allowed by default in California, but businesses have to provide consumers with an opt-out "right ... to direct a business that collects sensitive personal information about the consumer to limit its use of the consumer's sensitive personal information to that use which is necessary to perform the services or provide the goods reasonably expected by an average consumer who requests those goods or services ... a business that uses or discloses a consumer's sensitive personal information for purposes other than those specified ... shall provide notice to consumers ... that this information may be used, or disclosed to a service provider or contractor, for additional, specified purposes and that consumers have the right to limit the use or disclosure of their sensitive personal information".[1195,1196] Upon receipt of the aforementioned request from a consumer, the "business ... shall be prohibited ... from using or disclosing the consumer's sensitive personal information for any other purpose ... unless the consumer subsequently provides consent for the use or disclosure of the consumer's sensitive personal information for additional purposes".[1197] Sensitive data is in the VCDPA defined as "a category of personal data that includes: personal data revealing racial or ethnic origin, religious beliefs, mental or physical health diagnosis, sexual orientation, or citizenship or immigration status; the processing of genetic or biometric data for the purpose of uniquely identifying a natural person; the personal data collected from a known child; or precise geolocation data".[1198,1199] Unlike the CCPA, the VCDPA requires specific opt-in consent for the processing of sensitive personal data, prohibiting businesses to "process sensitive data concerning a consumer without obtaining the consumer's consent ...".[1200,1201] Finally, sensitive personal information that is 'publicly available' or 'manifestly made public' is excluded from both the CCPA's and the VCDPA's scope of application,[1202] which is in line with the U.S. First Amendment jurisprudence and the third-party doctrine set out above.

1194 CCPA § 1798.121.(d).
1195 CCPA § 1798.121.(a).
1196 Newell *et al.* (n229) 1082.
1197 CCPA § 1798.121.(b).
1198 VCDPA § 59.1-575.
1199 Newell *et al.* (n229) 1082.
1200 VCDPA § 59.1-578.A.5.
1201 Newell *et al.* (n229) 1082.
1202 CCPA § 1798.140.(ae); VCDPA § 59.1-575; Newell *et al.* (n229) 1084 and 1106-1111.

ii) *EU Sensitive Personal Data*

Prohibition of Discrimination – The categories of sensitive data protected by EU personal data protection law resemble the categories outlined in Article 14 ECHR prohibition of discrimination, which ensures that "the enjoyment of the rights and freedoms … shall be secured without discrimination on any ground such as sex, race, colour, language, religion, political or other opinion, national or social origin, association with a national minority, property, birth or other status".[1203] The prohibition of discrimination is also enshrined in Article 21 of the EU Charter, but the Explanatory Memorandum to this Charter clarifies that "in so far as this (Article) corresponds to article 14 of the ECHR, it applies in compliance with it".[1204] Article 8 of the 1995 Directive as well as its successor Article 9 of the 2016 GDPR include a prohibition, to which exemptions are possible, on the processing of sensitive personal data. Sensitive personal data consists of "personal data revealing racial or ethnic origin, political opinions, religious or philosophical beliefs, trade union membership, (and the processing of genetic data, biometric data for the purpose of uniquely identifying a natural person) and the processing of data concerning health or (a natural person's) sex life (or sexual orientation)".[1205] The processing of sensitive personal data can be justified by, among others, the individual's explicit consent, when necessary to carry out (contractual) obligations and exercise specific rights, when necessary to protect people's vital interests when they are themselves unable to, when necessary for a body's legitimate political, philosophical, religious or trade union activities, when the individual has made the data manifestly public, or when necessary for judicial purposes.[1206] The special category of sensitive data in EU personal data protection law has its origins in the prohibition of discrimination. Paul Quinn and Gianclaudio Malgieri observe that "the existence of sensitive data often revolve(s) around the need to prevent harmful forms of discrimination or related phenomena".[1207] Possible discriminatory consequences of profiling practices, direct and indirect, were exemplified in the introductory chapter.[1208] Maria Tzanou explains that a separate group of 'sensitive data' with additional protection is necessary "because the processing of such data can lead to illegal discrimination".[1209] While these observations are certainly accurate, it is important to notice that today's increasing computing power, interconnectedness,

1203 Article 14 ECHR.
1204 Explanations relating to the Charter of Fundamental Rights [2007] OJ C 303/24.
1205 Article 8.1 Directive 95/46/EC; Article 9.1 GDPR.
1206 Article 8.2 Directive 95/46/EC; Article 9.2 GDPR.
1207 Quinn and Malgieri (n36) 1585.
1208 See *Chapter 1, § 1, B.*
1209 Tzanou (n526) 91-92.

aggregated big data, and powerful machine learning algorithms provide for the ability to deduct sensitive information from any type of personal information.[1210] Colin Bennett explains that "the (discriminatory) harm results not from the information (or data) but from the *context* of that information (or data); it is what people do with (the data) that is the problem".[1211] EU personal data protection legislation focuses "erroneously ... on data as such, instead of harm arising from data uses",[1212] according to Lucas Bergkamp. Consequently, it would be useful to reconsider the current EU conceptualization where personal data, as such, is protected in a framework where personal data is protected in relation to the purposes for which it is employed.

C. INTERIM COMPARATIVE EU-U.S. ANALYSIS

Privacy versus Freedom of Speech – Publicly available information that is lawfully obtained and truthful is strongly protected in the United States by the First Amendment, which ensures freedom of speech. On the contrary, publicly available personal data is included in the scope of application of personal data protection legislation in the EU. A discrepancy emerges in the downstream dissemination of lawfully obtained truthful information, as in the United States the freedom to disseminate this information, and hence the freedom of speech, will often prevail, whereas in the EU a balancing exercise will be conducted that will likely tilt towards the right to privacy, and hence non-dissemination of the same information. The possibility to restrict Article 10 ECHR freedom of expression "for the protection of the reputation or rights of others"[1213] has also been explicitly enshrined in this Article. People's freedom of speech, and in particular democracies, can be endangered when diffused information is filtered based on other people's preferences, especially when this occurs without the former's knowledge. Individuals are confronted with an online world echoing the same ideas they hold, without being challenged in their thinking. Democracies are built on dialogue, the exchange of ideas, and cooperation, which is not reflected in the personalized webpages that people encounter. Freedom of speech and the right to privacy can, therefore, be interpreted as protecting democracy in a similar way; they both aim to stimulate political debate, ensure that information flows freely and "are meant to protect the individual citizen from excessive information power".[1214] Before the digital age, this information

1210 Enright (n198) 265; Gutwirth *et al.* (n32) 330; Quinn and Malgieri (n36) 1584 and 1605; Solove, 'Data Is What Data Does' (n16) 1081 and 1136-1137.

1211 Bennett (n140) 34-35.

1212 Bergkamp (n394) 42.

1213 Article 10.2 ECHR.

1214 Gutwirth *et al.* (n32) 294.

power was held by "speakers and publishers of content" at whom "old school speech regulation" was aimed; nowadays, the "digital infrastructure", such as social media providers or web hosting services, have taken over this role, as they manage what third parties are posting on their platforms.[1215] When these platforms engage in filtering practices, based on user preferences or profiling, they can silence selected groups intentionally or even unintentionally, resulting in "the author's speech (being) blocked, usually without explanation".[1216] Given the power of social media to govern "the flow of information … and … the behavior of the end-users and customers who employ the digital infrastructure … these companies, (such as) Facebook, YouTube, Twitter (now X), (or) Google, and their competitors and successors, are the new governors of digital expression",[1217] and should, according to Jack Balkin, abide by the same principles as public entities and the press have to do. The EU and the United States take a similar approach towards public persons, who will generally enjoy a lower level of privacy protection. Both sides of the Atlantic differ, however, in the exact level of protection afforded. The ECtHR requires that the disseminated information has to 'contribute to a debate of general interest' but will not accept the dissemination of the same information 'to just satisfy public curiosity'. The more lenient U.S. approach allowing the general dissemination of publicly available information is in line with the U.S. third party doctrine, according to which private information has to be actively secreted to enjoy Fourth Amendment protection. The third party doctrine is challenged by technological novelties and the digital world, where all information is shared with a digital third party in order to reach its recipient. This sharing does, however, not entail a wish to make this information publicly available. The U.S. Supreme Court seems to have adjusted the third party doctrine to this reality in the *Kyllo*[1218] and *Carpenter*[1219] cases, but it remains to be seen how other technological and digital cases will be decided as SCOTUS specified that its decision in these cases was only taken in the specific context of the case involved. The U.S. approach, which excludes information that was made publicly available from the scope of application of the Fourth Amendment as well as the California and Virginia consumer privacy acts, seems reasonable in a digital society when applied in a mediated context. People cannot expect to have privacy rights in information that they publicly share online when their settings do not restrict this information to being seen by 'only friends' or 'only specific users'. A certain degree of responsibility should be assigned to the people as a patriarchic approach, such as the current EU data protection approach, risks hollowing out people's decisional power. The EU requirement for consent for

1215 Balkin (n1068) 1174-1179.
1216 *Ibid.* 1178.
1217 *Ibid.* 1182-1188.
1218 *Kyllo* (n1083).
1219 *Carpenter* (n1085).

photos taken in public places or at public events is an example of a measure that tilts the balance too much towards patriarchism. If people decide to willingly participate in a public event and walk on the streets or squares, they can expect that an event photographer or a passing tourist will capture their image in a photograph. What is more relevant is what the photographer aims to do with the photograph. This leads the analysis back to the conclusion, which has already been reached a few times in this book, that the focus of personal data protection legislation should be on the purposes and the use of the collected/processed data, as opposed to the data as such. The U.S. concept of 'reasonable expectation of privacy', employed by the ECtHR, can provide a benchmark here. A person can (reasonably) expect that their photograph of participation in an international law program will be published on the university's website. The same person would not expect an unrelated law firm to use the same photo for commercial and advertising purposes. While the 'reasonable expectation of privacy' benchmark is, admittedly, a subjective one, it still seems more accurate than the current U.S. and EU approaches, which may both have tilted too much to one side of the spectrum (almost absolute free use versus prohibition of use).

Right to be forgotten – The European concept of 'the right to be forgotten' plays an important role in the discussion on the interplay between the right to privacy and freedom of speech. The right to be forgotten is often portrayed as a right to request deletion of lawfully obtained truthful information and to prevent its further dissemination, which is particularly problematic from a U.S. First Amendment perspective.[1220] The tension between these two interests can explicitly be found in § 1798.105.(d)(4) of the CCPA, which states that "a business ..., another service provider, or another contractor, shall not be required to comply with a consumer's request to delete the consumer's personal information if it is reasonably necessary for the business, service provider, or contractor to maintain the consumer's personal information in order to: ... Exercise free speech, (or) ensure the right of another consumer to exercise that consumer's right of free speech ...".[1221] Upon closer reading, this is not what the right to be forgotten aims to obtain, and also not what the CJEU decided in the *Google Spain*[1222] case. The CJEU targeted the search engine Google, which facilitated the distribution of personal information, and not the newspaper (press) that had published the article containing the information to which Google was referring.[1223] Peter Blume explains that it is "a right to have links removed (which) does not imply that the data disappears. The data is still out there. It is just more difficult to

1220 Cate (n193) 28; Fromholz (n74) 465; Peltz-Steele, 'American Privacy' (n240) 368-378; Rosen, 'Right to Be Forgotten' (n1092) 88; Jeffrey Rosen, 'A Grave New Threat to Free Speech From Europe' (*The New Republic*, 10 Feb 2012).

1221 CCPA § 1798.105.(d)(4).

1222 *Google Spain* (n733).

1223 Balkin (n1068) 1202-1203.

find".[1224] The right to be forgotten aims at "practical obscurity rather than complete censorship",[1225] according to Jack Balkin. Uta Kohl acknowledges this carefully formulated balance where "the right to be forgotten envisages that the relevant personal information is, and will, remain in the public domain, but (that it) should not be so easily traceable to the data subject".[1226] It is, as a consequence, more accurate to speak of a "right to be remembered with difficulty",[1227] instead of a 'right to be (completely) forgotten'. Compliance with the U.S. Fourth Amendment's third party doctrine of 'active secreting' of private information has become increasingly difficult, even almost impossible, in an online world where websites, social media, and email are used as means of communication.[1228] The right to be forgotten is a European way to balance the interests of freedom of speech and privacy in a digital era where the accessibility and proliferation of information has reached new levels. A comparison can be drawn with the online availability of court judgements.[1229] Before the digital era, people had to go to each court separately to actively consult and read available judgements. Nowadays, it suffices to type a query into an online database and consult the same information much more easily. Parties to the case are, therefore, usually anonymized to protect their privacy. The same evolution occurred for news items and media outlets. Where previously a person had to consult (physical) archives, a simple query in an online database that can be accessed from someone's home will suffice today to access the same information. Digitization has facilitated the proliferation of information to a very large extent, and search engines have extensively contributed to this evolution. Antoinette Rouvroy and Yves Poullet point out that "technological developments gradually brought about a situation where (a) there is virtually no limit to the amount of information that can be recorded, (b) there is virtually no limit to the scope of analysis that can be done ... and (c) the information may be stored virtually forever".[1230] Fred Cate, Julia Fromholz, and Lucas Bergkamp warn more broadly that "privacy ... facilitates the dissemination of false information ... (and) protects the withholding of relevant true information".[1231,1232] A lack of complete information impairs, after all, people's ability to make informed choices and decisions.[1233] Jeffrey Rosen observed in 2012 that the right to be forgotten "represents the biggest threat to

1224 Blume (n528) 10-11.
1225 Balkin (n1068) 1202-1203.
1226 Kohl (n398) 762.
1227 Blume (n528) 10-11; Peltz-Steele, 'American Privacy' (n240) 368-370.
1228 Orin Kerr and Greg Nojeim, 'The Data Question: Should the Third-Party Records Doctrine be Revisited?' (*ABA Journal*, 1 Aug 2012).
1229 Peltz-Steele, 'American Privacy' (n240) 402-403.
1230 Gutwirth *et al.* (n32) 68.
1231 Cate (n193) 28.
1232 Bergkamp (n394) 36; Fromholz (n74) 465.
1233 *Ibid.*

free speech on the Internet ... leading to a far less open Internet".[1234,1235] Nowadays, the selective filtering of content which is and is not shown to users could be added to this 'biggest threat to free speech on the Internet'. Lucas Bergkamp questions "whether the EU has any business regulating the possession and exchange of lawfully obtained and truthful information".[1236] From a U.S. perspective, the dissemination of lawfully obtained truthful information will indeed prevail, even when in conflict with someone's privacy interests. Jeffrey Rosen, Meg Ambrose and Jef Ausloos explain the distinct approach between the EU and the United States from a historical perspective: "In Europe, the intellectual roots of the right to be forgotten can be found in French law, which recognizes *le droit à l'oubli* – or the 'right of oblivion' – a right that allows a convicted criminal who has served his time and been rehabilitated to object to the publication of the facts of his conviction and incarceration. In America, by contrast, publication of someone's criminal history is protected by the First Amendment ...".[1237,1238] To understand the idea behind the EU conceptualization of the right to be forgotten, and the balance it aims to preserve between the right to privacy and freedom of speech, the findings of the first section of this chapter have to be reiterated. The EU right to personal data protection is grounded in the right to privacy, which is in its turn grounded in safeguarding the protection of people's human dignity, through the protection of people's reputation and their personal image (in public). The U.S. origins of data privacy, or privacy more broadly, can be traced back to the Fourth Amendment, which protects someone's home. It is in this context that Uta Kohl places the distinct EU and U.S. approach towards the right to be forgotten: "its distinctiveness does not lie in its apparent technicality but in its robust openness to privacy in public – an idea that is alien to the Anglo-American culture of privacy",[1239] as the latter is rooted in the inviolability of the home.[1240] A right to be forgotten which would require the deletion of all information available on all websites would completely undermine freedom of speech and information dissemination rights. The interpretation given by the CJEU, which is more accurately defined as 'a right to be remembered with difficulty', where the information is still available for those people who make the effort to actively look for it, strikes a fair balance between the right to privacy and freedom of speech. The decisional power over someone's personal data is, moreover, given back to the people whose personal data is involved, as opposed to the government or private companies.

1234 Rosen, 'Right to Be Forgotten' (n1092) 88.

1235 Peltz-Steele, 'American Privacy' (n240) 371-372; Rosen, 'Right to Be Forgotten' (n1092) 88; Rosen, 'Free Speech' (n1220).

1236 Bergkamp (n394) 35.

1237 Rosen, 'Right to Be Forgotten' (n1092) 88.

1238 Ambrose and Ausloos (n355) 1-9.

1239 Kohl (n398) 737.

1240 *Ibid.* 738-742.

Non-discrimination and sensitive data – Sensitive data deserve a higher level of protection as their (ab)use can result in a more serious level of (privacy) harm sustained by people in the form of discriminatory (profiling) practices.[1241] The similarity between the EU categories of sensitive data and the categories set out in Article 14 ECHR prohibition of discrimination enhances consistency in the protected types of data. The fragmented landscape in the United States, on the contrary, results in discrepancies between the protected categories enshrined in the different State consumer privacy acts, and more specifically in those of California and Virginia. An additional level of protection for specific categories of (sensitive) data can be useful, but only if these categories are defined similarly in the different jurisdictions where businesses are operational. Public sector activities are, by definition, location-based and delineated by their geographical territory, but private sector activities, especially in the digital era, can have a worldwide span. Interestingly, political opinions are in the EU considered sensitive data, requiring an additional level of protection, while this is not the case in the United States, and more particularly in California and Virginia.[1242] People must be able to express their political opinions freely to stimulate political debates, exchange and confront ideas and, eventually, to preserve democracy itself.[1243] Political opinions deserve a higher level of protection in the light of increased data processing and polarizing trends explained above, but it should be left to the legal systems concerned to decide how this protection should be provided. Bryce Newell *et al.* explain that "*information* is commonly understood as 'data + meaning', (which is) also consistent with the widely regarded idea that data, information, knowledge, and wisdom exist in a sort of pyramidic relationship in which each serves as the foundational element of the form that sits on top – that is, data + meaning = information; information + understanding = knowledge; and so forth".[1244] Paul Quinn and Gianclaudio Malgieri observe that "at present, the approach is mostly contextual in nature … (where) relatively little attention is paid to the intentions of the data controller".[1245] With the increasing abilities of technology and digitization, any data can reveal something about 'sensitive' data, turning all types of data into sensitive data requiring a higher level of protection. The EU GDPR excludes anonymous data from its scope of application as it only applies to 'personally identifiable data'.[1246] Private companies no longer need identified or identifiable information to 'categorize' a person. Bits and pieces of

---

1241 Solove, 'Data Is What Data Does' (n16) 1127.

1242 CCPA § 1798.140.(ae); VCDPA § 59.1-575; Mathias Möschel, 'European Anti-Discrimination Law' in Thomas Giegerich (ed), *The European Union as Protector and Promoter of Equality* (Springer 2020) 477; Newell *et al.* (n229) 1081-1082.

1243 Geschke *et al.* (n52) 145-146; Vogiatzoglou (n737) 166.

1244 Newell *et al.* (n229) 1087.

1245 Quinn and Malgieri (n36) 1584.

1246 Recital 26 GDPR.

information about the individual suffice for the former to, relatively accurately, categorize an anonymous person into a predefined consumer profile. Paul De Hert and Serge Gutwirth use the following example: "while prohibiting the processing of sensitive data about, for instance, Jewish people, is positive, it would be unwise not to observe that a simple list of names (ordinary data) can also convey the information required to target them and ought to be protected as well".[1247] Consequently, the GDPR is "completely toothless"[1248] in these situations, which can be qualified as an indirect form of discrimination. Given today's computing possibilities, Viktor Mayer-Schönberger's, Kenneth Cukier's, and Daniel Solove's suggestion of protecting personal data in function of the purposes (not discriminatory) for which the data are collected/processed, and consequently eliminating the distinction between different pre-defined 'categories' of personal data, should be endorsed. The focus of data privacy legislation should not be on the type of data as such, but on the uses of this data; "data is what data does".[1249,1250] This book advocates, therefore, a change of perspective from the current procedural point of view (*which type of data*) to a contextual point of view (*how the data is used*).

§ 3. LIBERAL MARKET HARM-BASED AND REGULATORY RISK-BASED CHARACTERISTICS

The final section of this chapter discusses the characterization of the U.S. approach as more 'liberal with a central position for the free market' and the EU approach as 'regulatory protective'. The aim is not to evaluate and determine which approach is better, but to discover similarities by placing each approach in its broader historical and cultural context. The findings show that the U.S. 'harm' approach can also be found in the jurisprudence of the European Court of Human Rights, and that the EU 'risk' approach in the area of data privacy is not that straightforward. Jonathan Wiener[1251] observed the deeper understanding behind the stereotypes already two decades ago:

> "Modern comparisons of risk regulation in the United States and Europe are often cast in stereotypes. They depict Europeans as risk-averse, afraid of the unknown (the ghost in the dark), afraid of new technologies (especially American) and of global markets, jumping to adopt precautionary regulations against the most remote and speculative

---

1247 Gutwirth *et al.* (n32) 25.

1248 Pałka, 'Data Management' (n44) 616.

1249 Solove, 'Data Is What Data Does' (n16) 1081.

1250 Viktor Mayer-Schönberger and Kenneth Cukier, *Big data: a revolution that will transform how we live, work, and think* (Houghton Mifflin 2013) 242p.; Solove, 'Data Is What Data Does' (n16) 1081.

1251 Wiener (n193) 208-209.

risks. Meanwhile Americans are seen as risk-indifferent or even risk-preferring, blustering blithely past risks (real and imagined), confident that new technology ... and the power of (American) markets will solve every problem and that precaution is a waste of time and a hindrance to progress. ... Despite some divisive rhetoric of late, U.S. and European systems of risk regulation are not divergent in the simple way in which they are claimed to be."

The U.S. and EU approaches towards data privacy are shaped by the involvement of different stakeholders. Robert Baldwin *et al.* identify "a triangle of shaping elements" in government regulation, consisting of market failure, public opinion, and lobby-driven stakeholders.[1252] These three voices are discussed in this section for the United States and the EU respectively to show how they contributed to shaping the so-called harm- and risk-centered policies that are in place today.

A. U.S. LIBERAL MARKET HARM-BASED CHARACTERISTICS

i) Liberal Market Approach

Passive government – The historical aim of the U.S. Bill of Rights, which includes the amendments to the U.S. Constitution, was to 'protect the people from the power of government', assigning a negative role to the government.[1253] The rights enshrined in the U.S. Constitution reflect people's distrust to a powerful central government, limiting concentrated governmental power, and provide citizens with rights to oppose governmental interventions, taking a critical stance towards government activity and involvement in people's lives.[1254] The United States adheres to the common law tradition, where legal principles and an evolutionary interpretation of, for example, the amendments, are primarily developed and updated by the courts' jurisprudence.[1255] Influential jurisprudence from courts at the U.S. States' level is also often codified (or modified) in State statutes.[1256]

1252 Robert Baldwin, Christopher Hood, and Henry Rothstein, *The Government of Risk* (OUP 2001) 61-62.

1253 Bygrave, *Data Privacy Law* (n37) 112; Cate (n193) 51 and 99; Hannah Fuson, 'Fourth Amendment Searches in First Amendment Spaces' (2020) 50 UnivMemphisLRev 231, 257-258 and 285; Marshall *et al.* (n1073) 752; Packard (n801) 261-262; Peltz-Steele, 'The pond betwixt' (n568) 17; Christopher Smith, 'The Bill of Rights after September 11th' (2004) 42 DuqLRev 259, 259.

1254 Bennett (n140) 29-30; Cate (n193) 44-51 and 99 and 123-130; Heisenberg (n66) 19; Kirtley (n795) 648-649; Wiener (n193) 246-247.

1255 Bennett (n140) 144; Cate (n193) 109; Morris Cohen, 'The Common Law in the American Legal System' (1989) 81 LawLibrJ 13, 14; Sheila Jasanoff, 'American Exceptionalism and the Political Acknowledgment of Risk' (1990) 119 Daedalus 61, 66; Solove and Hartzog (n61) 619 620.

1256 Legal Information Institute, 'Common Law' (*Cornell Law School*, 2020); Solove and Hartzog (n61) 619-620.

(Corrected) Liberal system – The U.S. market-oriented regulatory philosophy prioritizes market forces and enterprises to remedy issues and discrepancies before necessitating jurisprudential or legislative intervention in commerce by the government, contributing to a libertarian free market regime.[1257] Robert Baldwin *et al.* concretize some of these necessities, being "information deficiencies or asymmetries, inequalities of bargaining power, monopoly power, or spillover effects".[1258] When computerization and technological innovation started to emerge in the United States, with a predominant role for influential companies such as Microsoft, Google, Apple, and Facebook (now Meta), no specific legislation was issued, but it was rather left to the companies involved to self-regulate.[1259] The inequality of bargaining power, information asymmetries, and data privacy scandals (*see below*) contributed, however, to a necessary legislative intervention in the area of consumer privacy, albeit at the U.S. State level instead of at the federal level.[1260]

ii) Harm Approach

Strong Risk assessment – The primacy of U.S. courts' decision-making and jurisprudence had an influence on subsequent administrative risk regulation and assessment, which commenced in environmental and public health policy and expanded to other policy areas. When an administrative authority was confronted with scientific uncertainty regarding a subject that had to be regulated, the authority's decisions were, until the 1980s, often submitted to the courts for a regulatory check. This scrutiny resulted in the "adopt(ion of) formal analytical procedures, such as quantitative risk assessment, and (the building of) massive technical records to satisfy judicial demands for 'reasoned decision-making' and a 'hard look' at the evidence".[1261] In the case of scientific uncertainty, the possibilities for risk to materialize were overstated to make sure the administrative decision would pass the courts' test. This cautious approach was criticized for its use of "bad science to further an expensive and unrealistic strategy of zero risk".[1262,1263]

1257 Baldwin *et al.* (n1252) 63-70; Bygrave, *Data Protection Law* (n17) 54; Bygrave, *Data Privacy Law* (n37) 110; Marc Eisner, *Regulatory Politics in Transition* (Johns Hopkins press 1993) 171-172; Gutwirth *et al.* (n32) 188; Heisenberg (n66) 26-35; Peltz-Steele, 'The pond betwixt' (n568) 17-25; Peltz-Steele, 'American Privacy' (n240) 368; Richard Revesz, 'Rehabilitating Interstate Competition' (1992) 67 NYU LRev 1210, 1222; Vogel (n539) 30-31; Whitman (n392) 1161-1162.

1258 Baldwin *et al.* (n1252) 63.

1259 Bygrave, *Data Privacy Law* (n37) 107; Lynskey, *The foundations* (n42) 178; Scasserra and Martínez Elebi (n3) 4.

1260 Bygrave, *Data Protection Law* (n17) 54; see *Chapter 3, § 1, B.*

1261 Jasanoff (n1255) 66.

1262 *Ibid.* 68.

1263 *Ibid.* 66-68.

Political preferences – Between 1960 and 1980, the United States was more likely to adopt precautionary and stringent risk regulations than the EU, of which the 1974 Privacy Act[1264] is an example.[1265] Since the 1980s, the political landscape in the United States became more polarized and the regulatory philosophy changed completely, leading to stronger positions and less room for flexibility. In 1984 *Chevron U.S.A. v Natural Resources Defense Council*,[1266] SCOTUS afforded the decisional power to interpret and explain statutory policies back to the agencies, as opposed to the courts, because "federal judges – who have no constituency – have a duty to respect legitimate policy choices made by those who do (and the) responsibilities for assessing the wisdom of such policy choices and resolving the struggle between competing views of the public interest are not judicial ones: Our Constitution vests such responsibilities in the political branches".[1267] The Reagan "administration entered Washington (in the 1980s) with an explicit mandate to scale down the level of governmental intervention in business activity, even when the object was to safeguard public health and safety".[1268,1269] In that period, the United States was also confronted with "false positive policy errors (which) weakened the political credibility of new risk claims as well as the willingness of policymakers to enact more stringent regulations in response to them".[1270] Since this change in approach, Republicans have had a harm-focused voice in industrial risk management practices, preferring government-industry cooperation, and have been reciprocal to the business-lobbying sector, which was "opposed to more stringent consumer and environmental risk regulations".[1271] Regardless of the political side of future Presidents, Congress has become and remained polarized ever since.[1272] President Reagan promulgated Executive Order (EO) 12291[1273] in 1981 requiring regulatory agencies to conduct a cost-benefit analysis before issuing risk regulation.[1274] Peter Swire explains, however, that a cost-benefit analysis often relies on certain assumptions. These assumptions can be incorrect, as there are many uncertain factors in environmental law that cannot be perfectly measured or estimated.[1275] Reliance on a cost-benefit analysis might, therefore, be flawed, yet many of EO 12291's principles were re-promulgated by

---

1264 See *Chapter 3, § 1, A., ii)*.
1265 Jasanoff (n1255) 63.
1266 *Chevron U.S.A. v Natural Res. Def. Council* [1984] 467 U.S. 837; overturned in *Loper Bright Enterprises v Raimondo* [2024] 603 U.S. 369.
1267 *Chevron U.S.A.* (n1266) 866.
1268 Jasanoff (n1255) 70.
1269 Eisner (n1257) 188.
1270 Vogel (n539) 252.
1271 *Ibid.* 285.
1272 Peter Swire, 'The Race to Laxity and the Race to Undesirability' (1996) 14 YLPR 67, 69; Vogel (n539) 230-232.
1273 Sec.2(b) and Sec.3(d)(4) and Sec.6(a)(6) EO 12291, 17 Feb 1981.
1274 Eisner (n1257) 190.
1275 Swire (n1272) 94-99.

President Clinton in a new Executive Order 12866[1276] in 1993. The latter EO was upheld by the following Bush administration.[1277] The political changes led to a requirement adjustment from a strong to a light risk assessment. The focus shifted to concrete harms, where scientific "risk assessment (is) the cornerstone on which fundamental science decisions (are) based".[1278] Translated to the e-commerce market and data privacy, the focus was placed on concrete "harm arising from data uses",[1279] which were considered 'facts' based on "sound science"[1280] as opposed to risk speculations and precaution, often guided by public fear, which could "stifle innovation"[1281] and "(kill) the goose that (lays) the golden egg".[1282,1283] The concept of American risk-taking became a necessary precondition for progressive science, trade, e-commerce, and industrialization.[1284] The U.S. private sector succeeded to live up to its innovative promises, as the majority of big tech and e-commerce companies that we know today are predominantly U.S.-based companies.[1285]

a) Triangle of Shaping Elements in Government Regulation

Market failure – The "widespread concern about the perceived over-stringency and inefficiency of many precautionary standards"[1286] led to new risk regulations requiring a higher level of scientific evidence to prove their necessity.[1287] As the courts played an important role in this evolution, the change in approach can also be observed in U.S. case law.[1288] In 1976 *Ethyl Corp. v Environmental Protection Agency*,[1289] the Court of Appeals for the District of Columbia Circuit decided that "a significant risk of harm to the health of urban populations … is not arbitrary (or) capricious, (since it) has a rational basis in the evidence",[1290] without, however, defining the scope of the 'significant risk of harm'. In 1980

1276 Sec.1(a), (b)(6) and Sec.4(c)(B) EO 12866, 30 Sep 1993.

1277 Eisner (n1257) 171-192; Jasanoff (n1255) 63-70; Vogel (n539) 3-4 and 34-36 and 228-231 and 252-258 and 285; Wiener (n193) 214-221.

1278 Vogel (n539) 267.

1279 Bergkamp (n394) 41-42; Lynskey, *The foundations* (n42) 177-178.

1280 Vogel (n539) 9.

1281 Heisenberg (n66) 173.

1282 *Ibid.* 37 and 76.

1283 Wiener (n193) 214-215.

1284 Heisenberg (n66) 76; Vogel (n539) 9; Wiener (n193) 214-215.

1285 See *Chapter 1, § 1, A.*

1286 Daniel Bodansky, 'The Precautionary Principle in U.S. Environmental Law' in Tim O'Riordan and James Cameron (eds), *Interpreting The Precautionary Principle* (1st edn, Routledge 1994) 205; Vogel (n539) 261.

1287 Vogel (n539) 35 and 252-259 and 285.

1288 *Ibid.* 256-257; Wiener (n193) 211-213.

1289 *Ethyl Corp. v Environmental Protection Agency* [1976] 541 F.2d 1 (D.C. Cir. 1976).

1290 *Ibid.* 2.

Industrial Union Department v American Petroleum Institute,[1291] SCOTUS held, on the contrary, that there was no "unbridled discretion to adopt standards designed to create absolutely risk-free workplaces, regardless of cost"[1292] and that "safe is not the equivalent of risk-free".[1293] A similar approach was taken in 1983 *Gulf South Insul. v U.S. Consumer Prod*[1294] by the Court of Appeals for the Fifth Circuit that "the substantial evidence test (was put in place so that) the courts (would) scrutinize ... actions more closely than an arbitrary and capricious standard would allow".[1295] Mike Feintuck observes critically that the term 'scientific evidence' can arbitrarily be defined by the government and industries to suit their preferred scientific level of compliance. The definition of 'scientific evidence' can also be influenced by stakeholders and public demands, which renders the question of how 'scientific' the required 'scientific evidence' in the end actually be.[1296] In the area of data privacy, market failure occurred as the imbalance between powerful big tech companies and their users could not be remedied by market forces, and legislative intervention became necessary to restore this balance. The liberal market approach works effectively when consumers have the necessary knowledge, information, and leverage to negotiate with or pressure private companies. Dorothee Heisenberg points out that consumers were initially not aware of the potential harms that could result from data processing activities, and consequently did not exercise their negotiating power. Even today, many consumers still prefer to access the digital services provided regardless of the (privacy) costs, as informed decision-making will sometimes lead to the inconvenient necessity to renounce the use of the chosen service or product.[1297]

Public opinion and pressure – In the environmental area as well as in the area of data privacy, the initial reluctance to U.S. governmental intervention had to be remedied by legislative initiatives at the State level. David Vogel defines situations where policymakers are pressured to take legislative action by the public and media as 'momentary alarms'. The environmental area was dominated by these 'alarm' situations. Before the 1980s-1990s, public calls for regulatory intervention led to over-regulation as the "gap between the public's perceptions of the risks they consider both credible and unacceptable and the existing scope

1291 *Indus. Union Dept. v Amer. Petroleum Inst.* [1980] 448 U.S. 607.

1292 *Ibid.* 607-608.

1293 *Ibid.* 608.

1294 *Gulf South Insul. v U.S. Consumer Prod* [1983] 701 F.2d 1137 (5th Cir. 1983).

1295 *Ibid.* 1142.

1296 Mike Feintuck, 'Precautionary Maybe, but What's the Principle?' (2005) 32 JOLS 371, 387; Wiener (n193) 216; Bruce Yandle, 'The precautionary principle as a force for global political centralization' in Julian Morris (ed), *Rethinking Risk and the Precautionary Principle* (Butterworth-Heinemann 2000) 19.

1297 Heisenberg (n66) 132-136.

and stringency of government regulation"[1298] often differs, leading to 'false alarms'. Since the 1980s-1990s, this over-regulation has been counterbalanced by equal calls for less stringent intervention, leading to non-regulation as the starting point, corrected by regulatory intervention when pressured by the public.[1299] Robert Baldwin *et al.* define this approach as "the populist or opinion-responsive way (where) … public opinion and preferences" are a public policy correction mechanism for "the functional or market failure approach".[1300] A similar trend took place in the data privacy area, where it was initially left to the digital market and big tech companies to regulate e-commerce. U.S. citizens initially favored industry self-regulation, but as it failed to protect people's personal data adequately, a growing distrust led to a preference for legislative intervention from the federal government, namely Congress.[1301] The occurrence of data privacy scandals in the United States made U.S. citizens realize that their valuable personal data was insufficiently protected against government intrusion as well as against businesses' excessive (ab)use.[1302] The Snowden revelations[1303] provided a catalyst for protests against government intrusion of citizens' private communications, but even before those events, U.S. citizens were reluctant to "allow monitoring of phone calls and emails to fight international terrorism".[1304,1305] The 2012 Google Apple Safari activity-tracking cookies circumvented Apple's privacy features by installing cookies on user devices to track their activity when making use of Apple's web browser Safari, where this was normally blocked by default.[1306] The 2018 Cambridge Analytica scandal involved the sale of information on people's personal Facebook accounts through a massive data mining operation for political advertising purposes during the 2016 U.S. presidential elections without users' consent.[1307] The 2020 ClearView AI face scraping practices engaged in illegally 'scraping' photos of people's faces from internet websites, such as Facebook, Twitter, or YouTube, and using them to build

1298 Vogel (n539) 37.
1299 Feintuck (n1296) 388; Vogel (n539) 264-265.
1300 Baldwin *et al.* (n1252) 64.
1301 Brooke Auxier, 'How Americans see Digital Privacy Issues amid the COVID-19 Outbreak' (*Pew Research*, 4 May 2020); Bennett (n140) 39; Cate (n193) 123; Heisenberg (n66) 9-39 and 161.
1302 Bennett (n140) 39; Heisenberg (n66) 14-15.
1303 See *Chapter 1, § 2, A.*
1304 Heisenberg (n66) 37.
1305 Hartzog and Richards (n240) 1028; Heisenberg (n66) 140-141.
1306 Julia Angwin and Jennifer Valentino-DeVries, 'Google's iPhone Tracking' (*The Wall Street Journal*, 17 Feb 2012); Lee (n81) 94-95; Jonathan Mayer, 'Safari Trackers' (*Web Policy*, 17 Feb 2012).
1307 Baik (n193) 1; Gardner (n57) 185; Hartzog and Richards (n240) 1028; Lee (n81) 162; Pernot-Leplay (n193) 115.

ClearView AI's facial recognition database for law enforcement purposes.[1308] Increased public demand for federal regulatory intervention in data privacy took place, but as the federal initiatives were unsuccessful, the U.S. States stepped in legislatively.[1309]

Lobby-driven stakeholders – One of the factors that prevented the adoption of comprehensive data privacy legislation by the U.S. federal government, giving preference to maintaining a sectoral approach, was the strong lobbying power of big tech and digital businesses involved in the e-commerce sector.[1310] As mentioned above, a political forum was created for government-industry cooperation and the government was reciprocal to lobbying practices. Even though the concerns formulated by U.S. pro-privacy groups were similar to those in the EU, these groups were to a large extent excluded from the regulatory discussions. The dominant position of powerful businesses was, as a consequence, implemented in U.S. government policy.[1311] Big data business models rely on the availability and possibility to use collected personal data for targeted advertising, which is incompatible with certain data privacy principles, such as data minimization.[1312] It is, therefore, not surprising that in the State consumer privacy acts discussed in this book, namely the CCPA and the VCDPA, opt-in of personal data collection for targeted advertising has become the default norm, as opposed to the European default opt-out system.[1313] The business sector needs this personal data, after all, to fulfill its commercial purposes.[1314] Government authorities benefit from these extensive amounts of personal data for their own national security purposes as well, as they often access (with or without private companies' cooperation) the personal databases of these companies.[1315] Robert Baldwin *et al.* define this type of policymaking as "corporatist or interest-driven", where the actors involved consist of a group "of those business firms whose profits were most affected by regulation".[1316] Successful business lobbying results often in "business-friendly regulation".[1317]

1308 Kashmir Hill, 'The Secretive Company That Might End Privacy as We Know It' (*The New York Times*, 18 Jan 2020); Kashmir Hill, 'Clearview AI Used Your Face. Now You May Get a Stake in the Company' (*The New York Times*, 13 Jun 2024); Matsakis (n787); Katherine Tangalakis-Lippert, 'Clearview AI scraped 30 billion images from Facebook and other social media sites and gave them to cops' (*Business Insider*, 3 Apr 2023).

1309 See *Chapter 3, § 1, B.*

1310 Heisenberg (n66) 168.

1311 Bygrave, *Data Privacy Law* (n37) 107; Heisenberg (n66) 19 and 73-97.

1312 Hoofnagle *et al.* (n11) 78.

1313 CCPA § 1798.185.(a)(19)(A)(vi)(III) and § 1798.140.(k); VCDPA § 59.1-577.A.5.

1314 Ohm (n826) 1127-1128.

1315 *Ibid.* 1128; see *Chapter 5.*

1316 Baldwin *et al.* (n1252) 65.

1317 *Ibid.* 112-121; Newell *et al.* (n229) 1063.

b) Harm Approach and Data Privacy

Concretely sustained harm – For a case to be admissible in a U.S. federal court and for a party to have 'standing' under Article III U.S.C., SCOTUS stated in the landmark 1992 *Lujan v Defenders of Wildlife*[1318] case that "the plaintiff must personally have: 1) suffered some actual or threatened injury (namely, "an 'injury in fact' – an invasion of a legally protected interest which is (a) concrete and particularized ... and (b) actual or imminent, not 'conjectural' or 'hypothetical'"[1319]); 2) that injury can fairly be traced to the challenged action of the defendant; and 3) that the injury is likely to be redressed by a favorable decision".[1320,1321] Privacy harms (as opposed to the more procedural data privacy harms) are of a generally subjective nature, which may complicate the fulfillment of the 'standing' requirement. Samuel Warren and Louis Brandeis noticed already in the 1890s that "mere injury to (someone's) feelings",[1322] dignity, emotions, and personality was not adequately protected by U.S. (tort) law.[1323] Emmanuel Pernot-Leplay observes that still today many of the data privacy scandals cannot be adequately addressed by the victims under U.S. law.[1324] Paul Ohm concludes, therefore, that "judges seem to feel most comfortable with completed, measurable harm, ... (but) seem less willing to credit uncompleted but likely harm or completed but difficult-to-measure harm".[1325] Compensation is consequently not provided for intangible damage or harm.[1326] In 2002 *Smith v Chase Manhattan Bank*,[1327] the Second Department of the Appellate Division of the Supreme Court of New York held that "the offering of products and services via junk mail to customers whose confidential information had been allegedly sold to a third party by the bank did not qualify as an actual harm",[1328] while in the EU the same act would constitute a breach of the purpose limitation principle provided for by personal data protection law. Similarly, some people found out that they were wrongfully placed on a 'No-Fly List' as they were denied boarding an airplane, which caused concrete harm.[1329] Other people that were wrongfully

---

1318 *Lujan v Defenders of Wildlife* [1992] 504 U.S. 555.
1319 *Ibid.* 560.
1320 Legal Information Institute, 'Standing Requirement: Overview' (*Cornell Law School*, Oct 2024).
1321 *Lujan* (n1318) 560-561.
1322 Warren and Brandeis (n825) 197.
1323 Ohm (n826) 1163; Warren and Brandeis (n825) 197-198.
1324 Pernot-Leplay (n193) 115.
1325 Ohm (n826) 1167.
1326 Lynskey, *The foundations* (n42) 226-227.
1327 *Smith v Chase Manhattan Bank* [2002] 293 A.D.2d 598 (N.Y. App. Div.).
1328 *Ibid.*
1329 *FBI et al. v Fikre* [2024] 601 U.S._; Bill Mears, 'Judge: U.S. violated rights of those on 'no-fly' list' (*CNN*, 25 Jun 2014); Charlie Savage, 'Judge Rules Terrorism Watchlist Violates Constitutional Rights' (*The New York Times*, 4 Sep 2019).

placed on the same list, but were not aware of it as they did not board a commercial airplane during that time, could not vindicate this mistake as they did not sustain concrete harm as a result of it, even if they had gotten knowledge of this fact. The same situation would in the EU qualify as a personal data protection violation in the form of denial of the right to rectification and erasure.

Harm-averse or procedural? – While the U.S. approach towards personal data privacy is often portrayed as harm-based, the question can be asked if this is really the case. The promulgation of data breach notification acts at the State level, starting in 2002 in California, is laudable, but a closer look at these acts will also reveal that they are of a more procedural than harm-based nature. These acts prescribe security measures to be taken by private companies, which aim at enhancing consumers' privacy interests, but are as such procedural measures.[1330] Businesses will comply with their duties when they notify a data breach as prescribed by the law, but victims of data breaches can often not vindicate their 'harm' jurisprudentially in any meaningful way as it will be difficult to prove what their concretely sustained harm is. Daniel Solove's suggestion to focus on the uses of personal data, instead of on the data as such, could provide a middle ground in these situations, and a useful addition to the already existing data breach notification legislation. A broader interpretation of the harm approach would grant victims not only the possibility to vindicate their material harm, but also the psychologically sustained harm. Solove's broader definition of 'harm' "involves negative consequences from the collection, use, or transfer of personal data that affect individuals or society"[1331] and can be operationalized through Paul Ohm's 'threat modeling' approach. This model was developed in the framework of sensitive personal data to assess "the risk of harm in privacy law, borrowing from the computer security literature",[1332] but can also be applied to personal data more generally. The four factors in Ohm's model to determine whether a person sustained (material or psychological) harm encompass "1) the possibility of harm, 2) (the) probability of harm, 3) (the) presence of a confidential relationship, and 4) whether the risk reflects majoritarian concerns",[1333] excluding "information harms experienced by a very small number of relatively powerless individuals".[1334,1335] Solove's theory operationalized by Ohm's threat model could provide a practical basis for the recognition of (reputational) privacy harms as *sui generis* in U.S. tort law.

1330 Bygrave, *Data Privacy Law* (n37) 114; Ohm (n826) 1179; Zuiderveen Borgesius *et al.* (n180) 33-34.
1331 Solove, 'Data Is What Data Does' (n16) 1128.
1332 Ohm (n826) 1125.
1333 *Ibid.* 1161.
1334 *Ibid.* 1169.
1335 *Ibid.* 1125-1132 and 1169-1177; Solove, 'Data Is What Data Does' (n16) 1135-1136.

State-level regulation – The 'California Effect' is a concept developed by David Vogel to describe the 'Race to the Top' in environmental regulation, assuming that the strictest State law will eventually become the standard.[1336] This cutting-edge role in the United States is often taken by California. Similar to the EU, California shares the characteristics of a strong economic position in the consumer market and the ability to set high-level standards.[1337] The main regulatory idea is that the federal government should set out minimum standards and not act pre-emptively. States are then free to promulgate legislation implementing these minimum standards and can add more stringent standards, contributing to a competitive experimental regulatory laboratory where different rules can be tested. The result of this experimental regulatory laboratory leads assumably to the most successful standards becoming the default rule. Vogel continues his observation that, in the environmental area, "European regulatory policies … affected American public policies primarily at the State rather than the federal level, (and that) … the failure of the federal government to strengthen a wide range of risk regulations ha(d) created a policy vacuum which many American States ha(d) attempted to fill".[1338] This regulatory role was predominantly taken by California, "which has adopted a wide range of ("innovative, comprehensive, and stringent"[1339]) risk regulations similar to and often modeled on those of the EU".[1340,1341] A similarity can be found when considering U.S. data privacy policies, as the absence of federal governmental intervention led U.S. States to proactively enact (consumer) data privacy legislation themselves, with also California being the first State to promulgate stringent data privacy legislation in the form of the 2018 California Consumer Privacy Act[1342] following the example of the 2016 EU GDPR.

B. EU REGULATORY RISK-BASED CHARACTERISTICS

i) Regulatory Approach

Active government – The governments in EU Member States have an active role and duty to protect and enhance citizens' (fundamental) rights, and in particular the fundamental right to personal data protection, forming a socio-democratic

1336 Vogel (n539) 16.
1337 Zuiderveen Borgesius *et al.* (n180) 17.
1338 Swire (n1272) 68-71; Vogel (n539) 287.
1339 Vogel (n539) 228.
1340 *Ibid.* 15-16.
1341 Hadjipetrova and Poteat (n193) 14; Revesz (n1257) 1231; Swire (n1272) 81-86.
1342 See *Chapter 3, § 1, B., ii).*

regime.[1343] The majority of EU Member States are civil (Roman) law countries where regulation is enshrined in statutes and codes.[1344] Government interference in, for example, the economic (data) market is consolidated through legislative intervention, which is typical for a regulatory approach.[1345] Consequently, when computerization and e-commerce began to emerge, the European Commission was convinced that a regulatory framework, taking into consideration privacy and personal data protection, would benefit European consumers' trust and confidence in the upcoming digital age.[1346]

Protective system – The right to personal data protection obtained the status of a fundamental right in the EU regulatory framework.[1347] Personal data protection regulation mandates private companies (and the public sector to a certain extent) to protect people's personal data and to prevent mis- and abuse of their data.[1348] Advocate General Ruiz-Jarabo Colomer pointed to the 1995 Directive's "overriding importance of protecting individuals"[1349] in the 2009 *Rijkeboer* case. Dorothee Heisenberg shares the opinion that the EU regulatory approach in the area of the economic market consists of a "Protection system".[1350]

ii) Risk Approach

Precautionary principle – The EU risk approach towards personal data protection is, to a large extent, based on and has evolved from the precautionary principle, which originates in the German 'Vorsorgeprinzip' applied in the environmental area from the 1970s onward.[1351] The precautionary principle prescribes, according to Frank Cross, "that (the) government should take precautions to protect public health and the environment, even in the absence of clear evidence of harm and notwithstanding the costs of such action".[1352]

1343 Baldwin *et al.* (n1252) 4; Bygrave, *Data Privacy Law* (n37) 208; Cate (n193) 44 and 130; Heisenberg (n66) 14-27 and 76-80 and 97 and 135-136; Liddicoat (n355) 77; Lynskey, *The foundations* (n42) 84 and 177-178; Peltz-Steele, 'The pond betwixt' (n568) 15-30; Raghavan (n193) 241; Vogel (n539) 30-31; Wiener (n193) 213.

1344 Bennett (n140) 144; Cate (n193) 44.

1345 Heisenberg (n66) 26-27.

1346 Commission Eur. Communities, 'A European Initiative in Electronic Commerce' COM(97) 157 final, 12-18.

1347 See *Chapter 3, § 3, B., ii).*

1348 Bennett (n140) 144; Heisenberg (n66) 14; Lynskey, *The foundations* (n42) 178; Zuiderveen Borgesius *et al.* (n180) 19.

1349 Opinion of Advocate General Ruiz-Jarabo Colomer delivered on 22 Dec 2008 *College van burgemeester en wethouders van Rotterdam v M.E.E. Rijkeboer* App no C-553/07 para 70; Lynskey, *The foundations* (n42) 184.

1350 Heisenberg (n66) 14-26.

1351 Feintuck (n1296) 374; Peter Sand, 'The Precautionary Principle' (2000) 6 HERA 445, 446.

1352 Frank Cross, 'Paradoxical Perils of the Precautionary Principle' (1996) 53 Wash&LeeLRev 851, 851.

In the digital era, the former definition can be expanded to include a duty to proactively protect Europeans' fundamental right to personal data protection. A two-tier approach can be identified; a precautionary approach when no to very limited information on possible risks is available, and a risk approach requiring a balancing exercise when a certain amount of information on possible risks is available. The precautionary principle was enshrined in the 1992 Maastricht Treaty (on the European Union)[1353] in the area of EU environmental policy.[1354] In time, the principle's scope of application broadened to also encompass other policy areas. The principle was criticized by the EU Committee of the American Chamber of Commerce as the concept was vague and could enable protectionist EU measures.[1355] The European Commission issued, therefore, a Communication on the precautionary principle in 2000,[1356] where its scope of application was explained. The precautionary principle aims at reducing the level of risk for "potentially dangerous effects ... to the minimum acceptable level" when "scientific information is insufficient, inconclusive, or uncertain", while taking into account the public's sensitivity and fears.[1357,1358] David Vogel explains that the precautionary principle "enables ... policymakers to err on the side of caution ... by not requiring substantial or conclusive scientific proof of harm, (but only) a potential or reasonable likelihood of harm".[1359] Other authors[1360] correct Vogel's observation, since a broader, non-radical interpretation of the principle requires that *not only* scientific factors are taken into account, *but also*, as a correcting mechanism, "collective, often non-economic, democratically-derived interests".[1361] When a certain (limited) amount of information is available, the precautionary approach is transformed into a balancing risk approach. The CJEU favors precautionary and risk legislation to be adopted at the EU level, as opposed to the Member State level, as stringent national risk regulations could endanger the EU single market. While the initial legislative documents were still primarily focused on the environment, health, and safety, the foundation of the risk approach in the protection of personal data can also be traced back to the

1353 Article 130r(2) Maastricht Treaty on the European Union [1992] OJ C 191/1.

1354 Sand (n1351) 449.

1355 Gareth Harding, 'Arguments continue to rage over EU's use of the 'precautionary principle'' (*Politico*, 12 Apr 2000).

1356 Commission Eur. Communities, 'Communication from the Commission on the Precautionary Principle' COM(2000) 1 final.

1357 *Ibid.* 7-13.

1358 Case T-13/99 *Pfizer Animal Health S.A. v Council* [2002] paras 139-144 and 169-170; Vogiatzoglou (n737) 121-122; Wiener (n193) 217-219.

1359 Vogel (n539) 275.

1360 Feintuck (n1296) 380 and 398; Andrew Stirling, 'Risk, Precaution and Science' (2007) 8 EMBO Reports 309, 312-314; Oliver Todt and José Luján, 'Analyzing Precautionary Regulation' (2014) 34 RiskAnal 2163, 2163-2170.

1361 Feintuck (n1296) 398.

precautionary principle.[1362] Raphael Gellert observes that "data protection is first and foremost a legal framework for the regulation of the risks stemming from the development of computers", and that these risks consist of "the activity of (automated) personal data recordkeeping".[1363] The EU Commission requires, as a consequence, that a cost-benefit analysis has to be conducted, which "entails comparing the overall cost to the Community of action and lack of action, in both the short and long term".[1364,1365] Article 2 of the 1980 OECD Guidelines also states that they apply to "personal data, which, because of the manner in which they are processed, ... or the context in which they are used, pose a danger to privacy and individual liberties".[1366] A European risk approach to data privacy supports the idea "that creation and innovation should do no harm, and that regulation (should) be a driver of responsible technology development".[1367]

Political preferences – An interesting shift occurred in the recent history of the EU risk approach. Until the 1990s, the EU was more tolerant towards risk, taking a less precautionary attitude.[1368] Public demands changed this tolerant attitude in and around the 1990s, because 'false negatives' had contributed to regulatory policy failures, diminishing "public confidence in the capacity of scientific risk assessments".[1369] The EU's aim to take a strong global leadership position based on its internal market power provided for an additional economic motive to act legislatively and to act more strictly towards risk around the same time. This global-standard-setting-position was confirmed by European Commissioner for Justice Věra Jourová and former European Data Protection Supervisor Giovanni Buttarelli during the replacement of the 1995 Directive by the 2016 GDPR.[1370] Veerle Heyvaert identifies yet another motive for the EU's change in approach, which is of a defensive nature. It is, after all, "harder to argue that a risk management regime is unnecessary, disproportionate or unfair if it is endorsed by a significant proportion of the world's population".[1371] David Vogel explains that the most stringent rules often become the standard in global markets, as compliance with the most stringent rules also encompasses compliance with less stringent

1362 Commission (n1356) 2; Cross (n1352) 851-855; Feintuck (n1296) 371; Stirling (n1360) 309; Vogel (n539) 9 and 35-36 and 238-239 and 266-275; Wiener (n193) 211-212; Zuiderveen Borgesius *et al.* (n180) 19.

1363 Gellert (n219) 3.

1364 Commission (n1356) 4 and 17-19; Wiener (n193) 251.

1365 Feintuck (n1296) 377.

1366 Article 2 1980 OECD Guidelines; Gellert (n219) 3-7.

1367 Liddicoat (n355) 77.

1368 Jasanoff (n1255) 63-69.

1369 Vogel (n539) 252.

1370 Giovanni Buttarelli, 'The EU GDPR as a Clarion Call for a New Global Digital Gold Standard' (2016) 6 IDPL 77, 78; Heisenberg (n66) 169-170; Pernot-Leplay (n193) 109-110; Mark Scott and Laurens Cerulus, 'Europe's New Data Protection Rules Export Privacy Standards Worldwide' (*Politico*, 31 Jan 2018).

1371 Veerle Heyvaert, 'Globalizing Regulation' (2009) 36 JOLS 110, 116; Swire (n1272) 82.

legal frameworks.[1372] Peter Swire questions this assumption using Richard Revesz' analysis of the race-to-the-bottom phenomenon where "competition among the States (is expected) to create less stringent standards".[1373,1374] In the area of personal data protection, Vogel's theory on the strict EU legislative intervention became true, as not only a high level of personal data protection was achieved within the European Union, but was also exported through the GDPR's extraterritorial application.[1375] Anu Bradford calls this phenomenon, where the EU sets the standards for the rest of the world, the 'Brussels Effect'.[1376]

a) Triangle of Shaping Elements in Government Regulation

Market failure – The inclusion of the precautionary principle in the 1992 Maastricht Treaty incentivized EU officials to "enact more stringent regulations in (case of) scientific uncertainty (… and provided the) ability to ban or restrict existing commercial activities"[1377] if needed. This trend was complemented by the EU Commission's Action Plan "Simplifying and Improving the Regulatory Environment"[1378] and its Communication on Impact Assessment[1379] in 2002. The latter document required the introduction of "an integrated Impact Assessment process (that would) help improve the quality and coherence of policy design, (that would) increase transparency, communication and information … (but which was not) a substitute for the political decision".[1380,1381] The CJEU confirmed in the 2002 *Pfizer*[1382] case that "unless the precautionary principle is to be rendered nugatory, the fact that it is impossible to carry out a full scientific risk assessment does not prevent the competent public authority from taking preventive measures".[1383] Raphael Gellert points out that these impact or risk assessments, initially introduced in the environmental area, "have served as an inspiration for privacy (and data protection) impact assessments".[1384]

Public opinion and pressure – According to David Vogel, "Europeans … perceived more health, safety, and environmental risks caused by business to be

1372 Heisenberg (n66) 169; Swire (n1272) 81-82; Vogel (n539) 3-14 and 252.
1373 Swire (n1272) 70.
1374 Revesz (n1257) 1210-1254.
1375 Vogel (n539) 3-14 and 252; see *Chapter 3, § 3, B., iv), b).*
1376 Anu Bradford, *The Brussels Effect* (1st edn, OUP 2020) 25.
1377 Vogel (n539) 35-36.
1378 Commission Eur. Communities, 'Communication from the Commission: Action Plan "Simplifying and Improving the Regulatory Environment"' COM(2002) 278 final.
1379 Commission Eur. Communities, 'Communication from the Commission on Impact Assessment' COM(2002) 276 final.
1380 *Ibid.* 5.
1381 Wiener (n193) 221-222.
1382 Case T-13/99 *Pfizer Animal Health S.A.* (n1358).
1383 *Ibid.* para II – 3311.
1384 Gellert (n219) 12.

both credible and politically unacceptable than ... Americans"[1385] between 1990 and 2010. Consequently, "European regulatory law has, since roughly the late 1980s, become 'more precautionary' than U.S. regulatory law",[1386] contributing to, in Ulrich Beck's words, 'a risk society' where "human activity and technology ... produces as a side-effect risks that need specialized expertise (and) are collective, global, and irreversible in their impact, and thus potentially catastrophic on a scale never seen before".[1387,1388] If a potential risk can be prevented, legislative intervention will be endorsed, creating "the illusion of a risk-free society for which ever more drastic privacy intrusions are justified".[1389] Cass Sunstein warns that public pressure and fear do not always lead to adequate government reaction, as they can "produce unjustified infringements on liberty"[1390] and restrictions on economic activities and innovation. Aaron Wildavsky shares this concern that a one-sided approach focusing only on risk and safety "neglect(s), to the detriment of our common safety, opportunity benefits".[1391] This approach can be observed in the environmental area as well as in other policy areas, such as personal data protection. According to Viktor Mayer-Schönberger, "the first data protection laws were enacted in response to the emergence of electronic data processing within governments and large corporations".[1392] People did not trust the latter to adequately protect their data as companies could make large profits from their customers' personal data.[1393] The former was introducing the welfare (social security) State in many European countries around that time, requiring "government bureaucracies ... to constantly collect increasing amounts of information from the(ir) citizens".[1394,1395] Computers and technology aided governments setting up large databases for social security purposes, but as "many citizens ... had experienced quite distinctly and directly the potential dangers of unrestricted gathering and processing of personal data"[1396] during the Second World War, they opposed these developments.[1397] A growing number of "citizens requested individual privacy and data protection rights"[1398] that could safeguard

1385 Vogel (n539) 34.
1386 Wiener (n193) 209.
1387 Baldwin *et al.* (n1252) 3.
1388 Ulrich Beck, *Risk Society* (Sage 1992) 19-24.
1389 Rauhofer (n364) 186.
1390 Cass Sunstein, *Laws of Fear* (CUP 2005) 225.
1391 Aaron Wildavsky, *Searching for Safety* (Taylor and Francis 2017) 246.
1392 Agre (n193) 221.
1393 Bygrave, *Data Privacy Law* (n37) 21-22; EC, 'Towards a more dynamic' (n88); Heisenberg (n66) 9 and 26.
1394 Agre (n193) 222.
1395 Payal Arora, 'General Data Protection Regulation – A Global Standard?' (2019) 17 S&S 717, 719; Heisenberg (n66) 51-52.
1396 Agre (n193) 225.
1397 See *Chapter 4, § 1, B., i).*
1398 Agre (n193) 225.

their personal data from (ab)uses by businesses and government agencies alike, which were adopted by EU politicians in response.[1399] The social regulation of the emerging welfare State led, ironically, to the necessity to adopt even more regulation to 'regulate' governmental data collection practices enabling their own operation. Even after the Snowden revelations,[1400] the balance was upheld in Europe that the fight against terrorism does not justify all means and should be balanced with respect for other fundamental rights.[1401] Robert Baldwin *et al.* define this phenomenon as "the populist or opinion-responsive way" of regulation, since "public policy follows public opinion and preferences".[1402,1403] They warn, however, that public discussions can be 'hijacked' by activists or certain segments of the public that do not necessarily represent the broader public opinion through the "scream method",[1404] where attention is paid to those who scream loudest.[1405] This method was also employed by the lobby-driven stakeholders discussed below.

Lobby-driven stakeholders – While initially both the commercial and privacy value of personal data were stressed in EU personal data protection legislation, the balance tilted towards the privacy value (trumping the commercial value) in its further legal evolution.[1406] Two stakeholders can be identified for their influence on this evolution: privacy interest groups and the EU Parliament. Firstly, in the 1990s, pro-privacy groups increasingly emerged across the EU, "which (also) became more politically active".[1407] Dorothee Heisenberg holds that the tilted balance was due to the dominant voice in the negotiations, where "only pro-privacy interests (the data protection authorities of several Member States) were consulted, and businesses were unable to make significant changes to the (1995) Directive after it had been drafted by the EU Commission",[1408] resulting in the adoption of a Directive that resembled 80% of its first draft.[1409] The draft was interesting for pro-privacy groups as it was developed by national data protection authorities, which considered personal data protection a fundamental human right.[1410] European businesses complained, however, for being left out of the

1399 *Ibid.* 222-225; Gutwirth *et al.* (n32) 54-55; Heisenberg (n66) 9; Rauhofer (n364) 192; Vogel (n539) 34.
1400 See *Chapter 1, § 2, A.*
1401 EC, 'Towards a more dynamic' (n88); The Stockholm Programme (n181) 4 and 24.
1402 Baldwin *et al.* (n1252) 64.
1403 *Ibid.* 90.
1404 *Ibid.* 102.
1405 *Ibid.* 102-110.
1406 See *Chapter 3, § 3, B., iv), a).*
1407 Heisenberg (n66) 77.
1408 *Ibid.* 10.
1409 *Ibid.* 41.
1410 *Ibid.* 15-16 and 41-57; Lynskey, *The foundations* (n42) 16 and 47.

consultations, even though they constituted a "significant stakeholder group".[1411] Secondly, the EU Parliament called upon the EU Commission to promulgate homogeneous EU-wide personal data protection legislation, as differing Member State legislation in this area impeded the rights of EU citizens and the EU single market. In its role of "upholder of individual European rights",[1412] the Parliament needed four attempts (in 1975, 1979, 1982 and 1995) and 14 years before it could convince the Commission to act legislatively.[1413]

b) Risk Approach and Personal Data Protection

Protective risk approach – According to Orla Lynskey, the 1995 Directive took a "predominantly precautionary approach", while the 2016 GDPR moved "away from this precautionary approach towards a more risk-based approach".[1414] Firstly, the newly introduced data protection by design and by default of Article 25 GDPR requires personal data controllers to implement appropriate measures and necessary safeguards "to ensure a level of security appropriate to the risks represented by the processing and the nature of the data to be protected".[1415,1416] Secondly, the newly introduced data protection impact assessment of Article 35 GDPR requires data controllers to "carry out an assessment of the impact of the envisaged processing operations on the protection of personal data (where a type of processing in particular using new technologies is likely to result in a high risk to the rights and freedoms of natural persons)".[1417] Individuals can also themselves perform a 'risk assessment' when given the choice whether to share their personal data. The latter risk approach is linked to the exercise of individual control over someone's privacy.[1418] People's consent to data processing is often equaled with their understanding and acceptance of potential risks, which is an incorrect assumption. Entrusting data controllers, as opposed to individuals, with a risk assessment is preferable, since "people assess familiar (or mediatized) dangers as riskier than unfamiliar ones"[1419] and are more "interested when they are subjected to personal harm as a result of a specific violation … in specific contexts at specific times".[1420] Businesses can, moreover, estimate the potential risk and harm from their personal data collection and processing activities more

1411 Heisenberg (n66) 90.
1412 *Ibid.* 16 and 54.
1413 *Ibid.* 16 and 52-55; Nugter (n362) 29-31; see *Chapter 3, § 3, A.*
1414 Lynskey, *The foundations* (n42) 9.
1415 C-342/12 *Worten v Autoridade para as Condições de Trabalho* [2013] para 24.
1416 Article 25.1 GDPR; Vogiatzoglou (n737) 221.
1417 Lynskey, *The foundations* (n42) 82; Solove, 'Data Is What Data Does' (n16) 1129.
1418 Lynskey, *The foundations* (n42) 177-178.
1419 Rauhofer (n364) 191; Solove, 'Introduction' (n43) 1887; Sunstein (n1390) 35-37.
1420 Bennett (n140) 204.

accurately than the consumers that just make use of the former's services. Former European Data Protection Supervisor Giovanni Buttarelli shares the opinion that "the burden of assessing the legality and fairness of complex processing (should fall) primarily on controllers and regulators, not on the individual".[1421]

Risk-averse or procedural? – If EU personal data protection legislation is considered risk-based or risk-averse, which risks does the GDPR, and previously the 1995 Directive, aim to address? The first and second sections of this chapter point to risks related to the intrusion upon someone's private sphere and discriminatory practices. Daniel Solove lists the "known harms" as "discrimination, manipulation, emotional distress, and reputational damage, among other things".[1422] How do the GDPR's rules relate to these identified risks and harms? When considering the personal data protection principles and how they are enforced, they seem to be of a rather procedural nature; if a business 'ticks the boxes' of (procedural) requirements, it will comply with the GDPR's obligations.[1423] The CJEU's case law confirms that no actual material harm is required for a violation of the right to personal data protection; non-compliance with the GDPR's obligations suffices.[1424] The CJEU does not assess whether risk or, in an escalated stage, harm really occurred. Rather, the Court will engage in a mechanical check to see whether data controllers fulfill the rules set out by the GDPR.[1425] While the GDPR may seem to adopt a risk-based approach, it is actually a document of a more procedural nature "focus(ing) on whether data is used fairly and with due process".[1426] In the *Schrems* cases,[1427] the CJEU concluded that Europeans' personal data was not adequately protected because Schrems argued that there was a possibility under U.S. law for U.S. government agencies to access this data. Schrems never proved that his personal data was actually accessed by U.S. government agencies, let alone that he was harmed by this access. The purpose limitation and proportionality principles were not observed. The GDPR's aim consists of safeguarding the free flow of personal data on the single market while lowering the chance of harm materializing.[1428] The concept of risk is defined by Raphael Gellert as "the chance (understood as a probabilistic notion) that a danger (*i.e.* an event with harmful consequences) will happen",[1429] and risk regulation is then, in Robert Baldwin *et al.*'s definition,

---

1421 Buttarelli (n1370) 78.

1422 Solove, 'Data Is What Data Does' (n16) 1128.

1423 Pałka, 'Data Management' (n44) 623; Przemysław Pałka, 'Ciało obce: zasady RODO a gospodarka rynkowa' (2022) 5 IKAR 62, 62-81; Solove, 'Data Is What Data Does' (n16) 1111.

1424 See *Chapter 3, § 3, C.*

1425 Pałka, 'Data Management' (n44) 623.

1426 Hoofnagle *et al.* (n11) 70.

1427 See *Chapter 1, § 2, A. and B.*

1428 Bergkamp (n394) 32; Gutwirth *et al.* (n32) 329-330; Hoofnagle *et al.* (n11) 67; Lynskey, *The foundations* (n42) 85 and 195.

1429 Gellert (n219) 8.

"governmental interference with market or social processes to control potential adverse consequences to health",[1430] or broader, to fundamental rights. The Article 29 WP[1431] advocated a risk approach going "beyond a narrow harm-based-approach that concentrates only on damage and … (taking) into consideration every potential as well as actual adverse effects, assessed on a very wide scale ranging from an impact on the person concerned by the processing in question to a general societal impact".[1432,1433] The GDPR concretizes further that data controllers should take measures to reduce "the risks of physical, material, or moral damage as a result of data processing".[1434,1435] EU personal data protection legislation aims more generally to restore the balance between data processors and individuals by remedying the intangible harm of "a sense of individual powerlessness vis-à-vis data processors".[1436,1437] The risk for intangible harm resulting from data processing was also recognized by the CJEU in the 2014 *Digital Rights* case, as the large scale data retention possibilities could "allow very precise conclusions to be drawn concerning the private lives of the persons whose data ha(d) been retained",[1438] which was in breach with their right to privacy and personal data protection.[1439] Paul Schwartz explains that "in the context of privacy (it is) frequently difficult to show (actual damages)"[1440] as exemplified by U.S. case law, where "the Ohio Court of Appeals held that … while … a transaction revealed information about an individual's lifestyle, it did not cause *mental suffering, shame or humiliation to a person of ordinary sensibilities*".[1441] Risks resulting from personal data processing can be objectified and defined very broadly (as they relate to the GDPR's procedural dimension), whereas 'privacy risks' are subjective as they are linked to what someone defines as a privacy invasion.[1442] Orla Lynskey and Judith Rauhofer[1443] use Jeremy Bentham's panopticon-shaped prison to exemplify this subjective element. Actual surveillance, or concrete 'harm', was not needed for the panopticon to

1430 Baldwin *et al.* (n1252) 3.
1431 See *Chapter 3, § 3, B., i), b)*.
1432 Article 29 WP, 'Statement on the role of a risk-based approach in data protection legal frameworks' (WP218, 30 May 2014) 4.
1433 *Ibid.* 2-4; Lynskey, *The foundations* (n42) 86.
1434 Lynskey, *The foundations* (n42) 210.
1435 Recital 83 GDPR.
1436 Lynskey, *The foundations* (n42) 211.
1437 Article 29 WP, 'The Future of Privacy' (n478) 15-16; Gutwirth *et al.* (n32) 68; Lynskey, *The foundations* (n42) 210-213; Daniel Solove, '"I've got nothing to hide" and other misunderstandings of privacy' (2007) 44 San Diego LRev 745, 758.
1438 *Digital Rights* (n647) para 27.
1439 Lynskey, *The foundations* (n42) 225; see *Chapter 5, § 3, A.*
1440 Schwartz, 'Property' (n896) 2108.
1441 *Housh v Peth* [1956] 165 Ohio St. 35, 133 N.E.2d 340, 39; *Shibley v Time, Inc.* [1975] 45 Ohio App. 2d 69, 341 N.E.2d 337, 72; Schwartz, 'Property' (n896) 2108.
1442 Lynskey, *The foundations* (n42) 85-86.
1443 Rauhofer (n364) 193-194.

be effective; "the mere perception of surveillance suffic(ed) to inhibit individual behaviour"[1444] and change people's way of life.

C. INTERIM COMPARATIVE EU-U.S. ANALYSIS

Liberal Market versus Regulatory approach – The United States and the EU differ significantly regarding the acceptable level of government interference in people's lives. In the United States, a more liberal market approach is taken where the government is expected not to intervene in people's private affairs unless really necessary, giving preference to market forces and litigation, as citizens have to safeguard their own rights and interests. A more regulatory approach is taken in the EU, where government interference in people's private affairs is accepted and even expected, as governments should actively protect the rights of their citizens. In line with these cultural differences, Fred Cate identifies a core distinction between the United States and the EU, which influences their regulatory approach, namely that "European laws suggest that European citizens fear the invasive activities of private parties more than the involvement of the government; (whereas) in the United States, the opposite is true".[1445] The public outrage in the aftermath of the revelations on governments' spying operations and massive data collection practices was, for example, much larger in the United States than in the EU. This is an important cultural difference which has to be adequately taken into account in this discussion. Market failure, public opinion, and lobby-driven stakeholders were identified by Robert Baldwin *et al.* as the three shaping elements in government regulation. While the elements of market failure and public opinion will be discussed below, this part will focus on the element of lobby-driven stakeholders. Mike Feintuck points out that the conceptualization and definition of 'risk of harm' and 'scientific evidence' is dependent on the person or entity defining these terms, and that it is plausible that the responsible entity will opt for a definition that best suits its interests. David Vogel's analysis of the environmental area and Dorothee Heisenberg's analysis of the data privacy area confirm this observation. Vogel observed that "for most of the more stringent EU risk regulations …, there were no important differences …; American and European firms have lobbied against many of the risk regulations adopted by the EU",[1446] "the only difference is that, after 1990, producers became more successful in preventing the adoption (of risk regulation) in the United States (rather) than in Europe".[1447] On both sides

1444 Lynskey, 'Deconstructing' (n534) 589.
1445 Cate (n193) 130.
1446 Vogel (n539) 29.
1447 *Ibid.* 30.

of the Atlantic, however, businesses were opposing stringent risk regulations.[1448] Heisenberg made a similar observation during the EU-U.S. personal data transfer discussions, where pro-privacy interest groups were the predominant EU lobbying group, while the predominant lobbying group on the U.S. side were big tech and e-commerce businesses.[1449] The different EU and U.S. approaches reflect, as a consequence, not necessarily only cultural differences between the two continents, but also the predominant voices in policymaking.

Harm versus Risk approach – The origins of the stereotypical description where the U.S. approach towards data privacy is considered to be harm-based while the EU approach towards personal data protection is considered to be risk-based can be traced back to political and legislative developments in the environmental area. Jonathan Wiener defines this distinction in approach as quantitative (scientific harm approach) versus qualitative (public and lobbying interests risk approach).[1450] The historical overview has shown that neither the United States nor the EU is by definition harm- or risk-averse. Under- and overreactive political and legislative environmental decisions on both sides of the Atlantic provoked opposite reactions from the public. U.S. administrative authorities faced at that time jurisprudential scrutiny of their risk assessments, while this was not the case for EU regulatory bodies. Where in the United States, the public and stakeholders demanded less stringent regulations as over-regulation had taken place due to previous public calls for stronger legal intervention, in the EU, the public and stakeholders demanded a more precautionary approach in response to environmental legal market failures as the regulations in place at that time were too flexible. Sheila Jasanoff places this shift in trend in the United States around the 1980s when President Reagan came into office, while David Vogel places this shift around the 1990s. These approaches were transplanted afterward to the data privacy area. In the U.S. liberal market approach, people's personal data can, in general, be used freely by government agencies and private companies unless these practices would harm the people whose personal data is used. In contrast, in an EU precautionary risk approach, people's personal data can only be used by government agencies and private companies if there is a legal basis that provides them with this possibility.[1451] While the discussion showed that neither the United States nor the EU can be considered respectively as risk-taking or precautionary, the changes in approach had nevertheless and impact on the future regulation of data privacy by both sides of the Atlantic. Both approaches have their advantages and flaws, making none the ideal model. The United States may encounter "harms of inaction on false negatives", resulting in "preventable, and possibly irreparable" damage, while the EU may

1448 Heisenberg (n66) 9.
1449 *Ibid.* 19 and 165-166.
1450 Wiener (n193) 216.
1451 Heisenberg (n66) 14.

encounter "harms of overreaction to false positives", resulting in the imposition of "unnecessary costs on both producers and consumers, (less) technological innovation, and (unnecessary) public anxieties".[1452] The stereotypical harm- and risk-based approach of the United States and the EU, respectively, has not only alternated in time, but also between the regulatory fields concerned. Whereas environmental law and data privacy reflect a more precautionary stance on the EU side, the United States takes an extremely precautionary approach in cases of national security and terrorism, which is objected by the EU favoring a harm-based approach where human rights are to be respected at all times.[1453] President George W. Bush took a firm precautionary position in the context of the U.S. invasion of Iraq; "if we wait for threats to fully materialize, we will have waited too long".[1454] Jonathan Wiener observes that "the reality is that the United States and Europe both endorse precaution, just regarding different risks; and both criticize precaution when applied to risks they discount".[1455] An overly precautionary stance in the area of national security and terrorism, where the discourse is dominated by public pressure and fear, often results in "human rights violations of the most grotesque kind",[1456] such as unjustified discrimination, intrusions, and imprisonment.[1457] Judith Rauhofer warns in this context for far-reaching profiling practices, which can eventually lead to a social crediting system such as the one used in China, whether employed covertly or overtly.[1458] Risk management and finding the right precautionary balance to be struck between preventive and reactive measures is very difficult. A paramount focus on probability can lead to misconceptions and a *Minority Report*[1459] scenario, where people presumed to commit a future crime are arrested by the 'pre-crime police', without actually having committed the crime. Not every potential criminal is or will become a criminal, as many other factors are also relevant and should be taken into account. A similar approach can be taken with regard to harms resulting from personal data processing; there are risks that these harms will occur, but they may as well never materialize. The EU and U.S. interpretation of the *Schrems* cases[1460] can exemplify this distinction. From an EU perspective, the CJEU established a breach of the personal data

1452 Vogel (n539) 17; Wiener (n193) 223.

1453 Vogel (n539) 19-20; Wiener (n193) 209 and 239-241 and 258.

1454 The White House, 'President Bush Delivers Graduation Speech at West Point' (*archives.gov*, 1 Jun 2002); Vogel (n539) 19; Wiener (n193) 239.

1455 Wiener (n193) 241.

1456 Sunstein (n1390) 206.

1457 *Ibid.* 225-226.

1458 Rauhofer (n364) 194.

1459 *Minority Report* is a 2002 science fiction movie directed by Steven Spielberg, starring Tom Cruise, based on Philip Dick's 1956 book *Minority Report.* In the story, the Pre-Crime police stops crimes before they occur, by proactively arresting criminals based on predictions made by three future-seeing Pre-Cogs. Jonathan Wiener makes in his 2003 article *Whose precaution after all?* a similar reference to *Minority Report* on p.236-237.

1460 See *Chapter 1, § 2, A. and B.*

protection principles and consequently decided that the transatlantic frameworks were invalid as the protection provided by the U.S. system was not adequate to the EU's standards. From a U.S. perspective, one still wonders what the actual harm sustained by Schrems consisted of. He never proved that the personal data that he had provided to Facebook as a Facebook user was actually shared with, let alone accessed by, U.S. government authorities. While (subjective) privacy harms are very difficult to prove, as discussed in this section, the *Schrems* cases concerned a very hypothetical situation. The harm requirement to have standing before a U.S. court still predominantly focuses on concretely sustained harm, which is easier to prove for crimes involving physical harm than for mental harm or psychological suffering. Many authors[1461] point out that while mental harm is indeed more difficult to measure, as it is subjective, attention should also be paid to this type of harm, especially in the digital age, and the legal system should be adjusted to also include psychological suffering. EU, California, and Virginia data privacy legislation do currently not address nor remedy the (psychological) harm that people sustain resulting from a data breach or misuse of their personal data. Users will receive a notification of a data breach to inform them but are subsequently left with a feeling of impotence. It is almost impossible to foresee where users' personal data will end up in the aftermath of a data breach, and what consequences (appropriation, identity theft, sale on the black market, ...) it can have. Daniel Solove's comprehensive conceptualization of privacy as 'privacy-harmful activities' was, therefore, chosen in this book. The situations covered by Solove's definition do not require actual harm or damage to be sustained, but are sufficiently concrete to endanger someone's privacy (e.g. *Information Collection (Surveillance)*; watching, listening to, or recording people's activities, or *Information Processing*, including (unauthorized) *Secondary Use*), as opposed to the general 'risk' requirement formulated in EU personal data protection legislation.

Market Power and Data Privacy – Personal data protection legislation in both the U.S. and the EU private sector aims at restoring the power balance between e-commerce businesses and the consumers whose personal data is collected and processed by these businesses. In the U.S. liberal market system, a bottom-up movement took place with a request from the citizens to act legislatively to restore this balance, while in the EU regulatory system, this restoration occurred top-down by the EU legislators. While the U.S. Congress did not succeed in enacting federal data privacy legislation, the U.S. States took their own legal initiatives, starting with California. David Vogel identifies the 'California effect' in the United States, while Anu Bradford identifies the 'Brussels effect' in the EU. Both effects have the elements of a strong market power, a broad sphere of influence, and a dominant position to 'force' their standards upon others

---

[1461] Lynskey, *The foundations* (n42) 307p.; Ohm (n826) 1125-1196; Pernot-Leplay (n193) 101-124; Solove, *Understanding Privacy* (n194); Warren and Brandeis (n825) 197.

in common. California and Brussels differ, however, in their relation to their spheres of influence. Where the EU (Brussels) GDPR is a regulation that has to be exactly implemented in the Member States' legal systems and even extends its application outside the EU, the California Consumer Privacy Act was the first of its kind in the U.S. 'competitive experimental regulatory laboratory' that is formed by the U.S. States. Each of these approaches is typical for the legal system concerned; the United States prefers to work bottom-up, while the EU prefers to work top-down.[1462] The aim of this discussion is not to determine which approach is better, but rather to identify possible ways for cooperation. The EU should not take a static, imposing approach after adopting a certain type of legislation, but should rather take an open stance towards different regulatory initiatives and organically develop its legal framework in cooperation, not isolation, with other international players. If another legislative initiative, such as one of the U.S. State consumer privacy acts, turns out to provide a better solution or a better regulatory framework for the protection of personal data, the EU should take that into consideration and dare to admit that another approach may be more suitable by adjusting its own framework. Going back to the original purpose of personal data protection legislation, the main principles set out in the 1980 OECD Guidelines[1463] are still relevant, but the focus should be readjusted to concrete privacy and discriminatory risk-mediation, and how victims can address and redress their sustained psychological (and, if applicable, physical or material) harm. These legal adjustments should, however, not be undertaken by the EU or the United States alone, but at the international level. Daniel Solove's and Paul Ohm's privacy-harmful activities threat model can serve as a starting point for these discussions.

§ 4. INTERIM CONCLUSION

This chapter provided an overview of the historical-philosophical context in which (data) privacy originates in the United States and the EU, ranging from non-interference by the State in private affairs, the protection of people's human dignity, their personal image and reputation, over people's privacy, to individual control and property. Subsequently, the interplay between the right to (data) privacy and freedom of speech as well as the prohibition of discrimination were discussed, arguing for mutual understanding in the privacy – freedom of speech relationship, and for the abolition of the special category of sensitive data to prevent discriminatory practices, refocusing on the purposes for which all types of personal data are collected and used, instead of on certain types of personal

1462 Wiener (n193) 248.

1463 See *Chapter 3, § 2, A.*

data as such. Finally, the last section discussed the stereotypical characteristics of the U.S. liberal market and harm approach versus the EU regulatory and precautionary approach, as these characteristics influence regulatory attitudes towards data privacy on both sides of the Atlantic.

The first section found that the roots of the right to privacy originated in both the United States and the EU in the necessity to protect people against (unlawful) interferences by the government. The shared aim was to prevent the government, and later also private companies, from (ab)using the extensive number of citizens' personal data in their possession to subjugate the latter to the former's (unlimited) control and power. Data privacy legislation gives the individual control over personal data back to the people (albeit limited), as it enhances their self-authorship and self-determination. In the EU, this mainly relates to someone's reputation or public image, while in the United States, this is more related to the confines of someone's private sphere or home. However, with the conceptualization of information privacy, the United States also joined the idea that people have a certain degree of privacy in their personal information. The right to privacy is an old concept which has become a broad term encompassing many facets as it has to adapt over time to constantly changing circumstances. In an evolutionary interpretation, the newly constructed right to personal data protection can, as a consequence, be understood as a means to an end to protecting the people (and their privacy interests) behind the personal data. The idea of qualifying personal data as someone's property emerged in the United States but is not as such precluded by the wording of the ECHR. The U.S. reasoning where individual control would lead people to take rational decisions in function of their self-determination was, however, flawed, and eventually incentivized the government to intervene through (partial) regulation. The U.S. 'Notice & Choice' requirement and the EU consent requirement, as well as the U.S. opt-out system and the EU opt-in system, serve the same purpose of enhancing individual control and decisional autonomy, but fail to reach their goal due to power and information imbalances where a proliferation of players and incomprehensible data collection policies prevail. People's personal data is not just their property or their creation, it reflects their personality as they are the subject of it. U.S. and EU data privacy regulations resulted in a balancing exercise between privacy and commercial interests, as both systems initially tilted too much to one side but were subsequently corrected to find a more adequate balance. Partial privacy self-management in the form of limited government intervention is, consequently, necessary to remedy "the most objectionable personal data processing practices",[1464] but should also be limited to these practices only.

The second section discussed, firstly, the relationship between the right to privacy and freedom of speech. The interplay between these two rights in the

---

1464 Lynskey, *The foundations* (n42) 237.

context of lawfully obtained truthful information differs in the United States and the EU, as in the former freedom of speech will often prevail, and consequently the dissemination of this information, while in the latter the right to privacy will often be protected, consequently precluding this information's dissemination. A similar distinction can be further noted in the U.S. and EU approaches towards publicly available information, which can be disseminated in the former, but which is protected in the latter. Both sides of the Atlantic take a strong stance in one direction, but the overly lenient U.S. third party doctrine and the overly patriarchic EU protection of this information are challenged. The corrected 'reasonable expectation of privacy' principle may provide a solution in these situations, as people should, to a certain extent, realize that what they openly publish online cannot be considered private, but also that the sole fact that an email is sent through an email provider's website does not entail the intention of the sender to make this information publicly available. The United States and the EU take a similar approach towards public persons, who generally enjoy a lower level of privacy protection. The ECtHR requires, however, that the disseminated information has 'to contribute to a debate of general interest', while excluding the dissemination of information solely 'to satisfy public curiosity', whereas in the United States the latter form of dissemination is also allowed. The information power has shifted from public entities and the press to private companies, and to ensure that freedom of speech and freedom of information are preserved, it is important that these new players abide by the same information dissemination standards as their predecessors to prevent censorship. The European 'right to be forgotten' aims at mitigating the proliferation and accessibility of information in a digital world, as opposed to an analogue world. Where in the past information had to be consulted by going to physical databases, the same information can be accessed today by a quick query into an online search engine from behind someone's computer at home. The right to be forgotten does not lead to information being actually forgotten, it obscures rather than censors data that is available online. It is, therefore, more accurate to speak of a 'right to be remembered with difficulty', as it gives the decisional power back to the people involved. The information can still be consulted, but as in the past, it will require some effort from those people who would like to obtain it, and contributes to a fair balance between people's privacy interests and society's information rights. Secondly, the relationship between the right to (data) privacy and the prohibition of discrimination was discussed, and more particularly the conceptualization of sensitive data. While in the EU, the categories of sensitive data reflect the categories protected by the prohibition of discrimination, to prevent discriminatory practices, this is not the case in the U.S. State consumer privacy acts discussed in this book. Political opinions are, for example, excluded from U.S. data privacy law but were shown to have important implications for preserving democracy in an increasingly polarizing world with profiling practices. Different categories of data requiring different levels of protection complicate businesses' operations without necessarily obtaining their goal of preventing discrimination. In today's digital world, the approach where personal data is protected as such has become outdated, as even anonymous data can relatively easily be traced back to its original owners. This book advocated, therefore, shifting the focus from a definitional perspective (the data as such) to a purpose perspective (what is the collected/processed data used for).

The third section highlighted that cultural differences between the United States and the EU provide an explanatory factor for their decision-making processes, while not being determinant. The acceptable level of government interference in people's lives differs significantly between both sides of the Atlantic. Where in the United States, the government should not interfere unless strictly necessary, giving prevalence to market forces and people to pursue their own choices, contributing to a bottom-up regulatory system, the EU population expects the government to actively engage in protecting their interests through a regulatory top-down approach. The same reasoning can explain why Americans fear government intrusions more than those of private companies, while Europeans share the opposite feelings. As a consequence, actual harm is required in the United States before a plaintiff can have standing in court, while in the EU a certain degree of risk will suffice. These paradigms have resulted in legal frameworks where Americans' personal data can in general be used freely by government agencies and private companies unless these practices would harm the people whose personal data is used, whereas Europeans' personal data can only be used by government agencies and private companies if there is a legal basis that provides this possibility. The three elements that shape government intervention, namely market failure, public opinion, and lobby-driven stakeholders can, however, mediate these pre-defined differences between both sides of the Atlantic, and influence policies. U.S. businesses and EU pro-privacy activists were the main lobby-driven stakeholders that influenced data privacy policymaking in both regions. The market failure, where the EU initially took a too lenient regulatory stance and the United States a too strict one, led the population to pressure their governments to take, respectively, a stricter and more lenient approach. These regulatory attitudes are not generally applicable to both sides of the Atlantic and will depend on the regulatory field concerned.

While the EU was the first to strictly regulate personal data protection, this does not mean that its regulatory framework is (still) the best one. Consequently, the EU should adopt an open stance towards other regulatory approaches. The data protection regimes examined in this book do not address nor remedy psychological harm, which is a significant flaw that should be remedied. The most important goal of regulatory intervention, as it currently stands, is not necessarily to empower consumers, but to regulate data processors' behavior regarding the collected/processed data, to respect people's privacy, and not to engage in discriminatory practices.

CHAPTER 5

INTELLIGENCE AND DATA PRIVACY OVERVIEW

The different stakeholder interests in people's personal data were discussed in the introductory chapter. Where the third chapter focused more on the private sector and the commercial aspect of personal data (collection/processing), this chapter focuses on the intelligence aspect of personal data (collection/processing) for law enforcement and intelligence purposes. The terrorist attacks in New York in 2001, Madrid in 2004, London in 2005, Paris in 2015, and many more that followed gave rise to an increased focus on national security and the introduction of far-reaching surveillance laws, specifically regarding the access to and retention of personal communications data.[1465] The introduction of the USA Patriot Act in 2001 and the several (bulk) personal data retention laws of EU Member States scrutinized by the CJEU exemplify this trend. This chapter does not engage in a comprehensive discussion of all U.S. and EU Member States' national security laws, but is limited to those laws and cases relevant in the area of data privacy and EU-U.S. relations. The EU and U.S. approach towards the intelligence aspect of personal data and data privacy in a law enforcement and national security context is discussed to determine how both regions strike a balance between their national security interests and their citizens' fundamental rights, and will show that both sides of the Atlantic are actually not that different.

§ 1. BACKGROUND

WWII & Terrorism – The general distrust of the government in the United States led historically to a stricter regulation of government activities than commercial ones. In Europe, the memories of the Second World War and the atrocities to which government (ab)use of Jewish citizens' personal data had led were still vivid when digitization and computerization began to emerge around

1465 Greenwald, *No Place to Hide* (n16) 1-5; Gutwirth *et al.* (n32) 78 and 312-313; Yves Poullet, 'The Fight Against Crime and/or The Protection of Privacy' (2004) 18 IRLCT 251, 251-256; Purtova, *Property Rights* (n31) 28; Zalnieriute (n17) 199-200; Zuiderveen Borgesius *et al.* (n180) 17-18.

the 1970s.[1466] Both regions shared, consequently, caution when law enforcement and intelligence services wanted to engage in personal data collection and processing for crime fighting and national security purposes. Terrorist attacks have countered this caution in recent years, leading to a "globalized and networked society (that) has become a cross-border surveillance society"[1467] as governments were expected (or felt responsible) to take preventive measures, even when citizens did not agree with overly far-reaching encroachments on their constitutionally guaranteed rights.[1468] In periods of high security tension, such as terrorist attacks, national security interests will often prevail over other fundamental rights, including privacy, transforming the presumption of innocence into a presumption of guilt where everyone's personal data is collected and processed for intelligence purposes.[1469] According to the Article 29 WP,[1470] the alteration to 'preventive policing' includes several dimensions; "information … gathered and exchanged … to prevent possible criminal acts … focuses on a wider group of persons … not only on persons that are directly related to a crime such as suspects or witnesses, but also on wider groups of the population who are not involved in an investigation … information that is collected for a given, legitimate purpose is increasingly used for different, at times incompatible purposes … more authorities are involved in the use of information, not just police and judicial authorities … but also national security services, (consequently) the technological possibilities to easily combine information may have a profound impact on the privacy and data protection of all citizens and on … their fundamental rights".[1471] The EU tried to maintain the balance between respect for fundamental rights and the protection of national security as this balance remained a key element in the EU's antiterrorism and organized crime policies,[1472] and was (initially) upheld by the CJEU as will be shown in the case law overview below. The United States

---

[1466] See *Chapter 4, § 1, B., i)*.

[1467] Gutwirth *et al.* (n32) 177.

[1468] Greenwald, *No Place to Hide* (n16) 1-2; Heisenberg (n66) 140-141; Purtova, *Property Rights* (n31) 28-29.

[1469] Gutwirth *et al.* (n32) 78 and 216 and 312-313; Purtova, *Property Rights* (n31) 28; Plixavra Vogiatzoglou, 'Mass surveillance, predictive policing and the implementation of the CJEU and ECtHR requirement of objectivity' (2019) 10 EJLT 1, 4.

[1470] See *Chapter 3, § 3, B., i), b)*.

[1471] Article 29 WP, 'The Future of Privacy' (n478) 25.

[1472] For example, see the Stockholm Program which ensures a.o. personal data protection in the area of freedom, security, and justice.: Article 29 WP, 'Resolution by the Article 29 Working Party on the 2nd European Data Protection Day' (WP144, 5 Dec 2007) 2; Article 29 WP, 'The Future of Privacy' (n478) 6; Quirine Eijkman, 'Preventive counter-terrorism and non-discrimination assessment in the European Union' (2011) 22 SecurHumRights 89, 89; European Parliament, 'Mag terrorismebestrijding ten koste gaan van mensenrechten?' (*europa.eu*, 10 Apr 2012); The Stockholm Programme (n181) 10 and 25.

tilted towards the security side of the spectrum, setting up 'mass domestic warrantless surveillance programs' and engaging in 'preventive detention of suspected terrorists'.[1473] In order to prevent these 'momentary alarms' from escalating, to use David Vogel's conceptualization,[1474] Ivan Szekely[1475] and Yves Poullet[1476] suggest that 'impulsive' measures in response to a certain event, such as a terrorist attack, should be limited in time, subjected to several restrictions, and ideally brought together in a 'checklist'. Szekely continues that "the main criterion of such a limitation is reversibility ... (it) can be lifted after the danger has passed, so the guarantees to the information rights should be restored to their former level after the threat has expired ..."[1477] Can the terrorist threat in today's world, however, be considered as a danger that 'has passed'? And even if the terrorist threat would at any point in time reach a lower level, will there not be other potential threats to countries' national security which legitimize upholding strict surveillance measures?

Double standard & outsourcing – In the EU-U.S. personal data transfer (*Schrems*) saga,[1478] the U.S. national security exception, allowing U.S. intelligence agencies to access personal data transferred from the EU to the United States by private companies, was identified as one of the main problematic features. Whilst the EU, and more specifically the CJEU, condemned the United States for engaging in bulk (meta)data collection and accessing private companies' databases with consumer information, EU Member States were found to engage in similar practices upon scrutiny by the CJEU (*see below*). Colin Bennett predicted already in 1992 that "when asked today what it will take to get privacy back on the national (U.S.) agenda, commentators point to the occurrence of some random, unforeseen event that might again create an 'open window', for instance, a big horror story involving a massive abuse of enormous quantities of personal data, perhaps accompanied by a major class action suit".[1479] 20 years later this is exactly what happened with the 2013 Snowden revelations[1480] and resulted in regulatory intervention in the United States through the 2015 USA Freedom Act (*see below*).[1481] Edward Snowden

---

1473 Fiona De Londras, *Detention in the 'War on Terror'* (1st edn, CUP 2011) 8-9; Greenwald, *No Place to Hide* (n16) 1-5; Heisenberg (n66) 140; Sunny Hughes, 'U.S. Domestic Surveillance after 9/11' (2012) 27 CJLS 399, 399; Packard (n801) 262; Poullet, 'The Fight' (n1465) 256; Zuiderveen Borgesius *et al.* (n180) 17-18.

1474 See *Chapter 4, § 3, A., ii), a).*

1475 Gutwirth *et al.* (n32) 313-314.

1476 Poullet, 'The Fight' (n1465) 262-263.

1477 Gutwirth *et al.* (n32) 313.

1478 See *Chapter 1, § 2, A. and B.*

1479 Bennett (n140) 232.

1480 See *Chapter 1, § 2, A.*

1481 Kohl (n398) 740; Zuiderveen Borgesius *et al.* (n180) 17-18.

was not employed by the NSA, but was a contractor working for the private Dell Corporation and Booz Allen Hamilton companies. Glenn Greenwald observes that "while the NSA is officially a public agency, it has countless overlapping partnerships with private sector corporations, and many of its core functions have been outsourced".[1482] Historically, the responsibilities of the public and private sectors differed, subjecting these sectors to different legal frameworks. In the last decades, the rapid development of technology has increased privatization and modernization, leading to a "shared governance, with policy implementation apportioned between government and private sector actors, (in particular) information technology"[1483] being one of the outsourced areas.[1484] If there are, after all, specialized private companies, it is more convenient to rely on their expertise than to create new public enterprises for the same purposes. The OECD noticed this evolution already in 2011 and acknowledged that "governments have turned to outsourcing as a way of accessing external expertise and delivering services more cost-effectively".[1485,1486] When "governments … decide to pay a firm to deliver goods or services directly to the end user, (which) may include the outsourcing of "mainline" functions previously conducted by the government",[1487] the private company will become a public sector agent.[1488] If, on the contrary, law enforcement and intelligence agencies access private companies' databases without the latter's knowledge or mandate them to hand over the collected data, the different applicable (public versus private) legal frameworks cannot be observed. The purpose limitation principle can, in particular, not be fulfilled as the collected personal data will be used for different purposes (i.e. safeguarding national security and preventing crime) than it was initially collected for (i.e. providing commercial services).[1489] The exercise of the rights to access and correction will also be restrained by the interconnected web of service providers and intermediaries, which complicates the identification of all the parties in the chain due to which a compliance request will not always be able to reach all data processors. An individual will often not even know who all these parties are to begin with.[1490]

1482 Greenwald, *No Place to Hide* (n16) 101.

1483 Rachel Potter, 'Macro Outsourcing' (2022) 84 JOP 960, 960.

1484 Brewczynska (n401) 10; Carol Harlow, 'Public and Private Law' in Jason Varuhas and Shona Stark (eds), *The Frontiers of Public Law* (Hart Publishing 2019) 334; Rory Van Loo, 'The New Gatekeepers' (2020) 106 VaLRev 467, 467.

1485 OECD, *Government at a Glance 2011* (OECD Publishing, 2011) 168.

1486 Guibault and Bernt Hugenholtz (n533) 279.

1487 *Ibid.*

1488 Purtova, *Property Rights* (n31) 28.

1489 Gutwirth *et al.* (n32) 78 and 294.

1490 *Ibid.* 313.

§ 2. U.S. SURVEILLANCE LAWS

Overview – The intelligence and law enforcement agencies of the U.S. government are to a large extent restricted in their operations by the U.S. Constitution and the Bill of Rights. More specifically, for data privacy, the First and Fourth Amendments provide a legal framework that these agencies have to respect. A case law overview of the Fourth Amendment was provided in the previous chapter[1491] and will not be reiterated here. Instead, this section will focus on the different U.S. surveillance laws which contributed to and tried to remedy the invalidation of the EU-U.S. data privacy frameworks and which focus on the protection of U.S. national security.

1978 FISA – The Foreign Intelligence Surveillance Act (FISA)[1492] was enacted in 1978 to "authorize electronic surveillance without a (regular) court order ... to acquire foreign intelligence information for periods of up to one year if (the conditions set out in the Act are fulfilled)".[1493] FISA struck a balance between secret surveillance and judicial oversight by establishing a Foreign Intelligence Surveillance Court (FISC) with impartial and independent judges responsible for the issuance of a special court order to access and collect personal data in the form of foreign intelligence. The FISC is a secret court as its sessions as well as its orders are held and issued non-publicly. The proceedings are *ex parte*, meaning that the targeted (and surveilled) individuals cannot be present nor informed about the orders' existence, and the only party present during the hearings is the U.S. government.[1494] The U.S. Attorney General has to adopt safeguards in the form of "specific minimization procedures governing the retention and dissemination of the information received in response to an order".[1495] These procedures consist of, among others, making use of secure networks, restricting data collection, limiting access to the data approved by the order, and ensuring oversight by different bodies.[1496]

1981 Executive Order 12333 – President Ronald Reagan promulgated Executive Order (EO) 12333[1497] in 1981 to "enhance human and technical collection

1491 See *Chapter 4, § 2, A., i)*.
1492 1978 Foreign Intelligence Surveillance Act, 50 U.S.C. 1801, 95th Congress, 25 Oct 1978, 92 Stat. 1786 (FISA).
1493 Sec. 102(a)(1) FISA.
1494 Greenwald, *No Place to Hide* (n16) 127-128; McLaughlin (n139) 228-229; U.S. Department of Justice, 'The Foreign Intelligence Surveillance Act of 1978 (FISA)' (*Office of Justice Programs*, 2025).
1495 McLaughlin (n139) 228.
1496 Such as the U.S. Department of Justice, the FISC, Congress, and audits and program reviews by the intelligence agencies' privacy and civil liberties officers.: *Am.C.L.Union v Clapper* [2015] 785 F.3d 787 (2nd Cir. 2015) 797-798; McLaughlin (n139) 229.
1497 EO 12333 United States Intelligence Activities, 46Fed.Reg.59, 941, 4 Dec 1981.

techniques, especially those undertaken abroad, and the acquisition of significant foreign intelligence ..."[1498] by authorizing the Intelligence Community to collect, retain, and disseminate, among others, "(b) information constituting foreign intelligence or counterintelligence, including such information concerning corporations or other commercial organizations ...; (c) information obtained in the course of a lawful foreign intelligence, counterintelligence, international drug or international terrorism investigation; ... (i) incidentally obtained information that may indicate involvement in activities that may violate federal, State, local, or foreign laws; ...".[1499] The last situation is of particular importance as it significantly extends the intelligence agencies' data collection and retention competences. U.S. law foresees specific safeguards (such as those enshrined in the U.S. Constitution and Bill of Rights) for information collected on U.S. persons, which have to be observed when this information is collected directly. When the same information is collected 'incidentally' in the course of intelligence operations abroad, EO 12333 seems to imply that the provided safeguards and oversight mechanisms do not have to be observed, making "incidental collection ... a legal loophole that can be stretched very wide".[1500,1501] These intelligence practices can, moreover, be conducted without the need to obtain a court order or warrant. It suffices that intelligence operations are "in accordance with procedures established by the head of the Intelligence Community element concerned or by the head of a department containing such element and approved by the Attorney General ..., after consultation with the Director".[1502,1503] EO 12333 allows intelligence services to directly access the information from the lines of communication themselves, without the need "to notify or obtain consent of a company before collecting its users' data",[1504] enabling U.S. authorities to collect personal data outside the United States while in transit.[1505]

2001 USA Patriot Act – The Uniting and Strengthening America by Providing Appropriate Tools Required to Intercept and Obstruct Terrorism

1498 2.2 *Purpose* EO 12333.

1499 2.3 *Collection of information* EO 12333.

1500 John Tye, 'Meet Executive Order 12333: The Reagan rule that lets the NSA spy on Americans' (*The Washington Post*, 18 Jul 2014).

1501 Spencer Ackerman, 'NSA reformers dismayed after privacy board vindicates surveillance dragnet' (*The Guardian*, 2 Jul 2014); Tye (n1500).

1502 2.3 *Collection of information* EO 12333.

1503 McLaughlin (n139) 229; Tye (n1500).

1504 Tye (n1500).

1505 Drechsler *et al.* (n151) 17-28; McLaughlin (n139) 229-240; Faiza Patel, 'Bulk Collection Under Section 215 Has Ended ... What's Next?' (*Brennan Center for Justice*, 30 Nov 2015); Tye (n1500).

Act (USA Patriot Act)[1506] was enacted in 2001 "to deter and punish terrorist acts in the United States and around the world, to enhance law enforcement investigatory tools, and for other purposes".[1507] This Act updated some provisions of the 1978 FISA in the aftermath of the 9/11 terrorist attacks in New York in 2001 to make FISA fit for application in the new technological world. Of particular importance to the discussion on EU-U.S. data flows and data privacy is the introduction of new FISA Section 501. The USA Patriot Act stated in 'Section 215. Access to records and other items under the Foreign Intelligence Surveillance Act' that a new FISA Section 501 would replace the original FISA Sections 501 through 503, allowing "the Director of the (FBI ... to) make an application for an order requiring the production of any tangible things (including books, records, papers, documents, and other items) for an investigation to protect against international terrorism or clandestine intelligence activities ...",[1508] lowering "the standard the government needed to meet in order to obtain 'business records' from 'probable cause' to 'relevance'".[1509,1510]

2008 FISA Sec. 702 – The Foreign Intelligence Surveillance Act of 1978 Amendments Act of 2008 (FISA 2008)[1511] was enacted by Congress "to amend the Foreign Intelligence Surveillance Act of 1978 to establish a procedure for authorizing certain acquisitions of foreign intelligence, and for other purposes",[1512] and in particular to authorize the issuance of a FISC order "for a period of up to 1 year from the effective date of the authorization ... targeting ... persons ... located outside the United States to acquire foreign intelligence information".[1513] This Amendment Act stated in 'Section 101. Additional procedures regarding certain persons outside the United States' that a new 'Section 702. Procedures for targeting certain persons outside the United States other than United States persons' would be introduced in FISA.[1514] Section 702 provides the Intelligence Community, according to the Office of the Director of National Intelligence, with "a critical intelligence collection authority ... to collect, analyze, and appropriately share foreign intelligence information about national security threats ... (it) authorizes targeted intelligence collection of specific types of foreign intelligence information ...

1506 Uniting and Strengthening America by Providing Appropriate Tools Required to Intercept and Obstruct Terrorism Act, 107th Congress, 26 Oct 2001, 115 Stat. 272 (USA Patriot Act).

1507 *Ibid.*

1508 Sec. 215 USA Patriot Act, 115 Stat. 287.

1509 Greenwald, *No Place to Hide* (n16) 28.

1510 Sec. 215 USA Patriot Act, 115 Stat. 287-288; Kosta and Kamara (n37) 476.

1511 Foreign Intelligence Surveillance Act of 1978 Amendments Act of 2008, 110th Congress, 10 Jul 2008, 122 Stat. 2436 (FISA 2008).

1512 *Ibid.*

1513 *Ibid.* 122 Stat. 2438.

1514 *Ibid.* 122 Stat. 2437-2448.

(and) is not a bulk collection program ... every Section 702 targeting decision is individualized and documented, approved pursuant to a multi-step process embodied in specific targeting procedures, and reviewed by an independent oversight team".[1515] Whistleblower Edward Snowden revealed in 2013, however, that the controversial PRISM program[1516] was set up based on an extensive interpretation of this Section, stretching the 'targeted' requirement to entire countries or regions (geographical) and to broad search terms, creating a dragnet (subject matter), "an interpretation so broad that even the law's original authors were shocked to learn how it was being used".[1517,1518]

2014 PPD-28 – The Presidential Policy Directive 28 (PPD-28)[1519] was promulgated by President Barack Obama in 2014 to restrict foreign signals intelligence by, among others, taking into account that "all persons should be treated with dignity and respect, regardless of their nationality or wherever they might reside, and that all persons have legitimate privacy interests in the handling of their personal information",[1520] setting out restrictions such as minimizing the dissemination and retention of collected personal information.[1521] PPD-28 was a reaction to the EU's request after the Snowden revelations[1522] to restrict the use of the U.S. national security exception "to an extent that is strictly necessary and proportionate".[1523] The President announced to review intelligence collection programs by limiting "the use of signals intelligence collected in bulk"[1524] and extending privacy protections and data retention period limitations to non-U.S. citizens by protecting "the privacy and civil liberties of all persons, whatever their nationality and regardless of where they might reside".[1525] More specifically, PPD-28 stipulates four personal data protection principles which have to be observed when conducting signals intelligence: "i) *minimization*: ... minimize the dissemination and retention of personal information collected from signals intelligence activities ...; ii) *data security and access*: ... take appropriate steps to ensure that any personal information contained within that intelligence is secure ... personal

[1515] Office of the Director of National Intelligence, 'FISA Section 702: A One Page Overview' (*intel.gov*, 2025).

[1516] See *Chapter 1, § 2, A*.

[1517] Greenwald, *No Place to Hide* (n16) 112.

[1518] Ackerman, 'NSA reformers' (n1501); Greenwald, *No Place to Hide* (n16) 90-93; see *Chapter 1, § 2, A*.

[1519] The White House Office of the Press Secretary, Presidential Policy Directive/PPD-28, 17 Jan 2014.

[1520] PPD-28, 1.

[1521] Bender (n78) 120-122; EC, 'Rebuilding Trust' (n92); EC, 'Restoring Trust – FAQ' (n88); Monteleone and Puccio (n95) 10; Sheketoff (n95) 401.

[1522] See *Chapter 1, § 2, A*.

[1523] EC, 'Rebuilding Trust' (n92) 8.

[1524] PPD-28, 3.

[1525] *Ibid.*

information shall be processed and stored under conditions that provide adequate protection and prevent access by unauthorized persons, consistent with the applicable safeguards for sensitive information …; iii) *data quality*: … provide national security policymakers with timely, accurate, and insightful intelligence … inaccurate records and reporting can not only undermine our national security interests, but also can result in the collection or analysis of information relating to persons whose activities are not of foreign intelligence or counterintelligence value …; iv) *oversight*: … include appropriate measures to facilitate oversight over the implementation of safeguards protecting personal information … include periodic auditing against the standards required …".[1526,1527]

2015 USA Freedom Act – The Uniting and Strengthening America by Fulfilling Rights and Ensuring Effective Discipline Over Monitoring Act (USA Freedom Act)[1528] was enacted in 2015 "to reform the authorities of the Federal Government to require the production of certain business records, conduct electronic surveillance, use pen registers and trap and trace devices, and use other forms of information gathering for foreign intelligence, counterterrorism, and criminal purposes, and for other purposes".[1529] The USA Freedom Act amended FISA to a large extent by particularly 'Section 501. Prohibition on bulk collection', which provided the amendment to strike the word 'may' (access telephony records) in the official FISA text, and to insert 'may, using a term that specifically identifies a person, entity, telephone number, or account as the basis for a request' (access telephony records).[1530] Moreover, 'Section 402. Declassification of decisions, orders, and opinions'[1531] of the FISC reformed its operations to provide more transparency and "judicial review of some of the most sensitive intelligence activities – including the Section 702 FISA program targeting foreign individuals overseas and the Section 215 USA Patriot Act (introducing FISA Sec. 501) telephone metadata program".[1532,1533]

2022 *FBI v Fazaga* case – Recently, the U.S. Supreme Court tilted the balance between civil rights and national security towards the latter in the

---

1526 PPD-28, 5-7.

1527 Office of the Press Secretary, 'Fact Sheet: Review of U.S. Signals Intelligence' (*archives.gov*, 17 Jan 2014); Megan Slack, 'President Obama Discusses U.S. Intelligence Programs at the Department of Justice' (*archives.gov*, 17 Jan 2014).

1528 Uniting and Strengthening America by Fulfilling Rights and Ensuring Effective Discipline Over Monitoring Act, 114th Congress, 2 Jun 2015, 129 Stat. 268 (USA Freedom Act).

1529 *Ibid.*

1530 Sec. 501 USA Freedom Act, 129 Stat. 282.

1531 Sec. 402 USA Freedom Act, 129 Stat. 281-282.

1532 Office of the Press Secretary (n1527).

1533 Gerhard Peters and John Woolley, 'Barack Obama, Fact Sheet: The Administration's Proposal for Ending the Section 215 Bulk Telephony Metadata Program Online' (*The American Presidency Project*, 27 Mar 2014).

landmark 2022 *FBI v Fazaga*[1534] case. Members of the Islamic Center of Irvine filed a complaint about disproportionate and untargeted surveillance conflicting with their freedom of religion as their Muslim Mosque and community were targeted in a counterterrorism operation based on FISA. The FBI refused to share possible evidence based on the evidentiary 'State Secrets Privilege' "pursuant to which the executive branch can seek to remove evidence from litigation because it could endanger national security if made public".[1535] The U.S. District Court for the Central District of California[1536] upheld the evidentiary privilege in 2011, dismissing the case as a litigation of the claims "would require or unjustifiably risk disclosure of secret and classified information".[1537] The Ninth Circuit[1538] reversed the District Court's decision in 2019, rejecting the evidentiary privilege, favoring the application of Sec. 106(f) FISA which provides that the court "shall, notwithstanding any other law, if the Attorney General files an affidavit under oath that disclosure or an adversary hearing would harm the national security of the United States, review *in camera* and *ex parte* the application, order, and such other materials relating to the surveillance as may be necessary to determine whether the surveillance of the aggrieved person was lawfully authorized and conducted".[1539] SCOTUS[1540] reversed the Ninth Circuit's decision again in 2022, returning to the initial decision made by the District Court, upholding the evidentiary privilege, leading to the dismissal of the case.[1541]

2022 Executive Order 14086 – President Joe Biden promulgated Executive Order (EO) 14086[1542] in 2022 to enhance "safeguards for United States signals intelligence activities".[1543] EO 14086 was the first step in the process for a new trans-Atlantic data transfer framework (the third attempt), which would become the 2023 *Data Privacy Framework (DPF) adequacy decision*.[1544] To this end, the exact wording of the CJEU's *Schrems II*[1545] decision was enshrined in the Executive Order to accommodate the EU's concerns.[1546] Three data

1534 *FBI v Fazaga* [2020] 595 U.S. __.

1535 'National Security – Surveillance – Ninth Circuit Holds that FISA Displaces the State Secrets Privilege for Electronic Surveillance – *Fazaga v. FBI*, 916 F.3d 1202 (9th Cir. 2019)' (2020) 133 HarvLRev 1774, 1774.

1536 *Yassir Fazaga et al v Federal Bureau of Investigation et al* [2012] 884 F.Supp.2d (CD Cal. 2012).

1537 *Ibid.* 1028-1029.

1538 *Fazaga v FBI* [2019] 916 F.3d 1202 (9th Cir. 2019).

1539 Sec.106(f) FISA.

1540 *FBI v Fazaga* (n1534).

1541 *Ibid.*; De Schrijver (n148) 2; Scott and Manancourt (n146).

1542 EO 14086 Enhancing Safeguards for United States Signals Intelligence Activities, 87Fed. Reg.198, 62283, 7 Oct 2022.

1543 *Ibid.* 62283.

1544 See *Chapter 1, § 2, C.*

1545 *Schrems II* (n119).

1546 De Schrijver (n148) 1-2; NOYB, 'New US Executive Order' (n154).

privacy principles are introduced for signals intelligence activities, consisting of i) authorization "by statute or by Executive Order, proclamation, or other Presidential Directive ...; ii) ... appropriate safeguards (ensuring) that privacy and civil liberties are integral considerations ... so that: (A) signals intelligence activities ... are necessary to advance a validated intelligence priority ..., and (B) signals intelligence activities shall be conducted only to the extent and in a manner that is proportionate to the validated intelligence priority for which they have been authorized ...; iii) ... rigorous oversight in order to ensure that (signals intelligence activities) comport with the principles identified above".[1547] Subsequently, a list of 'legitimate objectives' is included for which signals intelligence collection activities can be conducted, as well as a list with 'prohibited objectives'.[1548] EO 14086 prioritizes targeted data collection, but does not prohibit data collection in bulk as long as "authorized only based on a determination ... that the information necessary to advance a validated intelligence priority cannot reasonably be obtained by targeted collection ... (and through the application of) reasonable methods and technical measures in order to limit the data collected to only what is necessary to advance a validated intelligence priority, while minimizing the collection of non-pertinent information".[1549] A novelty is the possibility for non-U.S. persons to file a complaint in case of an alleged mishandling of their personal data. First, the Civil Liberties Protection Officer (CLPO) of the Office of the Director of National Intelligence will conduct a review to determine whether a violation occurred "without confirming or denying that the complainant was subject to United States signals intelligence activities".[1550] Secondly, a new 'Data Protection Review Court' is established where "the complainant or ... the Intelligence Community may ... apply for review of the CLPO's determinations",[1551] and of which the appointed judges will "be legal practitioners with appropriate experience in the fields of data privacy and national security law ..., and who shall not be, at the time of their initial appointment, employees of the United States Government ... such judges shall not have any official duties or employment within the United States Government other than their official duties and employment as judges on the Data Protection Review Court".[1552] Upon completion of a review, the Data Protection Review Court will "inform the complainant, through the appropriate public authority in a qualifying State and without confirming or denying that the complainant was subject to United States signals intelligence activities, that

---

1547 EO 14086, 62283.
1548 *Ibid.* 62283-62285.
1549 *Ibid.* 62286.
1550 *Ibid.* 62290.
1551 *Ibid.* 62291.
1552 *Ibid.*

'the review either did not identify any covered violations or the Data Protection Review Court issued a determination requiring appropriate remediation'".[1553] If in a later stage the information concerned is declassified, the complainant will be notified that the information has become available.[1554] The establishment of the Data Protection Review Court was a direct response to the CJEU's finding that there was no adequate redress mechanism in the United States for Europeans whose personal data was supposedly mishandled for U.S. surveillance activities, as the previously established Ombudsperson was found to be inadequate by the CJEU.[1555] The Data Protection Review Court is, however, situated in the executive as opposed to the judicial branch as it is established by executive order and not by Article III U.S. Constitution, which sets out "the judicial power of the United States".[1556] The retention of the possibility to engage in data collection in bulk does still face criticism from the European side, but subsequent CJEU case law has shown that several EU Member States engage in similar surveillance practices.[1557]

Act ↔ Executive Order ↔ Presidential Policy Directive – The documents governing U.S. surveillance practices discussed in this section consist of different legal frameworks with each a different legal value. As some of these formats were criticized by the European side, the different types of documents will briefly be explained here. An Act of Congress (or statute/law) is a bill that is signed by the President after passing the Senate and the House in identical form. The Act or law is subsequently integrated into the 1926 United States Code (U.S.C.),[1558] which is a pre-existing body of compiled laws, organized by subject, and divided into separate titles.[1559] An Executive Order (EO) is an internal directive, with the effect and force of law, issued by the U.S. President

1553 *Ibid.* 62292.

1554 *Ibid.* 62292-66293.

1555 See *Chapter 1, § 2, B. and C.*

1556 Article III, Sec. 1 U.S.C.

1557 Bureau of Intelligence and Research, 'Executive Order 14086 – Policy and Procedures' (*state.gov*, 3 Jul 2023); De Schrijver (n148) 1-2; Drechsler *et al.* (n151) 17-19; EC, 'Joint Statement' (n145); EP, DPF Resolution (n155) 3-4; NOYB, 'New US Executive Order' (n154); Office of Civil Liberties, Privacy & Transparency, *Executive Order 14086: Signals Intelligence Redress Mechanism* (Office of the Director of National Intelligence Report, 2023); David Shepardson and Philip Blenkinsop, 'Biden signs order to implement EU-U.S. data privacy framework' (*Reuters*, 8 Oct 2022); The White House, 'Data Privacy Framework' (n149).

1558 Office of the Law Revision Counsel, 'United States Code' (*U.S. House of Representatives*, 15 Mar 2025).

1559 Library of Congress, 'Federal Statutes: A Beginner's Guide: United States Code' (*loc.gov*, 2025); United States Senate, 'Laws and Acts' (*senate.gov*, 2025).

to manage and shape federal government operations and policy. The legislative power to enact laws or Acts is vested in Congress and the executive power to 'execute' these laws or Acts is vested with the U.S. President. Consequently, EOs must yield to lawmaking by Congress, except insofar as the Constitution makes a clear and exclusive grant of authority for lawmaking on a specific subject to the President, which it does not do much, or when Congress delegates the lawmaking power on a specific matter to the President. U.S. Presidents have tried to make (extensive) use of this power through engaging in lawmaking while (sometimes) sidestepping Congress. The current or succeeding President can amend and revoke an EO at any time. In practice, Congress has also overridden presidential EOs by legislating on the same subject. Congress nor the courts can provide compliance oversight (lawfulness) of EOs as they do not provide enforceable rights nor judicial redress possibilities for individuals. Only if a party can prove injury resulting from the EO taking effect, will it have standing in court against the President and government officials/agencies executing the EO. Judicial review of the legality and compliance with the provisions of the U.S. Constitution is possible, but can rarely be requested by individuals (unless they can prove concretely sustained harm[1560]). EOs must be published in the Federal Register, where rules and laws are usually published, unless they 'do not have general applicability and legal effect' or are 'effective only against Federal agencies/persons in their capacity as officers/agents/ employees'.[1561] A Presidential Policy Directive or Presidential Directive (PD) has the same legal effect as an Executive Order. The U.S. President promulgates Presidential Directives to manage and shape federal government operations and policy, which do not provide enforceable rights for individuals. PDs are usually not published, unless they have 'general applicability and legal effect'.[1562] In conclusion, the promulgation of an Act has to follow the most rigorous

1560 See *Chapter 4, § 3, A., ii), b)*.

1561 *Schrems II* (n119) para 182; Drechsler *et al.* (n151) 17; EP, DPF Resolution (n155) 5; McLaughlin (n139) 232-233; NOYB, 'New US Executive Order' (n154); Office of Civil Liberties, Privacy & Transparency (n1557) 4; Harold Relyea, *Presidential Directives: Background and Overview* (CRS Report for Congress, 2008) 5-6; Kevin Richards, 'Executive Orders: An Introduction' (*CRS Products: Library of Congress*, 2021); Tye (n1500); Christopher Wright Durocher, 'What is an Executive Order and What Legal Weight Does it Carry?' (*American Constitution Society*, 19 Mar 2025); 'What Is an Executive Order?' (*American Bar Association*, 25 Jan 2021).

1562 PPD-28, 9; Steven Aftergood, 'What's the Difference Between an Executive Order and a Directive?' (*fas.org*, 14 Feb 2013); Gallagher Law Library, 'U.S. Presidential Documents: Presidential Directives' (*University of Washington School of Law*, 2023); Randolph Moss, *Legal Effectiveness of a Presidential Directive, as Compared to an Executive Order* (Dept. of Justice: Office of Legal Counsel, 2000) 29-30; Richards (n1561).

legislative process, as it has to pass the Senate and the House, and subsequently be signed into law by the President, and is, consequently, the most difficult to amend or revoke. Executive Orders and Presidential Directives differ in their level of publicity, and while having the same legal effect as Acts, they can much more easily be amended or revoked by a sole act of the President.

Public v. Private actors – For the discussion of personal data collection/retention/processing by public versus private actors, Sec. 501 FISA (introduced by Sec. 215 Patriot Act) and EO 12333 are of particular importance. Sec. 501 FISA allows "the Director of the (FBI … to) make an application for an order requiring the production of any tangible things (including books, records, papers, documents, and other items) for an investigation to protect against international terrorism or clandestine intelligence activities …",[1563] which was exemplified by the FISC order mandating telecom company Verizon to hand over its (U.S.) customers' personal data.[1564] The FISC is, however, criticized for being a 'rubber stamp' as it has approved over 20,000 requests and was initially located in the Department of Justice (executive branch), which brought the FISC's independence into question. The FISC had not refused a single NSA request between its inception in 1978 and 2002. In the period of 2002 until 2012, the FISC had only rejected eleven applications, which is negligible compared to the amount of requests that the Court has approved in its lifespan.[1565] The 2015 Freedom Act introduced a new oversight and transparency requirement for the Director of the Administrative Office of the United States Courts to issue a yearly report regarding, among others, the activities of the Foreign Intelligence Surveillance Court and the Foreign Intelligence Surveillance Court of Review.[1566] The reports are available at the United States Courts' website, which contained the yearly reports from 2015 until 2024 at the time of writing.[1567] The 2024 Report mentions, for example, that in summary the FISC received 352 requests, approved 267, modified 72, partially denied 15, and not denied any request in full during 2024.[1568] The oversight requirement can certainly be seen as a positive step forward in making the FISC's operations more transparent. In contrast to Sec. 501 FISA, which grants U.S. intelligence services the competence to mandate private companies to hand over their customers' personal data, intelligence services can, based on EO 12333, directly access information that is in transit from the lines of communication

1563 Sec. 215 USA Patriot Act.
1564 See *Chapter 1, § 2, A*.
1565 Greenwald, *No Place to Hide* (n16) 128-129 and 251.
1566 50 U.S.C. § 1873(a), Pub. L. No. 114-23.
1567 United States Courts, 'Director's Report on Foreign Intelligence Surveillance Courts' Activities' (*uscourts.gov*, 2025).
1568 United States Courts, *Report of the Director of the Administrative Office of the U.S. Courts on Activities of the Foreign Intelligence Surveillance Courts for 2024* (U.S. Courts Report, 2025) 1.

without the need "to notify or obtain consent of a company before collecting its users' data".[1569] This practice is problematic for private companies, which, at least in California and Virginia, have to comply with the purpose limitation requirement as set out in the CCPA and the VCDPA discussed in this book.[1570] If these companies collect their customers' data for the provision of telecommunications services, the use of the same data by intelligence services for national security purposes violates the purpose limitation principle which private companies have to observe when operating in California and Virginia. The practice as set out by EO 12333 should consequently be avoided, and preference should be given to the Sec. 501 FISA framework which requires a FISC order to obtain these data. As private companies are aware of the FISA framework, they can include this purpose of possible data processing in their privacy policies to ensure compliance with the purpose limitation principle.

Discussion – For law enforcement purposes, personal data is increasingly protected in the digital age by SCOTUS' Fourth Amendment jurisprudence as was shown in the previous chapter where the *Kyllo*[1571] and *Carpenter*[1572] cases were discussed, but as the Court made clear that its decisions were specifically tied to the circumstances of each particular case, future litigation will have to show whether the U.S. Supreme Court continues its protective approach limiting the application of the third party doctrine in these cases.[1573] For intelligence and national security purposes, the wording of FISA seems to provide safeguards against government abuse in the form of a required FISC order and minimization procedures that have to be adopted by the U.S. Attorney General. While Snowden revealed that FISA was extensively interpreted to an unforeseen level, the 2015 Freedom Act (should have) remedied many of these over-interpretations by restricting FISA's legal wording. The 2022 EO 14086 clarified, however, that these remedies do not include a limitation on the possibility to engage in bulk metadata retention for foreign intelligence purposes. The newly introduced yearly reports summarizing the FISC's operations (since 2015) improve the Court's transparency while protecting a certain level of secrecy which is necessary for national security cases. The decision in the 2022 *Fazaga* case, on the contrary, seems to overly tilt to the national security side of the balance. SCOTUS' acceptance of the evidentiary State Secrets Privilege resulted in the case being nonjusticiable. The alternative offered by Sec. 106(f) FISA consisting of an *in camera* and *ex parte* review seems to offer a solution to balance both parties' interests. It is understandable that

1569 Tye (n1500).

1570 See *Chapter 3, § 1, B.*

1571 *Kyllo* (n1083).

1572 *Carpenter* (n1085).

1573 See *Chapter 4, § 2, C.*

sharing sensitive information relating to national security with 'any' court for review, even when this information is not shared with the parties, can pose certain dangers, but this can be remedied by appointing, for example, only one specific court or judge to review the sensitive information. In the Belgian system, only the Chamber of Indictment is allowed to review Special Investigative Measures which are included in a 'secret' file that exists next to the 'public' file to protect certain sensitive investigative techniques and/or the identities of undercover agents. The appointment of one specific U.S. court or judge could also be beneficial to the U.S. system to ensure a certain degree of review in sensitive national security cases, instead of not providing any possibility for review at all. The distinction between legal safeguards for U.S. versus non-U.S. persons was criticized by the EU, but it is questionable whether EU Member States extend specific safeguards to non-EU citizens. As a reaction to the EU's criticism, the 2014 PPD-28 extended certain safeguards, such as data minimization and limitations on data dissemination and retention, to non-U.S. persons, which may be quite exceptional as it is doubtful that other States would extend the safeguards for their own citizens in national security matters to non-citizens. Executive Order 14086 will be discussed below from a comparative perspective in *§ 5. Interim analysis*.

§ 3. EU SURVEILLANCE LAWS

In the aftermath of the invalidation of the EU-U.S. data privacy frameworks and the CJEU's position on U.S. national security and surveillance laws, attention was turned back inward to scrutinize the (similar) data retention and transmission laws of EU Member States. Not only was a similar data retention directive enacted at the EU level, but several Member States implemented this directive into their own national (surveillance) laws. This section provides an overview of the national security and surveillance laws at the EU and (selected) Member State level, together with an overview of related CJEU case law, in the light of the EU-U.S. data privacy discussion. In the following section, a non-exhaustive overview of relevant ECtHR (national security) case law is included to compare both courts' position on this delicate topic. Finally, the analysis section will discuss the findings and compare the U.S. and EU perspectives on national security.

A. EU LEVEL

2016 LED – The prevention, investigation, detection or prosecution of criminal offenses is covered by a specific Law Enforcement Directive

(LED)[1574] containing "less stringent rules applicable to data processing for law enforcement purposes".[1575] The LED's rules are largely similar to those of the 2016 GDPR,[1576] with the main difference being that the exercise of some rights (such as a request for access or rectification) can be denied or delayed to not endanger ongoing criminal investigations.[1577] Regarding the purpose limitation principle, the LED states, like the GDPR, that "personal data (shall) be collected for specified, explicit and legitimate purposes and not processed in a manner ... incompatible with those purposes".[1578] A closer reading of the LED highlights two important elements. Firstly, a contradiction seems to emerge as the LED does explicitly "not apply to the processing of personal data in the course of an activity which falls outside the scope of Union law, activities concerning national security, activities of agencies ... dealing with national security issues",[1579] while certain LED Articles[1580] include public and national security in their scope of application. These ambiguities occur more often in EU law and will be discussed below. If national security is outside the scope of EU law (LED and GDPR), public sector activities outsourced to private companies for these purposes should be governed by Member State law. A distinction should hence be made between the outsourcing of personal data collection for national security purposes (Member State legislation) and for law enforcement purposes (EU LED). Secondly, the LED states that private companies "entrusted ... to exercise public authority and public powers ... should be bound by a contract or other legal act and by the provisions applicable to processors pursuant to (the LED), while the application of (the GDPR) remains unaffected for the processing of personal data by the processor outside the scope of (the LED)".[1581] In this case, private companies become government agents and are subjected to public law when they exercise public sector activities.[1582] Two legal frameworks will hence be

1574 Directive (EU) 2016/680 of 27 Apr 2016 on the protection of natural persons with regard to the processing of personal data by competent authorities for the purposes of the prevention, investigation, detection or prosecution of criminal offences or the execution of criminal penalties, and on the free movement of such data, and repealing Council Framework Decision 2008/977/JHA [2016] OJ L 119/89 (LED).

1575 Lynskey, *The foundations* (n42) 19.

1576 See *Chapter 3, § 3, B., iv), b)*.

1577 Article 13.3 and 15.1 LED; Teresa Quintel and Eleni Kosta, 'Background and evolution of the LED' in Eleni Kosta and others (eds), *The EU Law Enforcement Directive (LED)* (OUP 2024) 5.

1578 Article 4.1(b) LED.

1579 Recital 14 and Article 2.3(a) LED; Plixavra Vogiatzoglou and Stefano Fantin, 'National and Public Security within and beyond the Police Directive' in Anton Vedder and others (eds), *Security and Law* (1st edn, Intersentia 2019) 30.

1580 Article 13.3(c)(d) and 15.1(c)(d) LED.

1581 Recital 11 LED.

1582 Harlow (n1484) 329.

applicable to private companies. Plixavra Vogiatzoglou and Stefano Fantin observe that "the two key concepts delineating the (LED's) application are the *purpose* of the processing and the notion of competent authorities".[1583]

2002 e-Privacy Directive – The e-Privacy Directive[1584] was introduced in 2002 to harmonize "the provisions of the Member States ... to ensure an equivalent level of protection of ... the right to privacy ... (when) processing personal data in the electronic communication sector and to ensure the free movement of such data ... in the Community".[1585] The 2002 Directive replaces its predecessor, Directive 97/66/EC of 15 December 1997 concerning the processing of personal data and the protection of privacy in the telecommunications sector, as the latter had become outdated due to the "developments in the markets and technologies for electronic communications services".[1586] The 2002 e-Privacy Directive complements, similar to its predecessor, the 1995 Directive and now the 2016 GDPR as a 'lex specialis'[1587] for the electronic communications sector. Of particular importance is Article 15.1 of the e-Privacy Directive, which states that "Member States may adopt legislative measures to restrict the scope of the rights and obligations provided for in ... this Directive when such restriction constitutes a necessary, appropriate and proportionate measure within a democratic society to safeguard national security ..., and the prevention, investigation, detection and prosecution of criminal offences ... to this end, Member States may ... adopt legislative measures providing for the retention of data for a limited period".[1588] Interestingly, however, article 1.3 of the e-Privacy Directive also states that "this Directive shall not apply ... to activities concerning public security, defence, State security ... and the activities of the State in areas of criminal law",[1589] which seems to contradict the content of Article 15.1 of the same Directive mentioned earlier.[1590]

1583 Vogiatzoglou and Fantin (n1579) 29-30.

1584 Directive 2002/58/EC of 12 Jul 2002 concerning the processing of personal data and the protection of privacy in the electronic communications sector [2002] OJ L 201/37.

1585 Article 1 Directive 2002/58/EC.

1586 Recital 4 Directive 2002/58/EC.

1587 Recital 10 Directive 2002/58/EC states that "in the electronic communications sector, Directive 95/46/EC applies ... to all matters concerning protection of fundamental rights and freedoms, which are not specifically covered by the provisions of this Directive". *See also*: Recital 12 and Article 1.2 Directive 2002/58/EC.

1588 Article 15.1 Directive 2002/58/EC.

1589 Article 1.3 Directive 2002/58/EC.

1590 Article 29 WP, 'Working Document WP228' (n547) 36-37; Bygrave, *Data Privacy Law* (n37) 64-66; de Vries *et al.* (n525) 307-308.

2006 Data Retention Directive – The Data Retention Directive[1591] was introduced in 2006, after the terrorist attacks in Madrid and London, "to harmonise Member States' provisions concerning the obligations of the providers of publicly available electronic communications services or of public communications networks with respect to the retention of certain data which are generated or processed by them, in order to ensure that the data are available for the purpose of the investigation, detection and prosecution of serious crime, as defined by each Member State in its national law".[1592] The Data Retention Directive made a distinction between the content of the communications, which could not be retained, and metadata,[1593] which had to be retained.[1594] According to Article 6 of the Directive, the collected metadata had to be "retained for periods of not less than six months and not more than two years from the date of the communication",[1595] but an extension of this period was possible if "a Member State fac(ed) particular circumstances that warrant(ed) an extension for a limited period".[1596] Jack Maxwell and Joe Tomlinson observe that the Directive's wide scope of application "required communication providers to retain metadata for virtually every person in Europe",[1597] which was confirmed by the CJEU (*see below*).[1598] The EU legislator provided two distinct justification grounds for its intervention at the EU level, as opposed to the Member States' level, in the Directive's recitals. Firstly, recitals 5 and 6 referred to the establishment of the internal market, set out in Article 95 EC (now Article 114.1 TFEU), as Member States' introduction of varying national data retention laws for service providers "present(ed) obstacles to the (EU) internal market for electronic communications, since service providers (were) faced with different requirements regarding the types of traffic and location data to be retained and the conditions and periods of retention",[1599] rendering a harmonizing intervention at the EU level preferable and necessary.[1600] Secondly, recital 21 referred to the EU "principle

---

1591 Directive 2006/24/EC of 15 Mar 2006 on the retention of data generated or processed in connection with the provision of publicly available electronic communications services or of public communications networks and amending Directive 2002/58/EC [2006] OJ L 105/54.

1592 Article 1 Directive 2006/24/EC.

1593 Consisting of traffic and location data, data to identify the user, etc.: see *Chapter 1, § 1, A.*

1594 Article 1.2 and 2.2(a) and 5 Directive 2006/24/EC.

1595 Article 6 Directive 2006/24/EC.

1596 Article 12.1 Directive 2006/24/EC.

1597 Jack Maxwell and Joe Tomlinson, 'Privacy Int'l v. Secretary of State for Foreign & Commonwealth Affairs and La Quadrature du Net v. Premier ministre (C.J.E.U.)' (2021) 60 ILM 464, 464.

1598 Article 3 Directive 2006/24/EC.

1599 Recital 6 Directive 2006/24/EC.

1600 Recital 5-6 Directive 2006/24/EC; *Digital Rights* (n647) para 11; Bygrave, *Data Privacy Law* (n37) 67; Zalnieriute (n17) 200-201.

of subsidiarity as set out in Article 5 of the Treaty",[1601] because the objective of harmonizing communications providers' data retention obligations could not "be sufficiently achieved by the Member States and (could) therefore ... be better achieved at Community level".[1602,1603]

2014 *Digital Rights Ireland* case – The compatibility of the Data Retention Directive with the EU Charter's rights to privacy and personal data protection was assessed by the CJEU in the 2014 *Digital Rights Ireland*[1604] joined cases regarding the Irish and Austrian national laws implementing the Data Retention Directive. The Austrian Constitutional Court had observed that the Directive "allow(ed) the storing of many types of data in relation to an unlimited number of persons for a long time (and) that the retention of data affect(ed) almost exclusively persons whose conduct in no way justifie(d) the retention of data relating to them".[1605] Accordingly, the referring Court expressed "doubts as to whether (the Data Retention Directive was) able to achieve the objectives which it pursue(d) and as to the proportionality of the interference with the fundamental rights concerned".[1606] The CJEU agreed that the data which had to be retained according to the Directive could "allow very precise conclusions to be drawn concerning the private lives of the persons whose data ha(d) been retained, such as the habits of everyday life, permanent or temporary places of residence, daily or other movements, the activities carried out, the social relationships of those persons and the social environments frequented by them".[1607] The Court of Justice addressed the question whether the Data Retention Directive was unduly interfering with Articles 7 (privacy) and 8 (personal data protection) of the EU Charter, answering in the affirmative. The Court observed that the Directive "cover(ed), in a generalised manner, all persons and all means of electronic communication as well as all traffic data without any differentiation, limitation or exception being made in the light of the objective of fighting against serious crime"[1608] and "(did) not require any relationship between the data whose retention (was) provided for and a threat to public security".[1609] The Data Retention Directive did, moreover, "not lay down clear and precise rules governing the extent of the interference with ... articles 7 and 8 of the Charter, (as it entailed) a wide-ranging and particularly serious interference with those fundamental rights ..., without

---

[1601] Recital 21 Directive 2006/24/EC.
[1602] *Ibid.*
[1603] Bygrave, *Data Privacy Law* (n37) 66-68; de Vries *et al.* (n525) 265-266 and 308.
[1604] *Digital Rights* (n647).
[1605] *Ibid.* para 20.
[1606] *Ibid.*
[1607] *Ibid.* para 27.
[1608] *Ibid.* para 57.
[1609] *Ibid.* para 59.

such an interference being … limited to what is strictly necessary".[1610] As a consequence, the CJEU decided that the 2006 Data Retention Directive violated Articles 7 (privacy) and 8 (personal data protection) of the EU Charter and invalidated the Directive.[1611]

Internal market v. national security – The invalidation of the Data Retention Directive was not surprising to the Article 29 WP,[1612] which had already "voiced its concern (in Opinion 01/2014) that the blanket retention for all people's data held by EU telecommunications providers for 2 years … was a disproportionate interference with an individual's right to privacy … (and) that the Data Retention Directive lacked sufficient clarity and would breach the purpose limitation principle".[1613] After the CJEU's decision in the 2014 Digital *Rights Ireland* case, the Article 29 WP confirmed its position that there should be "no bulk retention of all kinds of data"[1614] in a new opinion[1615] and statement.[1616] It is of course a matter of interpretation what the Data Retention Directive exactly aimed to regulate. The EU aimed at harmonizing the different national security laws, namely the different national data retention laws, as they hindered the establishment of Article 114 TFEU's internal market, which is the widest and strongest area for the EU to regulate. In my opinion, however, the legal subject of the Data Retention Directive was national security, which is situated in the legislative *domaine réservé* of the Member States, and should, as a consequence, not be regulated at the EU level.[1617] Federico Fabbrini shares this point of view that "the Data Retention Directive (had) the aim of fighting terrorism and protecting national security".[1618] Recitals 9 and 10 of the Directive seem to also confirm this second interpretation by stating that "(b)ecause retention of data has proved to be such a necessary and effective investigative tool for law enforcement in several Member States, and in particular concerning … organised crime and terrorism, it is necessary to ensure that retained data are made available to law enforcement authorities for a certain period …",[1619] consequently, "the

---

1610 *Ibid.* para 65.

1611 *Ibid.* paras 69-71; Jenny Bergholm, 'The Data Retention Saga Continued – from Tele2 Sverige to Privacy Intl and La Quadrature du Net' (2021) 2 JFT 111, 111; Brewczynska (n401) 55-57; Brkan (n739) 871; Christofi and Verdoodt (n107) 21-22; Lynskey, *The foundations* (n42) 161-173; Maxwell and Tomlinson (n1597) 464; David Mollenkamp, *National Security, Privacy, and Possible Alterations in the CJEU's Case Law in Response to the Spyware Surveillance Crisis* (Stanford-Vienna EU Law Working Paper No.79, 2023) 2-4; Zalnieriute (n17) 201.

1612 See *Chapter 3, § 3, B., i), b).*

1613 Article 29 WP, 'Opinion 01/2014' (n631) 17.

1614 Article 29 WP, 'Statement on the ruling of the Court of Justice of the European Union which invalidates the Data Retention Directive' (WP220, 1 Aug 2014) 2.

1615 Article 29 WP, 'Opinion 04/2014' (n16) 5.

1616 Article 29 WP, 'Statement WP220' (n1614).

1617 Article 4.2 TEU.

1618 de Vries *et al.* (n525) 265.

1619 Recital 9 Directive 2006/24/EC.

Council ... condemning the terrorist attacks on London, (reaffirmed) the need to adopt common measures on the retention of telecommunications data as soon as possible".[1620] Even the CJEU stated in the 2014 *Digital Rights Ireland* case that "the material objective of that directive (was), therefore, to contribute to the fight against serious crime and thus, ultimately, to public security",[1621] but did not invalidate the Data Retention Directive on this ground, rather on its incompatibility with the EU Charter.

Legal basis – Recital 4 of the 2006 EU Data Retention Directive seems to 'grant' the possibility for Member States to enact data retention legislation based on the 2002 e-Privacy Directive, while national legislation concerning "national security remains the sole responsibility, (a *domaine réservé*), of each Member State" according to Article 4.2 TEU.[1622] Recital 11 of the 2002 e-Privacy Directive explains that "this Directive does not address issues ... related to activities which are not governed by Community law ... it does not alter the existing balance between the individual's right to privacy and the possibility for Member States to take the measures referred to in article 15.1 of this Directive, necessary for the protection of public security ... and the enforcement of criminal law".[1623] Jenny Bergholm concludes that, "intuitively, the provisions in article 15.1 on the one hand, and article 1.3 of the e-Privacy Directive and article 4.2 TEU seem to contradict each other".[1624] The CJEU explained in 2016 *Tele2 Sverige* (*see below*) that "admittedly, the legislative measures ... referred to in article 15.1 of (e-Privacy) Directive 2002/58 concern activities characteristic of States or State authorities ... the objectives which, under that provision, such measures must pursue, such as safeguarding national security, defence and public security and the prevention, investigation, detection and prosecution of criminal offences ... overlap substantially with the objectives pursued by the activities referred to in article 1.3 of that directive".[1625] When read in its broader context, Article 15.1 e-Privacy Directive does not seem to provide a 'legal basis' in itself, as the 2006 Data Retention Directive seems to suggest, but is instead a confirmation of the national security exemption as enshrined in Article 4.2 TEU.

1620 Recital 10 Directive 2006/24/EC.

1621 *Digital Rights* (n647) para 41.

1622 Cameron (n78) 453-455; Federico Casolari, 'Supranational Security and National Security in Light of the EU Strategic Autonomy Doctrine' (2023) 28 EurForeignAffRev 323, 323-324; Giacomo Di Federico, 'The Potential of Article 4(2) TEU in the Solution of Constitutional Clashes Based on Alleged Violations of National Identity and the Quest for Adequate (Judicial) Standards' (2019) 25 EPL 347, 354.

1623 Recital 11 Directive 2006/24/EC.

1624 Bergholm (n1611) 115.

1625 *Tele2 Sverige* (n1653) para 72.

"It is … interesting that the CJEU goes through sources of secondary law (namely the e-Privacy Directive) in order to explain why the exception of national security (in TEU primary law) is not applicable … according to the hierarchy of norms of EU law, sources of primary law have prejudice over secondary law … sources of primary EU law (should consequently, at least theoretically, be valued) higher than … secondary (EU) legislation".[1626] It is, therefore, not surprising that the EU Member States submitted the argument in the court cases discussed below that "(the e-Privacy) Directive 2002/58 (did) not apply to the national legislation at issue … as the purpose of that legislation (was) to safeguard national security (and) … activities of the security and intelligence agencies are essential State functions relating to the maintenance of law and order and the safeguarding of national security and territorial integrity, and, accordingly, are the sole responsibility of the Member States, as attested to by … article 4.2 TEU".[1627,1628] Jenny Bergholm and the CJEU had expressed their concern[1629] that "had the (national cases) … been solved stressing the exception of national security, the (2002) e-Privacy Directive, together with the purpose of protecting fundamental rights in relation to invasive data processing, would have been undermined".[1630] The CJEU has, moreover, held on many occasions that "the mere fact that a national measure has been taken for the purpose of protecting national security cannot render EU law inapplicable and exempt the Member States from their obligation to comply with that law",[1631] as to do otherwise would undermine the core values of the Union and "be liable to impair the binding nature of Community law and its uniform application".[1632] These statements are, however, not entirely justified. Article 51.1 of the EU Charter states that its provisions, *in casu* Articles 7 and 8, "are addressed to the institutions, bodies, offices and agencies of the Union … and to the Member States only when they are implementing Union law". A contradiction emerges because this would mean that the EU Charter's provisions are not applicable to Member States when their legislative acts are outside the scope of EU law, *in casu* the introduction of a national security measure.[1633] The Article 29 WP, as well as Frederik Zuiderveen Borgesius *et al.*,[1634] shared this opinion already

1626 Bergholm (n1611) 117.
1627 *Privacy International* (n1663) para 32; *Quadrature du Net* (n1680) para 89.
1628 Maxwell and Tomlinson (n1597) 465; Vogiatzoglou (n737) 81-83; Zalnieriute (n17) 202.
1629 *Tele2 Sverige* (n1653) para 73.
1630 Bergholm (n1611) 117.
1631 C-300/11 *ZZ v Secretary of State for the Home Department* [2013] para 38; *Privacy International* (n1663) para 44.
1632 C-387/05 *Commission v Italy* [2009] para 45.
1633 Article 29 WP, 'Working Document WP228' (n547) 22; Kuner *et al.* (n587) 1.
1634 Zuiderveen Borgesius *et al.* (n180) 15.

in 2014/2015 as "surveillance programmes run by the EU Member States will in general not be subject to EU law, following the national security exemption written into the European treaties, as well as … several EU regulations and directives, including the EU data protection directive 95/46/EC (replaced by the GDPR) … that does not mean however (that) such programmes are only subject to national law … even though EU law in general and the data protection directive (now regulation) in particular do not apply, the data protection principles following the European Convention on Human Rights and Council of Europe Convention 108 on the protection of personal data will for the most part still need to be respected by the intelligence services in order to lawfully perform their duties … this includes the need for all intrusions to be necessary and proportionate in relation to the purpose to be achieved".[1635] The Member States are, after all, also bound by the ECHR, which contains similar (yet distinct) provisions to the EU Charter.[1636] The right to privacy is, for example, explicitly subject to exceptions including national security in Article 8.2 ECHR, as opposed to Article 7 EU Charter.[1637] If a measure falls within an exception of Article 8.2 ECHR, it still has to fulfill the conditions of legality, necessity, and proportionality.[1638] The core EU values will, therefore, still be respected, albeit through the ECHR instead of the EU Charter, as EU Member States' national security laws will still have to comply with the ECHR and pass the ECtHR's test.

Why versus Who – It is understandable that the CJEU is hesitant to invalidate EU (secondary) law based on Article 4.2 TEU's national security provision, and by extension Article 2.2(d) GDPR, as this would limit the scope of application of EU law. However, the Court had already engaged in such a decision in the 2006 *Parliament v Council and Commission (PNR)*[1639] case. An EU adequacy decision[1640] for the United States was adopted in 2004, enabling the transfer of EU Passenger Name Records[1641] to U.S. customs

1635 Article 29 WP, 'Opinion 04/2014' (n16) 6.

1636 Kuner *et al.* (n587) 3.

1637 Cameron (n78) 455.

1638 Article 8.2 ECHR; Vogiatzoglou and Fantin (n1579) 36-37.

1639 Joined Cases C-317/04 and C-318/04 *Parliament v Council and Commission* [2006].

1640 Decision of 17 May 2004 on the conclusion of an Agreement between the European Community and the USA on the processing and transfer of PNR data by Air Carriers to the U.S. Department of Homeland Security, Bureau of Customs and Border Protection [2004] OJ L 183/83.

1641 PNR encompasses airline passengers' data, such as: reservation and intended travel date, full name, number of travelers, contact and billing information, travel agency, baggage and seat information, and special meal requests.: Brewczynska (n401) 57-58; U.S. Department of State, Agreement Between the USA and the EU (*state.gov*, 14 Dec 2011) 1-2; Vogiatzoglou, 'Mass surveillance' (n1469) 5.

authorities "following the terrorist attacks of 11 September 2001, (as) the United States (had) passed legislation ... providing that air carriers operating flights to or from the (United States) or across (U.S.) territory had to provide (U.S.) customs authorities with electronic access to the data contained in their automated reservation and departure control systems, referred to as Passenger Name Records (PNR)".[1642] The CJEU invalidated this adequacy decision in 2006 *Parliament*,[1643] as "processing operations concerning public security, defence, State security and the activities of the State in areas of criminal law"[1644] were excluded from the 1995 Directive's scope of application (Article 3.2), which was similar to Article 2.2 GDPR currently in force. The Court continued that "while the view may rightly be taken that PNR data are initially collected by airlines in the course of an activity which falls within the scope of Community law, namely sale of an aeroplane ticket which provides entitlement to a supply of services, (the adequacy) decision (on which the agreement was based) concerns not data processing necessary for a supply of services, but data processing regarded as necessary for safeguarding public security and for law enforcement purposes".[1645] The CJEU concluded that the adequacy decision "concern(ed) processing of personal data as referred to (in) article 3.2 Directive (95/46/EC), (which) does not fall within the scope of the Directive",[1646] and, by extension, within "community (EU) competence".[1647,1648] Some Member States relied on this decision and on the Court's PNR reasoning in the telecommunications cases discussed below, arguing that their national metadata retention laws were outside the 1995 Directive's / GDPR's scope of application as they concerned matters of national security.[1649] The CJEU, however, decided to change its approach. To preserve legal certainty and clarity, this book will argue in *C. Public versus Private actors* below that the division of competences should be respected by the EU legislator as well as by the CJEU, and that the focus should be placed on the *purpose* of the processing as opposed to *who* is processing the data.

1642 *Parliament* (n1639) para 33.

1643 *Parliament* (n1639).

1644 *Ibid.* para 54.

1645 *Ibid.* para 57.

1646 *Ibid.* paras 59 and 68.

1647 *Ibid.* para 67.

1648 The latest version of the remedied EU-U.S. PNR adequacy decision came into force in 2012: Decision of 13 Dec 2011 on the signing, on behalf of the Union, of the Agreement between the USA and the EU on the use and transfer of PNR to the U.S. Department of Homeland Security [2012] OJ L 215/1.: Kosta and Kamara (n37) 399; Quintel and Kosta (n1577) 2; Vogiatzoglou (n737) 80.

1649 *Privacy International* (n1663) para 27; *Quadrature du Net* (n1680) para 100; Zalnieriute (n17) 210.

The purpose approach would also clarify the legal situation surrounding the 2006 Data Retention Directive, as it was, as such, a national security measure within the Member States' *domaine réservé*, even though the CJEU did not (explicitly) share this opinion.

Table 5. Overview of frequently used articles

TEU	
Article 4.2 TEU	"The Union shall respect the equality of Member States before the Treaties as well as their national identities, inherent in their fundamental structures, political and constitutional, inclusive of regional and local self-government. It shall respect their essential State functions, including ensuring the territorial integrity of the State, maintaining law and order and safeguarding national security. In particular, national security remains the sole responsibility of each Member State."
2002 e-Privacy Directive	
Article 1.3 e-PD	"This Directive shall not apply to activities which fall outside the scope of the Treaty establishing the European Community, such as those covered by Titles V and VI of the Treaty on European Union, and in any case to activities concerning public security, defence, State security (including the economic well-being of the State when the activities relate to State security matters) and the activities of the State in areas of criminal law."
Article 15.1 e-PD	"Member States may adopt legislative measures to restrict the scope of the rights and obligations provided for in Article 5, Article 6, Article 8(1), (2), (3) and (4), and Article 9 of this Directive when such restriction constitutes a necessary, appropriate and proportionate measure within a democratic society to safeguard national security (i.e. State security), defence, public security, and the prevention, investigation, detection and prosecution of criminal offences or of unauthorised use of the electronic communication system, as referred to in Article 13(1) of Directive 95/46/EC. To this end, Member States may, *inter alia*, adopt legislative measures providing for the retention of data for a limited period justified on the grounds laid down in this paragraph. All the measures referred to in this paragraph shall be in accordance with the general principles of Community law, including those referred to in Article 6(1) and (2) of the Treaty on European Union."
2016 GDPR	
Article 2.2(d) GDPR	"This Regulation does not apply to the processing of personal data: (a) in the course of an activity which falls outside the scope of Union law; (b) by the Member States when carrying out activities which fall within the scope of Chapter 2 of Title V of the TEU; (c) by a natural person in the course of a purely personal or household activity; (d) by competent authorities for the purposes of the prevention, investigation, detection or prosecution of criminal offences or the execution of criminal penalties, including the safeguarding against and the prevention of threats to public security."

(continued)

Table 5. *continued*

2016 GDPR	
Article 23.1(d) & (h) GDPR	"Union or Member State law to which the data controller or processor is subject may restrict by way of a legislative measure the scope of the obligations and rights provided for in Articles 12 to 22 and Article 34, as well as Article 5 in so far as its provisions correspond to the rights and obligations provided for in Articles 12 to 22, when such a restriction respects the essence of the fundamental rights and freedoms and is a necessary and proportionate measure in a democratic society to safeguard: (d) the prevention, investigation, detection or prosecution of criminal offences or the execution of criminal penalties, including the safeguarding against and the prevention of threats to public security; (h) a monitoring, inspection or regulatory function connected, even occasionally, to the exercise of official authority in the cases referred to in points (a) to (e) and (g);"

B. MEMBER STATE LEVEL

National data retention laws – Upon enactment of the 2006 Data Retention Directive, which, in its turn, was based on the 2002 e-Privacy Directive, the Member States transposed the Directive into their national law.[1650] The invalidation of the Data Retention Directive in 2014 *Digital Rights Ireland* endangered, consequently, the national laws that implemented this Directive as well. The national data retention laws of five Member States, namely Sweden, the United Kingdom, France, Belgium, and Germany, were scrutinized by the CJEU for their compliance with EU law, and more specifically with Articles 7 and 8 of the EU Charter. The CJEU placed the national data retention legislation within the scope of the 2002 e-Privacy Directive. While this reasoning is interesting from an EU perspective to bring the data retention cases within the scope of EU law, it is not the most interesting legal basis from the Member States' perspective as they preferred to situate the measures within Article 4.2 TEU's *domaine réservé*. Following the 2006 Data Retention Directive, the national data retention laws mandated that only metadata (location and traffic data) had to be retained, not the content of the communications.[1651]

2016 *Tele2 Sverige* joined cases: Sweden and UK – The CJEU had to determine whether the Swedish and UK national (bulk) metadata retention

---

1650 *Tele2 Sverige* (n1653) para 15; *Quadrature du Net* (n1680) para 76; *SpaceNet* (n735) para 33; Bergholm (n1611) 112.

1651 Bergholm (n1611) 111-139; Maxwell and Tomlinson (n1597) 464-520; Zalnieriute (n17) 198-218.

laws "cover(ing), in a generalised manner, all subscribers and registered users and all means of electronic communication as well as all traffic data, provid(ing) for no differentiation, limitation or exception according to the objective pursued"[1652] were compatible with the 2002 e-Privacy Directive (*see above*) in 2016 *Tele2 Sverige*.[1653] The Court made an analogous assessment to 2014 *Digital Rights Ireland* and interpreted the Swedish and UK metadata retention laws in the light of Articles 7 (privacy) and 8 (personal data protection) of the EU Charter. Interestingly, the analysis was initiated by an examination of "whether and to what extent national legislation on the retention of traffic and location data and access to that data by the national authorities, for the purpose of combating crime, (fell) within the scope of (e-Privacy) Directive 2002/58"[1654] instead of a scrutiny of the scope of Article 4.2 TEU as the legislation at issue was related to national security and surveillance. Additionally, the CJEU assessed compliance with Article 11 (freedom of expression) of the EU Charter, because "even if ... (the) retention of the content of a communication (was not permitted) ..., the retention of traffic and location data could nonetheless have an effect on the use of means of electronic communication and, consequently, on the exercise by the users thereof of their freedom of expression, guaranteed in article 11 of the Charter".[1655] The same argument was formulated in 2014 *Digital Rights Ireland*,[1656] but was not assessed as the Court had already established a violation of Articles 7 and 8 of the EU Charter. Similarly, the CJEU found a violation of Articles 7, 8, and 11 of the EU Charter in the 2016 *Tele2 Sverige*[1657] joined cases. Firstly, "national legislation such as that at issue in the main proceedings exceed(ed) the limits of what (was) strictly necessary and (could not) be considered to be justified, within a democratic society".[1658] Secondly, the possibility for competent national authorities to access retained metadata was "not restricted solely to fighting serious crime ... (was) not subject to prior review by a court or an independent administrative authority, and ... there (was) no requirement that the data concerned should be retained within the European Union".[1659] Member States were, however, given the opportunity to adopt targeted, as opposed to bulk, metadata retention laws for national security purposes as, according to the CJEU, the 2002 e-Privacy Directive did "not prevent a Member State

---

1652 *Tele2 Sverige* (n1653) para 105.
1653 Joined Cases C-203/15 and C-698/15 *Tele2 Sverige AB v Post- och telestyrelsen, and, Secretary of State for the Home Department v Tom Watson, Peter Brice, Geoffrey Lewis* [2016].
1654 *Ibid.* para 65.
1655 *Ibid.* para 101.
1656 *Digital Rights* (n647) paras 25 and 28.
1657 *Tele2 Sverige* (n1653) para 107.
1658 *Ibid.*
1659 *Ibid.* para 125.

from adopting legislation permitting, as a preventive measure, the targeted retention of traffic and location data, for the purpose of fighting serious crime, provided that the retention of data is limited, with respect to the categories of data to be retained, the means of communication affected, the persons concerned and the retention period adopted, to what is strictly necessary",[1660] hence not precluding this practice all together.[1661]

2020 *Privacy International* case: UK – Subsequently, the CJEU was asked to assess the national metadata retention laws of the United Kingdom,[1662] France, and Belgium in two Grand Chamber cases. The referring court in the first 2020 *Privacy International*[1663] case requested the CJEU to assess the UK metadata transmission law, enabling "practices for the acquisition and use of bulk communications data by the various security and intelligence agencies of the United Kingdom, namely GCHQ,[1664] MI5 and MI6"[1665] in the light of Articles 15.1 and 1.3 (exclusion public security of scope of application) e-Privacy Directive read together with Article 4.2 TEU.[1666] The referring court explained that "the databases compiled by the security and intelligence agencies (were) subject to bulk, unspecific, automated processing, with the aim of discovering unknown threats ... so as to have a 'haystack' in order to find the 'needle' hidden therein".[1667] The defendants disagreed with the CJEU's ruling in 2016 *Tele2 Sverige*, because "the obligation to transfer data ..., access to that data and its use do not fall within the competences of the European Union, in accordance ... with article 4.2 TEU, according to which national security remains the sole responsibility of each Member State".[1668] Even if the CJEU would disagree and consider the UK metadata transmission law within the scope of EU law, the referring court stated "that the requirements (for metadata retention) set out in ... (2016 *Tele2 Sverige*) appear inappropriate in the context of national security and would undermine the ability of the security and intelligence agencies to tackle some threats to national

1660 *Ibid.* para 108.
1661 Bergholm (n1611) 112; Cameron (n78) 456-458; Global Freedom of Expression, 'Joined Cases Tele2 Sverige AB v Post- och telestyrelsen and Secretary of State for the Home Department v. Watson' (*columbia.edu*, 2016); Maxwell and Tomlinson (n1597) 464; Mollenkamp (n1611) 4-6; Zalnieriute (n17) 201-202.
1662 At the time of the court case in the transition period of Brexit, where "the CJEU (still had) the final say over any legal disputes" until 31 December 2020.: Tom Edgington, 'Brexit: What has happened since 31 January?' (*BBC News*, 15 Oct 2020); Tom Edgington, 'Brexit: What is the transition period?' (*BBC News*, 1 Jul 2020).
1663 C-623/17 *Privacy International v Secretary of State for Foreign and Commonwealth Affairs* [2020].
1664 British Government Communications Headquarters intelligence, security, and cyber agency.: GCHQ (n85).
1665 *Privacy International* (n1663) para 19.
1666 *Ibid.* paras 1 and 29.
1667 *Ibid.* para 25.
1668 *Ibid.* para 26.

security".[1669] The first question inquired whether national legislation requiring "a provider of an electronic communications network ... (to) provide bulk communications data to the security and intelligence agencies of a Member State"[1670] fell within the scope of application of EU law, which the Court answered in the affirmative.[1671] The second question inquired whether, in case the first question was answered in the affirmative, "national legislation enabling a State authority to require providers of electronic communications services to carry out the general and indiscriminate transmission of traffic data and location data to the security and intelligence agencies for the purpose of safeguarding national security"[1672] was precluded by EU law. In this regard, the CJEU observed that the "disclosure of data by transmission (as required by the UK national law) concern(ed) all users of means of electronic communication, without its being specified whether that transmission must take place in real-time or subsequently ... (and that) ... those operations do not require prior authorisation from a court or independent administrative authority and do not involve notifying the persons concerned in any way".[1673] Even though the Court acknowledged that "the objective of safeguarding national security is ... capable of justifying measures entailing more serious interferences with fundamental rights than those which might be justified by ... other objectives",[1674] the scrutinized UK metadata transmission law provided "general access to all retained data, regardless of whether there (was) any link, at least indirect, with the aim pursued, (which could not) be regarded as being limited to what (was) strictly necessary".[1675] Interestingly, and further discussed in § 5. *Interim analysis*, the CJEU stated that "the transmission of such data to public authorities is equivalent ... to access",[1676] because "such transmission has the effect of making that data available to the public authorities".[1677] Similar to the 2016 *Tele2 Sverige* case, the Member States retained the opportunity to adopt targeted "national legislation governing access to traffic data and location data ... (as long as this legislation relies) on objective criteria in order to define the circumstances and conditions under which the competent national authorities are to be granted access to the data at issue",[1678] hence once again not precluding this practice all together.[1679]

1669 *Ibid.* para 28.
1670 *Ibid.* para 29(e)(1).
1671 *Ibid.* para 49.
1672 *Ibid.* para 50.
1673 *Ibid.* para 52.
1674 *Ibid.* para 75.
1675 *Ibid.* para 78.
1676 *Ibid.* para 80.
1677 *Ibid.* para 79.
1678 *Ibid.* para 78.
1679 Bergholm (n1611) 112-126; Maxwell and Tomlinson (n1597) 464-466; Mollenkamp (n1611) 6-7; Zalnieriute (n17) 202-207.

2020 *Quadrature du Net* joined cases: France and Belgium – The referring courts in the second 2020 *Quadrature du Net*[1680] joined cases requested the CJEU to assess the French and Belgian bulk metadata retention laws against the "background of serious and persistent threats to national security ... in particular the terrorist threat",[1681] and "the effective punishment of sexual abuse of minors".[1682] The referring courts added a new justification ground to their requests, as compared to the previous cases, which consisted of "article 6 of the (EU) Charter ... (laying) down the right of every individual not only to liberty but also to security and (guaranteeing) rights corresponding to those guaranteed in article 5 of the ECHR".[1683] The CJEU took a milder approach in its analysis, concluding that, at the outset, "legislative measures which ... provide, as a preventive measure, for the general and indiscriminate retention of traffic and location data"[1684] were precluded by EU law, but that "for the purposes of safeguarding national security ... requiring providers of electronic communications services to retain, generally and indiscriminately, traffic and location data ... (when) ... the Member State concerned is confronted with a serious threat to national security that is shown to be genuine and present or foreseeable, where ... (this) ... is subject to effective review, either by a court or by an independent administrative body whose decision is binding ... and where ... only for a period that is limited in time to what is strictly necessary, but which may be extended if that threat persists"[1685] is allowed by EU law. The Court also reiterated that "for the purposes of safeguarding national security, combating serious crime and preventing serious threats to public security ... the targeted retention of traffic and location data which is limited, on the basis of objective and non-discriminatory factors ... for a period that is limited in time to what is strictly necessary, but which may be extended"[1686] is allowed by EU law, as well as "for the purposes of combating serious crime and ... safeguarding national security ... requiring providers of electronic communications services, by ... (a) competent authority ... subject to effective judicial review, to undertake, for a specified period of time, the expedited retention of traffic and location data in the possession of those service providers, provided that those measures ensure, by means of clear and precise rules, that the retention of data ... (complies) with the applicable substantive and procedural conditions and that the persons concerned have

---

1680 Joined Cases C-511/18, C-512/18, and C-520/18 *La Quadrature du Net v Premier ministre, and, Ordre des barreaux francophones et germanophone v Conseil des ministres* [2020].

1681 *Ibid.* para 68.

1682 *Ibid.* para 79.

1683 *Ibid.* para 123.

1684 *Ibid.* para 168.

1685 *Ibid.*

1686 *Ibid.*

effective safeguards against the risks of abuse".[1687] Additionally, the CJEU allowed the retention of not only metadata in specified circumstances set out in its decision, but included also IP addresses and data relating to the civil identity of users of electronic communications systems. Consequently, "the question whether the Member States may justify a limitation on the rights and obligations (set out in the e-Privacy Directive 2002/58) must be assessed by measuring the seriousness of the interference entailed by such a limitation and by verifying that the importance of the public interest objective pursued by that limitation is proportionate to that seriousness",[1688] which requires conducting a proportionality test. The CJEU specified that the above-mentioned requirements have to be fulfilled when engaging in bulk metadata retention and collection, but permitted this practice, even when 'general and indiscriminate', in situations of national security protection. Finally, the referring courts inquired whether "national legislation which requires providers of electronic communications services to implement, on their networks, measures allowing … the automated analysis and real-time collection of traffic and location data … but which (made) no provision for the persons concerned by that processing and that collection to be notified thereof" was allowed by EU law. The CJEU held that "automated analysis … limited to situations in which a Member State is facing a serious threat to national security … shown to be genuine and present or foreseeable, and … subject of an effective review, either by a court or by an independent administrative body whose decision is binding … (and that) … real-time collection of traffic and location data (metadata) … limited to persons in respect of whom there is a valid reason to suspect that they are involved in one way or another in terrorist activities and … subject to a prior review carried out either by a court or by an independent administrative body whose decision is binding …"[1689] is not precluded by EU law.[1690]

2022 *SpaceNet and Telekom* joined cases: Germany – Finally, the CJEU scrutinized in the 2022 *SpaceNet and Telekom*[1691] joined cases whether "a national legislative measure which, with certain exceptions, requires providers of publicly available electronic communications services … inter alia for the purposes of prosecuting serious criminal offences or preventing a specific risk to national security, to retain, in a general and indiscriminate way, most of the traffic and location data of the end users of those services, laying down a retention period of several weeks and rules intended to ensure the

1687 *Ibid.*
1688 *Ibid.* para 131.
1689 *Ibid.* para 192.
1690 Bergholm (n1611) 112-126; Kosta and Kamara (n37) 400-403; Maxwell and Tomlinson (n1597) 464-466; Zalnieriute (n17) 205-207.
1691 *SpaceNet* (n735).

effective protection of the retained data against the risks of abuse and against any unlawful access to those data"[1692] was in conformity with EU law. The referring court stressed that "the retention obligation provided for by the legislation at issue in the main proceedings concerns a smaller amount of data and a shorter retention period (namely, "4 weeks for location data and 10 weeks for traffic data"[1693]) than that provided for by the national legislation at issue in the … 2020 … *Quadrature du Net* (joined cases)"[1694] and "that the national legislation at issue in the main proceedings ensures the effective protection of retained data (namely, "state-of-the-art technical and organisational measures"[1695]) against the risks of abuse and unlawful access".[1696] The CJEU reiterated in its conclusion that "crime, even of a particularly serious nature, cannot be treated in the same way as a threat to national security",[1697] and upheld the 2020 *Quadrature du Net* decision that "unlike crime, even particularly serious crime, a threat to national security must be genuine and present, or, at the very least, foreseeable, which presupposes that sufficiently concrete circumstances have arisen to be able to justify a generalised and indiscriminate measure of retention of traffic and location data for a limited period of time".[1698,1699]

Types of crime – In the CJEU's 2020 *Quadrature du Net* decision, different types of crime were outlined, together with different conditions for possible engagement (or not) in bulk metadata retention. Terrorism, national security, child sexual abuse, and public security seem to allow bulk metadata retention activities by the Member States. However, in 2022 *SpaceNet* the Court held that 'crime cannot be treated in the same way as a threat to national security'. Neither in 2020 *Quadrature du Net* nor in 2022 *SpaceNet* did the CJEU engage in a discussion of each of these concepts. Regarding national security, the Court held in 2020 *Quadrature du Net* that it "corresponds to the primary interest in protecting the essential functions of the State and the fundamental interests of society and encompasses the prevention and punishment of activities capable of seriously destabilising the fundamental constitutional, political, economic or social structures of a country and, in particular, of directly threatening society, the population or the State itself, such as terrorist activities",[1700] but this definition is still sufficiently broad to

1692 *Ibid.* para 47.
1693 *Ibid.* para 33.
1694 *Ibid.* para 44.
1695 *Ibid.* para 17.
1696 *Ibid.* para 45.
1697 *Ibid.* para 94.
1698 *Ibid.* para 93.
1699 Foo Yun Chee, 'Germany's blanket data retention law is illegal, EU top court says' (*Reuters*, 20 Sep 2022).
1700 *Quadrature du Net* (n1680) para 135.

allow a wide margin of interpretation. The different categories of crime, and their distinctions, are also not further elaborated in the CJEU's case law.[1701] These types of (serious) crime can impact civil society equally seriously, and the Court's artificial distinction between them, without explaining what they entail, contributes to uncertainty and confusion. Most of the scrutinized cases relate directly to terrorism, and the adoption of the 2006 Data Retention Directive was a direct response to the occurrence of terrorist attacks, as enshrined in its recital 10. Terrorism can, consequently, be considered part of the national security *domaine réservé* of the Member States, where the EU should not intervene legislatively, unless in police cooperation to coordinate and facilitate actions and measures at the Member State level.[1702]

Evolution – The cases above show that the CJEU's position on bulk metadata retention by EU Member States evolved from a strong 'not allowed' in the 2014 *Digital Rights Ireland* case to 'maybe allowed' in the 2016 *Tele2 Sverige* joined cases to 'allowed' under certain conditions in the 2020 *Quadrature du Net* joined cases. The CJEU took a significantly milder approach when the Member States explicitly invoked Article 4.2 TEU and appealed to the national security and terrorist threat.[1703] This change of approach may not only have been a consequence of the terrorism and national security argumentation, but also of the resistance of EU Member States to comply with the strict CJEU ruling in the 2016 *Tele2 Sverige* joined cases, which was becoming stronger and more explicit in their written observations to every case that was referred to the CJEU.[1704] The case law overview provided above gives the impression that the referring national courts were consistently submitting the same type of bulk metadata retention laws for review and scrutiny by the CJEU, but each time their questions were formulated differently seemingly to influence the outcome of the decision. This can be exemplified by the Member States' strong position in the 2020 *Privacy International* and *Quadrature Du Net* cases that Article 4.2 TEU should be applied, which states that "national security remains the sole responsibility of each Member State".[1705] It can be argued that the Member States' resistance, at least partially, pressured the CJEU to take a milder approach regarding matters concerning national security, and to allow measures that the EU Member States deem necessary, even if they are 'far-reaching'.[1706] The positioning of the EU Member States on this matter

---

1701 Article 29 WP, 'Working Document WP228' (n547) 22-25; Bergholm (n1611) 131-135; Vogiatzoglou (n737) 74-76.

1702 Article 87-88 TFEU.

1703 Bergholm (n1611) 128-131.

1704 *Tele2 Sverige* (n1653) para 65; *Privacy International* (n1663) para 32; *Quadrature du Net* (n1680) para 89; Bergholm (n1611) 126-130; Zalnieriute (n17) 201-202.

1705 Article 4.2 TEU.

1706 Bergholm (n1611) 127-128.

is understandable as national security is assigned as a *domaine réservé* for the Member States in Article 4.2 of the TEU. Giacomo Di Federico goes even further to interpret Article 4.2 TEU as including "an explicit reference to national security as an exclusive competence of the Member States … (its) last sentence … restates … that competences not conferred upon the Union in the treaties remain with the Member States".[1707] Over the years, the CJEU has attempted to interpret the founding Treaties in a more activist way, bringing more competences and legislative areas within the scope of EU law.[1708] Member States' frustration with this activist practice is, therefore, understandable, especially in a field as sensitive as national security and serious crime prevention where Member States do not want to give up their legislative powers. The CJEU's formulation in 2020 *Quadrature du Net* that real-time metadata collection is allowed if limited to persons who are suspected of being involved 'in one way or another in terrorist activities' seems very broad when compared to the Court's initial decision in 2014 *Digital Rights Ireland* prohibiting bulk metadata retention altogether. Additional conditions and a requirement of prior review by a court or administrative body to justify the intervention were added, but the Court seems nevertheless to have listened or at least been influenced by the Member States' strong argument to respect their *domaine réservé* regarding national security.

C. PUBLIC VERSUS PRIVATE ACTORS

Why versus Who – In the case law overview above, the distinction between situations involving national security and situations involving other types of crime was decisive for the applicable conditions and legal framework. An additional dimension to this distinction was added by the opinion of Advocate General Manuel Campos Sánchez-Bordona in the previously discussed 2020 *Quadrature du Net* joined cases, where he introduced a shift from why the data is processed (for example, for national security purposes) to who is processing the data (private versus public actors). The Advocate General interpreted Article 1.3 e-Privacy Directive read together with Article 4 TEU as holding that "activities for national security purposes, conducted *solely* by State authorities, *without* the assistance of the private

1707 Di Federico (n1622) 354.

1708 Gunnar Beck, 'Judicial Activism in the Court of Justice of the EU' (2017) 36 UQLJ 333, 333; Fausto Comandè and Jan De Groof, 'Juridification, Judicialisation and Judicial Activism in Higher Education' in Cristina Sin and others (eds), *European Higher Education and the Internal Market* (Springer 2018) 75-78; Mark Dawson, Bruno de Witte, and Elise Muir, *Judicial Activism at the European Court of Justice* (Edward Elgar 2013) 1-6; Fabien Terpan and Sabine Saurugger, 'Assessing Judicial Activism of the CJEU' (2019) 41 JEurIntegr 543, 543.

actors, are *outside* the scope of the e-Privacy Directive (while) on the other hand, ... national data retention legislation that requires *private parties* such as electronic service providers to cooperate with the State authorities by retaining user data, and that permits State authorities to access the data collected by these private parties, is *within* the scope of the e-Privacy Directive and must comply with its data protection requirements, even if it is to address 'national security concerns'".[1709,1710] Jenny Bergholm shares the Advocate-General's opinion that, according to the CJEU, an *a contrario* reading of Article 2.2(d) GDPR[1711] in conjunction with Article 23.1(d) & (h) GDPR[1712] provides that since the former Article "does not apply to processing operations carried out 'by competent authorities' for the purposes of, inter alia, the prevention and detection of criminal offences, including the safeguarding against and the prevention of threats to public security, it is apparent from (the latter Article) that the processing of personal data carried out by individuals for those same purposes falls within the scope of that regulation".[1713,1714] Iain Cameron concludes from this interpretation that "if a State took ownership over (nationalized) part of its telecommunications infrastructure (e.g. the Internet exchange points), and gave its security and intelligence agencies access to the data flows, when they pass through the exchanges, then this would mean that the State would be 'using its own resources'",[1715] which would bring the activity outside the scope of EU law. In times of rapid information technology development, 'nationalizing' private companies to avoid compliance with EU law, subjecting them only to national surveillance laws, does not seem to be an optimal solution.

Discussion – Instead of an '*a contrario*' reasoning, the same analysis as provided in the '*Legal basis*' discussion above[1716] can be applied where the latter Article (23.1(d) & (h) GDPR) can be interpreted as a confirmation, rather

1709 Zalnieriute (n17) 203.

1710 Opinion of Advocate General Campos Sánchez-Bordona delivered on 15 Jan 2020 *Quadrature du Net* (n1680) paras 78-79.

1711 Which states that it "does not apply to the processing of personal data: ... by competent authorities for the purposes of the prevention, investigation, detection or prosecution of criminal offences or the execution of criminal penalties, including the safeguarding against and the prevention of threats to public security".: Article 2.2(d) GDPR.

1712 Which states that "Union or Member State law to which the data controller or processor is subject may restrict by way of a legislative measure the scope of the obligations and rights provided for ... when such a restriction respects the essence of the fundamental rights and freedoms and is a necessary and proportionate measure in a democratic society to safeguard: (d) the prevention, investigation, detection or prosecution of criminal offences or the execution of criminal penalties, including the safeguarding against and the prevention of threats to public security; (h) a monitoring, inspection or regulatory function connected ... to the exercise of official authority ...".: Article 23.1(d)&(h) GDPR.

1713 *Privacy International* (n1663) para 47; *Quadrature du Net* (n1680) para 102.

1714 Bergholm (n1611) 116; Vogiatzoglou (n737) 84-85; Zalnieriute (n17) 210-211.

1715 Cameron (n78) 459.

1716 See *Chapter 5, § 3, A.*

than a contradiction, of the former (2.2(d) GDPR). Since the GDPR does not apply when personal data is processed by public authorities of the Member State for national security purposes (Recital 16 and Articles 2.2(d) and 23.1(a), (c)-(d) GDPR), the EU Member States may also restrict private data controllers and processors by introducing legislative measures when they are processing data for the same purposes. In this interpretation, Article 23.1(d) & (h) GDPR is interpreted in the light of Article 2.2(d) GDPR, focusing on *why* the data is processed rather than by *whom* the data is processed. Monika Zalnieriute confirms that "the emphasis on the *purpose* of processing activities – as opposed to *who* does the processing – remains under the GDPR".[1717] The same reasoning was applied by the CJEU in 2006 *Parliament (PNR)*,[1718] which encompassed the same situation as the telecommunications cases discussed above. In both cases, a private company (respectively, an airline and a telecom company) had to transmit or retain personal data of its customers to a public institution (respectively, the U.S. Bureau of Customs and Border Protection and the EU Member States' national security and law enforcement agencies) for the purposes of safeguarding national security and preventing crime. The EU legislator seems to have embraced this change of approach in the 2017 "Proposal for a Regulation ... concerning the respect for private life and the protection of personal data in electronic communications and repealing (e-Privacy) Directive 2002/58/EC"[1719] by "clearly exclud(ing) national security activities, whether by the State or by providers, from its scope",[1720] and in the 2024 EU Artificial Intelligence Act[1721] by stating that AI systems "placed on the market, put into service, or used ... for military, defence or national security purposes ... should be excluded from the scope of this Regulation regardless of which type of entity is carrying out those activities, such as whether it is a public or private entity".[1722,1723] The 2017 e-Privacy Regulation proposal got stuck on data access and retention discussions by law enforcement and seems to have stalled as the last step in this procedure dates from February 2021 when the Proposal was discussed by the Council of the European Union and its

1717 Recital 19 GDPR; Zalnieriute (n17) 212.

1718 See *Chapter 5, § 3, A.*

1719 European Commission, 'Proposal for a Regulation concerning the respect for private life and the protection of personal data in electronic communications and repealing Directive 2002/58/EC' COM(2017) 10 final.

1720 Recital 26 *Ibid.*; Maxwell and Tomlinson (n1597) 466.

1721 Regulation (EU) 2024/1689 of 13 Jun 2024 laying down harmonised rules on artificial intelligence and amending Regulations (EC) No 300/2008, (EU) No 167/2013, (EU) No 168/2013, (EU) 2018/858, (EU) 2018/1139 and (EU) 2019/2144 and Directives 2014/90/EU, (EU) 2016/797 and (EU) 2020/1828 [2024] OJ L 2024/1689 (AI Act).

1722 Recital 24 AI Act.

1723 Article 2.3 AI Act; Vogiatzoglou (n737) 78-86.

preparatory bodies.[1724] While the CJEU emphasized *who* is conducting the data processing in an activist interpretation of the law, the EU treaties as well as the GDPR, the AI Act, and the e-Privacy Regulation proposal suggest emphasizing *why* the data processing is being conducted to determine the applicable legal framework.

Outsourcing – The legislation's *why* approach and the Court's adjusted *who* approach discussed above would result in the following situations. Under the Court's adjusted *who* approach, the applicable legal framework depends on the entity that conducts the data collection, retention, and processing activity. In times of increased government outsourcing, this would result in almost all activities being subject to EU law, severely restricting Member States' competences regarding national security. Under the legislation's *why* approach, the applicable legal framework depends on the purpose of the data collection, retention, and processing activities. If the data processing takes place for national security purposes, even if executed by a private company, Member States' national law will be applicable. If the data processing takes place for purposes other than national security, EU law will have to be observed. When "governments … decide to pay a firm to deliver goods or services directly to the end user, (which) may include the outsourcing of "mainline" functions previously conducted by the government",[1725] the regulatory framework set out in Article 6.1(e) GDPR and recital 11 LED will apply. More concretely, this means that if a government authority explicitly delegates a public sector activity to a private company for law enforcement purposes in accordance with the conditions set forth in the LED ('bound by a contract or other legal act'), the private company will be subject to the LED's provisions for this type of processing, and remain subject to the GDPR's provisions for other, private, processing purposes. It is important to stress that government outsourcing of public sector activities to private companies should occur explicitly. Only then will private companies be able to comply with their legal responsibilities and the purpose limitation principle. If, for example, a private company is required to retain or transfer its customers' data to government authorities, the company can include this purpose in its terms and conditions and will have to comply with a dual legal framework; compliance with the GDPR in relations with their customers and compliance with Member States' national security laws in relations with government authorities. Secret accessing of private companies' customer databases by intelligence agencies should be avoided at all times, as well as mandating private companies to hand over this data to the latter where there was no previous obligation to

1724 Eur-Lex, 'Document 52017PC0010: Procedure 2017/0003/COD' (*europa.eu*, 2024); Kosta and Kamara (n37) 95-113; Mollenkamp (n1611) 25-27.

1725 OECD (n1485) 168.

engage in this kind of activity. Transparency and compliance are necessary as they enhance legal certainty and ensure that protective measures are observed.

§ 4. ECtHR: NATIONAL SECURITY

Interference and justification – While national security measures will generally interfere with people's right to private life, and consequently, with Article 8 ECHR, the European Court of Human Rights (ECtHR) will subsequently engage in a three-step test to determine whether the interference can be justified. The three-step test consists of three justification grounds, specified in Article 8.2 ECHR, which have to be fulfilled cumulatively in order to justify the initial interference with someone's right to privacy.[1726] The legality requirement ensures that the interference must be 'in accordance with the law', the necessity requirement guarantees that the interference 'is necessary in a democratic society', and the proportionality requirement sets out a limitative list of situations which can justify the interference, of which 'in the interests of national security, public safety ..., (and) for the prevention of disorder or crime' is of particular importance for this discussion.[1727] Based on a non-exhaustive overview of the ECtHR's case law, this section will identify the main requirements for lawful (bulk) metadata retention and access practices by national intelligence agencies of the signatory States.

National security – Situations of national security, which are not (or should not) be covered by EU law as argued in the previous section, will still be subject to compliance with the ECHR and scrutiny by the ECtHR. The ECHR "obliges its Parties to secure to everyone within their jurisdiction a series of rights and freedoms, including the right to respect for private life and does not contain a general exemption for national security matters",[1728] but rather sets a balancing exercise forth where national security measures must comply with the principles of legitimacy, necessity, and proportionality (legitimate aim). National security cases are often centered around Articles 6 (fair trial) and 8 (privacy) of the ECHR.[1729] The ECtHR has held that "powers of secret surveillance of citizens, characterising as they do the police state, are tolerable under the Convention only in so far as strictly necessary for safeguarding the democratic institutions".[1730] The following exemplary non-exhaustive

1726 Bygrave, *Data Privacy Law* (n37) 90-91.
1727 Article 8.2 ECHR.
1728 Article 29 WP, 'Working Document WP228' (n547) 30.
1729 *Leander* (n401); *Rotaru* (n401); *Uzun v Germany* App no 35623/05 (ECtHR, 2 Sep 2010); *Szabó and Vissy v Hungary* App no 37138/14 (ECtHR, 12 Jan 2016); *Big Brother Watch 2018* (n83).
1730 *Klass* (n648) para 42; *Szabó and Vissy* (n1729) para 54.

ECtHR case law overview can provide more clarity. In 1978 *Klass and others v Germany*,[1731] the Court was asked to assess whether "legislation ... (where) the person concerned is not informed of the surveillance measures and cannot have recourse to the courts when such measures are terminated"[1732] violates Article 8 ECHR right to private life. The Court found an interference, but the legality[1733] and proportionality[1734] justification grounds were complied with. Regarding the necessity requirement, the ECtHR held that "it is ... not for the Court to substitute for the assessment of the national authorities any other assessment of what might be the best policy in this field ... nevertheless ... this does not mean that the Contracting States enjoy an unlimited discretion to subject persons within their jurisdiction to secret surveillance ... the Contracting States may not, in the name of the struggle against espionage and terrorism, adopt whatever measures they deem appropriate".[1735] After a detailed analysis of the legislative measure, the ECtHR decided that all the justification grounds were fulfilled and Article 8 ECHR was not violated.[1736] In 2010 *Uzun v Germany*,[1737] the Court held that GPS surveillance "for some three months, systematically collect(ing) and stor(ing) data determining ... the applicant's whereabouts and movements in the public sphere ... further record(ing) the personal data and us(ing) it ... to draw up a pattern of the applicant's movements, to make further investigations and to collect additional evidence at the places the applicant had travelled to, which was later used at the criminal trial against the applicant"[1738] interfered with the applicant's Article 8 ECHR right to private life. Subsequently, the ECtHR found that the legality,[1739] necessity, and proportionality[1740] requirements were fulfilled, which justified the interference. In 2016 *Szabó and Vissy v Hungary*,[1741] the Court decided that "the measures which the (Anti-Terrorism Task Force was) entitled to apply under ... the National Security Act"[1742] could subject "virtually any person in Hungary ... to secret surveillance ... (as) the legislation (did) not describe the categories of persons who ... may have their communications intercepted",[1743] which interfered with the applicants' Article 8 ECHR right to

1731 *Klass* (n648).
1732 *Ibid.* para 39.
1733 *Ibid.* para 43.
1734 *Ibid.* para 46.
1735 *Ibid.* para 49.
1736 *Ibid.* para 60.
1737 *Uzun* (n1729).
1738 *Ibid.* para 51.
1739 *Ibid.* para 74.
1740 *Ibid.* paras 80-81.
1741 *Szabó and Vissy* (n1729).
1742 *Ibid.* para 52.
1743 *Ibid.* para 66.

private life.[1744] The proportionality (legitimate aim)[1745] requirement was found to be fulfilled, but this was not the case for the legality and necessity requirements, because "the 'quality of law' ... implies that the domestic law must not only be accessible and foreseeable in its application (there was a law prescribing the measure[1746]), it must also ensure that secret surveillance measures are applied only when 'necessary in a democratic society', in particular by providing for adequate and effective safeguards and guarantees against abuse".[1747] Additionally, "anti-terrorism surveillance measures in Hungary ha(d) never been subjected to judicial control",[1748] and according to the ECtHR "supervision by a politically responsible member of the executive, such as the Minister of Justice, (did) not provide the necessary guarantees".[1749] Consequently, the Court found a violation of applicants' Article 8 ECHR right to private life.[1750] In 2021 *Centrum För Rättvisa v Sweden*,[1751] the ECtHR explained its position on "the relevant legislation and practice in Sweden on bulk interception of communications, also referred to as signals intelligence",[1752] and found that "while article 8 (ECHR) does not prohibit the use of bulk interception to protect national security and other essential national interests against serious external threats, and States enjoy a wide margin of appreciation in deciding what type of interception regime is necessary ... the margin of appreciation afforded to them must be narrower and a number of safeguards will have to be present".[1753] The Court acknowledged that (even) metadata can reveal sensitive and detailed information, and that "the interception, retention and searching of related communications data should be analysed by reference to the same safeguards as those applicable to content".[1754] The ECtHR stressed in its finding that "it is not its role to prescribe an ideal model for signals intelligence but rather to review ... the existing legal and practical arrangements (for Convention compliance), which vary conceptually and functionally from one Contracting Party to another",[1755] and consequently limited itself to such an exercise. In 2015 *Roman Zakharov v Russia*,[1756] the Court explained that "in its case-law on secret measures of surveillance, the Court has developed the following minimum safeguards that should be set out in law in order to avoid abuses of

1744 *Ibid.* para 53.
1745 *Ibid.* para 55.
1746 *Ibid.* para 60.
1747 *Ibid.* para 59.
1748 *Ibid.* para 76.
1749 *Ibid.* para 77.
1750 *Ibid.* para 89.
1751 *Centrum För Rättvisa v Sweden* App no 35252/08 (ECtHR, 25 May 2021).
1752 *Ibid.* para 152.
1753 *Ibid.* para 261.
1754 *Ibid.* para 277.
1755 *Ibid.* para 366.
1756 *Roman Zakharov v Russia* App no 47143/06 (ECtHR, 4 Dec 2015).

power: the nature of offences which may give rise to an interception order; a definition of the categories of people liable to have their telephones tapped; a limit on the duration of telephone tapping; the procedure to be followed for examining, using and storing the data obtained; the precautions to be taken when communicating the data to other parties; and the circumstances in which recordings may or must be erased or destroyed",[1757] which the Court applied *mutatis mutandis* to the interception of communications to determine whether the measures taken were lawful. Additionally, the ECtHR also examined the elements of 'Supervision of the implementation of secret surveillance measures' and 'Notification of interception of communications and available remedies'.[1758]

Landmark case – 2018 *Big Brother Watch* – The 2018 and 2021 *Big Brother Watch v United Kingdom*[1759] cases brought before the ECtHR are the British equivalent of the CJEU 2015 and 2020 *Schrems* cases[1760] where U.S. surveillance laws were scrutinized. Given the close cooperation between the U.S. NSA and the UK GCHQ, the Snowden revelations resulted not only in a scrutiny of U.S. surveillance practices, but also of those of the United Kingdom. The ECtHR was asked to assess the conformity of UK surveillance laws with Articles 8 and 10 ECHR, but the discussion in this section will focus on the former Article for comparative purposes, as the latter Article, in this case, addressed the monitoring of journalists and the potential uncovering of their sources, which is left out of the scope of this book. In the first 2018 Chamber hearing of the joined cases, the applicants addressed three problematic practices which interfered with their Article 8 ECHR right to private life, namely the bulk interception of communications, the intelligence sharing between the United Kingdom and the United States, and the permission for certain public authorities to acquire communications data from Communications Service Providers.[1761] Firstly, for the bulk interception of communications, the ECtHR reiterated "that the national authorities enjoy a wide margin of appreciation in choosing how best to achieve the legitimate aim of protecting national security … (especially) … in view of the current threats facing many Contracting States (including the scourge of global terrorism and other serious crime, such as drug trafficking, human trafficking, the sexual exploitation of children and cybercrime), advancements in technology which have made it easier for terrorists and criminals to evade detection on the Internet, and the unpredictability of the routes via which electronic communications are transmitted, the Court considers that the decision

---

1757 *Ibid.* para 231.
1758 *Ibid.* paras 238-305.
1759 *Big Brother Watch 2018* (n83); *Big Brother Watch 2021* (n83).
1760 See *Chapter 1, § 2, A. and B.*
1761 *Big Brother Watch 2018* (n83) para 269.

to operate a bulk interception regime in order to identify hitherto unknown threats to national security is one which continues to fall within States' margin of appreciation".[1762] The ECtHR emphasized that "it would be wrong automatically to assume that bulk interception constitutes a greater intrusion into the private life of an individual than targeted interception, which by its very nature is more likely to result in the acquisition and examination of a large volume of his or her communications".[1763] Bulk interception of communications does interfere with Article 8 ECHR right to privacy,[1764] but the justification grounds of legality and proportionality were fulfilled.[1765] The Court identified, nevertheless, "two principal areas of concern; first, the lack of oversight of the entire selection process, including the selection of bearers for interception, the selectors and search criteria for filtering intercepted communications, and the selection of material for examination by an analyst; and secondly, the absence of any real safeguards applicable to the selection of related communications data for examination"[1766] which did not comply with the justification ground of necessity, and hence violated Article 8 ECHR right to private life.[1767] Secondly, for the UK-U.S. intelligence sharing practices, and more generally regarding the compliance with Article 8 ECHR of the "receipt of information from foreign intelligence services",[1768] the ECtHR held that even though there is an interference with Article 8 ECHR,[1769] "the nature of global terrorism … requires a flow of information between the security services of many countries in all parts of the world … this 'information flow' was embedded into a legislative context providing considerable safeguards against abuse … resulting (in the) interference (being) kept to that which was 'necessary in a democratic society'",[1770] and hence justified.[1771] In both scenarios, the Court assessed the justification grounds in light of the six minimum requirements set out in 2015 *Roman Zakharov v Russia* (*see above*).[1772] Thirdly, for the permission for certain public authorities to acquire communications data from Communications Service Providers (CSPs), the ECtHR followed the decision of the CJEU regarding access to retained data by service providers (*see above*), and concluded that "any regime permitting the authorities to access data retained by CSPs (must limit this) access to the purpose of combating

1762 *Ibid.* para 314.
1763 *Ibid.* para 316.
1764 *Ibid.* para 321.
1765 *Ibid.* para 323.
1766 *Ibid.* para 387.
1767 *Ibid.* para 388.
1768 *Ibid.* para 389.
1769 *Ibid.* para 419.
1770 *Ibid.* para 446.
1771 *Ibid.* paras 447-448.
1772 *Ibid.* paras 322-388 and 423-446.

'serious crime', and the access (must) be subject to prior review by a court or independent administrative body ..., the ... regime (in question) ... is not subject to prior review by a court or independent administrative body ... it cannot be in accordance with the law within the meaning of article 8 (ECHR)".[1773]

Landmark case – 2021 *Big Brother Watch* – The Chamber's 2018 decision was referred to the Grand Chamber, which reviewed the case[1774] in 2021. Regarding the first practice of bulk interception of communications, the Grand Chamber reiterated that an extended version of 2015 *Roman Zakharov v Russia*'s 'six minimum safeguards' should be observed,[1775] and upheld the Chamber's decision entirely. More specifically, "the Court (examined) whether the domestic legal framework clearly defined: 1. the grounds on which bulk interception may be authorised; 2. the circumstances in which an individual's communications may be intercepted; 3. the procedure to be followed for granting authorisation; 4. the procedures to be followed for selecting, examining and using intercept material; 5. the precautions to be taken when communicating the material to other parties; 6. the limits on the duration of interception, the storage of intercept material and the circumstances in which such material must be erased and destroyed; 7. the procedures and modalities for supervision by an independent authority of compliance with the above safeguards and its powers to address non-compliance; 8. the procedures for independent *ex post facto* review of such compliance and the powers vested in the competent body in addressing instances of non-compliance".[1776] Regarding the interception of the content of communications,[1777] the ECtHR found that the first, second, fourth, fifth, sixth, seventh, and eighth conditions were fulfilled, but the finding for the third condition that "strong selectors linked to identifiable individuals were nevertheless not subject to prior internal authorization"[1778] was found problematic.[1779] For the interception of communications data or metadata, the ECtHR found that "the storage provisions concerning related communications data were sufficiently robust, even though they differed in substance from the provisions relating to content".[1780] In conclusion, the Court decided that "bulk interception is of vital importance to Contracting States in identifying threats to their national security ... nonetheless ... there is considerable potential for bulk

1773 *Ibid.* para 467.
1774 *Big Brother Watch 2021* (n83).
1775 *Ibid.* paras 335 and 348-364.
1776 *Ibid.* para 361.
1777 *Ibid.* paras 368-414.
1778 *Ibid.* para 383.
1779 *Ibid.* paras 371, 376, 383, 391, 398-399, 405, 412-415.
1780 *Ibid.* para 423.

interception to be abused in a manner adversely affecting the rights of individuals to respect for private life … when viewed as a whole, the … regime, despite its safeguards … did not contain sufficient 'end-to-end' safeguards to provide adequate and effective guarantees against arbitrariness and the risk of abuse … in particular … the absence of independent authorisation, the failure to include the categories of selectors in the application for a warrant, and the failure to subject selectors linked to an individual to prior internal authorisation … these weaknesses concerned not only the interception of the contents of communications but also the interception of related communications data".[1781] Consequently, the ECtHR held that the regime "was … incapable of keeping the "interference" to what was "necessary in a democratic society",[1782] violating Article 8 ECHR right to private life.[1783] Regarding the second practice of intelligence sharing between the United Kingdom and the United States, the Grand Chamber also upheld the Chamber's decision that "the regime for requesting and receiving intercept material was compatible with article 8 (ECHR … given that) there existed clear detailed rules … (regarding) … the circumstances in which and the conditions on which the authorities were empowered to make a request to a foreign intelligence service; domestic law contained effective guarantees against the use of such requests to circumvent domestic law and/or the United Kingdom's obligations under the Convention; the United Kingdom had in place adequate safeguards for the examination, use, storage, onward transmission, erasure and destruction of the material; and the regime was subject to independent oversight by the IC Commissioner and there was a possibility for *ex post facto* review by the IPT",[1784] resulting in a justification of the interference, and hence no violation of Article 8 ECHR right to private life.[1785] Regarding the third practice of the permission for certain public authorities to acquire communications data from Communications Service Providers, the Grand Chamber noticed that "the Government did not contest the Chamber's findings before the Grand Chamber"[1786] and concluded that there is "no ground on which to disagree with the Chamber's conclusions",[1787] upholding the decision that Article 8 ECHR was violated.[1788] In conclusion, the 2021 Grand Chamber upheld the 2018 Chamber's decision in its entirety with regard to Article 8 ECHR compliance.

[1781] *Ibid.* paras 424-425.
[1782] *Ibid.* para 426.
[1783] *Ibid.* para 427.
[1784] *Ibid.* para 513.
[1785] *Ibid.* para 514.
[1786] *Ibid.* para 521.
[1787] *Ibid.*
[1788] *Ibid.* para 522.

Discussion – The signatory States to the ECHR enjoy a higher level of discretion in adopting national security measures, but must nevertheless comply with the rights and conditions set out in the ECHR. This section focused on the ECtHR's case law regarding Article 8 ECHR right to private life compliance, and found that while national security measures do interfere with people's right to private life as protected by Article 8 ECHR, the interference can be justified if the measure is in accordance with the law (legality), necessary in a democratic society (necessity), and pursues a legitimate aim or interest, of which national security is one explicitly mentioned (proportionality). The signatory States enjoy a wide margin of appreciation regarding national security measures, but the Court has stressed that 'this does not mean that the Contracting States enjoy an unlimited discretion … (and) … may not … adopt whatever measures they deem appropriate'. The ECtHR developed, as a consequence, 'six plus two' requirements that national surveillance measures have to fulfill in order to avoid abuse of State power in the 2015 *Roman Zakharov v Russia* case. These requirements must be set out in law and consist of: '1. the grounds on which national surveillance measures may be authorised; 2. the circumstances in which an individual can be subjected to the surveillance measure; 3. the procedure to be followed for granting authorisation; 4. the procedures to be followed for selecting, examining and using intercept material; 5. the precautions to be taken when communicating the material to other parties; 6. the limits on the duration of the surveillance measure, the storage of intercept material and the circumstances in which such material must be erased and destroyed; and 1. the procedures and modalities for supervision by an independent authority of compliance with these six requirements and this authority's powers to address non-compliance; 2. the procedures for independent *ex post facto* review of such compliance and the powers vested in the competent body in addressing instances of non-compliance'. The ECtHR does not prohibit signatory States from engaging in bulk metadata retention as a national surveillance measure, but when engaging in this practice the 'six plus two' requirements must be observed. Metadata retention was, moreover, found to be of equal sensitivity as content retention, resulting in the applicability of similar safeguards. The ECtHR seemed to also prefer, but not require, supervision by an independent judicial authority over supervision by an executive authority to ensure its independence. Regarding situations in which government authorities seek access to telecommunications service providers' customer data and content, the ECtHR aligned itself with the CJEU's decision on this matter, albeit allowing this practice for 'purposes of serious crime', which seems broader, and in line with the margin of appreciation of the signatory States, than the CJEU's focus on national security and terrorism.

§ 5. INTERIM COMPARATIVE EU-U.S. ANALYSIS

Bulk metadata retention – The Snowden revelations about bulk metadata collection and access by the U.S. intelligence services contributed to a large extent to the invalidation of the legal frameworks for transatlantic personal data transfers in the two *Schrems* cases.[1789] The CJEU scrutinized, among others, the U.S. national security exception as applied to personal data transfers in the first *Schrems* case, as criticism of the mass U.S. surveillance practices emerged in the EU. After the invalidation of the transatlantic framework for personal data transfers, the CJEU turned its view inward and scrutinized the bulk data collection and retention practices of its own Member States. Those practices turned out to be very similar to those of the United States. Both regions enacted bulk metadata retention laws in the aftermath of terrorist attacks on their soil, respectively Sec. 501 and 702 FISA after the 9/11 terrorist attacks in New York, and the EU Data Retention Directive after the terrorist attacks in Madrid and London. While it is true that the CJEU invalidated the EU Data Retention Directive for violating Articles 7 and 8 of the EU Charter and prohibited bulk metadata collection and retention in the 2014 *Digital Rights Ireland* case, the Court gradually evolved to a 'maybe allowed' position in the 2016 *Tele2 Sverige* case, and eventually allowed bulk metadata collection and retention for national security purposes by the EU Member States in the 2020 *Quadrature du Net* case, albeit under strict conditions. The CJEU invalidated the EU-U.S. *Safe Harbour* data transfer framework in the 2015 *Schrems I* case, which was in line with the Court's position prohibiting bulk metadata retention and collection in 2014 *Digital Rights Ireland*. The following EU-U.S. *Privacy Shield* invalidation took place in the July 2020 *Schrems II* case, after the Court's 2015 *Tele2 Sverige* ruling, which did not preclude bulk metadata retention all together, and shortly before the CJEU's October 2020 *Quadrature du Net* decision which eventually conditionally allowed bulk metadata retention and collection practices by the EU Member States. Even though the United States had implemented additional safeguards based on the initial *Schrems I* decision in the run-up to *Privacy Shield*, the CJEU still considered the introduced safeguards to be insufficient. The United States consequently criticized the Court for applying a double standard as it had invalidated the transatlantic personal data transfer frameworks to a large extent based on U.S. bulk metadata collection and retention practices that its own EU Member States were also engaging in. The situation could have been different if there had been a European

---

1789 See *Chapter 1, § 2, A. and B.*

whistleblower *à la* Snowden before the U.S. practices were revealed. If the European countries' engagement in (past and probably still present) personal data collection and retention practices as a source of intelligence had been revealed prior to the U.S. national security practices, the 'momentary alarm', to reuse David Vogel's conceptualization,[1790] of outrage about the U.S. surveillance practices would probably have been (completely) different.

Division of competences – The EU Member States firmly disagreed with the CJEU's encroachment on their Article 4.2 TEU national security *domaine réservé* in the bulk metadata retention case law. A similar feeling was shared by the United States when the CJEU assessed U.S. surveillance laws, and more in particular its bulk metadata retention practices, in the *Schrems I* and *Schrems II* cases based on the provisions of the EU GDPR. Moreover, the CJEU was judging the United States from an EU perspective, applying EU law to U.S. intelligence practices, while the CJEU was not entirely acting within its own competences when adjudicating EU Member States' surveillance laws which were situated in their national security *domaine réservé*. Article 2.2(d) GDPR explicitly excludes the processing of personal data for national security from the GDPR's scope of application.[1791] Article 45.2(a) GDPR requires, in a contradictory way, the Commission "(to) take account of ... relevant legislation, ... including concerning public security, defence, national security and criminal law and the access of public authorities to personal data ... when assessing the adequacy of the level of protection"[1792] of a third country. The provision in Article 45.2(a) GDPR should be amended as it creates a legal discrepancy and unjustified distinction between the treatment of EU Member States and third countries. The CJEU can, after all, not judge a third country on an account that it cannot even judge its own Member States on. Consequently, the Court cannot validly condemn the United States for its national security practices, especially not based on a (questionable) GDPR provision for an adequacy decision. The practice of misinterpretation or overly extensive interpretation of legal provisions is shared by U.S. and EU courts and lawmakers as well. Sec. 702 FISA was drafted in a cautiously limited way, but the overly extensive interpretation given to its wording surprised even its own drafters. Moreover, the CJEU followed this over-interpretation in the *Schrems II*[1793] case when it held that "as regards the surveillance programmes based on Section 702 of the FISA, the Commission found ... that, according to that Article, 'the FISC does not authorise individual surveillance measures;

1790 See *Chapter 4, § 3, A., ii), a)*.

1791 Recital 16 and Article 2.2 and 23.1 GDPR.

1792 Article 45.2(a) GDPR.

1793 *Schrems II* (n119).

rather, it authorises surveillance programs (like PRISM, UPSTREAM[1794]) on the basis of annual certifications prepared by the Attorney General and the Director of National Intelligence (DNI)' ... the supervisory role of the FISC is thus designed to verify whether those surveillance programmes relate to the objective of acquiring foreign intelligence information, but it does not cover the issue of whether 'individuals are properly targeted to acquire foreign intelligence information' ... Section 702 of the FISA does not indicate any limitations on the power it confers to implement surveillance programmes for the purposes of foreign intelligence or the existence of guarantees for non-U.S. persons potentially targeted by those programmes".[1795,1796] While the latter observation is true, it is also questionable whether the surveillance laws of EU Member States foresee specific safeguards for non-(EU-)citizens' information collected in the course of foreign intelligence, which should, as will be argued below, in any case not be adjudicated by the CJEU. Regarding the CJEU's former observation that 'FISA does not indicate any limitations', it has to be clarified that FISA 2008, at least in the written text of the law, includes a requirement to adopt targeting and minimization procedures by the Attorney General, in consultation with the Director of National Intelligence.[1797] The CJEU may have too quickly judged the U.S. FISA surveillance law based on a momentary overbroad interpretation of its content as was revealed by Edward Snowden, instead of acknowledging that the given interpretation was too broad, but that the text of the Act as such may have been legally sound if the additional adopted procedures proved to be adequate. This book argues in any case that the CJEU does not have the competence to adjudicate national surveillance laws, whether enacted by EU Member States or third countries, and that the CJEU should not engage in judging national security laws, especially those of third countries. In a similar way, the CJEU brought private sector actors within the scope of application of EU law by extending the law's focus from why personal data is processed (in the case of national security, outside EU law) to who is processing the data (only subjecting public actors to Member States' law). The criticism and confusion that resulted from this case law was, once again, remedied by the EU lawmaker who explicitly wrote into the new legal provisions that data processing for national security purposes is excluded from the EU acts' scope of application, 'regardless whether it is a public or private entity' engaging in the processing activity. It is understandable that these instances try to bring as areas as possible into their (legal) spheres of influence, but in order to act in accordance with the law, the safeguards and

---

1794 See *Chapter 1, § 2, A.*

1795 *Schrems II* (n119) paras 179-180.

1796 Drechsler *et al.* (n151) 22; Greenwald, *No Place to Hide* (n16) 74; McLaughlin (n139) 232; Patel (n1505).

1797 FISA 2008, 122 Stat. 2439.

limitations built into legislation should be respected. Therefore, it is important to stay closer to the wording of the legislation and the intention behind the careful wording of its drafters, rather than to allow too broad and even contradictory interpretations of legal provisions that were never foreseen to have the wide stretch they are being given by their subsequent interpreters. The EU's aim to protect its citizens' personal data is laudable, but the so-called 'pampering' should not take over all responsibilities of EU citizens. Users in EU Member States should be aware that when they make use of certain American services, their personal data will be transferred to U.S. companies where it will be subject to a different protection regime. People should retain their decisional autonomy and be correctly informed to understand these processes in order to estimate the potential risks and benefits when using services offered by a third country, in this case the United States. The third chapter advocated, therefore, more basic global standards instead of too strict regional, *in casu* European, standards.

Admissibility/Merits – The U.S. Supreme Court did not even consider the merits in the 2022 *FBI v Fazaga* case as the Court decided that the case was inadmissible based on the evidentiary State Secrets Privilege. It remains to be seen whether SCOTUS' decision was limited to this particular case, or whether the Court will uphold the evidentiary State Secrets Privilege in its future case law, rendering national security cases in the United States nonjusticiable. If a similar case was brought to court in the EU, the Member States' courts would likely declare the case admissible and decide that the surveillance measures involving hundreds of Muslims were disproportionate (proportionality requirement) and not limited to what is strictly necessary (necessity requirement).[1798] The EU Member States' strong position in the bulk metadata retention cases to respect their national security *domaine réservé* enshrined in Article 4.2 TEU would probably also result in Member State national security cases being nonjusticiable by the CJEU in the EU conferred powers framework. Jenny Bergholm agrees that "had the CJEU opted for a literal interpretation of the TEU, the data retention obligations introduced by the Member States for protecting national security could (easily) have been excluded from the scope of the e-Privacy Directive and EU law as a whole … (in this reading) the CJEU would not have been able to rule on these cases, and even less to interpret them in the light of the Charter",[1799] but could still be reviewed by the Member States, subject to ECtHR scrutiny. In a literal reading based on the wording of the TEU for the EU and based on the evidentiary State Secrets Privilege for the United States, national security cases are nonjusticiable at the EU level as well as in the United States.

[1798] De Schrijver (n148) 1-2.

[1799] Bergholm (n1611) 129-130.

Private sector transmission v. retention – In today's digital era, both sides of the Atlantic engage extensively in the outsourcing of public sector activities to specialized private companies. Glenn Greenwald observed already in 2014 that while "the NSA itself employs roughly thirty thousand people ... the agency also has contracts for some sixty thousand employees of private corporations, who often provide essential services".[1800] The same trend can be observed in the European Union. In order to ensure compliance with the corresponding legal frameworks for specific public or private sector duties, private companies engaging in public sector activities should explicitly be bound by a contract setting out their duties and responsibilities as government agents and the specific (public) legal framework applicable to them when operating in this role of public authority. In the EU, the regulatory division between personal data processing for public sector activities outsourced to the private sector has been brought back to the focus on why processing takes place (not by whom). The purpose of the processing will subsequently determine which legal framework is applicable (EU or Member State law). The adoption of the 2017 Proposal for a Regulation amending the e-Privacy Directive, which explicitly excludes activities for national security purposes from its scope of application regardless of the type of entity (public or private) engaging in these activities, would be welcomed as it would bring clarity to the currently conflicted legal landscape. In the United States, the use of Sec. 501 FISA should be prioritized over the use of EO 12333. Sec. 501 FISA provides U.S. intelligence services with the possibility to mandate private companies to hand over their customers' personal data, while EO 12333 allows intelligence agencies to directly access information from the lines of communication without private companies' knowledge. Sec. 501 FISA provides safeguards for public authorities' requests of private companies' customer data, such as FISC orders and minimization procedures. The improvements to the FISC's system of operation and yearly reporting duty are a welcome effort by the U.S. government to enhance the FISC's transparency. The (consumer) data privacy laws of the U.S. States of California and Virginia as well as the EU include a purpose limitation principle for personal data processing that has to be fulfilled by private companies. Secret access by government authorities to private companies' databases should, consequently, be avoided, and private companies should specify in their privacy policies that their customer data may be accessed by public authorities for their intelligence activities in order to comply with the purpose limitation principle. Public sector access to private companies' databases should, moreover, only take place within a legal framework setting out rules and safeguards for public-private cooperation. In this context, the CJEU's distinction between the obligation for private companies to transmit versus to

[1800] Greenwald, *No Place to Hide* (n16) 101.

retain their customers' (meta)data for intelligence purposes is also remarkable. The Court interpreted the requirement for private companies to transmit their customers' (meta)data to government authorities as being equivalent to the latter accessing that data. On the contrary, the CJEU subsequently held in the 2020 *Quadrature du Net* joined cases that the requirement for private companies to retain their customers' (meta)data on behalf of and for potential use of government authorities as not being equivalent to the latter accessing that data.[1801] The Member States were of the opinion, exemplified by the UK's written observations to the 2016 *Tele2 Sverige* joined cases, that "only legislation relating to the retention of data, but not legislation relating to the access to that data by the competent national law enforcement authorities, falls within the scope of (EU law)",[1802] as the latter situation was situated in the Member States' *domaine réservé* regarding national security. Is the distinction between data retention for, transmission to, and access by government authorities really a distinction that can be made in practice? And is the CJEU's equation to government access to transmitted, as opposed to retained, personal data by private companies really justified? The retention of customers' (meta)data by private companies is likely to be for government authorities to request and, if necessary, use. It is not the aim of this book to address how intelligence agencies and law enforcement operate with regard to retained metadata, but given their aim to protect society, it is plausible that intelligence agencies do 'screen' retained (meta)data. The intelligence programs revealed by Snowden and the Member States' bulk metadata retention legislation have, moreover, shown that intelligence agencies can have access to retained (meta) data. The distinction between transmission, retention, and access might therefore, in practice, be a sole theoretical one.

2023 EU-U.S. Data Privacy Framework – The 2023 EU-U.S. Data Privacy Framework, discussed in *Chapter 1, § 2, C.*, owes its existence mainly to the promulgation of EO 14086 by President Joe Biden. The inclusion of the CJEU's 'necessity and proportionality' wording for U.S. surveillance practices and the establishment of a new U.S. Data Protection Review Court were deemed sufficient to adopt a new adequacy decision for the United States, providing a legal framework for transatlantic personal data transfers and protection. From an outsider's perspective, EO 14086 concedes extensively to the EU's concerns and requests, which should not be taken for granted by the EU. It is quite uncommon that a foreign legal system agrees to implement conditions and concepts of another legal system, as it conflicts with the former's independence

1801 Bergholm (n1611) 122.
1802 *Tele2 Sverige* (n1653) para 65.

and sovereignty. While the EU can legitimately be concerned about the format of these concessions, which were enshrined in an Executive Order and can be revoked by a U.S. President at any time, it should be up to the EU to take precautions instead of criticizing a third country for its legal system. If the EU decided to base its adequacy decision on a, maybe legally weaker, Executive Order, the EU should have included safeguards, conditions, a temporary backup plan, and a review mechanism into the adequacy decision in case EO 14086 would be revoked. This book advocates mutual understanding and respect by the EU for foreign legal systems, instead of taking a position where the EU tries to dictate and impose its rules on the world.

New U.S. Data Protection Review Court – One of the important new features for transatlantic personal data protection in the U.S. system is the establishment of a Data Protection Review Court. While the status of the Court is criticized by the EU, as it is set up as an executive administrative body, it was not possible in the U.S. legal system to set up a new judicial Article III U.S.C. court as the EU requested and preferred. Instead, the United States managed well to navigate the legal landscape and develop a solution to the EU's persistent request. The CJEU held in *Quadrature du Net* in 2020 that surveillance practices, and in particular bulk metadata retention practices, should be 'subject to an effective review, either by a court or by an independent administrative body whose decision is binding'. The ECtHR held in 2021 *Big Brother Watch* that 'the Court (will examine) whether the domestic legal framework clearly define(s) … the procedures for independent *ex post facto* review of such compliance (namely, with the requested safeguards) and the powers vested in the competent body in addressing instances of non-compliance'. For some countries, it may not be possible to set up a dedicated court. Therefore, independence should be judged from the perspective of the legal system concerned instead of from an EU perspective. The EU criticized, in addition, the 'general responses' that the Data Protection Review Court will provide, namely that 'the review either did not identify any covered violations or that a determination was issued requiring appropriate remediation'. While the EU explains that these general responses are insufficient to comply with EU law, the CJEU determined in the 2020 *Quadrature du Net* joined cases that the French commission for review of national security activities issues the exact same response upon scrutiny of a case, namely a notification to "the complainant that the necessary investigations have been carried out, without confirming or denying their implementation".[1803] As already pointed out above, the EU and CJEU should first turn inward to establish Member States' internal practices, which could be used as a benchmark, before judging third countries

[1803] *Quadrature du Net* (n1680) para 38.

for engaging in similar practices. This book maintains, moreover, that while the EU can ask for certain safeguards to be respected with regard to Europeans' personal data that is transferred to third countries, these safeguards should be in compliance with globally accepted safeguards and should be judged from the perspective of the legal system concerned.

§ 6. INTERIM CONCLUSION

This chapter provided an overview of the intelligence and national security context in which data privacy principles have to be applied in the United States and the EU. Upon scrutiny of the U.S. and EU surveillance laws, and more specifically the bulk metadata retention practices in the aftermath of terrorist attacks allowing access to private companies' customers' (meta)data, this book has found that the practices in which both regions engage are actually very similar. The EU and CJEU famously criticized the U.S. national security exception, allowing far-reaching surveillance measures, but EU Member States have shown to attach similar importance to their own Article 4.2 TEU *domaine réservé* regarding national security, making the national security exception not that exceptional at all. The jurisdictional consequence of this exception may render national security cases on both sides of the Atlantic nonjusticiable and non-admissible. The U.S. evidentiary State Secrets Privilege tilts, however, too much to the national security side of the balance, as potential victims have no possibility at all to ask for a review of their case. The EU Member States' *domaine réservé*, when applied in accordance with the law, would render national security cases non-justiciable by the CJEU, but could still be reviewed by Member State courts subject to ECHR compliance. The U.S. and EU courts and lawmakers share, moreover, an activist practice of interpreting the wording of legislation in an overbroad and sometimes even contradicting manner in order to bring more activities in their scope of influence and application. This practice has led to intervention by lawmakers on both sides of the Atlantic to restrict and clarify the wording of the legislation to bring it back to its initial scope and to prevent future misinterpretations and overextensions, ensuring conformity and 'accordance' with the law. Similarly problematic is the practice where government authorities access private companies' databases without the latter's (prior) knowledge. Historically, private and public sectors had different responsibilities and were, therefore, governed by separate legal frameworks. The increased digitization and privatization have resulted in an equal increase in government outsourcing of public sector activities to the private sector. To ensure that private companies can still comply with the different (public and private) purposes in which they are engaged, both the EU and the United States should develop clear legal frameworks for outsourced public sector activities. This clarity will enable private companies to comply with the purpose limitation principle as they can include an intelligence purpose in their privacy policies.

The surveillance practices of both sides of the Atlantic reveal that the balance has tilted towards national security. This finding is not necessarily contradictory to citizens' fundamental rights, as one of these rights is also their right to security, but it does undermine other fundamental rights such as privacy and freedom of speech. Peter Swire confirms that "as fellow members of the North Atlantic Treaty Organization, the U.S. and many (EU) Member States have a shared interest in countering threats, including terrorism and nation-state attacks … (it is) better to build layers of safeguards onto needed intelligence activities … than to block those activities"[1804] altogether. Both sides of the Atlantic share the aim of protecting personal data privacy, but also of safeguarding national security. The EU Member States engaged, and are likely still engaging, in some form of bulk metadata retention and collection practices for intelligence purposes. It is, therefore, important to first determine the status quo regarding the national security exception as used by EU Member States, before judging third countries for their national security practices. Instead of condemning third countries, the EU should adopt an open stance towards the practices of other foreign legal systems, align its intra- and extra-EU case law, and engage in mutual understanding.

1804 Peter Swire, '"Schrems II" Backs the European Legal Regime into a Corner – How Can It Get Out?' (*iapp Blog*, 16 Jul 2020).

CHAPTER 6
COMPARATIVE EU-U.S. ANALYSIS

§ 1. SECTORAL APPROACH: PUBLIC V. PRIVATE SECTOR

The regulatory distinction between the United States and the EU in the area of data privacy can be explained by their respective historical, cultural, regulatory, and philosophical origins. From a civil society perspective, a historical similarity can be identified in citizens' fear of government overreach and abuse of personal data. The U.S. Constitution reflects the spirit of the American republican revolution, which resulted in a strong stance against government interference in people's private affairs, and more specifically to 'protect the people from the (potentially abusive) power of government'. Citizens in the EU similarly witnessed the disastrous consequences of the government's abuse of power during the Second World War, when Jewish citizens' personal data was abused to localize, arrest, and eventually kill many of them. Both sides of the Atlantic are hence aware that personal data protection legislation is necessary to protect citizens from the power of government. For the private sector, the transatlantic division seems more explicit, with the United States favoring a liberal market approach, whereas the EU prefers a regulatory market approach. Both approaches are also grounded in the role that individuals have in the pursuit of their happiness. In the United States, this role is predominantly reserved for individuals themselves. Americans' successes and life achievements are generally attributed to personal achievements. This characterization also explains the emphasis on litigation as people should actively oppose uses of their personal data that they disagree with. Several authors[1805] define the starting point of the U.S. approach as 'a general permissibility to collect and use personal data unless there is an explicit law that prohibits certain of these uses or unless these uses cause harm'. In the European Union, a wider social security system is in place where governments are expected to not only respect but also actively enhance citizens' fundamental rights and well-being. If people face certain difficulties in their lives, European governments are expected to provide (temporary) support for people to help them to get their

1805 Berka (n58) 177; Bygrave, *Data Privacy Law* (n37) 111; Hoofnagle *et al.* (n11) 76; Zuiderveen Borgesius *et al.* (n180) 19.

lives back on track. This characterization also explains the primary focus on regulatory intervention to prevent harm from occurring, instead of litigation afterward to remedy harm that has already occurred. Several authors[1806] define the starting point of the EU approach as "a general prohibition to collect and use personal data unless there is an explicit law that allows certain of these uses".

Co-supervisor Przemysław Pałka added the following observation to this transatlantic division. The legal framework within which the public and the private sectors can respectively operate was, historically, rooted in the same division; the government can only act upon the powers that are conferred upon it, whereas private companies can act within the framework of the law as long as an activity is not explicitly prohibited or does not cause harm to people. This distinction is maintained in U.S. law, where the 1974 Privacy Act sets out strict conditions for the federal government to collect and use citizens' personal data, while the private sector can (or, more accurately, could) collect and process personal data freely unless explicitly prohibited.[1807] One can subsequently ask how the EU's initial focus on government regulation of personal data collection and use evolved to also include the private sector? The EU's legal-historical data privacy overview (*Chapter 3*) explained the initial reluctance of the EU Commission to intervene legislatively in the area of data privacy, as it was considered a Member State affair and 'primarily a public sector concern regarding the regulation of government databanks where the EU Commission did not have jurisdiction to regulate these public sector issues'. The increase in data collection and processing activities and the regulatory patchwork that began to emerge in the EU, with several Member States adopting personal data protection laws, inhibited, however, the EU's project to establish an internal Single market. The internal market legal basis provided the EU with the possibility to regulate personal data protection for the private sector, and while the public sector was initially excluded from this regulatory framework and regulated in a separate document, 'the distinction in treatment was removed by the European Parliament', but needed to be remedied. The broad public sector exemptions to the scope of application included in the 1995 Directive and the 2016 GDPR still reflect this regulatory division between the EU and the Member States.

The intelligence and data privacy overview (*Chapter 5*) even strengthens this regulatory public-private division as attempts by the CJEU to bring national security matters and legislation within its jurisdiction were heavily opposed by the EU Member States, which argued that their Article 4.2 TEU *domaine réservé* regarding national security should be respected. The CJEU extended the law's focus from why personal data is processed (in the case of national security, outside EU law) to who is processing the data (only subjecting public actors to Member States' law). In an era of increased outsourcing of public sector activities

[1806] Berka (n58) 111; Hoofnagle *et al.* (n11) 76; Zuiderveen Borgesius *et al.* (n180) 19.
[1807] Zuiderveen Borgesius *et al.* (n180) 19.

to private companies that have the required technological expertise, bringing the activities of these private actors into the scope of EU law extends the EU's scope of influence significantly. The Member States did not agree with this encroachment on their competences and the EU lawmaker remedied the CJEU's activism by explicitly adding to the legal provisions that 'data processing for national security purposes is excluded from the EU acts' scope of application, regardless of whether it is a public or private entity engaging in the processing activity'. A similar activism can be noticed in the United States, where the wording of Sec. 702 FISA was interpreted so extensively that even its own drafters could not have foreseen what scope of application would be attributed to it. Here also, the U.S. lawmaker intervened and specified that telephony records may only be accessed 'using a term that specifically identifies a person, entity, telephone number, or account as the basis for a request'. EU and U.S. courts and lawmakers share, consequently, the practice of misinterpretation or overly extensive interpretation of legal provisions in order to bring as many areas as possible into their (legal) spheres of influence. This practice should be objected to. An evolutionary interpretation is advocated in this book, which is not the same as a contradictory interpretation. Laws are drafted carefully and include safeguards and limitations on their use. It is therefore important to act in a legally correct way by staying closer to the wording of the legislation and the intention behind the careful wording of its drafters, to ensure that one acts 'in accordance with the law'. To this end, Article 45.2(a) GDPR, which requires to take third countries' national security legislation and the possibilities for public authorities' access to personal data into account for an adequacy decision, should be amended in order to align it with the EU's internal *domaine réservé* division, excluding national security from the EU's scope of application, and to align the intra- and extra-EU policy. The CJEU can, after all, not judge a third country on an account that it cannot even judge its own Member States on. The United States criticized the CJEU accurately for acting outside its competences when assessing U.S. surveillance laws based on the EU Charter and a GDPR provision. Especially since the CJEU eventually conceded to the EU Member States' pressure to allow the same bulk metadata retention practices, albeit under strict conditions, as it prohibited the United States from engaging in. Both regions enacted bulk metadata retention laws in the aftermath of terrorist attacks on their soil, and in both regions this legislative initiative was grounded in the protection of national security. The U.S. surveillance practices were the first to be revealed, attracting prominent public attention, but the subsequent revelation of similar surveillance practices in EU Member States shows that both regions are actually not that different in their national security policies. In order to preserve legal certainty and democracy, national security cases should be admissible and justiciable by the courts of the country concerned. The EU Member States should engage in judicial review of their surveillance laws at the national level, while the United States should prioritize the *in camera* and *ex parte* review procedure set out in Sec. 106(f)

FISA over the evidentiary State Secrets Privilege, which obstructs review of U.S. surveillance laws altogether.

The findings in this book partly support and partly object Przemysław Pałka's preference for 'a sectoral approach over a one-fits-all format for personal data protection legislation as the stakes and values involved differ significantly'. For the private versus public sector division, the findings in this book support a sectoral approach. The 'comprehensive' EU approach includes many public sector exemptions, and activist attempts by the CJEU to bring national security matters within its jurisdiction were heavily opposed by the EU Member States. Article 4.2 TEU's *domaine réservé* regarding national security should be respected as it is a core aspect of Member States' identity. To this end, EU Member States should adopt personal data protection legislation on a national level for the public sector, providing guidance and information to ensure democracy and transparency, and to facilitate cross-border cooperation with other law enforcement and intelligence services when necessary. The EU Member States remain subject to legal scrutiny by the ECtHR for this type of regulation. The United States already has a separate legal framework in place for federal agencies, in the form of the 1974 Privacy Act, but the U.S. States should also adopt personal data privacy legislation for State agencies if that was not yet the case.

For the different sub-sectors within the private sector, the findings in this book object a sectoral approach. A similar legislative evolution can be noticed on both sides of the Atlantic. Firstly, regulators in several EU Member States became aware of the risks of personal data collection and processing by private companies, and decided to step in legislatively to protect their citizens against businesses' overreach and abuse. These legislative initiatives hindered the establishment of the internal market, which led to legislative intervention at the EU level to harmonize the rules to protect citizens' personal data by providing one framework for all sub-sectors operating in the private sector. A dual privacy and economic approach was consequently taken. Secondly, the United States initially favored different sectoral data privacy laws to be adopted through self-regulation. Large-scale data privacy scandals, such as Google's Apple Safari activity-tracking cookies, Facebook's Cambridge Analytica, or ClearView AI's face-scraping practices, made U.S. citizens, however, aware that their valuable personal data was insufficiently protected against businesses' excessive overreach and that consumers had almost no bargaining power against big tech companies. Congress was requested to step in legislatively by adopting federal consumer data privacy regulation, but as proposals kept being rejected, the U.S. States decided to step in legislatively. Initially, only the State of California had a California Consumer Privacy Act in place. At the time of writing, the number of U.S. States with consumer privacy acts had already grown to 20 States. The United States is currently in a similar stage to where the EU was when its Member States began to enact national personal data protection rules to protect their citizens' data privacy. The need for trans-State and international commerce will likely also in the United States lead to a convergence of U.S. State consumer privacy acts, where the 'experimental regulatory laboratory' will presumably lead to the most successful standards becoming the default rule. Based on these evolutions, it can be concluded that comprehensive data privacy legislation for the private sector is desirable as it facilitates regional and global trade, but a separate legal framework should be adopted for the public sector (government and law enforcement) and private sector (businesses) as their interests, tasks, and purposes differ significantly, which should be addressed adequately when legislating.

§ 2. PRIVATE SECTOR: GENERAL DATA PRIVACY PRINCIPLES

The EU's protective and paternalistic legal framework with strict and procedural rules has become too burdensome for businesses and hampers competition. The original aim to return the decisional power and individual control to the people should be restored, by setting out strictly necessary basic data privacy principles in the form of one clear minimum standard instead of multiple ones, to prevent the most flagrant abuses of personal data. In the privacy-commerce balance, individuals should be informed and educated to make conscious choices about whether to share their data through self-management, which would restore their decisional power. At present, data privacy regulation is addressed mainly at private companies, and while the aim to incentivize private companies to engage in responsible data processing activities that do not adversely affect their consumers is laudable, the balance of responsibility should be restored to include both the private companies and the individuals involved. People's personal data and privacy cannot be adequately protected in a globalized world where personal data is transferred across jurisdictions if each of these jurisdictions adopts different data privacy rules. Similarly, private companies cannot operate smoothly on a global or even international scale if different rules are in place in different countries and regions. A consistent global framework can safeguard people's data privacy interests and facilitate private companies' commercial interests. Several attempts have already been made on several levels to develop universal, or at least regional, data privacy principles based on different legal frameworks. This book used the examples of the OECD Guidelines, the CoE Convention, U.S. State acts, and EU law.

One of the core issues that universal, or at least regional, principles are confronted with is enforcement. While the EU's introduction of high fines for violations has a deterrent effect, data privacy violations still occur as the enforcement system is found to be defective from a consumer's point of view.[1808] The U.S. system of a

1808 Gentile and Lynskey (n780) 799-801; Publications Office EU, *The Future of Data Protection* (n780) 14.

cure period could provide a solution for these problems, as it provides consumers with a right to directly contact the businesses involved, and provides the businesses with a limited time to remedy the identified issues in order to avoid (high) fines. This procedure shortens the chain of parties involved and may provide quick relief. Unwilling businesses that refuse to comply will, in a second phase, still face high fines through enforcement by the appointed administrative authority or court. To this end, a general private right of action for consumers should be introduced in the United States. Consumers' expectations are converging on both sides of the Atlantic. The U.S. FTC has already expanded its regulatory authority to not only verify whether businesses comply with the promises they make in their privacy policies, but also to take into account consumers' expectations.[1809] A codification of these changing consumer expectations as applied in the FTC's settlements and litigations on a continuous basis would be advantageous for legal certainty and transparency. Such codification would, moreover, reveal common transatlantic trends in consumers' expectations, facilitating the development of common data privacy principles.

The EU and the United States have changed places as global trendsetters in diverse policy areas since the 1990s.[1810] Notwithstanding the transatlantic differences regarding personal data privacy, the EU 1995 Directive, replaced by the 2016 GDPR, did succeed in setting an international standard. The rules and requirements set out in these influential legal documents enacted by the European Union were transposed to the legal systems of many countries worldwide, such as those of Japan and Australia.[1811] The EU 1995 Directive was the first legal document to largely implement the principles set out in the 1980 OECD Guidelines, which contributed to the Directive's success, but other OECD Member countries[1812] also followed by adopting their own version of personal data protection legislation implementing the OECD's fair information principles for the private sector.[1813] Emmanuel Pernot-Leplay[1814] analyzes the implementation of the EU GDPR (and its predecessor the 1995 Directive) in the national laws of third countries from the point of view of a legal transplant. The implementation of an already existing system is a cost-saving decision, as these countries do not have to spend time and money developing new personal data protection laws from scratch. Moreover, third countries were (and to a certain extent are) incentivized to implement the principles set out in EU personal data protection law by its strict extraterritorial component requiring 'an

1809 Solove and Hartzog (n61) 667-672.

1810 Vogel (n539) 4.

1811 Arora (n1395) 718-723; Bygrave, *Data Privacy Law* (n37) 208; Heisenberg (n66) 2-11 and 26 and 169-170; Pernot-Leplay (n193) 101-105; Solove, 'Data Is What Data Does' (n16) 1091.

1812 Such as Australia, Canada, Greece, Japan, Turkey, and the United States.; Heisenberg (n66) 103.

1813 *Ibid.* 165.

1814 Pernot-Leplay (n193) 101-110.

adequate level of protection' for personal data transfers to third countries outside the European Union. Compliance with EU data protection principles results, after all, in a relatively smooth transfer of personal data between third countries and the European Union.[1815] The EU's trendsetting position is enabled by its strong market power and ability to impose legislation top-down on a relatively large geographical scale, also called 'the Brussels effect'. The U.S. counterpart is 'the California effect', as the State of California shares the elements of a strong market power, a broad sphere of influence, and a dominant position to 'force' its standards upon others. This effect is, however, mediated in the United States. The U.S. bottom-up approach leads to a 'competitive experimental regulatory laboratory' where States can compete to set 'the best' standard, which will often eventually become the dominant standard. The EU may have been the first one to adopt a strong binding regional regulatory framework, but it should not become fixated on this position as it has already been extensively criticized. The regulatory initiative is laudable, but the EU should take an open stance towards different regulatory initiatives that have developed in other regions and organically revisit its legal framework in cooperation, not isolation, with other international players.

Several authors conclude that data privacy legislation is not chiefly addressed to individual consumers, but rather to private companies involved in data processing practices. Daniel Solove observes that "perhaps the greatest practical impact of privacy self-management is not in informing individuals and improving their privacy management, but in informing the companies that are collecting and using the data and in improving the companies' management of privacy".[1816] Fred Cate and Viktor Mayer-Schönberger point to the shift in "the responsibility for data protection away from the data subject (the people) towards the data user (the data processor)".[1817] Paul Blume acknowledges that "almost all rules are addressed to the controller (the data processor) and the data subject (the people) in some sense is (are) only given a secondary role in European data protection law".[1818] EU personal data protection law aims, therefore, at changing the processing behavior of market players and private companies, rather than at changing the behavior of people regarding their personal data. "In the European view, compliance (with the data protection rules) means monitoring the organizations that handle data to ensure that they do it correctly",[1819] as private companies have to implement and adjust their business models to the stringent rules set out in the GDPR, rather than the individuals that the regulation aims

1815 Heisenberg (n66) 11 and 121 and 169-170.
1816 Solove, 'Introduction' (n43) 1900.
1817 Cate and Mayer-Schönberger (n362) 70.
1818 Blume (n528) 5-6.
1819 Heisenberg (n66) 15.

to protect, as the latter do not make as much use of the micro-rights foreseen in the GDPR.

The EU global trendsetting approach can also be perceived as an imposing method by other countries and regions, dictating unilaterally EU rules to the rest of the world, which is criticized. Fred Cate considers EU data protection legislation a protectionist measure, as it forces multinational companies, which engage in the processing of personal data on an international and global scale, to comply and implement EU rules.[1820] Payal Arora reminds the EU that "there is a moral responsibility to rethink, in global terms, the implications of legal reforms on audiences well beyond the EU market",[1821] because "laws and regulations have deep political interests often rooted in neocolonial ideologies (which) are not necessarily designed and executed for the protection of all citizens, (also privacy) laws may evoke different meanings among the world's marginalized communities, far from the sacrosanct position they hold among many in the West".[1822] Julia Fromholz observes that "although the Directive (and now the GDPR) may affect the entire world, the fact remains that only fifteen countries (now 27) agreed to it ..., a unilateral decision by a small group of countries is not the most effective way to create a widely accepted standard ... EU data protection law) in effect forces the United States, along with all other non-EU countries, to abide by its regulations, to negotiate with the EU in order to win an interpretation that is more flexible than the words of the (law) suggest, or to suffer the ill consequences of not being able to transfer data out of the EU ... in addition to attempting to impose a foreign set of cultural values on American entities, the Directive (and its successor, the GDPR) also may be trying to impose rules that are not well suited to today's technology",[1823] as was acknowledged by the EU Draghi Report. The EU has succeeded, to a large extent, in achieving a global trendsetting standard (unilaterally) in the area of personal data protection, but the EU should not engage in a similar unilateral regulatory intervention of future technological global markets. The neocolonialist criticism of third countries regarding the EU's one-sided rule-imposing approach with global consequences in the form of heavy fines is well-founded, as the EU is not the only player in the global technology market. The EU reacted, moreover, with the same criticism of the United States for similar one-sided Passenger Name Record practices (*see below*). While the EU's aim to protect personal data is laudable, this matter should be discussed and regulated in multilateral fora on a global level, including all (private, public, civil society) stakeholders.

The EU's unilateral legislative initiative also triggered certain other countries or regions to set a global personal data transfer standard, different from the

---

1820 Cate (n193) 126-127.
1821 Arora (n1395) 723.
1822 *Ibid.* 718.
1823 Fromholz (n74) 474-475.

EU's requirements. Russia[1824] and China decided, for example, to adopt their own type of personal data protection legislation. In 2021, China adopted the Personal Information Protection Law, which introduced even stricter rules than the GDPR.[1825] Up until today there is, however, no adequacy decision for China,[1826] as its specific legal system allows for "numerous exceptions ... to data protection in an extensive surveillance legal framework",[1827] even though this book argued above that countries' national security and surveillance laws cannot be a valid criterion for adequacy determination as the EU has to respect their Member States' legislative *domaine réservé* regarding national security, and can consequently not judge third countries' national security laws if it cannot judge its own Member States' national security laws as this would create a double standard. Multilateral fora, such as the Organization for Economic Cooperation and Development (OECD), could provide a more acceptable space to develop common standards. As an intergovernmental organization with globally dispersed members,[1828] the OECD meets on regular occasions and could provide a more democratic way of developing and introducing rules by all these countries together. The OECD was, together with the Council of Europe, one of the first organizations to take initiative in regulating personal data protection and data flows.[1829] Their 1980 Guidelines were criticized for being disregarded and unenforced as they consisted of non-binding soft law. The 1995 EU Directive was created to include and enforce (some of) the principles enshrined in the initial 1980 OECD Guidelines through EU law.[1830] It is true that the EU has

---

1824 For an overview of the Russian data protection regime as compared to the EU, mainly relying on Standard Contractual Clauses for EU data transfers, before the Ukraine war: Jan Czarnocki and others, *Report on Government access to data in third countries* (EDPB Report, 2021) 40-54, and Stanislav Rumyantsev, 'Russia: Harmonising data protection laws with the EU' (*Gorodissky*, 13 Feb 2019); and after the Ukraine war: EDPB, 'Statement 02/2022 on personal data transfers to the Russian Federation' (*europa.eu*, Feb 2022).

1825 Josh Ye, 'With new privacy law, China could reshape cross-border data rules similar to Europe's GDPR' (*South China Morning Post*, 30 Aug 2021).

1826 "The EC has so far recognized Andorra, Argentina, Canada (commercial organizations), Faroe Islands, Guernsey, Israel, Isle of Man, Japan, Jersey, New Zealand, Republic of Korea, Switzerland, the United Kingdom under the GDPR and the LED, and Uruguay as providing adequate protection".: Laurens Cerulus, 'Europe eyes privacy clampdown on China' (*Politico*, 4 Feb 2019); European Commission, 'Adequacy decisions: How the EU determines if a non-EU country has an adequate level of data protection' (*europa.eu*, 2024).

1827 Czarnocki *et al.* (n1824) 12-26.

1828 Consisting not only of most EU Member States and the United States, but also of a number of other industrialized pro-western countries, such as Japan, Australia, New Zealand, Korea, Israel, Chile, and Mexico.: Hans Gassmann, 'OECD Guidelines Governing the Protection of Privacy and Transborder Flows of Personal Data' (1981) 5 ComputNetw 127, 127; Christopher Kuner, *Transborder Data Flows and Data Privacy Law* (OUP 2013) 35.

1829 See *Chapter 3, § 2.*

1830 Gassmann (n1828) 127; Heisenberg (n66) 8-9 and 25-27 and 52-54; Kuner, *Transborder* (n1828) 35-36; OECD, *OECD Guidelines on the Protection of Privacy and Transborder Flows of Personal Data* (OECD Publications Service, 2001) 7-8; OECD, *The OECD Privacy Framework* (OECD, 2013) 3-5.

strong leverage through the imposition of fines and the enforcement by the CJEU, but it is also understandable that, in particular, countries in the Global South do not agree with this imposing approach, sometimes even qualifying it as neocolonialism.[1831]

EU commissioner Frits Bolkestein reacted to the Passenger Name Record (PNR) framework,[1832] introduced by the United States in the fight against terrorism, that "the American way of proceeding by unilateral action and threats of penalties is unacceptable",[1833] as European airlines were required to send their PNR data to U.S. authorities. The same statement can be made about the EU's decision to act unilaterally in the area of personal data protection by introducing the 2016 GDPR with a strong enforceable extraterritorial component and heavy fines.[1834] The EU has been criticized for allowing data transfers to countries with more questionable data protection standards than the United States, which do likely also not fulfill the EU's 'adequate or equivalent level of protection' requirement.[1835] Peter Swire points out that "transfers of personal data to authoritarian countries, such as China and Russia" are more problematic than data transfers to the United States, even though they still occur on a regular basis.[1836] European Data Protection Supervisor Wojciech Wiewiórowski shares this concern, and "fear(s) more for data that was destined for China than the United States, which ... was 'much closer' to the EU in terms of values".[1837] It is, therefore, interesting to note that EU-U.S. data transfers, and with them the adequacy decisions and court cases, are given predominant attention,[1838] as opposed to Chinese, Russian, or other data protection regimes which have more questionable adequacy levels, but which keep occurring on a daily basis.

When taken in a global context, transatlantic personal data transfers are not that problematic. The United States adheres, after all, to the 1980 OECD Guidelines, which principles were enshrined in the EU 1995 Directive, succeeded by the 2016 GDPR, and the EU and the United States share the values of democracy and human rights. A commitment of both regions to a common set of principles can consequently be identified. A global instrument setting out enforceable general data privacy principles for the private sector is preferable, as the present-day fragmented landscape impedes commercial activities and people's data privacy.

1831 Arora (n1395) 718; Jacqueline Hicks, "Digital colonialism': why some countries want to take control of their people's data from Big Tech' (*The Conversation*, 26 Sep 2019); Imtiaz Muqbil, 'GDPR – Another chapter in the book of European extra-territorial neocolonialism' (*Travel Impact Newswire*, 9 Jun 2018).

1832 See *Chapter 5, § 3, A.*

1833 Heisenberg (n66) 143.

1834 Hoofnagle *et al.* (n11) 66-69.

1835 Heisenberg (n66) 106-112; Swire, '"Schrems II"' (n1804).

1836 Swire, '"Schrems II"' (n1804).

1837 Vincent Manancourt, 'The EU court ruling that could blow up digital trade' (*Politico*, 13 Jul 2020).

1838 Bygrave, *Data Privacy Law* (n37) 107.

The following six general personal data protection (or data privacy) categories, consisting of several data privacy principles, were in this book deduced and developed from the (evolution of the) selected legal instruments:

1) data quality is enhanced when the collected data is adequate, accurate, and up-to-date for its intended use, and limited to the information needed for data processing purposes.[1839] The following data privacy principles are situated within this category:
   - *purpose limitation & purpose specification:* the collected personal data can only be used for the purposes it was initially collected for and as was communicated to the person involved at the time of collection;
   - *data minimization:* the collected personal data has to be relevant for and limited to what is necessary for the stated and intended use of the data;
   - *time and storage limitation:* the collected personal data cannot be retained for longer than necessary to fulfill the stated or intended purposes, as this impedes its accuracy and correctness;
2) legitimate processing requires the *lawful* collection of personal data, which can be determined based on:
   - a legal basis or legitimate aim;
   - people must be provided with opt-in/opt-out options for the collection of their personal data;
   - people's consent is required for certain types of processing (such as, but not limited to: when people can adversely be affected or when the processing cannot be foreseen based on the information provided);
   - the observance of non-discriminatory practices by data processors;
   - the provision of a right to object to illegitimate forms of processing without adverse consequences for exercising people's data privacy rights;
3) notification and transparency require data processors to provide people with certain information regarding data processing:
   - possibly in a *privacy policy*;
   - information relating to *data processing practices* (e.g. quality, legitimacy, accuracy, rights);
   - information relating to the *data processor* (e.g. address, contact details);
   - information relating to *appeal bodies* (administrative and/or courts);
   - information about possible *disclosure* of people's personal data *to third parties*;
   - the provision of a *right of access* to personal data held on the people concerned;
   - a *data breach notification* has to be sent out by data processors in case of a data breach involving someone's personal data;

[1839] Sebastian-Coleman (n770) 39-41.

4) data accuracy prescribes that the collected data has to be *accurate* and kept *up-to-date*, which is enhanced by:
   - *correction rights* which provide people with the opportunity to correct incomplete or inaccurate personal data held on them;
   - *deletion rights* which provide people with the opportunity to request the erasure of incomplete or inaccurate personal data held on them (subject to a balancing exercise with other competing rights);
   - the requirement that data processors have to *notify third parties* with whom the data was shared to comply with the formerly mentioned requests (if reasonably possible);
5) data security to keep the collected personal data safe from unauthorized access and destruction through the implementation of technical and/or practical measures;
6) effective enforcement is ensured through people's access to an effective *remedy* (sanction or remediation) enforced by an *administrative body* and/or a *court* in case of non-compliance with the data privacy principles.

The content and interpretation of these principles should be developed on an international level by multidisciplinary working groups consisting of (at least) business representatives, privacy lawyers, civil society representatives, and government officials to determine standards that are feasible and desirable by the stakeholders involved, and to ensure a uniform interpretation of the data privacy principles and concepts agreed upon. These stakeholders also reflect Robert Baldwin *et al.*'s 'three shaping elements in government regulation', namely market failure, public opinion, and lobby-driven interests, which were used in this book. A discussion of each of these elements showed, after all, that the EU-U.S. division is not that much culturally or sociologically defined, but rather fluctuant based on specific situations and reactions. Neither the United States nor the European Union are 'by definition' liberal market harm-based or regulatory risk-based. These approaches were rather the result of market failures (respectively too strict and too lenient regulations), public opinion (demanding respectively more lenient and stricter regulatory intervention), and the involvement of lobby-driven stakeholders (respectively businesses and pro-privacy groups). It is, therefore, important to provide all stakeholders in the discussion with an equal voice to develop a framework that can be widely supported by the private sector, the public sector, and civil society.

§ 3. PERSONAL DATA PRIVACY

The qualification of 'the right to personal data protection' is, at first sight, fundamentally distinct between the EU and the United States, but upon closer inspection the privacy-commerce balance can be found in data privacy regulations on both sides of the Atlantic. The U.S. approach initially emphasized the commercial side of the balance, by qualifying people's personal data as a commercial asset. A remnant of this qualification can still be found in U.S. State consumer privacy acts where the default opt-in system is used, and people have to actively opt out if they do not want their personal data to be processed by private companies. The 'Notice and Choice' model exemplifies that consumers are expected to make informed choices, based on private companies' privacy policies or 'notices', about whether to share their data for the benefits they can obtain in return. The uneven bargaining power corrected this approach, however, as people did not really have a choice and personal data could not only be perceived as a commodity. Personal data reflects people's personality and characteristics of who they are as a person. In the U.S. approach to privacy, people have an active duty to secrete information that they want to keep private. Information that is made public loses, consequently, its protection. Strong emphasis is placed on people's decisions and individual control to decide which information they want to share and with whom. The 'secrecy paradigm' also results in the prevalence of freedom of speech interests over privacy interests in the United States. Publicly available information that is lawfully obtained and truthful is, as a consequence, strongly protected and can almost freely be disseminated. The digital era has, however, complicated this approach as 'private' communications are enabled by third-party operators, which require the information to be shared with a third party. The EU roots of the newly introduced fundamental right to personal data protection can be traced back to the right to privacy and the protection of people's human dignity. This conceptualization is preoccupied with someone's public image, and how people's reputation and identity are presented to the world. The ability to determine for oneself and exercise individual control over which personal information is shared with the (digital) world is, therefore, crucial. This approach explains why privacy interests often prevail over freedom of speech interests in the European Union. Even when lawfully obtained truthful information is disseminated, the person concerned will often be able to block this dissemination, whether through reputation rights or through the 'right to be forgotten'. The right to be forgotten should be re-defined to a 'right to be remembered with difficulty' as the former conceptualization seems to suggest that personal data will be completely deleted upon an individual's request. Rather, a balancing exercise will be conducted between the person's privacy interests and the public's information interests to determine whose interests should prevail in the particular case. The EU right to be forgotten is preoccupied with the ease and speed with which information can be found, not necessarily with the fact that the information is out there. The Court limited its decision, therefore, to requiring the deletion of the information from search engines (which facilitate access and dissemination of information), as opposed to news outlets which were allowed to retain the information concerned on their websites. The 'right to be remembered with difficulty' is a good example of restoring the balance between an individual's privacy interests and the public's information interests in a digital age where information has become easily available in vast amounts. An overly extensive interpretation of 'the right to be forgotten' could, after all, lead to a situation where individuals have the opportunity to actively obscure unfavorable truthful information under the 'privacy' justification. This practice hampers other parties from making informed choices and decisions about the person or situation concerned, and can be related to the necessity to enable debates and discussions instead of blocking or pre-selecting content that is shared with users, as both situations eventually endanger democracy and a democratic society.

The privacy-commerce balance was initially well-maintained in the EU as the 1995 Directive placed emphasis on both sides of the spectrum. As the EU did not have the competence to enact fundamental rights legislation (at that time), the protection of people's privacy interests in their personal data was grounded in the internal (trade) market and the facilitation of its 'free flow', which combined a privacy and a property approach. The subsequent elevation of the protection of personal data to a separate self-standing fundamental right in EU primary law in 2007 is quite unique. Even though the commerce dimension can still be found in recital 101 of the 2016 GDPR where "flows of personal data to and from countries outside the Union and international organisations are necessary for the expansion of international trade and international cooperation",[1840] and the EU's duty to uphold and promote free and fair trade in its relations with the wider world is enshrined in Article 3.5 TEU, a shift to the privacy side of the spectrum, or better, to a more protective and procedural approach, can be noticed. This is confirmed by, on the one hand, the EU preference for a default opt-out system where individuals have to actively give their permission to private companies for personal data processing activities, and on the other hand, by the recent emphasis placed by the CJEU and the EDPB on people's consent as predominant legitimizing basis for data processing activities, as opposed to other equal legitimizing grounds foreseen by the GDPR, which are considered inferior, contrary to the wording of the GDPR. In a digital world which only offers individuals the choice between 'yes I share my personal data' or 'no I do not use the service or product', the 'consent' legitimizing basis for data processing activities can hardly be considered an effective empowerment tool. The EU's emphasis on the privacy and procedural side of the spectrum has been criticized in recent years, as it hampers the competitiveness of EU businesses and burdens the EU commercial market. Both regions' data privacy systems are, consequently, grounded in individual control, self-determination, and self-authorship.

The concept of privacy has a long history and encompasses a broad range of aspects as it has to adapt over time and space. Where initially personal data protection was strongly grounded in the right to privacy enshrined in

[1840] Recital 101 GDPR.

Article 8 ECHR, its subsequent detachment and individualization can be questioned. While it is true that the EU concept of personal data protection encompasses more elements than the 'classical' right to privacy, as it was tailored to the digital age, the same result could have been achieved by an evolutionary digital interpretation of the right to privacy. The uncomfortable artificial detachment of this newly created fundamental right from its privacy origins can still be noticed in the CJEU's case law, where both rights are consistently conflated and used together, and in the discrepant discussion on the 'essence' of personal data protection. The conclusion of the 'essence' discussion points to a procedural conceptualization where data security measures to protect privacy interests seem to constitute the 'essence' of this newly created fundamental right. As a consequence, the protection of personal data is only a procedural means (data security measures, where certain 'boxes' must be ticked for compliance) to protect and achieve a privacy protection end. The added value of this newly introduced fundamental right is, therefore, redundant, as it essentially protects people's privacy interests, albeit through procedural requirements. The procedural conceptualization has led to the paradox that personal data is protected as such in the EU, instead of retaining the focus on the protection of the people behind the data, which can also be noticed in the U.S. State consumer acts of California and Virginia as they followed the example of the EU. The procedural nature of 'personal data protection' was already present in the early 1970s in the United States, where a dual focus on the protection of people's privacy interests through the respect for and provision of due process rights was emphasized.

Three situations can exemplify the EU's excessive focus on the procedural aspect of the protection of personal data, which is also employed in the U.S. States that followed the GDPR's example, where the data as such is protected instead of the privacy interests of the person behind the data. Firstly, the EU's protection of publicly available information which was knowingly shared by the person concerned is a very restrictive and paternalistic measure. It unduly restricts people's individual control and decisional autonomy, as individuals should be aware of the consequences of their actions in order to act accordingly. From a U.S. perspective, it is hypocritical to claim privacy rights in information that is posted on the Internet by making it publicly available for everyone to read. In a similar way, the sole act of taking a photograph of someone in a public area should not be considered as a violation of someone's personal data protection, as that person chose knowingly to be in a public area. More importantly, the law should be concerned about what this information is used for in order to protect people's privacy interests. This book suggested adopting 'a reasonable expectation' benchmark in these cases, where use of the photograph will be allowed for 'reasonably expected purposes' related to the circumstances in which the photograph was taken. Secondly, the EU's introduction of a special category of 'sensitive data', followed by the U.S. States of California and Virginia, requiring an additional level of protection, as the processing of this particular information involves a heightened risk of discriminatory practices occurring, has become outdated due to fast-paced advancements in big data analytics. The emphasis on the protection of data as such disregards today's possibilities to deduce 'sensitive' information from regular or even anonymous data. A change of approach must, therefore, occur, where the emphasis is placed on the intentions of data processors, and, hence, the purposes for which the collected and processed data will be used. The GDPR and the CCPA already include such provisions, but they consist of a minority. Discriminatory uses that can harm individuals, whether directly or indirectly, should be prohibited, unless they can be justified. The procedural aspect of personal data protection rules contributes to preserving people's privacy interests by granting them individual control over their personal data, but this should take place in a broader, well-informed context. A change of perspective for regulatory initiatives from the current procedural point of view (*which type of data*) to a contextual point of view (*how the data is used*) is therefore recommended, as 'data is what data does' or broader 'what is done with it'. Thirdly, individuals' psychologically sustained harm is often not taken into account in EU and U.S. regulatory frameworks, as companies will fulfill their data protection duties when they can 'tick the boxes'. Even when a data breach occurs, private companies will not be held accountable if they have fulfilled the data protection requirements. Individuals will be notified of the data breach, but can subsequently not do more than worry about where their data will end up. A shift in approach should therefore be endorsed by both sides of the Atlantic to include psychologically sustained harm in the form of a re-conceptualization of (data) privacy to Daniel Solove's comprehensive 'privacy-harmful activities' categorization. The privacy-harmful activities model can subsequently be operationalized by Paul Ohm's 'threat modeling' approach, where a person's sustained (material or psychological) harm can be quantified by determining the chances of (1) the possibility of harm occurring, (2) the probability of harm occurring, (3) the presence of a confidential relationship, which can be operationalized by an average consumer's expectation, and (4) whether the risk would be perceived as 'serious' by the majority of population, in order to exclude personal sensitivities from the test.[1841] Psychological harm has become even more prevalent in the digital age, and legal systems on both sides of the Atlantic should consequently include psychological suffering in their regulatory frameworks.

The EU's disentanglement of the right to personal data protection from the right to privacy is criticized and, as the 'essence' of personal data protection was shown to consist of data security measures to protect people's privacy, the U.S. concept of 'data privacy' is perceived as more adequate than 'personal data protection' as it still reflects the privacy origins of this newly created concept and

[1841] Ohm (n826) 1161.

its delineation that the protected privacy interests are limited to personal data. For data privacy legislation to be effective, it is necessary that a dual privacy and commerce approach is taken in order to effectively protect people's privacy interests while enhancing personal data flows and businesses' economic activities in the digital age. The regulatory framework should, moreover, focus on the purposes of data collection and processing rather than the procedural approach that is currently taken where the data as such is protected instead of the people behind the data.

CHAPTER 7
CONCLUSION

This book aimed at deepening the understanding of, and determining the differences and convergences between, the U.S. and EU legal approaches towards personal data protection. An analysis was conducted on three levels, representing the three core stakeholders in the data privacy debate, namely, the private sector, civil society, and the public sector, consisting of government intelligence and law enforcement agencies. Each of these levels plays a fundamental role in the development of a roadmap for the U.S. and EU approaches towards data privacy to co-exist, and coherence and convergence at each of these levels are necessary to find a long-lasting solution to the transatlantic personal data transfer issues. The findings in this book confirm that it is possible for the U.S. and EU legal approaches towards data privacy to co-exist, and that convergences can be found at each of the three levels.

For the public-private sector distinction, a separate legal framework can be identified on both sides of the Atlantic, albeit explicitly in the United States and implicitly in the European Union. The European Union proclaims that it takes an 'omnibus' regulatory approach, but a closer look at the system reveals substantial exemptions for public sector activities, including law enforcement and national security. U.S. and EU citizens also share the feeling that their personal data has to be protected from the power of government. A separate regime is necessary for these sectors as their stakes and purposes differ significantly. Public sector interests relate to countries' core national interests and should be left to the countries involved to regulate. The United States and the EU Member States have experienced terrorist attacks and are aware that they have to protect their citizens while ensuring respect for their fundamental rights. The national security exception is, as a consequence, embraced by all countries involved, whether on the U.S. or the EU side, and they foresee a specific legal framework for the operations of intelligence and law enforcement agencies. U.S. and EU courts and lawmakers should, however, adhere more closely to the wording of carefully drafted surveillance laws in order to preserve their restrictive interpretation, and align their domestic and foreign policy to ensure coherence.

For the private sector, a trend is shared between both sides of the Atlantic to move towards comprehensive data privacy legislation, which should equally address businesses' commercial concerns and individuals' privacy concerns. A coherent global framework will not only facilitate regional and global trade but will also ensure that citizens' personal data is equally protected by each private actor in the data processing chain. The EU has attempted to set a global standard, but without international discussion, its approach is rather perceived to be imposing than mutually agreed upon. The strict and procedural rules have also drifted away from the aim of restoring people's individual control and decisional power, to a merely mechanical instrument where private companies have to 'check the boxes' in order to comply. This book argues to return to the initial idea of setting out strictly necessary basic data privacy principles in the form of one clear minimum standard which prevents the most flagrant abuses of personal data. Within that framework, individuals have the decisional power to subsequently decide whether they want to share their personal data for commercial purposes. To this end, six data privacy categories, consisting of several data privacy principles, were developed in this book, based on the legal instruments consulted. The first 'data quality' category includes the purpose limitation, purpose specification, data minimization, time limitation, and storage limitation principles. The second 'legitimate processing' category includes the requirement for a legal basis, legitimate aim or consent for data processing, opt-in/opt-out options, the non-discrimination principle, and the right to object to illegitimate processing. The third 'notification and transparency' category includes the requirement to provide information, possibly in a privacy policy, regarding data processing practices, the data processor, appeal bodies, possible disclosure of personal data to third parties, an individual's right of access, and a data breach notification. The fourth 'data accuracy' category includes the requirement that collected data has to be accurate and kept up to date, to provide data correction and deletion rights, and to notify the exercise of these rights to third parties with whom the personal data was shared. The fifth 'data security' category includes the requirement to implement technical and/or organizational measures to protect personal data from unauthorized access and destruction. The sixth 'effective enforcement' category includes the requirement to provide an effective remedy in the form of a sanction or remediation enforced by an administrative body and/or a court in case of non-compliance. To ensure that these principles are equally applied and understood, they should be made operational on an international level, including stakeholders from all three levels (private sector, public sector, civil society).

The qualification of the right to personal data protection or data privacy seems, from a civil society perspective, fundamentally different between the two sides of the Atlantic, but also here many common elements can be distinguished upon closer scrutiny. Consumer expectations are converging on both sides of the Atlantic, and their voice should be taken into account when determining which data processing activities are considered harmful. The privacy-commerce balance can be identified in U.S. and EU data privacy legislation, as both legal frameworks are grounded in the protection of people's privacy interests. Neither the United States nor the European Union are 'by definition' liberal market harm-based or regulatory risk-based, but rather became conceptualized like this as a result of market failures, dominant public opinion, and the weight of certain lobby-driven stakeholders in the development of data privacy policies. The U.S. and EU approaches fluctuate depending on specific situations and public reactions, rather than being grounded in cultural, historical, or sociological differences. Instead of creating a new fundamental right, personal data protection can be perceived as an evolutionary digital interpretation of the right to privacy. This is endorsed by the observation that 'the essence' of personal data protection seems to consist of data security measures to protect privacy interests, which reflects the U.S. elements of privacy and due process that were already present in data privacy legislation in the 1970s. The protection of personal data can be perceived as a procedural means to achieve a privacy protection end, but in recent years the focus has shifted to protecting the data as such, instead of the people behind the data. This book advocates a reconceptualization from a procedural approach to a privacy harmful activities' framework, to restore the focus on the protection of people's privacy interests and non-discrimination instead of a procedural framework where private companies comply with their duties by mechanically ticking the boxes. Psychological harm should be adequately addressed in regulatory frameworks, and a change of perspective from the current procedural point of view (*which type of data*) to a contextual point of view (*how the data is used*) can contribute to this aim, focusing on what the data 'does'.

Many wonder whether the EU-U.S. Data Privacy Framework, the third attempt to establish a transatlantic legal framework, will survive the CJEU's scrutiny. Instead of unilaterally imposing EU rules on the rest of the world, especially in a global domain such as technology and data privacy, this book advocates mutual understanding and respect by the EU for foreign legal systems. The EU can ask for certain safeguards to be respected with regard to Europeans' personal data that is transferred to third countries, but these safeguards should be in compliance with globally developed and accepted norms. The six broad data privacy categories developed in this book, consisting of several data privacy principles, can be used as a starting point for this endeavor. It is important that all involved stakeholders, namely the private and public sector, and civil society, have an equal voice in this process, and that commercial, intelligence, and privacy concerns are taken into account. In a globalized world where technology knows no physical borders, the use of national or even regional standards has become outdated. Data privacy principles developed in several parts of the world and by several organizations share many elements in common. All actors and sectors involved need clarity and legal certainty. It is time that actors and regions decide to cooperate and engage in mutual understanding, instead of unilaterally imposing their own ideas on the rest of the world.

REFERENCES FOR FURTHER READING

1. LEGISLATION AND LEGAL INSTRUMENTS

INTERNATIONAL

Council of Europe [1950] European Convention for the Protection of Human Rights and Fundamental Freedoms (ECHR).

OECD Guidelines on the Protection of Privacy and Transborder Flows of Personal Data [1980] C(80)58/FINAL.

Explanatory Memorandum to the 1980 OECD Guidelines.

Council of Europe [1981] Convention for the Protection of Individuals with regard to Automatic Processing of Personal Data, *European Treaty Series – No. 108* (Convention 108).

OECD Guidelines on the Protection of Privacy and Transborder Flows of Personal Data (updated 2013) [2013].

Council of Europe [2018] Protocol amending the Convention for the Protection of Individuals with regard to Automatic Processing of Personal Data (ETS No. 108) CM(2018)2-final.

Council of Europe [2018] Protocol amending the Convention for the Protection of Individuals with regard to Automatic Processing of Personal Data (CETS No. 223) CM/Inf(2018)15-final (Convention 108+).

EUROPEAN UNION

Directive 95/46/EC of the European Parliament and of the Council of 24 October 1995 on the protection of individuals with regard to the processing of personal data and on the free movement of such data [1995] OJ L 281/31.

Commission Decision 2000/520/EC of 26 July 2000 pursuant to Directive 95/46/EC of the European Parliament and of the Council on the adequacy of the protection provided by the safe harbour privacy principles and related frequently asked questions issued by the U.S. Department of Commerce [2000] OJ L 215/7.

Directive 2002/58/EC of the European Parliament and of the Council of 12 July 2002 concerning the processing of personal data and the protection of privacy in the electronic communications sector (Directive on privacy and electronic communications) [2002] OJ L 201/37.

Directive 2006/24/EC of the European Parliament and of the Council of 15 March 2006 on the retention of data generated or processed in connection with the provision of publicly available electronic communications services or of public communications networks and amending Directive 2002/58/EC [2006] OJ L 105/54.
Explanations relating to the Charter of Fundamental Rights [2007] OJ C 303/17.
Treaty of Lisbon amending the Treaty on the European Union and the Treaty establishing the European Community [2007] OJ C 306/1.
Treaty on the European Union [2012] OJ C 326/13 (TEU).
Treaty on the Functioning of the European Union [2012] OJ C 326/47 (TFEU).
Charter of Fundamental Rights of the European Union [2012] OJ C 326/391 (EU Charter).
Regulation (EU) 2016/679 of the European Parliament and the Council of 27 April 2016 on the protection of natural persons with regard to the processing of personal data and on the free movement of such data, and repealing Directive 95/46/EC [2016] OJ L 119/1 (GDPR).
Directive (EU) 2016/680 of 27 April 2016 on the protection of natural persons with regard to the processing of personal data by competent authorities for the purposes of the prevention, investigation, detection or prosecution of criminal offences or the execution of criminal penalties, and on the free movement of such data, and repealing Council Framework Decision 2008/977/JHA [2016] OJ L 119/89 (LED).
Commission Implementing Decision (EU) 2016/1250 of 12 July 2016 pursuant to Directive 95/46/EC of the European Parliament and of the Council on the adequacy of the protection provided by the EU-U.S. Privacy Shield [2016] OJ L 207/1.
Commission Implementing Decision EU 2023/1795 of 10 July 2023 pursuant to Regulation (EU) 2016/679 of the European Parliament and of the Council on the adequate level of protection of personal data under the EU-US Data Privacy Framework [2023] OJ L 231/118.

UNITED STATES

Bill of Rights to the U.S. Constitution, 15 December 1791.
First Amendment to the U.S. Constitution, 15 December 1791.
Fourth Amendment to the U.S. Constitution, 15 December 1791.
The 1914 Federal Trade Commission Act (1914 FTC Act), 15 U.S.C., §§41-58 (Sec.1-Sec.27).
The 1974 Privacy Act (As Amended), 88 Stat. 1896, Public Law 93-579, as codified at 5 U.S.C. 552a.
The 1978 Foreign Intelligence Surveillance Act, 50 U.S.C. 1801, 95th Congress, 25 October 1978, 92 Stat. 1786 (FISA).
Executive Order 12333 United States Intelligence Activities, 46Fed.Reg.59, 941, 4 December 1981 (EO 12333).
Executive Order 12866, 30 September 1993.
Restatement (Second) of Torts (1997).
The Uniting and Strengthening America by Providing Appropriate Tools Required to Intercept and Obstruct Terrorism Act, 107th Congress, 26 October 2001, 115 Stat. 272 (USA Patriot Act).

The Foreign Intelligence Surveillance Act of 1978 Amendments Act of 2008, 110th Congress, 10 July 2008, 122 Stat. 2436 (FISA 2008).
The White House Office of the Press Secretary, Presidential Policy Directive/PPD-28, 17 January 2014.
The Uniting and Strengthening America by Fulfilling Rights and Ensuring Effective Discipline Over Monitoring Act, 114th Congress, 2 June 2015, 129 Stat. 268 (USA Freedom Act).
Title 1.81.5. California Consumer Privacy Act of 2018, Cal.Civ.Code §§1798.100–1798.199 (CCPA).
The 2020 California Privacy Rights Act, Assembly Bill No. 1194 Chapter 567, An Act to Amend Sections 1798.99.31, 1798.145, and 1798.185 of the Civil Code, Relating to Privacy, Approved By Governor October 08, 2023, Filed With Secretary of State October 08, 2023 (CPRA).
Code of Virginia, Chapter 53. Consumer Data Protection Act of 2021, §§59.1-575–59.1-585 (VCDPA).
Executive Order 14086 Enhancing Safeguards for United States Signals Intelligence Activities, 87Fed.Reg.198, 62283, 7 October 2022 (EO 14086).

2. CASE LAW

German Bundesverfassungsgericht, Census Judgment of the First Senate of 15 December 1983, 1 BvR 209, 269, 362, 420, 440, 484/83.

CJEU

Joined Cases C-317/04 and C-318/04 *Parliament v Council and Commission* [2006] ECLI:EU:C:2006:346.
Joined Cases C-293/12 and C-594/12 *Digital Rights Ireland Ltd v Minister for Communications* [2014] ECLI:EU:C:2014:238.
C-131/12 *Google Spain SL and Google Inc. v Agencia Española de Protección de Datos (AEPD) and Mario Costeja González* [2014] ECLI:EU:C:2014:317.
C-362/14 *Maximilian Schrems v Data Protection Commissioner* [2015] ECLI:EU:C:2015:650 (*Schrems I*).
Joined Cases C-203/15 and C-698/15 *Tele2 Sverige AB v Post- och telestyrelsen, and, Secretary of State for the Home Department v Tom Watson, Peter Brice, Geoffrey Lewis* [2016] ECLI:EU:C:2016:970.
C-311/18 *Data Protection Comr v Facebook Ireland Ltd, Maximillian Schrems* [2020] ECLI:EU:C:2020:559 (*Schrems II*).
C-623/17 *Privacy International v Secretary of State for Foreign and Commonwealth Affairs* [2020] ECLI:EU:C:2020:790 (*Privacy International*).
Joined Cases C-511/18, C-512/18, and C-520/18 *La Quadrature du Net v Premier ministre, and, Ordre des barreaux francophones et germanophone v Conseil des ministres* [2020] ECLI:EU:C:2020:791.

Joined Cases C-793/19 and C-794/19 *Bundesrepublik Deutschland v SpaceNet AG and Telekom Deutschland GmbH* [2022] ECLI:EU:C:2022:702.

ECtHR

Roman Zakharov v Russia App no 47143/06 ECLI:CE:ECHR:2015:1204JUD004714306 (ECtHR, 4 December 2015).
Big Brother Watch and Others v United Kingdom App nos 58170/13, 62322/14, and 24960/15 ECLI:CE:ECHR:2018:0913JUD005817013 (ECtHR, 13 September 2018).
Big Brother Watch and Others v United Kingdom App nos 58170/13, 62322/14, and 24960/15 ECLI:CE:ECHR:2021:0525JUD005817013 (ECtHR, 25 May 2021).

UNITED STATES

Katz v United States [1967] 389 U.S. 347.
United States v Knotts [1983] 460 U.S. 276.
Kyllo v United States [2001] 533 U.S. 27.
Yassir Fazaga et al v Federal Bureau of Investigation et al [2012] 884 F.Supp.2d (CD Cal. 2012).
Carpenter v United States [2018] 585 U.S. __.
Fazaga v FBI [2019] 916 F.3d 1202 (9th Cir. 2019).
FBI v Fazaga [2022] 595 U.S. __.

3. LITERATURE

BOOKS

Bennett Colin, *Regulating Privacy* (Cornell University Press 1992) 263p.
Bradford Anu, *The Brussels Effect* (1st edn, OUP 2020) 404p.
Bygrave Lee, *Data Protection Law* (Kluwer 2002) 426p.
Bygrave Lee, *Data Privacy Law* (OUP 2014) 233p.
de Vries Sybe, Bernitz Ulf, and Weatherill Stephen (eds), *The EU Charter of Fundamental Rights as a binding instrument* (Hart Publishing 2015) 413p.
Eisner Marc, *Regulatory Politics in Transition* (Johns Hopkins press 1993) 246p.
Greenwald Glenn, *No Place to Hide* (Hamish Hamilton 2014) 259p.
Guibault Lucie and Bernt Hugenholtz P (eds), *The Future of the Public Domain* (Kluwer 2006) 377p.
Gutwirth Serge, Poullet Yves, De Hert Paul, de Terwangne Cécile, and Nouwt Sjaak (eds), *Reinventing Data Protection?* (Springer 2009) 356p.
Heisenberg Dorothee, *Negotiating Privacy* (Lynne Rienner Publishers 2005) 219p.
Kosta Eleni and Kamara Irene (eds), *Data Retention in Europe and Beyond* (OUP 2025) 490p.

Lynskey Orla, *The foundations of EU data protection law* (1st edn, OUP 2015) 307p.
Nugter A.C.M., *Transborder Flow of Personal Data within the EC* (Kluwer 1990) 430p.
Purtova Nadezhda, *Property Rights in Personal Data* (Kluwer 2012) 308p.
Solove Daniel, *Understanding Privacy* (HUP 2008) 257p.
Sundmaeker Harald, Guillemin Patrick, Friess Peter, and Woelffle Sylvie (eds), *Vision and Challenges for Realising the Internet of Things* (CERP-IoT 2010) 229p.
Vermesan Ovidiu and Bacquet Joël (eds), *Next Generation Internet of Things* (River Publishers 2018) 352p.
Vogel David, *The Politics of Precaution* (PUP 2012) 317p.
Westin Alan, *Privacy and Freedom* (Athenaeum 1967) 487p.

ARTICLES

Balkin Jack, 'Free Speech in the Algorithmic Society: Big Data, Private Governance, and New School Speech Regulation' (2018) 51 UC Davis Law Review 1149, 1149-1210.
Bergholm Jenny, 'The Data Retention Saga Continued – from Tele2 Sverige to Privacy Intl and La Quadrature du Net' (2021) 2 Juridiska Föreningen i Finland 111, 111-139.
Bergkamp Lucas, 'EU Data Protection Policy: The Privacy Fallacy: Adverse Effects of Europe's Data Protection Policy in an Information-Driven Economy' (2002) 18 Computer Law & Security Report 31, 31-47.
Blume Peter, 'It Is Time for Tomorrow: EU Data Protection Reform and the Internet' (2015) 18 Journal of Internet Law 3, 3-13.
Buitelaar J C, 'Privacy: Back to the Roots' (2012) 13 German Law Journal 171, 171-202.
Cannataci Joseph and Mifsud-Bonnici Jeanne, 'Data Protection Comes of Age: The Data Protection Clauses in the European Constitutional Treaty' (2005) 14 Information & Communications Technology Law 5, 5-15.
Cate Fred, 'The EU data protection directive, information privacy, and the public interest' (1995) 80 Iowa Law Review 431, 431-444.
Cate Fred and Mayer-Schönberger Viktor, 'Tomorrow's privacy: Notice and consent in a world of Big Data' (2013) 3 International Data Privacy Law 67, 67-73.
Chander Anupam, 'The Internet of Things: Both Goods and Services' (2019) 18 World Trade Review s9, s9-s22.
Cohen Julie, 'Examined Lives: Informational Privacy and the Subject as Object' (2000) 52 Stanford Law Review 1373, 1373-1438.
de Beer Jeremy, Belanger Jules, and Sethi Mohit, 'Consumer Contracts, Copyright Licensing, and Control over Data on the Internet of Things' (2020) 18 Canadian Journal of Law and Technology 161, 161-211.
De Schrijver Steven, 'Privacy Shield 2.0 – een stap naar Schrems III?' (2023) 1 Computerrecht 1, 1-3.
de Terwangne Cécile, 'Council of Europe convention 108+: A modernised international treaty for the protection of personal data' (2021) 40 The Computer Law and Security Report 105497 1, 1-18.
Enright Harrison, 'What a Data Privacy Law Should Look like in West Virginia: Balancing Competing Interests of Consumers and Businesses' (2022) 125 West Virginia Law Review 263, 263-298.

Feintuck Mike, 'Precautionary Maybe, but What's the Principle? The Precautionary Principle, the Regulation of Risk, and the Public Domain' (2005) 32 Journal of Law and Society 371, 371-398.

Floridi Luciano, 'On Human Dignity as a Foundation for the Right to Privacy' (2016) 29 Philosophy & technology 307, 307-312.

Fromholz Julia, 'The European Union Data Privacy Directive' (2000) 15 Berkeley Technology Law Journal 461, 461-484.

Garyiene Javier, 'State Privacy Law Developments' (2021) 77 The Business Lawyer 255, 255-262.

Gellert Raphael, 'Understanding Data Protection as Risk Regulation' (2015) 18 Journal of Internet Law 3, 3-16.

Hadjipetrova Ganka and Poteat Hannah, 'States Are Coming to the Force of Privacy in the Digital Era' (2014) 6 Landslide 13, 13-71.

Hartzog Woodrow, 'The case against idealising control' (2018) 4 European Data Protection Law Review 423, 423-432.

Hartzog Woodrow, 'The Public Information Fallacy' (2019) 99 Boston University Law Review 459, 459-522.

Hoofnagle Chris, van der Sloot Bart, and Zuiderveen Borgesius Frederik, 'The European Union general data protection regulation: what it is and what it means' (2019) 28 Information & Communications Technology Law 65, 65-98.

Jasanoff Sheila, 'American Exceptionalism and the Political Acknowledgment of Risk' (1990) 119 Daedalus 61, 61-81.

Karsenti Nicolas, 'Privacy and Connected Objects' (2019) 17 Canadian Journal of Law and Technology 34, 34-58.

Kirtley Jane, 'The EU Data Protection Directive and the First Amendment: Why a Press Exemption Won't Work' (1995) 80 Iowa Law Review 639, 639-650.

Kohl Uta, 'The Right To Be Forgotten in Data Protection Law and Two Western Cultures of Privacy' (2023) 72 International and Comparative Law Quarterly 737, 737-769.

Lemley Mark, 'Private Property: A Comment on Professor Samuelson's Contribution' (2000) 52 Stanford Law Review 1545, 1545-1557.

Limpert Bradley, 'App. 13.15 – The Internet of Things: An introduction to privacy issues with a focus on the retail and home environments' [2016] Technology Contracting: Law, Precedents and Commentary 1, 1-18.

Lynskey Orla, 'Deconstructing data protection: the 'added-value' of a right to data protection in the EU legal order' (2014) 63 The International and comparative law quarterly 569, 569-597.

Maxwell Jack and Tomlinson Joe, 'Privacy Int'l v. Secretary of State for Foreign & Commonwealth Affairs and La Quadrature du Net v. Premier ministre (C.J.E.U.)' (2021) 60 International Legal Materials 464, 464-520.

McLaughlin Edward, 'Schrems's Slippery Slope: Strengthening Governance Mechanisms to Rehabilitate EU-U.S. Cross-Border Data Transfers after Schrems II' (2021) 90 Fordham Law Review 217, 217-260.

Newell Bryce, Purtova Nadezhda, Moon Young, and Paterson III Hugh, 'Regulating The Data Market: The Material Scope of American Consumer Data Privacy Law' (2024) 45 University of Pennsylvania Journal of International Law 1055, 1055-1143.

Ohm Paul, 'Sensitive Information' (2015) 88 Southern California Law Review 1125, 1125-1196.

Pałka Przemysław, 'Data Management Law for the 2020s: The Lost Origins and the New Needs' (2020) 68 Buffalo Law Review 559, 559-640.

Peltz-Steele Richard, 'The New American Privacy' (2013) 44 Georgetown Journal of International Law 365, 365-410.

Peltz-Steele Richard, 'The pond betwixt: differences in the US-EU data protection/ safe harbor negotiation' (2015) 19 Journal of Internet Law 15, 15-30.

Pernot-Leplay Emmanuel, 'EU Influence on Data Privacy Laws: Is The U.S. Approach Converging With The EU Model?' (2019) 18 Colorado Technology Law Journal 101, 101-124.

Poullet Yves, 'Data protection legislation: What is at stake for our society and democracy?' (2009) 25 Computer Law & Security Review 211, 211-226.

Prosser William, 'Privacy' (1960) 48 California Law Review 383, 383-423.

Purtova Nadezhda, 'The illusion of personal data as no one's property' (2015) 7 Law, Innovation and Technology 83, 83-111.

Quinn Paul and Malgieri Gianclaudio, 'The Difficulty of Defining Sensitive Data – The Concept of Sensitive Data in the EU Data Protection Framework' (2021) 22 German Law Journal 1583, 1583-1612.

Rauhofer Judith, 'Privacy is dead, get over it! Information privacy and the dream of a risk-free society' (2008) 17 Information & Communications Technology Law 185, 185-197.

Schwartz Paul, 'Property, Privacy, and Personal Data' (2004) 117 Harvard Law Review 2056, 2056-2128.

Solove Daniel, 'Introduction: Privacy Self-Management and the Consent Dilemma' (2013) 126 Harvard Law Review 1880, 1880-1903.

Solove Daniel, 'Data Is What Data Does: Regulating Based on Harm and Risk Instead of Sensitive Data' (2024) 118 Northwestern University Law Review 1081, 1081-1137.

Solove Daniel and Hartzog Woodrow, 'The FTC and the New Common Law of Privacy' (2014) 114 Columbia Law Review 583, 583-676.

Tzanou Maria, 'Data Protection as a Fundamental Right next to Privacy? 'Reconstructing' a Not so New Right' (2013) 3 International Data Privacy Law 88, 88-99.

Warren Samuel and Brandeis Louis, 'The Right to Privacy' (1890) 4 Harvard Law Review 193, 193-220.

Whitman James, 'The Two Western Cultures of Privacy: Dignity Versus Liberty' (2004) 113 The Yale Law Journal 1151, 1151-1221.

Wiener Jonathan, 'Whose Precaution After All? A Comment on the Comparison and Evolution of Risk Regulatory Systems' (2003) 13 Duke Journal of Comparative & International Law 207, 207-262.

Zalnieriute Monika, 'A Struggle for Competence: National Security, Surveillance and the Scope of EU Law at the Court of Justice of European Union' (2022) 85 Modern Law Review 198, 198-218.

REPORTS, WORKING PAPERS, AND DOCTORAL THESES

Christofi Athena and Verdoodt Valerie, *Exploring the essence of the right to data protection and smart cities* (CiTiP Working Paper, 2019) 80p.

Draghi Mario, *The future of European competitiveness* (European Commission Report, 2024) 70p.

Freeman Wilson, *California Dreamin' of Privacy Regulation: The California Consumer Privacy Act and Congress* (CRS, 2018) 5p.

Lissens Sylvia, *The U.S. and EU approach towards personal data protection: "A collision of tides or a convergence of waves?" A legal exploration of the differences and convergences between the United States and the European Union* (Doctoral Thesis KU Leuven, 2025) 340p.

Mulligan Stephen and Linebaugh Chris, *Data Protection Law: An Overview* (CRS, 2019) 75p.

Mulligan Stephen and Linebaugh Chris, *Data Protection and Privacy Law: An Introduction* (CRS, 2022) 3p.

U.S. Department of Health, Education & Welfare, *Records, Computers, and the Rights of Citizens* (Report of the Secretary's Advisory Committee on Automated Personal Data Systems, 1973) DHEW Publication No. (OS) 73-94 (1973 HEW Report) 346p.

Vogiatzoglou Plixavra, *The Era of Pre-Crime: How Mass Data Surveillance and Predictive Policing Intersect and Interfere with Privacy, Data Protection and Due Process Rights in the EU* (Doctoral Thesis KU Leuven, 2023) 393p.

Zuiderveen Borgesius Frederik, Hagenauw Dominique, and Hijmans Hielke, *Privacy Bridges: EU and US privacy experts in search of transatlantic privacy solutions* (37th International Privacy Conference Amsterdam, 2015) 50p.

www.ingramcontent.com/pod-product-compliance
Ingram Content Group UK Ltd.
Pitfield, Milton Keynes, MK11 3LW, UK
UKHW051832301026
9729IPUK00005B/51

9 781839 706561